Research and Development in Expert Systems IX

THE BRITISH COMPUTER SOCIETY CONFERENCE SERIES

Editor: P. HAMMERSLEY

The BCS Conference Series aims to report developments of an advanced technical standard undertaken by members of The British Computer Society through the Society's conference organization. The series should be vital reading for all whose work or interest involves computing technology. Volumes in this Series will mirror the quality of papers published in the BCS's technical periodical *The Computer Journal* and range widely across topics in computer hardware, software, applications and management.

British Computer Society Conference Series 6

Research and Development in Expert Systems IX

Proceedings of Expert Systems 92, the Twelfth Annual Technical
Conference of the British Computer Society Specialist Group
on Expert Systems, London, December 1992

Edited by

M. A. Bramer
University of Portsmouth

R. W. Milne
Intelligent Applications Limited

Published on behalf of
THE BRITISH COMPUTER SOCIETY
by

 **CAMBRIDGE**
UNIVERSITY PRESS

Published by the Press Syndicate of the University of Cambridge
The Pitt Building, Trumpington Street, Cambridge CB2 1RP
40 West 20th Street, New York, NY 10011-4211, USA
10 Stamford Road, Oakleigh, Victoria 3166, Australia

© British Informatics Society Ltd 1993

First published 1993

Printed in Great Britain at the University Press, Cambridge

Library of Congress cataloguing in publication data available

British Library cataloguing in publication data available

ISBN 0 521 44517 5

Contents

Preface

This volume contains the refereed papers presented in the technical stream at Expert Systems '92, the twelfth annual conference of the British Computer Society Specialist Group on Expert Systems, held at Churchill College, Cambridge in December 1992.

On behalf of the programme committee I should like to thank those who took part in the refereeing this year. Their names are listed below.

I should also like to thank all those who have contributed to the organisation of this conference, in particular Rob Milne who again acted as the chairman of the conference organising committee and Ian Graham who organised the applications stream of the conference.

Thanks are also due to this year's conference organisers, Applied Workstations Limited, for their many efforts in making this conference possible, not least for their help in the preparation of this volume.

Max Bramer
Programme Chairman, Expert Systems '92

Conference Organising Committee
Rob Milne   (Conference Chairman)
Max Bramer   (Programme Chairman)
Alex Goodall
Ian Graham   (Organiser of Applications Stream)
David Lloyd
Ann Macintosh

Programme Committee
Max Bramer   (Chairman)
Tom Addis
Ian Graham
David Lloyd
Ann Macintosh
Robin Muir
Tim Rajan

Referees (in addition to Programme Committee members)

Alan Black	Jonathan Killin
Paul Brna	John Kingston
Flavio S Correa da Silva	Ian Lewin
Brian Drabble	Rob Milne
Ian Filby	Dave Robertson
Terry Fogarty	Nigel Shadbolt
Richard Forsyth	Peter Sharpe
Ian Harrison	Gail Swaffield
Sheila Hughes	Mike Uschold
Richard Kamm	Mike Yearworth

Introduction and Overview

M.A.BRAMER

Department of Information Science
University of Portsmouth
Locksway Road
Milton, Southsea   PO4 8JF
England

In 1980, when the British Computer Society's Specialist Group on Expert Systems was established, it was remarked that the number of operational expert systems in the world could be counted on the fingers of one mutilated hand.

Expert Systems and its parent field Artificial Intelligence, which were then barely known outside a few specialist academic institutions, are now accepted parts of most degree courses in Computer Science.

Moreover, the history of expert systems in the last ten years is a highly successful example of technology transfer from the research laboratory to industry.

Today there are thousands, possibly tens of thousands of expert systems in use world-wide. They cover a very wide range of application areas, from archaeology, through munitions disposal to welfare benefits advice (see, for example, Bramer 1987, 1988, 1990).

Many of these systems are small-scale, developed in a few months (or even weeks) and often comprising just a few hundred rules. However, even relatively straightforward expert systems can still frequently be of great practical and commercial value.

The Department of Trade and Industry recently produced a series of 12 case studies of commercially successful expert system applications in the UK which included systems for tasks as diverse as product design at Lucas Engineering, corporate meetings planning at Rolls-Royce and personnel selection at Marks and Spencer (DTI, 1990). However, despite explosive growth in the last ten years, it seems clear that we are still only scratching the surface of possible applications.

Although much of the early work was concerned with standalone systems - particularly consultation systems - which were principally rule-based, both the computational techniques employed and the nature of the systems themselves have broadened considerably in recent years.

Attention is increasingly becoming focused on forming links
between expert systems and the conventional problems of data
processing and commercial computing, including the interface
between expert systems and database management systems, the
development of intelligent front ends to complex software packages
and information retrieval systems, and applications in real-time
process control.

There is also an increasing interest in high-value applications
(particularly financial ones, such as insurance underwriting),
where substantial sums of money are involved and considerable
increases in a company's profits can be made by improvements in
performance which are only marginal, without any need for an
expert system to achieve anything remotely approaching perfect
performance.

As well as the conventional mode of use, it is likely that in the
future we shall see more 'mobile' expert systems in use for
outdoor applications. These might for example be mounted in a
maintenance engineer's van and connected via a radio link with a
mainframe back at his or her base (for example, for database
access) or incorporated in a small hand-held portable computer.

It is not long ago that expert systems were considered by many to
be insufficiently safe for 'safety-critical' applications. Now
these too are seen as a legitimate area of use.

It has been reported (AAAI, 1991) that a number of expert systems
were used in support of 'Operation Desert Storm' in the Gulf War,
including PRIDE (Pulse Radar Intelligent Diagnostic Environment),
SABRE (Single Army Battlefield Requirements Evaluator), TOPSS
(Tactical Operation Planning Support System), TACOS (The Automated
Container Offering System) and AALPS (Automated Air Load Planning
System).

The programming techniques used by expert system developers have
also changed considerably, from the 'first generation' systems
which relied purely on heuristic knowledge in the form of rules,
through 'second generation' systems combining heuristic reasoning
based on rules with deep reasoning based on a causal model of the
problem domain, to systems employing other representations - many
of them first developed in the Artificial Intelligence community -
such as frames, blackboards, conceptual graphs and objects.

The very short development times recorded for many expert systems
and for 'conventional' systems developed using similar
representational techniques are reminiscent of the introduction of
high-level languages such as FORTRAN and COBOL thirty years ago
and the drastic improvement in development times, compared with
the earlier use of assemblers and autocodes, obtained by the use
of more problem-oriented representations.

There have also been substantial advances in the area of development methodologies which have made the development of expert systems considerably more systematic than the early pioneering efforts (see for example Harris-Jones et al., 1992).

In my view, we are seeing a paradigm shift occurring in our perception of computing. It is not surprising that the initial use to which computers were put was to solve problems with well-defined, analytical solutions. Increasingly we are seeing that they can also be used to tackle ill-defined, 'inexact' problems, even those with no clear-cut solutions. It is in this latter area that the largest rewards may ultimately lie.

Expert system techniques provide facilities for modelling a problem domain in a way that is appreciably more meaningful to both the system designer and the user, and this promises benefits for conventional as well as Artificial Intelligence applications.

As well as the obvious immediate commercial benefits a major potential benefit of expert systems technology is the development over a period of time of improved codifications of expert knowledge.

This would be by no means a new phenomenon. Historically, it is the ability to record its knowledge (in the form of books, or in earlier times in stories, songs, etc.) that has enabled each generation to develop by building on the skills of those that have gone before. There are two aspects to this. Not only does the expertise of the most skilled person in a field in one generation progressively 'filter down' to the ordinary participants in that field in future generations, but the capability of starting at a much higher level enables the most skilled in succeeding generations to progress even further.

The development of expert systems may enable a major acceleration of this process to occur. Computer programs have important advantages over books etc. as media for the recording of knowledge in that not only can they be updated rapidly but they are necessarily precise and unambiguous. Any dispute over the meaning of a program can ultimately be solved by running it.

The availability of the expertise of a leading practitioner in a field in a fully precise and directly testable form may well enable others to find improved ways of codifying that knowledge, to look for simplifications, to identify errors or omissions, or to find improved ways of teaching the underlying skills. A refined form of the knowledge might again be stored in the form of an expert system, but might instead be communicated in the more conventional form of textbooks, etc.

Expert Systems have come a long way in the last ten years. The
field has advanced beyond its early successes with small
declarative rule-based systems by drawing on techniques such as
rule induction (White and Liu, 1992), case-based reasoning
(Bezirgan, 1992), truth maintenance (Hinde and Bray, 1992) and
temporal reasoning (Tolba et al., 1992) from the wider field of
Artificial Intelligence and established techniques from psychology
such as repertory grids (Shaw and Gaines, 1992).

There are many more techniques in the research laboratory waiting
to be brought into action to tackle the challenging applications
likely to be required in the future. Despite a decade of success
the era of expert systems is only just beginning.

REFERENCES

AAAI (1991). AI Magazine, Vol.12, No.2, Summer 1991, p.16.

Bezirgan, A. (1992). An Application of Case-Based Expert System
    Technology to Dynamic Job-Shop Scheduling. [This Volume.]

Bramer, M.A. (1987). Expert Systems in Business: a British
    Perspective. Proceedings of the First International Symposium
    on Artificial Intelligence and Expert Systems, Berlin, May,
    1987. Reprinted in Expert Systems, Vol.5, No.2, pp.104-117,
    May 1988.

Bramer, M.A. (1988). Applying Expert Systems in Business: A
    Critical Overview. Proceedings of the Second International
    Symposium on Artificial Intelligence and Expert Systems,
    Berlin, June 1988, Part C, pp.17-39.

Bramer, M.A. (1990). Practical Experience of Building Expert
    Systems. John Wiley and Co.

DTI (1990). Expert Systems Opportunities. [A pack of 12 case
    studies plus guidelines and video.] HMSO.

Harris-Jones, C., Barrett, T., Walker, T., Moores, T. and Edwards,
    J. (1992). A Methods Model for the Integration of KBS and
    Conventional Information Technology. [This Volume.]

Hinde, C.J. and Bray, A.D. (1992). Concurrent Engineering using
    Collaborating Truth Maintenance Systems. [This Volume.]

Shaw, M.L.G. and Gaines, B.R. (1992). On the Relationship between
    Repertory Grid and Term Subsumption Knowledge Structures:
    Theory, Practice and Tools. [This Volume.]

Tolba, H.A., Charpillet, F. and Haton, J.-P. (1992). Combining
    Qualitative and Quantitative Information for Temporal
    Reasoning. [This Volume.]

White, A.P. and Liu, W.Z. (1992). Fairness of Attribute Selection
    in Probabilistic Induction. [This Volume.]

CONSULTANT: Providing Advice for the Machine Learning Toolbox[*]

Susan Craw[†]   D. Sleeman

Nicolas Graner Michael Rissakis   Sunil Sharma

Department of Computing Science
University of Aberdeen
Aberdeen AB9 2UE

Abstract

The Machine Learning Toolbox (MLT), an Esprit project (P2154), provides an integrated toolbox of ten Machine Learning (ML) algorithms. One distinct component of the toolbox is Consultant, an advice-giving expert system, which assists a domain expert to choose and use a suitable algorithm for his learning problem. The University of Aberdeen has been responsible for the design and implementation of Consultant.

Consultant's knowledge and domain is unusual in several respects. Its knowledge represents the integrated expertise of ten algorithm developers, whose algorithms offer a range of ML techniques; but also some algorithms use fairly similar approaches. The lack of an agreed ML terminology was the initial impetus for an extensive, associated help system. From an MLT user's point of view, an ML beginner requires significant assistance with terminology and techniques, and can benefit from having access to previous, successful applications of ML to similar problems; but in contrast a more experienced user of ML does not wish constant supervision. This paper describes Consultant, discusses the methods used to achieve the required flexibility of use, and compares Consultant's similarities and distinguishing features with more standard expert system applications.

---

[*]Suggested short form *"S. Craw, D. Sleeman et al: CONSULTANT - MLT's Adviser"*

[†]Seconded from The Robert Gordon University, Aberdeen, September 1991 - August 1992.

CONSULTANT: Providing Advice for the Machine Learning Toolbox

SUSAN CRAW†, D. SLEEMAN, NICOLAS GRANER, MICHAEL RISSAKIS, SUNIL SHARMA

Department of Computing Science
University of Aberdeen
Aberdeen AB9 2UE

1 INTRODUCTION

The Machine Learning Toolbox (MLT), an Esprit project (P2154), provides an integrated toolbox of ten Machine Learning (ML) algorithms. One distinct component of the toolbox is Consultant, an advice-giving expert system. It provides domain experts with assistance and guidance on the selection and use of tools from the toolbox, but it is specifically aimed at experts who are not familiar with ML and its design has focused on their needs.

Consultant combines the normal functions of an expert system: asking questions, integrating evidence and summarising advice, with an extensive, easily used help system, providing assistance with ML terminology and approaches. The MLT project has experience gained from successful application-algorithm "marriages" and this information is available within Consultant's help system as additional assistance to the domain expert.

Consultant's knowledge and domain is unusual in several respects. Its knowledge represents the integrated expertise of ten algorithm developers, whose algorithms offer a range of ML techniques; but also some algorithms use fairly similar approaches. The lack of an agreed ML terminology was the initial impetus for an extensive, associated help system. From an MLT user's point of view, an ML beginner requires significant assistance with terminology and techniques, and can benefit from having access to previous, successful applications of ML to similar problems; but in contrast, a more experienced user of ML does not wish constant supervision.

MLT is an integrated toolkit containing Consultant [Graner (1992)], ten ML algorithms and a Common Knowledge Representation Language [Morik et al (1991)]. This paper focuses on Consultant, but we briefly introduce the algorithms here, since

---

† Seconded from The Robert Gordon University, Aberdeen, September 1991 - August 1992.

Consultant represents their features in its knowledge base so that it can advise on their use. The algorithms cover a wide range of ML approaches [1]:

- **APT** [Nedellec (1991)]: a learning apprentice system for problems solved by decomposition;

- **CIGOL**: induces FOL[2] rules from positive and negative examples;

- **NewID, CN2** [Clark (1991)], **LASH** [Hutber (1987)]: induce discrimination trees or rules from examples expressed as attribute-value pairs;

- **MAKEY**: induces discrimination rules from concept descriptions;

- **KBG** [Bisson (1992)]: a FOL clustering and generalisation tool;

- **MOBAL** [Morik (1991)]: a FOL modelling and knowledge acquisition tool;

- **DMP** [Parsons (1989)]: a symbolic clustering algorithm; and

- **SICLA**: a set of statistical, symbolic and numerical data analysis tools.

This paper describes Consultant, discusses the methods used to achieve the required flexibility of use, and compares Consultant's similarities and distinguishing features with more standard expert system applications. Section 2 gives an overview of Consultant and its evolution during the MLT project. A typical run of Consultant appears in Section 3. Sections 4 and 5 describe the components of Consultant in greater detail. The testing of Consultant is outlined in Section 6, and finally Section 7 summarises the main decisions in the development of Consultant.

2 OVERVIEW OF CONSULTANT

Consultant interviews the user about his learning task and represents features of the task and the data set which are important for selecting an algorithm from the toolbox. Therefore, Consultant is a classification expert system where the user is interrogated about features of the learning task, and Consultant classifies this task as requiring one of the ten MLT algorithms.

2.1 Approach

Consultant comprises two main components: an advising module and a help system. (These components are described more fully in Sections 4 and 5.) They can be accessed by the user in parallel. He can thus be using the advising module, but consult the help system to allow him to understand his interaction with the advising

---

[1]In addition to the references given, Specification Documents and User Guides for each of these algorithms exist as deliverables within the MLT project.

[2]First Order Logic (Predicate Calculus).

module; e.g. he does not know some terminology, he wants to find out about the currently recommended algorithm, he wants to know if his data is suitable for this algorithm, etc. Consultant's users range from ML experts experimenting with various ML algorithms, to domain experts who are beginning to use ML. These users have very different knowledge about, and expertise in, ML. Hence their requirements with respect to Consultant are very different. In this paper, we shall refer to the ML expert as Consultant's expert user; the domain expert will be called the beginner.

The advising module asks the user questions about his learning task. From the user's answers, Consultant builds a Description Set representing the Task, TDS, and a knowledge base links features of the TDS with pieces of advice. The evidence in the knowledge base for and against algorithms is triggered by the TDS, and "knowledge functions" integrate these pieces of evidence before presenting them to the user in a range of displays. The help system consists of a glossary and a set of help files together with a **smooth** means of accessing relevant topics from them.

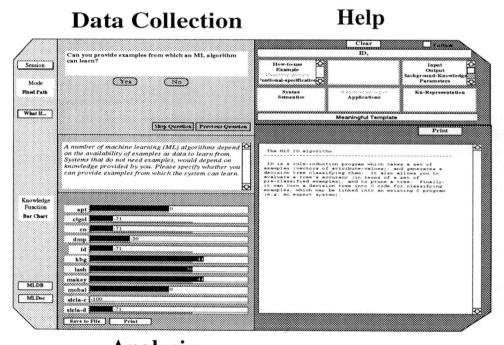

Figure 1: **Consultant's User Interface**

Consultant, in common with the other toolbox components, uses the HyperNeWS 1.4 HCI [van Hoff (1990)] (available from the Turing Institute), running on top of OpenWindows 2.0, to provide a user-friendly interface. Figure 1 shows Consultant's user interface with the control panel at the extreme left, the advising module to the left and the help system to the right.   The figure indicates that the HyperNeWS environment allows a very straightforward user interaction, a mouse-based interface and default settings are provided where appropriate; e.g. the default mode is fixed path – appropriate for a beginner.

2.2 Evolution

Consultant has evolved over the lifetime of the MLT project to incorporate the features specified in the project plan, the improvements suggested by evaluations and new developments in algorithm functionalities. The various versions of Consultant correspond to the releases of the MLT.

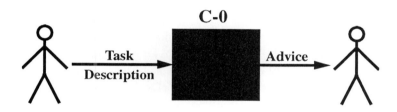

Figure 2: **Consultant-0's Functionality**

The initial version, Consultant-0 [WP5 (1990)], was a rule-based expert system implemented using Nexpert™. Compared to later versions of Consultant, Consultant-0 behaved very much like a black box: the user answered questions and at the end of questioning the recommendation appeared, Figure 2. This behaviour was found to be inappropriate. Evaluations showed that the ML expertise of domain experts was wide ranging. This had implications for suitable questioning approaches and appropriate help facilities. An ML expert can more easily understand questions about his learning task whereas a beginner needs substantial support in the form of easily accessible help. The shortcomings of Consultant-0 highlighted where improvements were required.

Consultant-1 [Sleeman (1991)] specified the same functionality as Consultant-0. However, this involved a major redesign of the system. Firstly, to overcome the restrictions of expert system shells, Consultant-1 was implemented in Sun Common LISP. In this way a tailored system was provided. Consultant-1 offers a flexible control of questioning and an extensive help system, Figure 3. The number of questions was also drastically reduced because a recommendation is based on knowledge which differentiates between the algorithms, rather than knowledge about the features of each algorithm. This paper focuses on Consultant-1, the currently implemented system, and Sections 4 and 5 describe it in detail.

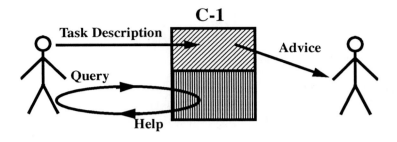

Figure 3: **Consultant-1's Functionality**

The next version of Consultant, Consultant-2, has been specified [Craw (1992)] and is **currently** being implemented. It extends the functionality of Consultant-1 by giving advice on **improving** the performance of the recommended algorithm for the application. The pre-run advice of Consultant-1 has been supplemented by post-run advice, suggesting refinements to the use of an algorithm in response to the output produced by running the algorithm. Figure 4 indicates this 2-phase functionality.

Consultant-2's pre-run module is a refined version of Consultant-1. In addition, it will be more closely integrated with the MLT algorithms by providing algorithms with initial parameter settings which are more finely tuned to suit the description of the task as represented in the TDS, than the default settings, within each algorithm, where the task description is not available. Consultant-2's post-run module develops the approach used for pre-run, but in addition to the TDS it acquires a description of the run of an algorithm and, from these, recommends refinements to the parameter settings. In addition, it will also advise on representation and data changes, and suggest the use of new post-processing tools available within MLT.

During the final phase of MLT, Consultant-3 will be specified. When using Consultant-2, the user still instigates the advising/testing phases in the use of MLT, but Consultant-3 will be a further development: an experimentation tool which designs its own trial runs for algorithms, runs them and analyses the results of learning.

3 A TYPICAL RUN WITH CONSULTANT-1

This section contains an edited log of a session with Consultant-1. Here are some of the questions and their answers.

Q: Which of the following best describes what you want to do?

    1. Select the most appropriate from two or more options

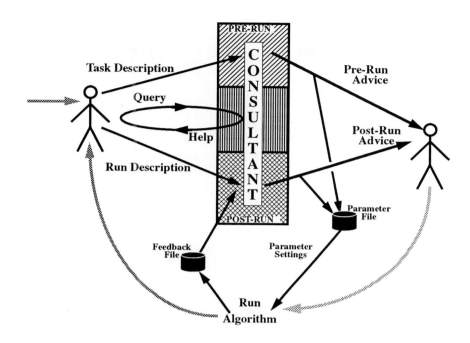

Figure 4: **Consultant-2's Functionality**

2. Optimise the performance of a particular system

3. Predict recurring events from past behaviour

4. Group entities with similar properties

5. Find an ordered sequence of actions to solve a problem

6. Detect instances of a pattern in data

7. Build or refine a model of a domain

A: Select the most appropriate from two or more options

Q: How many options (classes) are there? **A:** 10

Q: Are the classes mutually exclusive? **A:** NO

Q: Can you provide examples from which an ML algorithm can learn? **A:** YES

Q: How many examples could you provide? **A:** 100

Q: Can your data be noisy or inaccurate? **A:** YES

⋮

Q: Could you classify examples artificially generated by the system? **A:** YES

Q: Would you prefer the output to be in the form of:

1. A decision tree

2. A set of IF-THEN rules

3. A recognition function

   A: A decision tree

Q: Do you need the resulting rules (or tree or function) to completely cover the example space? **A:** YES

Below, a table corresponding to the barchart after all the questions were answered, is presented. The recommendations have been ordered and presented in three columns, containing the algorithm name and its overall certainty, expressed as a percentage.

Most Recommended		Not Recommended		Very Unfavoured		Definitely Not Suitable	
Name	%	Name	%	Name	%	Name	%
APT	55	MOBAL	-26	LASH	-68	MAKEY	-100
NewID	35	KBG	-33	SICLA-D	-72	SICLA-C	-100
		CN2	-38	CIGOL	-99		
		DMP	-44				

APT is the most highly recommended and we may ask for an explanation:

> There is significant evidence for APT, because you can classify artificial examples generated by the system; and

> there is small evidence for APT, because you need complete coverage of the example space; and

> there is slight evidence for APT, because an expert is available for an interactive session; and

> there is slight evidence for APT, because there are facts in the background knowledge.

Instead of asking for the similar explanation for NewID, we can compare its evidence with that for APT:

There is significant evidence for APT but no evidence for or against NewID since you can classify artificial examples generated by the system; and

there is slight evidence for APT but no evidence for or against NewID since an expert is available for an interactive session; and

there is slight evidence for APT but no evidence for or against NewID since there are facts in the background knowledge; and

there is no evidence for or against APT but large evidence for NewID since you can provide one hundred examples; and

⋮

there is no evidence for or against APT but slight evidence for NewID since there is noise in your data; and

there is no evidence for or against APT but large evidence against NewID since the different classes may overlap.

We may feel that the evidence for APT is not very definite, and when we consider the comparison, we notice that the last item counts heavily against NewID. On reflection we may decide that, in fact, classes do not overlap and so we re-answer the appropriate question as follows:

Q: Are the classes mutually exclusive? **A:** YES

This updates the barchart:

Most Recommended		Not Recommended		Very Unfavoured		Definitely Not Suitable	
Name	%	Name	%	Name	%	Name	%
NewID	87	MOBAL	-26	LASH	-68	MAKEY	-100
CN2	68	DMP	-44	CIGOL	-93	SICLA-C	-100
APT	55	KBG	-46				
SICLA-D	28						

The explanation for APT has not changed, so we now investigate the new top two recommendations:

There is significant evidence for NewID, because you want to choose among a set of decisions; and

there is large evidence for NewID, because you can provide one hundred examples; and

there is slight evidence for NewID, because there is noise in your data; and

$\vdots$

there is small evidence for NewID, because you need complete coverage of the example space.

The explanations for NewID and CN2 are very close, as can be seen from the following comparison:

There is small evidence for NewID but large evidence against CN2 since you would like the output to be a decision tree.

We may proceed by considering if we really do wish decision trees, etc.

4 ADVISING MODULE

The architecture diagram in Figure 5 represents the advising module as composed of the data collection and analysis tasks. This section gives detailed descriptions of the components of the advising module; the help system appears in Section 5.

4.1 Data Collection

Acquisition of the TDS is achieved by questioning the user about his learning task. The ACKnowledge project's (ESPRIT P2576) Knowledge Engineering Workbench is a sort of "knowledge acquisition toolbox". It assists the user with knowledge acquisition by allowing him to progressively refine a model of the target system [van Heijst (1992)]. In contrast, Consultant assumes its user has a clear idea of his learning task and the type of knowledge to be acquired, and provides much more help to allow the user to articulate the requirements of his task, as an ML application.

Consultant's user is presented with questions; an example appears at the top of the data collection area in Figure 1. The expert user will easily understand what this question is asking. However, the beginner can make use of the elaboration which appears underneath each question, again see Figure 1. At any point the user may choose to use the help facilities to assist in choosing his answer.

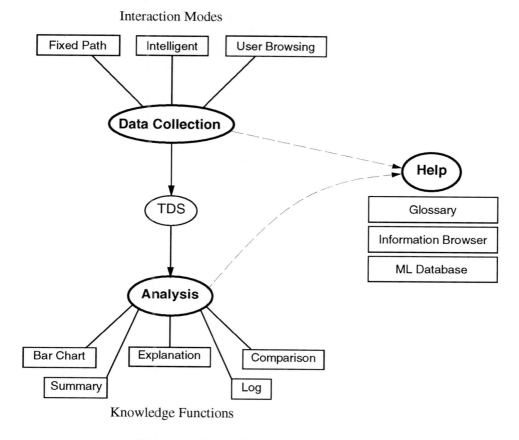

Figure 5: **Consultant's Architecture**

The expert user and the beginner may differ in the order they wish the questions to be presented to them. Consultant allows three modes of operation to suit different styles of interaction:

- **Fixed Path Mode** is suitable for the beginner. Questions are presented in a focused, logical manner where all related questions are grouped together. Although its name implies that the same sequence of questions is asked, the answers to early questions restrict the questions which are asked later, because the questions are structured using dependency links.

- **User Browsing** is suitable for the expert user. He is able to select which questions he wishes to answer. However, to use this mode successfully, the user must know which questions are relevant for his application. Therefore, it is not suitable for a beginner to build a representation of his task this way.

- **Intelligent Mode** provides the most efficient questioning – by asking the fewest questions. Consultant chooses the next question so that it has the most impact on the advice; i.e. the one that discriminates most between the recommended algorithms. However, the questions are not asked in a "logical" order, and therefore might confuse a beginner.

The user is able to return to previous questions. This may be appropriate for several reasons:

- he may have skipped a question and now feels that he can answer it;

- he may have altered his view of his learning task because later questions caused him to rethink his learning task; or

- he may wish to rethink a question because he had been unsure when he chose the answer.

The user may step back through the questions one at a time and reanswer them. Alternatively, he can enter the Whatif facility which allows him to save the current state of advising and start user-browsing mode to select questions whose answers he wishes to change. Typically the Whatif mode is used after all the questions have been asked.

The flexibility of this questioning regime, together with its varied support facilities, is not available in widely applicable, commercial shells, and therefore precludes the use of an "off the shelf" shell.

4.2 Knowledge Base

The knowledge base is a network of properties which link features of the learning task with the suitability of the various algorithms. Those properties which contain algorithm recommendations indicate the level of suitability using a certainty factor, a number between -1 and 1. A positive certainty indicates the property supports the algorithm, negative certainties act against the recommendation, a certainty of 1 represents conclusive evidence for the algorithm, -1 excludes the algorithm from the recommendation, and zero certainty neither supports nor detracts from this algorithm's recommendation. The overall algorithm suitability is calculated using MYCIN's integration function for certainty factors [Davis (1984)], this being a standard method for handling uncertain evidence in classification systems. Individual pieces of positive evidence are able to accumulate and provide more certain evidence, positive and negative evidence balance each other, and negative evidence increasingly weighs against a recommendation. In addition, evidence which totally precludes the use of algorithm can never be balanced or reduced. However, the certainties attached to

Consultant's properties need not be very accurate, because Consultant wishes only to rank the various algorithms and describe the evidence using an eleven point scale, see Section 4.3.

The process of acquiring Consultant's knowledge was unusual in two respects. Firstly, no **one** expert was available from whom to elicit the knowledge. Knowledge acquisition from multiple experts normally implies that more than one expert for the domain exists and the consensus of their knowledge must be represented. For Consultant, the acquisition was further complicated by the experts having expertise in **related**, but **disjoint** areas, namely the individual algorithms. One outcome of this was that a common terminology had to be defined which was suitable for all the algorithm developers. This lack of an established, unambiguous ML terminology further supports the need for elaborated questions and ML help facilities, even for ML experts.

Secondly, Consultant's knowledge base does not represent general ML expertise for choosing suitable ML approaches. Instead, distinguishing features of MLT's algorithms must be represented, and detailed knowledge is only required when several algorithms with similar approaches must be compared for suitability. Advising on the use of such diverse tools as are contained in MLT makes Consultant distinct from multistrategy learning systems [Michalski (1991)] where the selection of one, or several collaborating approaches, is made from a set of similar algorithms. The basic nature of Consultant's knowledge enables fairly simple, basic questions to be asked and this ensures that the beginner does not need to answer questions involving the subtleties of ML methods, which would be beyond his understanding at this stage.

The application types covered by Consultant are: select the most appropriate from two or more options (**classification**), optimise the performance of a particular system (**optimisation**), predict recurring events from past behaviour (**prediction**), group entities with similar properties (**clustering**), find an ordered sequence of actions to solve a problem (**planning**), detect instances of a pattern in data (**pattern detection**) and build or refine a model of a domain (**modelling**). Here, we briefly indicate some of the types of knowledge Consultant uses to recommend an algorithm for a classification application -

Classes: number, whether they overlap, ...
Examples: number, complexity, distribution among classes, noise, availability of negative examples, representation, ...
Interaction: availability of expert, ability to classify artificial examples, preferred output format, ...
Background knowledge: availability, format, ...

MLT's algorithms generate self-contained knowledge bases which can be used with one or more problem solving methods. Hence Consultant's recommendation is not dictated by the underlying problem solver. In contrast, many learning systems are designed for, or actually include, a particular problem solving method, e.g. PRODIGY [Carbonell (1991)], SOAR [Laird (1991)], and the choice of the learning system is heavily biased by the required problem solving paradigm.

4.3 Analysis

Although the underlying method of assembling evidence is based on certainty factors, it is not desirable to rely on them as exact, precise values. Therefore, Consultant offers several means of presenting its recommendations and justifications for its recommendations:

- The **barchart** represents the certainty attached to each algorithm recommendation as a bar. In Figure 1 we see that KBG and Makey are most favoured and SICLA-c has been eliminated as a possible algorithm for this learning task. The barchart display is shown while questions are being answered and is continually updated to reflect the current status. The bars have narrow shadow bars underneath to reflect the previous bar position before the current question was answered. This display has been well liked by domain experts because they value the immediate feedback, and in some cases have rethought the answer to a question when they saw its effect. The barchart is the only display which shows the "raw" certainties.

- An **explanation** provides textual justification for the level of support for an algorithm. Each piece of evidence for or against an algorithm is shown, but instead of quoting the raw certainties, the importance of the evidence is described on an eleven point scale: conclusive, large, significant, small, slight evidence for and against and no evidence for or against.[3] The user may ask for a justification of the recommendation for some or all of the algorithms. Section 3 contained explanations for APT and NewID.

- A **comparison** contrasts the discriminating task features which have contributed to the support for two algorithms, often chosen because they were closely recommended. The user may choose which algorithms to compare, but the default is the two most highly recommended algorithms. Section 3 contained comparisons for APT with NewID, and NewID with CN2.

- The **summary** recommends the most favoured algorithm, or lists all those leading algorithms which are closely rated to the most favoured one(s).

- The **log** records all the questions which have been asked so far, and the answers which have been given. This was used to provide part of the log in Section 3.

---

[3]The names for these levels will change in the next version to: conclusive, large, moderate, small, tiny evidence for and against and no discriminatory evidence exists; also the certainties they represent change slightly.

5 HELP SYSTEM

Consultant's help facilities are an important feature for assisting a domain expert. They must be extensive and supportive for a beginner, but should not be dictatorial or oppressive for an ML expert. The architecture diagram in Figure 5 also indicates the three help mechanisms available within Consultant:

- **Glossary:** an easy way to present brief help to a beginner;

- **Information Browser:** a comprehensive source of help files on ML and MLT topics, useful and accessible for both beginner and expert users of MLT; and

- **ML Database:** a collection of current ML abstracts, more relevant for ML experts.

The glossary contains short entries for basic terminology in ML. It is accessed by clicking on keywords which are displayed in red when they appear in dialogue text. This ensures that the user is able to get help at the point where the unfamiliar word has been used. The glossary entry for 'example' (or 'case') contains:
"The term Case or Example refers to the description of an object based on observed (or calculated) descriptors. A case can be a collection of several facts about an object, about a state or about an event, which are all related to each other; alternatively, simply an attribute-vector may be used to describe an object. An example differs from a case in that a case need not be classified as belonging to a particular class. That is, if a case is classified as a member of a particular class, the classified case is a positive example for the class."

The more extensive help system is available in parallel with the advising module and can be accessed by the user at any time. It consists of a large collection of help files with an easily used retrieval system. The help files include information on MLT algorithms and their requirements, more general ML topics, descriptions of MLT applications and successful "marriages" with algorithms. A help file is retrieved by assembling a collection of keywords for it. To assist this process, Consultant highlights those keywords which make sense if added to the existing list. In Figure 1 the keyword list, comprising only ID, can be extended by clicking on the highlighted words: How-to-use, Example, Parameters, Applications, etc., but the ID keyword alone has retrieved an overview help file for ID; more specific lists of keywords retrieve more specific help files.

Combinations of keywords are arranged in a hierarchical **lattice** structure[4]. The nodes in this keyword lattice represent **meaningful** concepts described by conjunctions of keywords. The lattice allows even a novice user to easily navigate through

---

[4]Many hierarchies of concepts are trees, but if some nodes in a hierarchy can be reached by more than one route then it forms a lattice.

the range of topics. Not only is he presented with suitable keywords, one of which he may be seeking, but it encourages him to explore files which he may not have considered retrieving.

Finally, Consultant provides ML assistance by allowing access to the ML database [Morales (1990)], a selection of ML relevant topics retrieved from the Turing Institute's ever growing database of references.

6 VALIDATION AND TESTING

The algorithm developers have inspected the knowledge about their algorithm. To ease this process, a natural language translator for Consultant's knowledge base has been written. As inconsistencies in the knowledge are reported and new features are incorporated in algorithms, refinements to the knowledge base are implemented.

All partners, but in particular applications partners, have tested Consultant by using it with in-house learning tasks. Some of this testing was done by MLT members, but much of the testing of Consultant was carried out by domain experts who were new to ML. Testing highlighted questions which were commonly misunderstood or were difficult to understand. The questions are being continually updated in response to such comments. Valuable testing was achieved by comparing Consultant's recommendations with those given by ML experts advising on suitable MLT algorithms. Such testing revealed that Consultant's advice compared favourably with those of ML experts.

A principled approach to the validation of expert systems is a current research issue, [VIVA (1992)]. Since, Consultant is simply an advice system for an expert; its recommendations need not be followed, and so rigorous validation is not appropriate. Our testing has been achieved by using an ML expert to verify Consultant's recommendations, and update the KB as necessary, during extended use at partner sites.

One of the aims of MLT has been to explore the use of ML algorithms for real-sized applications. The available applications cover a wide range of domains; e.g. design, medical, financial planning, fault diagnosis, etc. Consultant has been used with all these applications, and domain experts from a wide range of disciplines have been exposed to sessions with Consultant. It is noticeable that the speed of answering Consultant's questions varies with the expert's level of computer, and in particular ML, exposure. However computer-confident experts often rush through questions, hence misinterpreting certain questions and thus giving inappropriate answers. In contrast, more naive users answer the questions more carefully and are more willing to read the elaborations and investigate the help system. Therefore, a naive user often gets more useful advice on the initial run, although the more expert user often subsequently adjusts his replies to questions in response to receiving explanations from Consultant which alert him to his wrongly answered questions. Consultant allows the beginner to gradually articulate his learning task and encourages him to rethink earlier answers.

7 SUMMARY

Consultant is an integrated advice system for MLT to assist a domain expert to choose and use an ML algorithm; particularly a beginner in ML. Consultant has developed from the rigid, restrictive, black-box system, Consultant-0, through the well-liked, successful, flexible advice environment, Consultant-1 to the currently developing Consultant-2 system which allows a feedback loop through the algorithm runs. Consultant has been judged by partners and domain experts to be a supportive system giving appropriate, and useful, advice on applying MLT algorithms.

Consultant has some unusual features as an expert system. It embodies expertise not otherwise available in one source. This difficult knowledge acquisition task is eased by being restricted to discriminating knowledge about a relatively small set of often dissimilar ML algorithms. The need for a flexible control mechanism precluded the use of a standard shell. Consultant is tailored for use with MLT and the toolbox interface provides a common "look and feel" among Consultant and the MLT algorithms.

8 ACKNOWLEDGEMENTS

Knowledge for the various versions of Consultant and testing of existing implementations has been provided by other members of the consortium: Alcatel Alsthom Recherche (F), British Aerospace (UK), Foundation of Research and Technology – Hellas (Gr), Gesellschaft für Mathematik und Datenverarbeitung (D), INRIA (F), ISoft (F), Siemens AG (D), The Turing Institute (UK), Universidade de Coimbra (P), Université de la Réunion (F) and Université de Paris-Sud (F). In particular we thank Robert Davidge and Rüdiger Oehlmann, Aberdeen University, who implemented Consultant-0, and Chris Moore, British Aerospace, who implemented the knowledge functions for Consultant-1 and the natural language translator for Consultant's knowledge base. The development of Consultant is supported by the CEC as part of the Esprit II *"Machine Learning Toolbox"* project, P2154. Finally, we thank an anonymous reviewer for his useful comments.

9 REFERENCES

[Bisson (1992)] G. Bisson. Learning in FOL with a Similarity Measure. In *Proc. 11th National Conference on Artificial Intelligence*, 1992.

[Carbonell (1991)] J. G. Carbonell, C. A. Knoblock, and S. Minton. PRODIGY: an integrated architecture for planning and learning. In K. VanLehn, editor, *Architectures for Intelligence*. Lawrence Erlbaum, Hillsdale, NJ, 1991.

[Clark (1991)] P. Clark and R. A. Boswell. Rule induction with CN2: Some recent improvements. In Y. Kodratoff, editor, *Proc. Fifth European Working Session on Learning (EWSL)*, pages 151–163. Springer Verlag, 1991. No. 482 of Lecture Notes in Artificial Intelligence.

[Craw (1992)] S. Craw, N. Graner, M. Rissakis, S. Sharma, and D. Sleeman. Specification of Consultant–2. Deliverable 5.5, Machine Learning Toolbox ESPRIT Project P2154, 1992.

[Davis (1984)] R. Davis. Interactive transfer of expertise. In B. Buchanan and E. H. Shortliffe, editors, *Rule-Based Expert Systems*, pages 171–205. Addison-Wesley, Reading, MA., 1984.

[Graner (1992)] N. Graner, S. Sharma, D. Sleeman, M. Rissakis, C. Moore, and S. Craw. The Machine Learning Toolbox Consultant. Technical Report AUCS/TR9207, University of Aberdeen, 1992.

[Hutber (1987)] D. Hutber and P. Sims. Use of Machine Learning to Generate Rules. In *Proceedings of the Third Alvey Vision Conference*, 1987.

[Laird (1991)] J. Laird, M. Hucka, S. Huffman, and P. Rosenbloom. An analysis of Soar as an integrated architecture. *SIGART Bulletin*, 2(4):98–103, 1991.

[Michalski (1991)] R. S. Michalski and G. Tecuci, editors. *Proceedings of the First International Workshop on Multistrategy Learning (MSL–91)*, George Mason University, Fairfax, VA, 1991.

[Morales (1990)] E. Morales. The Machine Learning Toolbox Database. Deliverable 5.8, Machine Learning Toolbox ESPRIT Project P2154, 1990.

[Morik (1991)] K. Morik. Underlying assumptions of knowledge acquisition and machine learning. *Knowledge Acquisition Journal*, 3, 1991.

[Morik et al (1991)] K. Morik, K. Causse, and R. Boswell. A Common Knowledge Representation Integrating Learning Tools. In R. S. Michalski and G. Tecuci, editors, *Proceedings of the 1st International Workshop on Multi-Strategy Learning (MSL–91), West Virginia (USA)*, pages 81–96, 1991.

[Nedellec (1991)] C. Nedellec. A Smallest Generalization Step Strategy. In L. Birnbaum and G. Collins, editors, *Proceedings of the Eighth International Workshop on Machine Learning (IWML 91)*, pages 529–533. Morgan Kaufmann Publishers, Inc., 1991.

[Parsons (1989)] T. J. Parsons. Conceptual clustering in relational structures: An application in the domain of vision. *EWSL89, Proceedings of the Fourth European Working Session on Learning*, pages 163–177, 1989.

[Sleeman (1991)] D. Sleeman, S. Sharma, N. Graner, M. Rissakis, R. Davidge, and R. Oehlmann. Specification of Consultant–1. Deliverable 5.3, Machine Learning Toolbox ESPRIT Project P2154, 1991.

[van Heijst (1992)] G. van Heijst, P. Terpstra, B. Wielinga, and N. Shadbolt. Using generalised directive models in knowledge acquisition. In *Proceedings of EKAW 92*, 1992.

[van Hoff (1990)] A. van Hoff. HyperNeWS 1.4. Technical report, The Turing Institute, Glasgow, Scotland, 1990.

[VIVA (1992)] VIVA Partners Verification, Improvement & Validation of Knowledge Based Systems. Technical report, ESPRIT III Project 6125, 1992.

[WP5 (1990)] WP5 Partners. Overview of Consultant–0. Deliverable 5.2a, Machine Learning Toolbox ESPRIT Project P2154, 1990.

A Methods Model for the Integration of KBS and Conventional Information Technology

C. HARRIS-JONES*, T. BARRETT*, T. WALKER†, T. MOORES‡, J. EDWARDS‡

* BIS Information Systems, Ringway House, 45 Bull Street, Colmore Circus, Birmingham, B4 6AF
† Expert Systems Ltd, The Magdalen Centre, Oxford Science Park, Oxford, OX4 4GA
‡ Aston Business School, Aston University, Aston Triangle, Birmingham, B4 7ET

1.   INTRODUCTION

The last few years has seen a significant change in commercial KBS development. Organisations are now building KBS to solve specific business problems rather than simply to see what the technology can do. There has also been a move away from building KBS on stand alone PCs to using the corporate resources of networks, mini and Mainframe computers, and existing databases. As a result of these changes, two significant questions are now being regularly asked by organisations developing or interested in developing KBS:

- How can KBS be linked into existing systems to enhance their processing functions and make better use of data already held?

- What methods can be used to help build commercial applications using KBS techniques?

The key to these questions is the use of an integrated approach to the development of all IT systems. There are many methods available for conventional systems development, such as Information Engineering, SSADM, Jackson and Yourdon. There are also a number of KBS methods available or under development such as KADS, KEATS, and GEMINI. However, commercial organisations with well established procedures for conventional development do not want to use two different methods side-by-side, nor do they wish to discard their current conventional development method and replace it with a method claiming to cover all aspects of conventional and KBS development.

Organisations therefore require some way of integrating KBS methods into their existing methods.

This paper presents a framework, currently under development, which allows the integration to be carried out in a consistent and coherent manner. It is being developed at a relatively high level, and is aimed at the integration process itself and the subsequent use of the integrated method. Metrics are also being developed to answer project management questions, such as the cost and duration of the project and the expected quality of the hybrid products.

This research is part of a collaborative project between BIS Information Systems (Project leaders), Expert Systems Ltd and Aston University, under the Information Engineering Advanced Technology Programme (project number IED4/1/1426) and is jointly funded by the DTI, SERC and the industrial project partners. Much of the work has been based on the extensive experience of methods installation and integration, and development of KBS that exists within the consortium partners.

2.   INTEGRATED PROJECTS

2.1.   The integration problem

The increasing maturity of KBS technology has led to its wider application and an appreciation of the benefits it can bring to new or existing computer systems. For instance, a recent commercial project sought to develop an allocation and scheduling system which made use of conventional data entry, Operational Research algorithms and knowledge-based rules to generate and optimise a schedule. Such a system typifies the increasingly close relationship between KBS and conventional systems; the KBS and conventional elements are closely related with substantial data requiring conventional data analysis techniques and knowledge-based scheduling requiring KBS techniques. This type of project could be carried out by separating out the KBS elements and developing them using a KBS method, while using a conventional approach for the other parts of the project. However, attempting to run two different methods which use different terminology, different deliverables, and different management styles within a single project is not very satisfactory — particularly when there is a common database involved to which both the conventional and KBS elements need access. In some cases, the relationship between the KBS and conventional elements is so close that an integrated method is the only solution.

One way of approaching the problem of methods integration is to develop a method which allows for both conventional and KBS components. However, this would simply add to the plethora of existing methods and potential users would have to reject their current method and way of working and substitute the "new" method. This approach is very unlikely to gain commercial acceptance simply because of the large sums of money involved in methods installation and training. An alternative is to develop a framework allowing the integration of existing conventional and KBS methods. This would then only require organisations to supplement their existing expertise rather than replace it with new skills.

Another important issue in the use of methods is the need to tailor methods to individual projects. All projects are different and no single method can possibly fit all projects. Development methods, although targeted towards a particular type of application (for example business transaction processing or real-time process control), are usually intended to support the production of a wide range of applications within the target area. Many methods available provide a set of many hundreds of tasks, products and techniques. One of the problems observed in many organisations using such methods is that they will frequently use the whole method regardless of the nature of the project. The consequence is that a considerable amount of time can be spent "following the method" rather than actually building the intended system.

2.2.   Methods modelling
In line with the rise in the number of different development methods over the last decade several models of what a method "is" have been produced. These range from high level abstract models (Glasson, 1989) to very detailed models (AMADEUS, Loucopolous, *et al* 1987). These two are described below as representatives of methods modelling work. Other work includes Iivari (1990a and 1990b) and Ould & Roberts (1988).

Glasson's meta-model. Glasson describes a meta-model of system development which uses three main concepts — system evolution, system states and development deliverables. He takes the view that information systems are constantly evolving and uses system states to describe the process. At any given time the system is in a particular state, for example *Identified problem* or *Specified requirements*, and these describe the evolution of the system. The model provides a structure which allows sets of states to be organised into a system development sequence which is appropriate for a given project. The process of getting to a particular state is not described. This allows total flexibility in terms of the techniques which are used. For example, sets of techniques from many methods would allow a project to reach the state *Data analysis complete* even though there can only be one state where data analysis is complete. System states are comprised of, and defined by, a set of deliverables. The focus here is on the 'what' rather than the 'how'. One set of states and deliverables can be configured into a number of different life cycles depending on the requirements of the project.

AMADEUS. This project recognises the need for a multi-method approach, although it is not specifically considering KBS/conventional methods. The AMADEUS project is attempting to integrate methods at the semantic level (AMADEUS = A Multi-method Approach to Developing Unified Specifications). The aim of AMADEUS is to produce "a *unified conceptual model* which is rich enough semantically to maintain system specifications derived from any of the leading contemporary development methods" (Loucopolous, *op cit*). It identifies two views of system development methods: *process control* which looks at the steps and transformations applied during analysis, and the *model representation* view which looks at the deliverables of the process. AMADEUS concentrates on the latter, and attempts to develop a way of modelling the contents of methods such that all methods can be converted into a common model and then converted back into a different method. This is interfaced to tools so that the user of the tools does not need an awareness of how AMADEUS operates.

3.   METHODS MODELLING

The primary purpose of our project is to develop a framework which describes conventional and KBS methods in such a way that different methods can be integrated into a coherent whole. This will enable organisations to take their existing conventional method and integrate it with a KBS method. The integration process will also take account of information about the project on which the method is to be used, tailoring its contents appropriately. In this way, not only is a fully integrated method generated, but it also provides a sound basis for detailed project planning. This project is taking a high level approach closer to that of Glasson than AMADEUS. However, there is no reason why this high level approach should not eventually meet the very detailed approaches (such as AMADEUS).

A wide range of both KBS and conventional methods (including SSADM, Information Engineering, Modus, KADS, GEMINI and KEATS) have been analyzed and a methods model developed. This consists of three major parts — the *Structural Model*, the *Perspectives Model*, and the *Methods Process Model*. These models are outlined in the following sections.

3.1.   Structural Model

The purpose of the Structural Model is to provide a generic definition of the contents of methods and show the relationships between individual elements. It was developed by looking in detail at the contents of methods. The model has three layers of increasing abstraction (see Figure 1). The most abstract layer (3) contains a generic description of methods, identifying the individual components that go to make up development methods such as tasks, techniques and products; over 100 different components have so far been

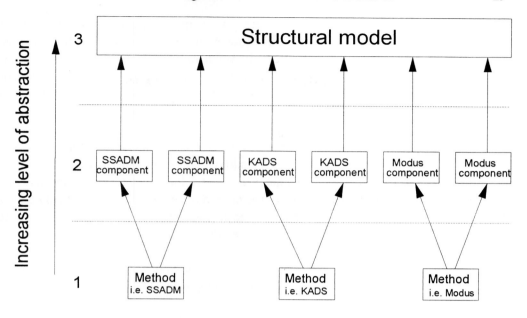

Figure 1: Diagram of 3 layer Structural Model

identified. This is not an attempt to develop an idealised method; the Structural Model simply takes those elements which already exist in methods and attempts to model them. The bottom layer (1), the least abstract, contains the methods descriptions as provided by the methods' vendors. The intermediate layer (2) provides the mapping of the individual methods onto the methods model. This middle layer takes the contents of the development methods and provides a library of discrete methods components in a format which allows them to be manipulated easily. One of the main purposes of the Structural Model is to act as a reference model against which the models of the source methods are constructed (ie SSADM, KADS, etc). This enables the methods to be assessed in terms of their coverage of the development process allowing omissions and overlaps to be identified.

3.2.   Perspectives Model

The Perspectives Model looks at the types of components which have to be modelled during systems development. The concept of a perspective has existed for a number of years and was initially used to classify development methods into either data-oriented or process-oriented. This was enhanced in the 1980s by a behaviour perspective. These have been described in detail by Olle *et al* (1988). The data perspective describes the data that are required in a system, typically through the use of data normalisation techniques and Entity-Relationship diagrams. The process perspective describes the processes which take place and is documented using techniques such as functional decomposition and process dependencies. The third perspective, behaviour, is less well defined: it describes how the system responds to events and is usually most developed in methods aimed at real-time systems. The use of these three views of systems development can also be found in a number of other authors including Kung & Sølvberg (1986) who describe Structure, Activity and Behaviour modelling; and Iivari (1990) who describes Structure, Function and Behaviour abstractions. These views can also be found in a number of object oriented methods, including Ptech (Martin & Odell, 1992).

Comparing the three perspectives with the scope of KBS methods it becomes clear that some additional features are needed. KBS methods tend to be particularly strong in two main areas — problem solving behaviour and domain knowledge. The problem solving aspects map onto many of the aspects of the behaviour perspective and consequently we have expanded the scope of this perspective to take account of these features. The domain knowledge — in particular the semantics of the domain — are not modelled anywhere in the current definition of the perspectives. We have therefore added a fourth perspective — knowledge. The "map" of methods thus provided by the perspectives shows the areas in which conventional and KBS methods need to be integrated. The relationship between the four perspectives is shown in figure 2.

Static vs dynamic. The data and knowledge perspectives contain "static" information which is manipulated by the process and behaviour perspectives. Ideally the static

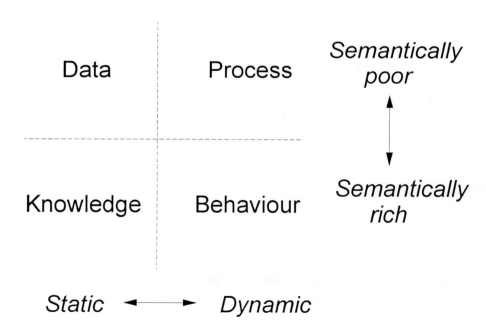

Figure 2: Diagram of four quadrant perspectives model

information is application-independent. This has some degree of truth in well designed corporate databases, it is also the ideal to which some KBS methods aspire, but very few KBS applications have yet achieved. One view is that this is due to a lack of understanding of what knowledge actually is, and to a lack of appropriate software tools. The opposing view is that it is impossible to analyse knowledge in a task-independent manner.

Semantic content. The process and data perspectives contain very little semantic information which can be used directly by the application. To some extent this is a truism since much of conventional analysis is aimed at removing as much meaning from data and processes as possible, for example data normalisation reduces all data to a common level and the links between data relations are purely cross-references. At the opposite extreme, modelling of domain knowledge attempts to capture as much of the semantics as possible. This semantic information is typically conveyed through the use of structures such as consists-of hierarchies, classification hierarchies and semantic nets. The middle ground appears to be occupied by object oriented techniques since these attempt to model some semantics while retaining an analysis of data necessary for conventional data-intensive applications. There is a similar correspondence of semantic content between the process and behaviour perspectives. The process perspective analyses the processes carried out in a system in a purely deterministic fashion. Some conventional IT methods capture behavioural information in as much as they record how the system responds to events — this is particularly true for real-time methods. Entity Life Histories provide high level behavioural information although this technique is often used purely for checking data and processes rather than a way of capturing behaviour to be coded explicitly. Knowledge-rich systems contain much semantic information which can be used to determine how to carry out actions and to structure tasks dynamically. This can also be used to generate explanations and to modify their own behaviour, for example so that the interaction with the user changes according to their level of expertise.

Perspectives evolution. Each component in the perspectives undergoes a transformation through the life of a development project and are usually referred to by different names at each stage. The top state of the perspectives is in the real world before any analysis has been carried out. Each component that is of relevance to the system being developed undergoes a series of transformations.

For example:

> form → entity → data structure → database table definition
> job → task → function definition → program specification

The evolution of the perspectives components is modelled as part of the Perspectives Model.

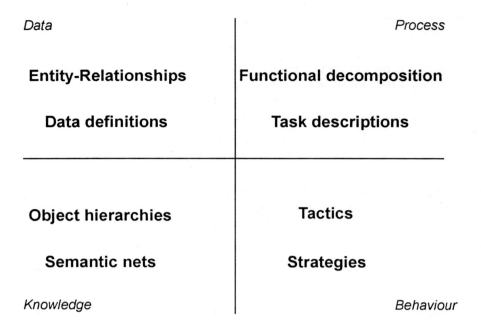

Figure 3: Details of the four quadrants: Analysis

Perspectives components. The contents of the four perspectives have been defined in some detail and is partly based on the work of Olle *et al* (1988). An overview of the components found in analysis is given in figure 3. Methods usually provide techniques for modelling a sub-set of the components contained in the model. They also provide techniques which straddle the boundaries and thus provide inter-perspective links. The most obvious example of this is the standard data flow diagram which relates the tasks to the data entities. There is a similar correspondence between the knowledge and behaviour perspectives exemplified by the inference structures found in KADS (Breuker, 1987). These document metaclasses which are abstract classifications of objects in the knowledge perspective, and knowledge sources which are descriptions of the ways in which knowledge can be used from the behaviour perspective. Object oriented methods are now appearing which do not make the separation of data and process in the same way, such as SOMA (Graham, 1991). These approaches can still be mapped onto the perspectives model since it represents the type of information which is captured rather than the way in which it is actually captured. Techniques from individual methods can then be mapped onto the model as appropriate.

3.3.   Methods Process Model

The Methods Process Model (MPM) shows how the various elements of the Structural Model fit together to configure a life cycle for a development project. Some methods describe this explicitly but very few provide detailed descriptions of process models. The MPM is the dynamic model which supports the production of a project plan. It is important not to confuse methods and life cycles. The former describe the tasks, techniques and products which can be used (and is described by the Structural Model), the latter describe how the tasks are configured for use on a specific project. Typical life-cycles are the waterfall model and prototyping; the structures within these high-level models are described by the MPM. One consequence of this explicit separation is that similar methods components can be used within different life cycles. This is graphically illustrated with the rise of Rapid Development Methods. Many of the same methods components used in projects with a waterfall approach are used in Rapid Development Methods.

The MPM is used largely in the configuration process where the detailed tasks are put together to produce a complete plan for an application development. Once the selected KBS and conventional development methods have been integrated using the Structural and Perspectives Models, the MJ M is used to configure the life cycle. The most abstract level of the model shows the four principle types of tasks defined in the Structural Model

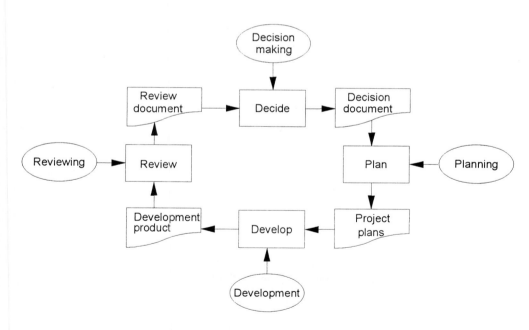

Figure 4: Diagram of the top level of the MPM

(see figure 4) in the sequence in which they are normally carried out. This is used to guide the high level configuration of tasks. More detailed levels of the Methods Process Model are then used to configure the project plan in detail.

The top level of the MPM bears a significant resemblance to Boehm's spiral model (Boehm, 1988). This is not surprising since both Boehm's model and our model have been derived from best current practice. The major difference is the renaming of the Risk quadrant to Decision. This was done because it was felt that it reflected the systems development process more accurately. At this point in a project a decision has to be made about the next step. Although an assessment of the risk is a very significant element in the decision making process, there are other elements including, for example, internal political issues. These can often kill a project far more efficiently than risk factors.

4.   METRICATION

Even with a well-constructed method in place, whether the proposed system is developed at all could well depend on the project manager's ability to accurately estimate certain properties of the project. In particular, the client would like to know the likely cost and duration of the project, while the project manager would need to be able to assess the expected quality of the products. If mistakes are made over these properties then at best there will be a strain on limited personnel and hardware resources, and at worst, the project could be cancelled due to costs outweighing any remaining benefits.

Metrics have been developed since the early 1970s to provide answers to these questions of cost, duration and quality for conventional systems. 'Metrics' are measurements of some aspect of the development process or products which are then used to develop estimating tools. For instance, COCOMO (Boehm, 1981) represents the relationship between person-months of effort (E) and thousands of lines of delivered source instructions (KDSI) with the model

$$E = 3 * (KDSI)^{1.12}$$

Where the inputs to these models are known early in the development process and the model proves to give accurate results, a tool which calculates the outputs from the model would provide valuable support for the project manager's estimating decisions.

Given that the systems being dealt with by the methods integration tool contain both conventional and KBS components, it might seem reasonable to follow the classic process and develop an estimating tool which can be applied to both types of components. However, the usefulness of following this process can be doubted. Firstly, there appears to be some resistance to the use of estimating tools amongst project managers (IPL, 1989; van Genuchten & Koolen 1991). Secondly, even where they are used, evidence suggests estimating tools are not accurate (Kusters *et al*, 1991). In the face of these problems, following the same process to build a hybrid metrics model would seem to be pointless.

It was decided to investigate these issues, and it was found (Moores & Edwards, 1992; Moores, 1992; Edwards & Moores, 1992) that the problem lay not with the process of developing estimating tools, but with the nature of the final product and what was being modelled. Specifically, although project managers often produce estimates even before drawing up a project plan, this is not regarded as a "true" estimate.   Instead, project managers see estimation as a bottom-up task first performed when a detailed (top-down) plan is produced.   Although a number of commercially available tools can give task-based estimates, this form of estimation is not their primary mode of generating an estimate and so it is no surprise that managers fail to perceive the relevance of estimating tools to their work.

So, while the existing process of developing estimating tools would seem to remain appropriate, it is a task-based model which seems to be the more useful model for project managers. A clear definition of the range of tasks involved in hybrid software development is being formulated within the methods model. However, a second feature of a hybrid metrics model is that it must be equally applicable to both conventional and KBS components. But these components are portrayed as being very different in character (eg. Bader *et al*, 1988), and so it is unclear whether any metric can be applied to both conventional and KBS components and produce meaningful data. Without the data, no hybrid model can be built. The question therefore becomes: "Are there any hybrid metrics?"

An experimental approach is being taken which is investigating the feasibility of building on existing work by extending three well-known conventional metrics (Halstead, 1977; McCabe, 1976; Henry & Kafura, 1984) to a KBS language. Prolog has been chosen as the KBS language. The approach is experimental because the concepts behind these conventional metrics do not have exact analogues in the KBS world. Halstead's program length metric talks of operators and operands. What should be counted as an operator in Prolog? McCabe's cyclomatic complexity metric suggests that once the structure of a program exceeds a certain level the number of bugs will dramatically increase. What is this level for Prolog? Henry and Kafura's data-flow metric suggests that high data-flow indicates a component which will require more reworking if other components are changed. Is this also true for a language like Prolog?

To answer these and other questions a tool has been developed which applies all three metrics to static Prolog code. The next step is to allow a number of commercial companies to use the tool to analyse their own library of programs. By also collecting development time and error-rate data, it will then be possible to establish whether these three simple metrics can indeed form the basis of an accurate and useful hybrid estimating tool.

5.   TOOL SUPPORT

So far the theoretical basis for methods integration work has been described. The project also has a practical stream: the construction of a tool for supporting the integration and configuration of methods. There are two reasons for undertaking this work:

- It is necessary to undertake some form of validation. Building a tool shows up gaps in the theory and forces clarification of concepts. It also provides quicker test results than attempting the process "by hand".

- For the project's results to have their desired practical application, they will need to be made widely available in an easy to use form.

The tool being constructed is called Russet. It runs in Microsoft's Windows 3.1 environment, and is written in the language *Prolog-2 for Windows 3*, from Expert Systems Ltd.

5.1.   Methods Representation

The representation chosen for the methods and the Structural Model is a frame-like structure. This gives ease of use to the methods engineers encoding the source methods, together with the power of inheritance in the resulting hierarchy.

```
Class                :    Plan
Class membership     :    \Product
Subclasses           :    Terms of reference, Project
                          plans report, Development plan,
                          Phase plans, Standards,
                          Resources
Class description    :    Plan products are used to
                          coordinate the usage of the
                          method
Cardinality          :    1:1
Perspective          :    null
```

Figure 5: A product frame from the Structural Model

An example of a frame (for the generic product *Plan*) in the Structural Model is shown in figure 5. The "Class membership" slot refers to its place in the Structural Model; "Subclasses" refers to the frames directly below in the Structural Model; "Cardinality" tells us there should only be one such classification per method; and the "Perspective" slot maps onto the Perspectives Model. The perspectives Model is represented in a similar way, but requires more complex links because of the time progression element; both the Structural Model and the Perspectives Model are loaded automatically every time Russet is consulted.

The source methods themselves are represented in a similar way to the Structural Model. Figure 6 shows a product from the KADS KBS method in this form. As can be seen, there are considerably more slots than for the Structural Model. Information contained here includes references to the Structural Model (the "Class membership" slot) and the Perspectives Model (the "Perspectives" and "P-Components" slots). Once the entire method's product hierarchy has been encoded in this form the method may be read by Russet.

```
Product name      :   Inference Layer
Method            :   KADS
Parent product    :   Model of Expertise
Class membership :   \Product\Development\System
                      options\Alternative solutions
Abbreviated name :   M4
Cardinality       :   1
AKO               :   null
Child products    :   null
Description       :   A specification of the inferences
                      which may be performed over the
                      knowledge base
Perspectives      :   Knowledge, Behaviour
P-Components       :   \Perspective\Knowledge\Object, etc,
                      etc
P-Representations:   Inference Structures, Knowledge
                      Sources, Metaclasses
Document support :   Interpretation Model Library
Tasks             :   Construct Model of Expertise
Techniques        :   ...
```

Figure 6: A KADS product in its Russet-prepared format

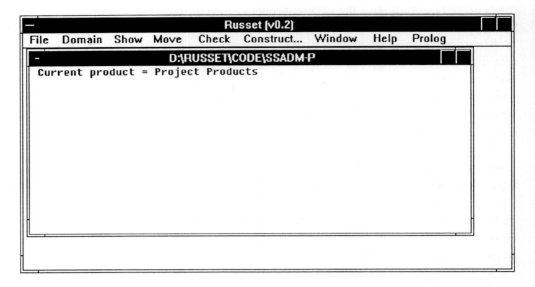

Figure 7: The Russet tool after the opening of SSADM

5.2.   The Russet Tool in Use

The version of Russet described in this paper (0.2) has been used to validate the work of the project to date, as described in earlier sections.

Russet runs in the Microsoft Windows environment, and follows the Multiple Document Interface format (IBM, 1989); it is built around the notion of "methods windows". At the start of a session the user will open a methods document referring to one of the source methods. Figure 7 shows the state of the application after the SSADM product hierarchy has been loaded.

A brief description of each of the menus — and hence the system's functionality — follows:

File   Covers all the standard Windows file manipulation actions: New, Open, Save, Print, etc. Files which have been opened from the textual frame descriptions can be saved in Prolog's internal format, thus speeding up later consultation.

Domain   Allows the user to select which type of methods components (Products, Tasks or Techniques) to display and integrate.

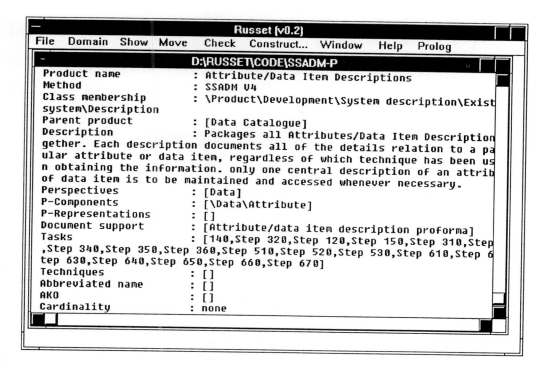

Figure 8: The "Details" of one of SSADM's products

Show   Has three options, and all operate on the currently active methods window. These are:

- "Details" which shows the contents of the current product (whose name is displayed in the methods window) in a frame-like format — see figure 8 for an example.

- "Hierarchy" which displays the entire (product) hierarchy of the current method, indented.

- "Structural Model" which displays the Structural Model, indented, together with the products in the current method which reference it.

Move   Navigates the product hierarchy: the menu options consist of a series of movement commands (Up, Down, Next, etc). There are plans to replace this with a graphical "point-and-click" view of the hierarchy.

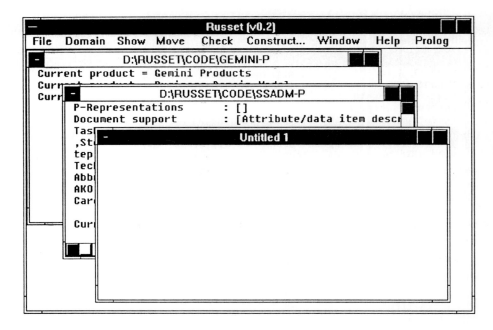

Figure 9: Russet before creating an integrated method

Check   Contains a series of consistency checks that the user may perform on the current method. Although used on single methods as a debugging aid, the real use of these functions is on newly created integrated methods.

Construct...   Prompts the user for further methods to load into the current Methods window. Figure 9 shows Russet with three Methods windows open, SSADM, GEMINI and a new, "Untitled" method. Using "Construct..." both SSADM and GEMINI may be integrated to create a new method.

Window   Covers the standard windows manipulation functions: Tile, Cascade, etc.

Help   Provides access to Windows Help files.

Prolog   A debugging option only; will not appear in any final release.

5.3.   The Future of Russet

At present Russet is a fairly primitive prototype primarily designed to verify the theoretical results of the project.

It is ultimately seen as a methods expert's workbench — using knowledge based technology to make sensible decisions in integrating and configuring methods. It will still, however, require some input from human experts. It is not designed to be usable by people completely unfamiliar with information systems and KBS methods; it will be usable by practitioners skilled in methods, but not necessarily those methods that they are integrating.

Eventually, it is envisaged that there will be a number of source methods descriptions available to potential users on a plug-in basis. In this way all the popular methods can be covered, but users will only need those which are appropriate to their organisation.

Once a suitable integrated method has been constructed Russet should be able to configure the hybrid method to fit the development in question — ensuring that only the necessary tasks are undertaken. Once such detailed task lists have been constructed, then it is possible to use the task-based estimating tools when planning the project, and then project management tools for monitoring and controlling the project as it progresses.

6.   CONCLUSIONS

The project is attempting to produce a model of conventional and KBS methods which guides the integration for use on hybrid commercial development projects. Three models have been built and work has started on a prototype to validate the approach and provide automated support.

The approach being taken has worked to date although the methods model is far from complete. However, it has already been used successfully in a number of different areas :

*   The methods model has been used to assist in the structuring of a set of methods to be delivered in hypertext format.

*   It has been used to check the completeness of manually integrated methods before they have been used on projects.

*   It is currently being used on a major development project building tools to support RDBMS design which requires the use of a hybrid method.

The need for a task-based estimating tool has also been clearly identified, with doubts over the classic process of developing estimating tools being overcome. A metrics tool has been developed to help in the collection of the data upon which the hybrid estimating tool is to be based. Three relatively simple metrics are being applied (implementation size, cyclomatic complexity, data flow), with early results suggesting that these metrics are both accurate and useful.

7.   REFERENCES

Bader J., Edwards J.S., Harris-Jones C., & Hannaford D., (1988) Practical Engineering of Knowledge Based Systems, *Information and Software Technology*, **30**(5), 266-277.

Boehm B.W., (1981) *Software Engineering Economics*. Prentice-Hall, Englewood Cliffs, New Jersey.

Boehm B.W., (1988) A spiral model of software development and enhancement, *Computer*, May 1988, pp61-72.

Breuker J. (Ed.), Weilinga B., van Someren M., de Hoog R., Schreiber G., de Greef P., Bredeweg B., Weilemaker J., Billeaut J-P., Davoodi M., Hayward S., *Model Driven Knowledge Acquisition Interpretation Models*, Deliverable D1, task A1, Esprit project 1098, Feb 1987.

Edwards, J.S. & Moores, T.T. (1992) Metrics and project management models in the development of hybrid information systems. To appear in *The Proceedings of the International Conference on Economics/Management and Information Technology*, Tokyo, 31 August-4 September, 1992.

van Genuchten, M. & Koolen, H. (1991) On the use of software cost estimating models. *Information & Management*, **21**, pp37-41.

Glasson B.C. (1989), Model of system evolution, *Information and Software Technology*, **31**, No 7, Sept 1989.

Graham I. (1991), *Object Oriented Methods*, Addison Wesley, 1991.

Halstead, M.H. (1977) *Elements of Software Science*. Elsevier North-Holland, New York.

Henry, S. & Kafura, D. (1984) The evaluation of software systems' structure using quantitative software metrics. *Software — Practice and Experience*, **14**(6), 561-571.

IBM (1989) *Common User Access: Advanced Interface Design,* International Business Machines Corp., Document No. SY0328-300-R00-1089, 1989.

Iivari J. (1990a), Hierarchical spiral model for information system and software development. Part 1:Theoretical background, *Information and Software Technology,* **32**, No 6, July/August 1990.

Iivari J. (1990b), Hierarchical spiral model for information system and software development. Part 2: design process, *Information and Software Technology,* **32**, No 7, Sept 1990.

IPL (1989) *Software Quality Survey*. Confidential report cited with permission from Information Processing Limited, Eveleigh House, Grove Street, Bath.

Kusters, R.J., van Genuchten, M. & Heemstra, F.J. (1991) Are software cost-estimating models accurate? In *The Economics of Information Systems and Software* (Veryard. R, Ed), pp155-161, Butterworth-Heinemann, Oxford.

Kung C.H. & Sølvberg A. (1986), Activity modelling and behaviour modelling, in Olle T.W. Sol H.G. and Verrijn-Stuart A.A. (Eds) *Information Systems Design methodologies: Improving the practice,* Elsevier Science 1986.

Loucopolous P., Black W.J., Sutcliffe A.G. & Layzell P.J. (1987), Towards a unified view of system development methods, *Int Jnl of Information Management,* V7, pp205-218, 1987.

Martin J. & Odell J., *Object Oriented Analysis and Design,* Prentice Hall, 1992.

McCabe, T. (1976) A complexity measure. *IEEE Transactions on Software Engineering,* **SE-2**(4), 308-320.

Moores, T.T. (1992) On the use of software cost estimating tools. *Doctoral Working Paper No.6 (NS),* Aston Business School, Aston University, April 1992.

Moores, T.T. & Edwards, J.S. (1992) Could large UK corporations and computing companies use software cost estimating tools? — a survey. *European Journal of Information Systems,* **1**(5), 311-319.

Olle T.W., Hagelstein J., Macdonald I.G., Rolland C., Sol HG, Van Assche FJM, Verrijn-Stuart AA, (1988), *Information Systems Methodologies : A Framework for Understanding,* Addison Wesley, 1988.

Ould M.A. & Roberts C., *Defining formal models of the software development process,* Software Engineering Environments, Ellis Horwood, 1988.

KBS Methodology as a framework for Co-operative Working

John Kingston

Knowledge Engineering Methods Group

AIAI

University of Edinburgh

Abstract

This paper describes the development of the Injection Moulding Process Expert System (IMPRESS). The IMPRESS system diagnoses faults in injection moulding machinery which lead to dirt or other contamination appearing in the plastic mouldings which are produced. This KBS has recently been put into use at Plastic Engineers (Scotland) Ltd, and is proving useful both as an expert assistant when technical help is otherwise unavailable, and as a training aid.

The IMPRESS system was built by a member of Plastic Engineers' staff with assistance from a KBS consultant. It was decided that the project would be based around a KBS methodology; a 'pragmatic' version of the KADS methodology was chosen. The methodology was used not only to formalise and guide the development of the KBS itself, but also to act as a framework for dividing the work between the two members of the project team. By gaining an understanding of the methodology, the staff member from Plastic Engineers was able to understand the knowledge analysis and KBS design documents produced by the consultant, and to use these documents to implement part of the KBS, both during the development of the system and when system maintenance was required.

The use of a methodology for this project on this project had both benefits and weaknesses, which are discussed at the end of the paper.

1 Introduction

In January 1992, Plastic Engineers (Scotland) Ltd obtained funding from Scottish Enterprise to help them in the development of a knowledge based system (KBS) for fault diagnosis. Plastic Engineers manufacture precision plastic mouldings, such as casings for PCs, or control panels for video recorders. They have a reputation for high quality, which they want to maintain. However, from time to time, problems with their injection moulding machines mean that substandard mouldings are produced, and these have to be scrapped to maintain the reputation for quality. While Plastic Engineers have technicians who are very competent at solving these problems, these technicians have a variety of roles to perform. If a technician is working on an urgent task, or is absent through holidays or illness, it may take some hours before diagnostic expertise is available. Shift leaders are able to provide some backup to technicians, but they have even more demands on their time than the technicians do. As a result, there are times when no-one with diagnostic knowledge is available, particularly during some night shifts.

After attending a seminar organised by AIAI and the Scottish Office in the summer of 1991, the idea of building a KBS to help with the diagnostic process was born. The project was set up in January 1992 with Plastic Engineers releasing one member of staff to work on the project for two days per week. This member of staff [JM] was a newly recruited graduate in Polymer Technology with knowledge of the process of injection moulding, but very little computing experience. AIAI were engaged to provide JM with initial training in KBS programming, knowledge elicitation and knowledge engineering (a total of 7 days' training) and then to provide 15 man days' consultancy spread over the 4-month duration of the project. The intention was that by the end of the project, JM would be fully conversant with the techniques used to develop the KBS, and would therefore be able to maintain the system if any changes were needed after installation.

AIAI decided to use a methodological approach to this project. The use of KBS methodology in the commercial world is still in its infancy, but AIAI were sufficiently convinced of the benefits of methods to use a simplified version of the KADS methodology on this project. However, in this project, the methods were used not only to formalise and guide the development of the KBS itself, but also to act as a framework for the division of labour and transfer of KBS expertise. This paper describes the benefits and drawbacks of using a methodology in this way.

Before any development could take place, however, a number of factors needed to be established to ensure that the KBS project stood a good chance of success. These included:

- Economic considerations. Plastic Engineers do have a genuine problem with quality control - they scrap around 2% of their production each month. The KBS is likely to make a significant improvement to the availability of diagnostic expertise, and to the early detection of faults, thus reducing scrap rates.

- Technical considerations. Diagnosis is known to be a task type which KBS are well suited for; also, the technicians currently take between several minutes and a few hours to solve problems, so there are unlikely to be any stringent requirements for real-time problem solving.

- Personnel considerations. The project was initiated by Plastic Engineers' General Manager, so management support was assured. The users - the machine operators - are likely to appreciate any help their shift leaders can give them in diagnosing faults. However, the commitment of the shift leaders and technicians themselves was unclear, so the AIAI consultant [JK] made a presentation to these people, which included a demonstration of a very simple KBS which diagnosed three different faults in the plastic moulding process. While the underlying structure of this demonstration system was very shallow in its reasoning, and drew knowledge from just one day of knowledge acquisition, it was sufficient to convey the concept of a KBS to the shift leaders and technicians, and to excite their curiosity so that they began to ask questions about the capabilities of the system. This was deemed to be sufficient commitment for the project to proceed.

The project was named IMPRESS (the Injection Moulding PRocess Expert SyStem project).

2   The framework of the IMPRESS project

The KADS methodology divides the process of KBS development into three phases: knowledge elicitation and analysis, KBS design and KBS implementation. The IMPRESS project was set up with a number of intermediate milestones accompanied by deliverables; these milestones were based around the phases specified by KADS. The phases specified in the project plan were:

- Knowledge elicitation and analysis - 6 weeks.

- KBS design - 4.5 weeks

- KBS implementation - 4.5 weeks

- Testing and installation - 2 weeks

The workload was divided between JM and JK in a manner which was intended to get the project completed within the deadline, but also to give JM a sufficient awareness of KBS development and the contents of the IMPRESS system to enable him to update it. The policy pursued was for both JK and JM to attend knowledge elicitation sessions; then for JK to perform the knowledge analysis and KBS design while JM undertook background reading on KADS so that he understood the deliverables which JK produced; and finally for JM to undertake the lion's share of the implementation, and to carry out user acceptance testing, any consequent alterations, and installation. The plan was adhered to fairly closely, and JM was indeed able to make alterations to the KBS himself in response to comments from the users.

3   Progress of the project

3.1   Knowledge Elicitation

Knowledge elicitation for the IMPRESS system was carried out at Plastic Engineers' premises in Ayrshire. The first interview was with one of the shift leaders, who was asked to provide a general overview of the problems which arise in the plastic moulding process. The interview was guided using the "laddered grid" knowledge elicitation technique [6]. This technique supplies a number of template questions which are designed to prompt experts to supply further information about a taxonomic hierarchy - for example, the question "Can you give me some examples of *Class*" will supply information about instances or subclasses of the class *Class*. The technique can also be used to elicit procedural information. In the interview with the shift leader, the resulting grid comprised both a detailed description of some of the faults which arise in the plastic moulding process, including descriptions of different symptoms and associated faults, and also explanations and corrective action for some faults. While it is not desirable for analysis purposes for the expert to be allowed to mix taxonomic and procedural information in his replies, this interview nevertheless provided a concise introduction to the domain and the diagnostic task.

The next interview was with the Quality Manager, who provided a breakdown of the five main categories of fault. These categories are

- Contamination - dirty marks of some kind on the final moulding

- Shorts - certain parts of the mould do not fill with plastic

- Burns - discolouration due to plastic being overheated

- Degate - human error when trimming with a knife

- Others

The Quality Manager keeps detailed statistics of the number of times each fault has occurred, and how long it takes to solve. From examination of these statistics, it became obvious that contamination was the most frequently occurring problem, and that contamination problems took an average of almost 2.5 hours to solve. Based on this information, it was decided that the KBS would initially be limited to diagnosing contamination problems only.

All other knowledge elicitation interviews were conducted with technicians, who are the day to day diagnostic experts. Most of these interviews used a "20 questions" knowledge elicitation technique [1]. This technique is normally used after several knowledge elicitation sessions, because it requires the knowledge engineer to be fairly familiar with the task. The knowledge engineer selects a potential fault, which the expert is required to diagnose; the expert does this by asking questions, which the knowledge engineer answers. As JM had some knowledge of the injection moulding process and of Plastic Engineers' machinery, it was possible to use this technique from a very early stage.

A typical "20 Questions" session is shown below. The hypothesised fault was dust entering the machine via the drier which dries the raw material. The technician was told that there were "black specks on the moulding". JM's answers to the technician's questions are shown in brackets.

```
What's the tool? [155]
Where are the marks? [Back face, sides - all over]
How long has the job been running? [2 days]
Has the problem been present since start up? [Yes]
Is the problem getting worse? [Yes]
Have you cleaned the shims? [Yes, it caused a little improvement, but
the problem recurred]
Is the temperature unstable, or too high? [No]
Check the thermocouplings [OK]
Check the condition of the screw, and look for black specks on the
screw [OK]
```

On being told the answer, the technician commented that dust from the drier was almost never a problem because of the reliability of the drier's filtration system.

The technician was then asked to explain his reasons for asking each question. The information which was extracted from the conversation described above and the subsequent explanation included:

- Possible faults include dirty shims, incorrect temperature settings, loose thermocouplings, and dirt on the screw.

- Some faults are more prevalent on certain machine tools - usually tools which produce large mouldings.

- If the marks had appeared only on the bottom edges of the moulding, this would have been a very strong indicator of one particular fault.

- Certain faults only occur shortly after the machine has been started up. Many of these are due to the machine not being cleaned properly before being shut down.

- If the problem only occurs for a short time, then the fault is likely to be contamination in a single batch of raw material.

- If the problem is getting worse, then it is likely to be due to some material which is trapped in the machine and slowly degrading

- Dust in the drier hardly ever causes a problem because it is filtered out

The "20 Questions" technique proved to be very helpful for eliciting diagnostic information, with a lot of useful information obtained in a concise format in a short period of time.

3.2   Knowledge Analysis

The technicians' knowledge divides into three main categories:

- Declarative knowledge - the workings of the machine, and knowledge of all faults which may occur.

- Procedural knowledge - knowing how to test for and how to fix faults.

- Control knowledge - performing tests in a sensible order.

The declarative and procedural knowledge was relatively straightforward to extract from the results of the "20 Questions" sessions, but the control knowledge required a little more thought. It was eventually determined that the likelihood of a fault occurring, and the time required to perform a particular test, were the most important factors in deciding the order in which tests should be performed. For example, in the "20 Questions" session quoted above, the technician asked about the condition of the screw last, because it takes a couple of hours to dismantle the machine sufficiently to expose the screw, and he did not ask about dust in the drier at all, because it is such a rare fault.

It turned out that there are quite a number of rare faults. However, as JM spent much of his time on the shop floor when he was not working on the KBS, it was decided that JK would press ahead with the analysis phase while JM completed the elicitation of all possible faults from the experts. The final KBS contains about 40 faults (broken down into five subclasses) and a similar number of tests.

3.3   KBS design, implementation, testing and installation

The analysed knowledge was transformed into a KBS design using techniques based on the KADS methodology (these techniques are outlined in section 4). The KBS was then implemented in KAPPA-PC version 1.2 on an Apricot 486 PC. The resulting design suggested that faults, tests, and test results should be represented using individual objects, while inference should be implemented primarily using a mixture of rules and functions, with a little use of object-oriented methods and demons. However, it transpired that some of the desired rule functionality was unavailable in KAPPA-PC; it also became clear that the time taken to execute a rule which matched on a set of objects was similar to the time taken for a function to iterate over the same objects. As a result, it was decided that rules would not be used at all, and so much of the inference in the IMPRESS system was implemented using functions.

The KBS was subjected to testing by developers concurrently with the implementation of the user interface, and was installed in the first week of August 1992. At the time of writing, few firm results were available, because there have been relatively few occasions since the installation of the KBS when there has been no technical expert available to answer questions. However, the fact that the system can be used "off-line" has been appreciated, and the KBS has been used several times for training purposes by interested machine operators.

4   Using KADS for the IMPRESS project

The KADS methodology for KBS development [2] is intended both to guide and to formalise KBS development. To this end, it provides guidance on obtaining knowledge, analysing it, and transforming it into a detailed design for an implemented KBS. The IMPRESS project did not use the KADS methodology in its entirety, but instead followed the "pragmatic KADS" approach described in [3].

4.1   Knowledge analysis: interpretation models

Once some knowledge has been acquired, the KADS methodology recommends selection of an *interpretation model*. Interpretation models are task-specific breakdowns of the inferences and items of knowledge required in a typical task of that type. These models are intended both to formalise acquired knowledge and to guide further knowledge acquisition. For the IMPRESS system, it was obvious from the start that the task type was diagnosis; however, KADS offers several different interpretation models for different methods of performing diagnosis. Eventually, it was decided that the interpretation model for *systematic diagnosis* was the most appropriate. This model is shown in Figure 1 below; the ovals are known as "inference functions", and the boxes as "knowledge roles"[1].

---

[1]Strictly speaking, Figure 1 represents only one component of an interpretation model. However, under "pragmatic KADS", the other component is not used, and so the structure shown in this diagram is described as an interpretation model throughout this paper.

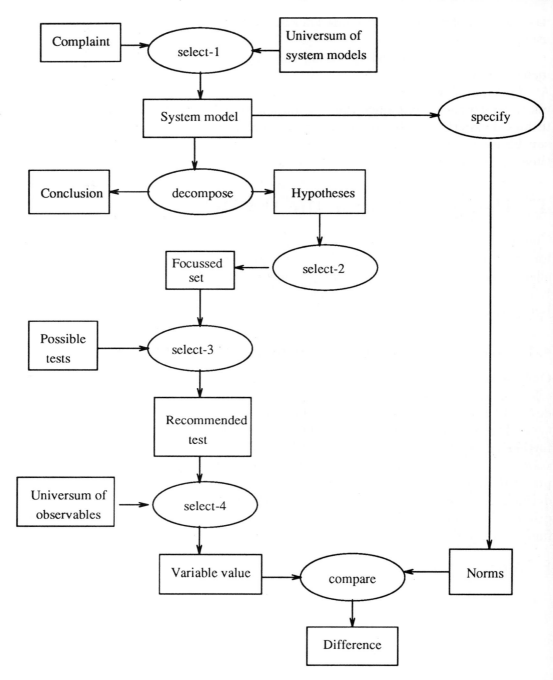

Figure 1: Interpretation model for systematic diagnosis

This model represents the inference which is expected to be performed when a task involving systematic diagnosis is executed. For example, if a user reports a problem with a machine, it is expected that a particular system model representing the correct operation of that machine will be selected, and a number of faults will be suggested. Based on a 'focussed' subset of these faults, a number of characteristics of the machine will be measured and compared with their expected values in the system model.

This model was then adapted to the domain of the IMPRESS system, as shown in Figures 2 and 3 below (Figure 3 is an expansion of the **select-1*** inference function in Figure 2), to produce a problem-specific *inference structure*. This inference structure indicates that the IMPRESS system will identify a set of possible faults (hypotheses) based on the reported contamination problem. A test is then recommended, based on the likelihood of the hypotheses, the time required to perform a test and the time required to alter the state of the machine so that the test can be performed. Once it has been decided which test will actually be performed, the test is carried out, and the actual result is compared against a set of expected results (see below) in order to update the set of hypotheses.

It can be seen that the adaptation from the interpretation model to the inference structure involved a number of changes. Most of these changes are relatively minor, such as the removal of the focussing of the set of hypotheses into a smaller set; it was felt that the set of hypotheses was sufficiently small that such a step was not necessary. However, one of the changes implies a fundamental change to the approach taken to reasoning. This change involved the interpretation model's suggestion of comparing values against a system model, which is a *model-based* approach to KBS construction. While a model-based approach would have worked adequately for the IMPRESS system, it was felt that explicitly representing injection moulding processes was not worth the effort, primarily because all Plastic Engineers' machines operate in the same manner, and so only one "system model" would be required. Instead, it was decided that for every known fault, the expected results of each test would be represented. For example, if the fault was "Contamination of raw material due to the box of material being left open", then a check on the material currently being fed into the machine should produce the result *Contamination present*, while a check on a fresh box of material should produce the result *Contamination absent*. These values were explicitly represented, and compared against the actual results of tests, as shown at the bottom of Figure 2.

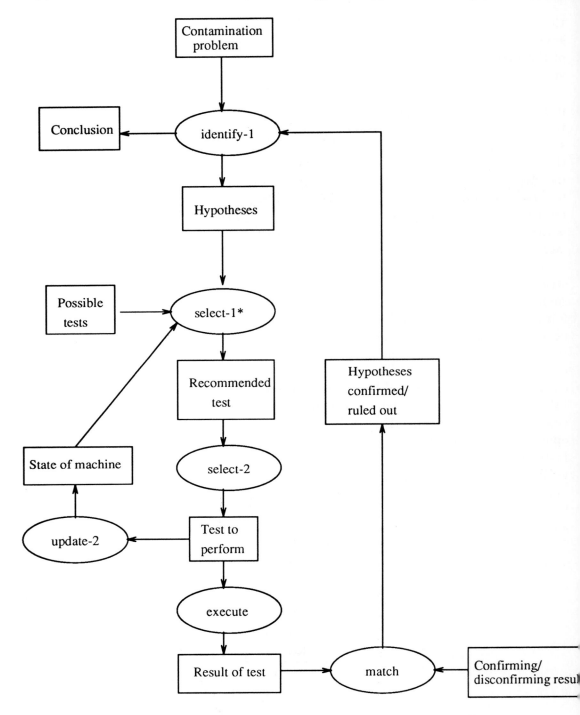

Figure 2: Inference structure for IMPRESS system

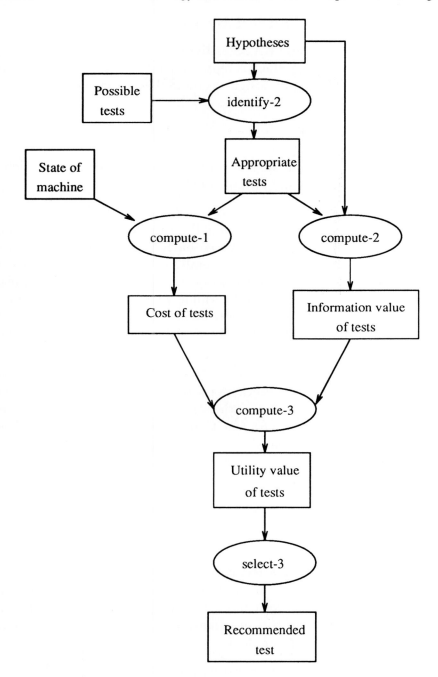

Figure 3: Inference structure for test selection in IMPRESS system

4.2   Further guidance provided by pragmatic KADS

The remaining stages of the pragmatic KADS analysis and design phases gradually extend and transform the knowledge which is represented in the inference structure into a detailed KBS design, with any design decisions being explicitly recorded. These stages are:

Knowledge analysis:

- The *task structure* identifies the flow of control between inference functions, and also identifies any inputs and outputs of the KBS.

- The *model of interaction*, an addition to the KADS methodology used by AIAI [4], assigns inference functions to the KBS, the user, or the two working together. The model of interaction is based on KADS' "model of cooperation", which is used to determine which overall task(s) should be performed by a knowledge based system. The model of interaction performs a similar function *within* a single KBS; it helps determine which of the inference functions should be performed by the system, which by the user, and which by the two working together. It also explicitly identifies every input and output within the system.

  The main decision made when developing the model of interaction for the IMPRESS system was that the selection of a test to perform would be done by the KBS and user in conjunction, rather than by the KBS alone; in other words, the KBS would recommend a test to perform, but the user would be free to reject the recommendation.

KBS design:

- *Functional decomposition* involves laying out the inference functions, knowledge roles and inputs/outputs in a single diagram, and identifying the data flow between them.

- *Behavioural design* involves the selection of AI "design methods", such as best-first search, blackboard reasoning, or truth maintenance, to implement each function in the functional decomposition. AIAI's pragmatic KADS approach makes use of a set of *probing questions*, based on the work of Kline & Dolins [5], to recommend design methods.

- *Physical design* involves the selection of rules, objects, or other low-level design techniques to implement the chosen design methods. This proved to be the most difficult of all the analysis and design stages, partly because the behavioural design stage did not produce many strong recommendations for particular design methods.

KADS recommends that the selection of a KBS implementation tool should be based on the results of this stage; however, an implementation tool has often been chosen by the time this stage of the project is reached, and so it is sensible if the capabilities of the KBS tool are borne in mind when performing physical design.

Once the physical design is complete, KADS suggests using conventional software engineering methods. While these methods are likely to work for implementation, they may not be adequate for verification and validation, which may differ significantly between a KBS and conventional computer programs [7].

4.3   Technology transfer using KADS

During the stages of knowledge analysis and KBS design, technology transfer was accomplished by introducing JM to KADS. This was achieved during JM's initial training. JM was also asked to read sections of the best current single reference on KADS[2]. With this background, JM was able to understand the deliverables from the analysis and design phases at a detailed level, and to use these deliverables as a basis for the implementation of the IMPRESS system.

The aim of using KADS for technology transfer was that JM would understand the KADS models sufficiently well that, should the occasion arise, he would be able to make a change to the inference structure and propagate the change through all the remaining stages in order to produce a revised physical design. This change would then be implemented in the KBS, and the revised set of models would serve as up to date documentation for the system. This purpose appears to have been achieved.

5   Benefits and weaknesses of methods for the IMPRESS project

The use of pragmatic KADS for the IMPRESS project provided a number of benefits, but also had some weaknesses. These are outlined below.

Benefits: The major advantage of KADS from the point of view of technology transfer is the large number of models which are produced during the development of the KBS. These models represent the KBS from a number of different viewpoints, so a novice stands a much greater chance of understanding the workings of the KBS from these models than from any single document describing the KBS. The variety of models also helps greatly when a new piece of knowledge or a new procedure must be added to the KBS, and it is difficult to decide where this new information fits into the previous structure. These models also force the KBS developer to document design decisions explicitly, which is almost essential for successful long-term maintenance, and can constitute a set of deliverables from each stage of the project for the management or project monitoring officer.

KADS itself has some particular advantages. The library of interpretation models is widely thought to be the most useful contribution of KADS to knowledge engineering, and it certainly provided a lot of assistance for the IMPRESS project. There is also some reasonably comprehensible background reading available on KADS which helps introduce novices to the methodology.

Weaknesses: Perhaps the biggest disadvantage of using KADS, when compared with a "rapid prototyping" approach to KBS development, is that implementation does not begin until relatively late in the project. While the preparation of a design which has been thought out and documented well provides plenty of justification for KADS' approach, late implementation carries disadvantages both for technical development and for technology transfer.

From the viewpoint of technical development, KADS' approach loses the advantages of iterative prototyping for knowledge acquisition and investigating possible implementation techniques. KADS does not rule out the use of prototyping as a knowledge acquisition technique, but it is time-consuming to build a prototype based on an uncertain system design which will eventually be thrown away, and it was decided that this approach was not worthwhile for a small-scale project such as the IMPRESS project. Iterative prototyping is also very useful for identifying omissions or misunderstandings in knowledge acquisition and analysis, and the fact that most of KADS' models are based on the analysed knowledge (directly or indirectly) means that errors in knowledge acquisition and analysis are costly, because they require almost all the models to be updated. A CASE tool for KADS would go a long way towards alleviating this difficulty.

From the viewpoint of technology transfer, KADS' approach means that a novice KBS programmer (JM in this project) is thrown into programming at the deep end, rather than being gradually introduced to implementation techniques as the prototype is built. While JM was given some training and programming exercises in KAPPA-PC while the analysis and design phases were being conducted, it is received wisdom that the only way to understand a KBS implementation tool fully is to use it to develop a full-scale KBS, and this project reinforced that belief. This unfamiliarity was a major contributor to the fact that the implementation phase overran by about 3 weeks, the only phase to show a significant deviation from the initial plan.

Two other features of KADS were noted which were minor disadvantages in the IMPRESS project:

- KADS provides little guidance on user interface design, which is something of a disadvantage since the development of user interfaces may take up a large proportion of the code and the development time for a KBS. For the sake of simplicity, the IMPRESS project used KAPPA-PC's built-in user interface facilities (menus, message boxes and text windows) to develop its user interface.

- The physical design stage should take into account the features of the chosen KBS implementation tool. KADS recommends that a tool should be chosen based on the results of the physical design stage, but in practice a tool has almost always been chosen before this stage. For example, the physical design for the IMPRESS system recommended the use of a series of demons on the slots of the **State of the machine** object to calculate the total time required for the machine to be put into a particular state. However, demons in KAPPA-PC do not return a value, so instead of using a return value, the technique had to be implemented using a global variable to accumulate the total time.

6   Conclusion

On the whole, the use of a methodology as a framework for technology transfer worked well on the IMPRESS project, and is recommended for other projects. However, a number of factors must be considered carefully when doing so:[2]

- Considerable effort is required to make sure that knowledge analysis is done properly, because of the effort required to correct errors at a later stage. In larger projects, or other projects where the knowledge to be acquired is particularly complex, it may well be worth developing a prototype to assist in knowledge acquisition.

- The implementation stage should be given at least as much time as the analysis stage, if not more, unless the chief programmer is **fully** conversant with the KBS implementation tool before the implementation stage is reached.

- Documentation should be prepared in a format which is fairly easy to update, since it is expected that the documentation will change over time.

- The features of the chosen implementation tool should be taken into account at the physical design stage (or equivalent stage in the chosen methodology).

---

[2]These comments assume that the methodology uses the three phases of analysis, design and implementation.

References

[1] Burton A M, Shadbolt N R, Rugg G and Hedgecock A P. Knowledge Elicitation Techniques in Classification Domains. In *Proceedings of ECAI-88: The 8th European Conference on Artificial Intelligence*, 1988.

[2] F. Hickman, J. Killin, L. Land *et al. Analysis for knowledge-based systems: A practical introduction to the KADS methodology.* Ellis Horwood, Chichester, 1989.

[3] J. Kingston. Pragmatic KADS: A methodological approach to a small KBS project. *Submitted to Expert Systems: The International Journal of Knowledge Engineering.* This paper is also available as AIAI Technical report AIAI-TR-110.

[4] J. Kingston. The model of interaction. *Newsletter of the BCS Methodologies Interest Group*, (1), August 1992. Also available from AIAI as AIAI Technical Report AIAI-TR-115.

[5] Kline, P J & Dolins, S B. *Designing expert systems : a guide to selecting implementation techniques.* Wiley, 1989.

[6] Shadbolt N.& Burton, M. Knowledge elicitation. In J. Wilson and N. Corlett, editor, *Evaluation of Human Work: A Practical Ergonomics Methodology*, pages 321–346. Taylor and Francis, 1990.

[7] T.J. Lydiard. A survey of verification and validation techniques for KBS. *Knowledge Engineering Review*, 7(2), June 1992.

Project Management for the Evolutionary Development of Expert Systems

Ian Watson

EDESIRL PROJECT
Department of Surveying, University of Salford,
SALFORD, M5 4WT. ☎ + 44 (0)61-745-5227
EMAIL: I.WATSON@SURVEYING.SALFORD.AC.UK

Abstract

The development of expert systems is inherently uncertain and so involves a high degree of risk. This paper describes a project management method that helps manage this uncertainty. It has been tailored to the Client Centred Approach — an expert system development method that is being designed for use by small and medium sized enterprises. This context implies that the management technique and its accompanying documentation must not over burden the resources of a smaller developer. The helix method of project management introduced in this paper represents a different view of Boehm's Spiral Model. It accepts that conventional linear project planning methods are not always suitable for developers of expert systems. Having accepted this, the helix method allows plans to be made for each development stage within the Client Centred Approach. We believe the Client Centred Approach is applicable wherever prototyping is used, and we contrast it with the methods being developed by KADS-II.

1. INTRODUCTION

This paper describes proposals for handling project management within the Client Centred Approach (CCA). The principles of the CCA are described in Basden [1989]. The thinking behind the approach, and its current state of development, are described in greater detail in Basden *et al.* [1991] and Watson *et al.* [1992]. Although the technique described here is applicable for any project that uses prototyping to develop a system (around forty five per cent of all commercial expert system projects according to a recent survey [DTI, 1992]), it has been developed specifically for small and medium sized enterprises (SMEs), rather than larger organisations. The DTI's report [1992] shows that forty per cent of expert system (ES) applications are being developed by SMEs (*i.e.*, companies with less than five hundred employees).

While ESs remained within the research labs as largely experimental demonstrators, there was less necessity to manage their development. That is, an ES would take as long to develop as the research grant provided for, or its development would last until a doctoral thesis was submitted [Inder & Filby, 1991]. However, as the development of ESs has become more routine, insofar as many are now being developed by and for commercial companies, project management is becoming a central area of concern [Bright *et al.*, 1991; Klahr, 1991; Taylor *et al.*, 1991; Thomas, 1991].

For conventional systems development (*e.g.*, databases), the main determiners of the size of the eventual system are the number of data items, functions performed on them, and input/output routines of the desired system. The quantities of each of these can be estimated reasonably accurately at the start of the project. From these estimates, development time scales can be calculated from experience. However, with ESs this is rarely possible [Thomas, 1991], although attempts are being made to evaluate metrics for ES development [Moores & Edwards, 1992].

Expert systems contain human knowledge that is used for problem solving. This expertise is the main determinant of the project size and complexity. However, there is no accurate way of estimating the effort involved in obtaining, structuring and representing this knowledge until a substantial amount of work has been done [Thomas, 1991]. Project planning must therefore be flexible, since early plans will not be accurate. The managers of expert system projects therefore need a project management technique that controls the flexibility while maintaining the visibility and accountability for all aspects of the project.

The CCA addresses this by making the development of an ES more visible through a well-defined project management method that explicitly deals with threats; *i.e.*, areas of uncertainty or risk that may jeopardise the project.

This paper first outlines the CCA's background and stages. It then describes a different perspective (or view) of Boehm's Spiral Method. The types of documentation that should accompany the evolving system are described, along with the project management activities. The paper concludes by outlining the potential benefits of the CCA's project management method to ES developers.

2. THE CLIENT CENTRED APPROACH

2.1.   The Background

Basden [1989] argues that a problem common to most current ES development methods is that they are technology centred. They place too much emphasis on the activities used to develop the systems, such as "elicitation," "implementation," and "verification," and not enough emphasis on what the clients can see and understand. It has been argued that by putting people at the centre of the development process [Diaper, 1987 & 1989] there is a greater chance of the resulting system being useful. The DTI advises that *"involving the users in all aspects of the system development from the outset will help to avoid potential problems"* [DTI, 1992].

Basden, however, identifies the *"client"* as an individual or group distinct from the eventual end users of the system. Thus, in a corporate environment the client may be the senior management commissioning the system and not the eventual end users. The CCA covers the full development life cycle of an ES providing milestones to guide the project. These milestones refer to what the clients can see being demonstrated and not to the conventional tasks such as elicitation, acquisition, representation. This accepts that the clients may not understand the jargon or the distinction between the tasks involved in development but will be able to perceive demonstrable changes in the system.

2.2.   An Overview of the CCA

The stages of the CCA are illustrated in Figure 1 and are described in more detail below. The CCA is divided into two broad activities:

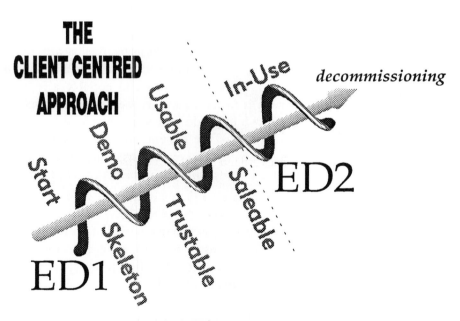

Figure 1. Seven Stages of the CCA

- **Evolutionary development part one (ED1).** This considers the development of the ES and takes it to a saleable stage. Each stage is a deliverable that the client can see, and that the developers must meet and plan for.

- **Evolutionary development part two (ED2).** This considers how the system can be kept in regular beneficial use, and considers such factors as training of users and most importantly the maintenance of the system. This phase only ends when the ES is decommissioned.

- *Start (the 5 hurdles)*

  The purpose, roles, benefits, and stakeholders are identified. The impact of the system on the client organisation is discussed, and those involved with the project get to know each other. As part of this process developers should considering five crucial questions or hurdles:

    1. Is the problem suitable for computerisation?
    2. Is the problem suitable for expert systems?
    3. Is the knowledge available to solve the problem?
    4. Is the system worth developing?
    5. Will the system be used?

  An ES is considered appropriate only if *all* the hurdles are crossed. The deliverables are documents outlining the feasibility of the project giving a "holistic picture" of the project.

- *Skeleton System*

  The deliverable is a mock-up that behaves and looks as the final system might but contains little knowledge. It is simply a set of interactive screens that show a few dummy questions, provide some dummy examples and possibly a report. The purpose of the Skeleton System is to let the clients see what the system might eventually be able to do, and how it might do it. It is also a vehicle for discussing the form of the inputs and outputs of the system, and is therefore a tool for knowledge elicitation. It can also be used to explore user interface requirements and other aspects of system functionality, similar to Colebourne *et al.* [1992]

- *Demonstration Systems*

  During this stage and the following stages iterative cycles of prototyping occur. Therefore, there may be several demonstration systems, each demonstrating a different aspect of the system's functionality. The first prototypes contain real domain knowledge, but can only produce acceptable results in a limited subset of the domain. Nonetheless, they demonstrate to the client that the system can solve the problem or let the project to be re-evaluated if necessary. This stage is used to explore issues relating to knowledge representation and system architecture before committing to a particular approach. The deliverables are the demonstration systems.

- *Trustable System*

  The knowledge in this deliverable is complete and correct. It gives correct results to all the problems the system will encounter. However, it will be difficult to use (even by its creators) and will be prone to operational problems.

- *Usable System*

  This deliverable has a usable interface and can link to external software if necessary. It also provides useful explanations, "what-if" facilities, and reports. This version could be used for real business benefit by those sympathetic to the system. Meeting this deliverable should involve evaluating the usability of the ES, possibly using techniques such as Evaluative Classification of Mismatch [Booth, 1990 & 1991].

- *Saleable System*

  This is the final deliverable version of the ES. The term "saleable" does not necessarily imply that the system will be sold for money. Instead the term is used to mean that the system may have to be "sold" to people who are not committed to its use (*e.g.*, given to other departments or other sites within an organisation). Its release involves the production of user documentation, training materials, and help lines (if required). The ES will have been introduced to a wider community (*e.g.*, alpha and beta releases). Appropriate changes will have been made and system bugs fixed.

- *In Use*

  This ensures that the system is used correctly by checking that the clients, users, and their organisations understand the strengths and weaknesses of the ES. Importantly, it also involves maintaining the knowledge base and updating the functionality of the system on a regular basis. This ensures that the ES remains in beneficial use over the longest possible time, thereby maximising the return on the investment in its development. The deliverables of this stage are the continuing business benefits that the organisation receives from using the system.

The CCA is an "evolutionary" methodology insofar as it supports the continuing evolution of an ES and because it is accepted that the methodology itself will evolve with time. The stages of the CCA state what should be delivered during the ES project. The CCA does not prescribe how each deliverable should be met or how the ES developers should work, and what tools and techniques they should use. The stakeholders in the project are free to use their own experience to decide this. However, the CCA does offer advice and guidance, and it can help the stakeholders plan for each deliverable and manage the project. This is described below.

3. THE SPIRAL MODEL

Boehm's spiral model for project management [1986 & 1989] is gaining in popularity, even among conventional software developers. It is specifically designed to manage risk and is being used by the KADS-II consortium [Bright *et al.*, 1991; Killin *et al.*, 1991]. Risk may be defined as, *"an event or situation that will have a negative impact on the project goals, schedules or budgets and whose probability is not known"* [Bright *et al.*, 1991].

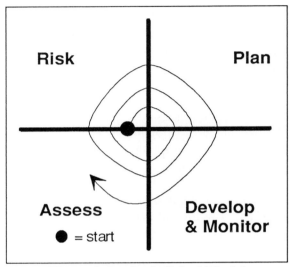

Figure 2. Boehm's Spiral Model

Essentially, the spiral model, shown in Figure 2, provides a way of visualising risk management. The process is divided into quadrants that represent management activities. In the first quadrant (Risk) the project team and their management assess areas of risk that may affect the project by compiling a list of risks. Boehm provides ten areas:

- personnel shortfalls,
- unrealistic schedules and budgets,
- developing the wrong software functions,
- developing the wrong user interface,
- gold plating of functions,
- continuous requirement changes,
- shortfalls in externally provided components,
- shortfalls in performed tasks,
- real time performance capabilities, and
- straining computer science capabilities.

To this list one may add risks that are specific to ES projects or to one's individual circumstances, for example

- poor access to experts,
- uncooperative experts,
- lack of commitment of users, and
- variation in user population.

After compiling a list of risks, managers should rate their assessment of each risk. One can use LOW, MEDIUM, and HIGH, 1 to 5 or any convenient rating. Having prepared this estimate of risk the managers next consider what options can be taken to reduce the risk in high areas.

Initially all possible options should be considered, including completely fanciful ones. Each option is then considered in turn against the project's known constraints. This quickly removes those that are impractical leaving options that could benefit the project.

At this point, one enters the second quadrant (Plan) as the managers prepare a plan for the next cycle. This plan will include the new options decided upon during the Risk quadrant. The plan should outline the targets for the cycle, including deliverables, responsibilities, and budgets if necessary. This results in a new work package plan that each member of the development team can use.

During the third quadrant (Development & Monitor) development work continues and is monitored daily by the project leader if necessary. This quadrant concludes with the production of project progress reports, and deliverable software and documentation as specified in the work package plan.

The progress reports and deliverables are then assessed by project managers during the assessment quadrant to see if they meet expectations. This process can be carried out by a steering or review committee if one has been established to guide the project. This is followed by further cycles of risk assessment, planning, development, and assessment until the system is embedded in use.

Although the spiral model is divided into four equal quadrants, these will not occupy equal lengths of time. The time spent on development may, of course, be greater than all the others. However, the spiral model shows that each activity is equally important to the success of the project.

4. THE HELIX METHOD

A large ES shell producer and consultancy has warned that the spiral model can confuse managers, and misrepresents progress, since it implies that the project is going round in circles [*pers comm*. Klahr, 1991]. The spiral model can be represented more intuitively, as shown in Figure 3, as a helix showing that the project does not continually cover the same ground, and that the development is progressing towards the project's goals. It also demonstrates (as the original spiral model does) that the management activities are regularly repeated during the project's development.

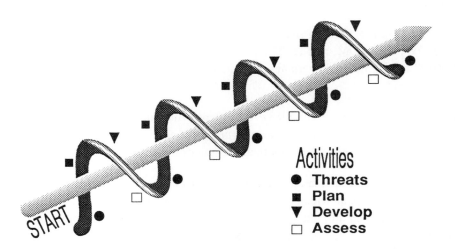

Figure 3. The Helix Method *(a different view of Boehm's Spiral)*

5. DOCUMENTATION

Assessment of the project's progress is a key activity within the helix or spiral models. To do this successfully, managers need the following documents:

- a clear statement of the objectives of the project,
- a clear statement of the expected benefits,
- clear milestones with planned deliverables, and
- clearly defined roles for all the stakeholders in the project.

Some of these will be represented as project documents. This documentation lets managers make informed decisions based on progress. The documentation also becomes a permanent record of the project and is a vital resource during ED2 when the system is maintained.

KADS is an expert system development method that is gaining in popularity. It describes a very comprehensive set of project documentation [Bright *et al.*, 1991]. However, KADS is designed for and by large organisations (*e.g.*, Siemens, Touche Ross, Lloyd's Register) and may not be suitable for use by smaller companies and smaller projects [*pers. comm.* Wielinga, 1991]. Developers using KADS sometimes make statements like,

> *"KADS is exactly the kind of methodology that one can follow most by slavishly applying least"* [Killin *et al.* 1991].

This implies that developers tend to "pick and choose" elements of KADS that they find useful. The documentation set that accompanies the KADS method involves a minimum of fifty documents (and in practice many more). These range from documents that detail the motivation and aims of the project through to documents that define every functional block within the system.

Whilst we believe that comprehensive project documentation is useful, the heavy documentation burden of KADS is one aspect that reduces its suitability for SMEs. In particular, small development teams would find the generation and maintenance of this documentation very time consuming. We are not advising developers to ignore documentation. Instead we are proposing a rational approach that combines effective (but possibly minimal) documentation with efficient use of project resources.

Section 7 outlines the contents of the documents that should accompany the CCA. These documents need not be lengthy, but each item should be addressed if only to say that it is not applicable. These documents are produced when necessary and may be amended to reflect changes in the evolving system. The management activities that accompany each stage are also described in section 7. Both the content of the documentation and the management activities are derived from those of the KADS-II Framework [Bright *et al.*, 1991] and from Boehm [1986 & 1989]. However, they have been simplified to suit the more limited resources of SMEs.

6. MAINTAINING THE SYSTEM

Because knowledge changes over time, maintaining ESs is significantly different from maintaining conventional systems [Chee & Power, 1990; Pau & Kristinsson, 1990, Killin *et al.*, 1991; Bench-Capon & Coenen, 1992; Coenen & Bench-Capon, 1992]. There may be many maintenance cycles within ED2. Depending on the resources available, the nature of the system, and its expected life, each management cycle may occur every quarter, bi-annually, annually, or at other periods. However, regular management meetings should be scheduled to plan the maintenance of the system. The following documentation should be in place by this stage:

System Documentation. This includes the location of all the project documents: the requirements, architectural, functional and knowledge specifications, along with source code. It should also record what changes have been made to the system's functionality or knowledge, why they were made, when, and by whom.

User Documentation. This records the latest version of the user documentation that accompanies any system updates, including training materials, installation instructions, trouble shooting advice, and work-arounds.

7. REVIEW OF THE HELIX METHOD

As with other aspects of the CCA we do not intend to be prescriptive (*i.e.*, the CCA states "what" and "when" actions should be taken, not "how" they are performed). Details will vary between projects and with individual management styles. Indeed, on small projects it is feasible for the system to be its own functional specification and for its knowledge base to be the statement of knowledge included in it. Essentially, the project management documentation should be made up of the following components at each stage:

- a document recording the conclusions of the progress assessment,
- a document describing the current requirements and architecture specifications of the developing system (in smaller projects the knowledge base of the system can form this document itself),
- a document describing the knowledge included in the current system (in smaller projects the knowledge base of the system can form this document itself),
- an interim "optimistic" project plan (*i.e.*, what could be achieved in a perfect world),
- a document describing the threats assessment, and
- a "realistic" project plan for the next stage detailing deliverables and task allocation.

These reflect the management activities that occur during each project management cycle. These activities or tasks are described as follows:

- assess progress,
- prepare interim project plan,
- identify threats,
- consider alternatives,
- consider constraints,
- select valid alternatives,
- prepare plan,
- gain acceptance, and
- develop & monitor.

It is not essential for developers following the CCA to use the helix method, but it does provide a way of managing the uncertainty inherent in developing expert systems. The management activities need not be time consuming. For each cycle they may be reduced to just a few hours. The documentation can also be reduced, so that the developing system is its own specification. However, developers should remember that the lack of system documentation may later become a threat to the successful maintenance of the system.

8. CONCLUSION

The helix method of project management recognises that conventional project planning is not always suitable for the inherently uncertain and risky process of implementing an expert system. Having accepted this the helix method allows plans to be made for each development stage within the CCA. At its simplest, there could be one management cycle round the helix for each deliverable within the CCA. The helix method combined with the CCA has the following potential advantages:

- It closely involves all the stakeholders in the system in the development process.
- It provides a clearly defined set of natural milestones for development, which can serve as auditing points.
- It provides a project management technique that guides development stage by stage.
- It visualises the threats to the project's success, reducing the risk of costly failure.
- It is directly suitable for smaller organisations since it does not overburden developers either with exhaustive documentation or time consuming management techniques.
- It accepts that an expert system's knowledge base requires ongoing maintenance and provides a way of managing that maintenance.

Although this project management method has been informed by KADS-II and especially Boehm, it places great emphasis on the reduction of effort, particularly regarding documentation. This is an acceptance that small developers may not have the resources to support a method as exhaustive as KADS but will still benefit from a staged method. Moreover it explicitly recognises that the development of an expert system does not stop once it is brought into use, and that its maintenance will require planning.

9. ACKNOWLEDGEMENTS

This research was funded under the IEATP Program, Project No. IED4/1/2062. We would also like to acknowledge our collaborators: The Royal Institution of Chartered Surveyors, Inference Europe Ltd., Imaginor Systems, and the members of our project user group.

10. REFERENCES

Basden, A. 1989, *A Client Centred Methodology for Building Expert Systems*, in **People and Computers, V**. Sutcliffe, A., & Macaulay, L. (Eds.), Cambridge University Press, Cambridge, UK.

Basden. A., Watson, I.D., & Brandon, P.S. (1991).
The evolutionary development of expert systems. In: **Research & Development in Expert Systems VIII**, (eds. Graham, I.M., & Milne, R.W.), pp.67-81 Cambridge University Press, Cambridge, UK.

Bench-Capon, T.J.M., & Coenen, F. (1992).
   The Maintenance of Legal Knowledge Based Systems. **AI Review,** Vol **6**: pp.129-43.
Boehm, B. (1986).
   A spiral model for software development and enhancement. **IEEE Computer,** May 1988.
Boehm, B. (1989).
   Software Risk Management. IEEE Computer Society Press.
Booth, P.A. (1990).
   ECM: A scheme for analysing user-system errors. In Diaper, D. et al., (Eds.), Human-
   Computer Interaction - Interact '90: Proc. of the 3rd. IFIP Conf. on HCI, pp.47-54. Elsevier
   Science Publishers B.V. (North-Holland).
Booth, P.A., (1991).
   Errors and theory in human-computer interaction. **Acta Psychologica, 78**: pp.69-96.
Bright, C., Martil, R., Williams, D., & Rajan, T. (1991).
   The KADS-II Framework for KBS Project Management. Proc. Ist SGES Int. Workshop on
   Knowledge-Based Systems Methodologies.
Chee, C.W.J., & Power, M.A. (1990).
   Expert Systems Maintainability. Proc. of the Annual Reliability & Maintainability Symposium,
   pp.415-18.
Coenen, F., & Bench-Capon, T.J.M. (1992).
   Maintenance & Maintainability in Regulation based Systems. ICL Technical Journal, May,
   pp.76-84.
Colebourne, A., Sawyer, P., & Sommerville, I. (1992).
   Evolutionary Development of Interactive Systems. Dept. of Computing, Lancaster University,
   UK. pers comm.
Diaper, D. (1987).
   POMESS: a People Orientated Methodology for expert System Specification, in Proc. 1st.
   European Workshop on Knowledge Acquisition for Knowledge Based Systems. Addis, T.,
   Boose, J., & Gains, B. (Eds.).
Diaper, D. (1989).
   Knowledge Elicitation: Principles, Techniques & Applications. Ellis Horwood Ltd.,
   Chichester, UK.
Department of Trade and Industry (1992).
   Knowledge Based Systems Survey of UK Applications. Report performed by Touche Ross and
   commisioned by the DTI, February, 1992
Inder, R., & Filby, I. (1991).
   Survey of Methodologies & Supporting Tools. Proc. Ist SGES Int. Workshop on Knowledge-
   Based Systems Methodologies.
Killin, J., Morgan-Gray, L., & Porter, D. (1991).
   Knowledge Engineering Within Software Engineering - Similarities & Differences. Proc. Ist
   SGES Int. Workshop on Knowledge-Based Systems Methodologies.
Klahr, P., (1991).
   Strategic Implications of KBS Methodologies. Proc. Ist SGES Int. Workshop on Knowledge-
   Based Systems Methodologies.

Moores, T.T., & Edwards, J.S. (1992).

  Could large UK corporations and computing companies use Software Cost Estimating tools? A survey. In, **European Journal of Information Systems**, in print.

Pau, L.F., & Kristinsson, J.B. (1989).

  SOFTM: A Software Maintenance Expert System in Prolog. **J. of Software Maintenance: Research & Practice,** 2(ii): pp.87-111.

Taylor, R.M., Bright, C., Martil, R., & de Hoog, R. (1991).

  The management of knowledge-based systems development and maintenance under KADS-II. In: **Research & Development in Expert Systems V111,** (eds. Graham, I.M., & Milne, R.W.), pp.52-66. Cambridge University Press, Cambridge, UK.

Thomas, M. (1991).

  What Constitutes a KBS Methodology. Proc. Ist SGES Int. Workshop on Knowledge-Based Systems Methodologies.

Watson, I.D., Basden, A., & Brandon, P. (1992).

  A client centred approach to the development of expert systems. In, **Proc. 12th. International. Workshop on Artificial Intelligence, Expert Systems & Natural Language,** in print.

The Specification and Development of Rule-Based Expert Systems

Pete Maher

Department of Mathematics and Computer Science University of Missouri - St. Louis, St. Louis, MO 63121 USA.

Owen Traynor

FB 3 Informatik und Mathematik, Universität Bremen, Bremen 33, Germany.

1 Abstract

This paper describes and illustrates the use of a methodology suitable for the formal development of expert systems. It addresses the problems of verification and validation of expert systems in a realistic way, though the methods are not advocated as a general tool for expert system development. The framework described allows for both the specification of Knowledge and the specification of the Inference methods which provide the basis for deduction. A flexible and extensible environment for the development and testing of specific types of expert system is presented. Various tools and results are shown to be useful in determining properties of both the knowledge base and the inference system when these are developed within the proposed framework.

The framework is based on exploitation of the transformational model of software development in combination with techniques from algebraic specification.

2 INTRODUCTION

The development of expert systems, within a formal development framework (see [Krieg-Brückner and Hoffmann 91]), can be seen as a significant advance in expert system technology. The benefits accrued from such an approach are substantial. In particular the following are notable: a formal foundation for reasoning about properties of the knowledge base and inference system is provided. Inductive and deductive methods are available to help in both the construction of the expert system and as a tool for analysis of the knowledge bases. A well defined language, with well defined semantics, provides the basis for specifying both the expert system and the associated knowledge bases. This results in a unified development framework.

The same methodology used for developing an efficient expert system can be used for developing an efficient knowledge base. Existing support systems may be exploited

in constructing expert systems using such a methodology. The methodology and system also support redevelopment, maintenance, and reuse of both knowledge base definitions (and developments) and inference system definitions (and developments). The
approach to constructing expert systems may be classified as follows: an inference
system is constructed by defining an algebraic type which models the computational
components of the desired inference system [Krieg-Brückner 88]. The algebraic type is
then developed, using a transformational development system [Krieg-Brückner and
Hoffmann 91], to an implementation of the inference engine. The inference engine is
subsequently incorporated as a development method within the transformational development system. A prototype system is operational. For further details see [Krieg-
Brückner and Hoffmann 91] and [Krieg-Brückner et al 91].

A *type* system is constructed to accommodate the knowledge base. *Relations* may be
specified as mappings (functions), *classes* of objects as types, and *productions* as axioms. The inference system now exists as a transformational development method.
This method may then be used in combination with the other development rules of the
system, to optimize, manipulate, and deduce properties of the knowledge base.

The specification language used is an algebraic language with high level structuring
mechanisms from Ada [Ada 83]. Type hierarchies can be generated using subtyping,
higher order functions and genericity can be used to specify general properties over
classes of objects.

Development of an expert system can then be seen as a two level activity, both activities carried out within the same general development framework; specification of the
inference system(s) and specification of the knowledge base(s). Figure 1 illustrates
the structure of the overall development framework.

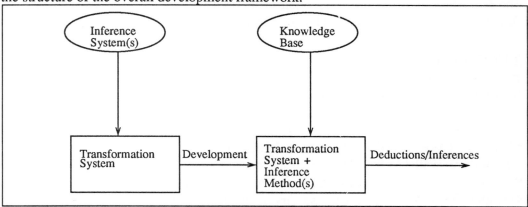

Figure 1. The development model

In order to construct the inference system in the manner outlined above, there must be
some domain (type) over which the specification of the inference system is made. In
fact this is a formulation of the actual specification language itself as an algebraic type.

The inference system is then a specification of how to manipulate terms of the specification language when these terms represent a knowledge base.

The signature of the algebraic type (used as the foundation for constructing the knowledge base) generates the Herbrand Universe for any knowledge base. Axioms and relations are used to structure the admissible terms of the Herbrand universe. The inference system then manipulates the terms defined by the knowledge base in order to answer queries or to perform deductions/inductions. General purpose tools may also be used to determine the consistency of the knowledge base and verify the implementation of the inference system.

In addition to the basic mechanisms for development, a library management system also provides refinement management. The Library represents and maintains the complete development history of programs from their specifications. This provides automated support for the redevelopment activity. It also allows for straight forward backtracking during a development. This is achieved by simply ascending the development tree.

3 GOALS AND ADVANTAGES OF THE METHOD

The logic programming paradigm has been advocated as an effective means of constructing expert systems. The declarative nature of logical languages allow, for example, rule based expert systems to be expressed in a concise and comfortable way. This paradigm alone, however, does not address the pressing problem of verification and validation in expert system development [Plant 90]. Also, such development frameworks lack, for example, secure type systems and effective analysis tools. Such languages make verification and validation difficult and provide few means to raise the level of confidence in the finished product.

The methods advocated here are not meant as a replacement to the traditional tried and tested mechanism for developing expert systems. They are proposed as an alternative development paradigm which more effectively supports the verification and validation needs of many expert system application domains.

A secure and well developed type system is provided which alone raises the level of confidence that even knowledge based specifications are consistent and free from the sort of inadvertent errors which can creep in when a logical (untyped) language such as Prolog is used. In addition, tools can be used to test for the consistency of such specifications before they ever get used operationally.

The declarative style of definition is still supported, and refinement, perhaps even to Prolog programs, is possible. Currently, projection of detailed designs to an Ada subset, a Functional language, and C are supported. Most importantly perhaps is that all development is done within a formal framework, which can be exercised to verify and validate at all stages in the development of an expert system, from construction of the inference mechanisms to the definition of knowledge bases and rules.

4 THE FORMAL FRAMEWORK

When undertaking formal development of programs of any kind, a vital issue is that of a formalism which will support the quest for formality. This generally means a **formal** specification language of one kind or another. We distinguish formality from rigour since rigorous construction of software does not require a demonstration of correctness but merely an intuitive 'hunch' or confidence that the resulting software is correct. This is reasonable since *care* was taken in its construction and the development methods are based on sound underlying mathematical foundations. Formality on the other hand, guarantees that the software is correct with respect to some, initial, formal requirements specification. This implies that the language used to construct the requirements specification must have a clear and well defined semantics. It must also be flexible enough to make the task of writing formal specifications more attractive than actually writing (constructing) implementations.

The approach taken here is that of the specification of *abstract data types* together with the definition of *computational structures* over these abstract types. The formal framework and semantics of languages allowing such specification is well developed [Ehrig and Mhar 85]. Specifically, a language called PA^{nn}dA-S will be the formalism used to construct specifications (for details of the language see Vol II of [Krieg-Brückner and Hoffmann 91]).

4.1 The Specification Language

The specification language used to illustrate the proposed framework is based on the PA^{nn}dA language, a wide spectrum language used in the PROSPECTRA project [Krieg-Brückner and Hoffmann 91]. The specification subset of this language is called PA^{nn}dA-S (meaning Prospectra **AdA A^{nn}A** Specification subset) It has the following notable features:

• Structuring and information hiding constructs from Ada: packages (including with clauses), subtypes, generics, and derived types.

• Higher order functions.

• Non- Strict functions.

• Predicates (including equality).

• Partial functions.

An example of a simple specification in PA^{nn}dA-S is given below.

```
with NAT_S;
Package sqrt_nat Is
  sqrt: NAT --> NAT;
  axiom for all N, K: NAT  =>K = sqrt(N)  -> sqr(K) <= N  and not(sqr(succ(K)) <= N);
end  sqrt_nat
```

Figure 2. An example specification

To explain: sqrt is defined as a function from NAT to NAT. The axiom part then defines
the constraints on the sqrt function. These are that, if the result of applying sqrt to N
is K then K satisfies the two conditions that (i) K squared is less than or equal to N
and (ii) that K+1 squared is greater than N. This specification outlines those properties that should be exhibited by a function which computes the square root of a natural
number. The package NAT_S, mentioned in the *with clause*, contains the definition of
functions such a sqr, <=, and so on.

Specifications are typically non-constructive. *What* should be done is specified, not
how it should be achieved. The production of the design and implementation is left to
the developer. Thus, the above specification is a *requirements specification* for
square root. The full developments of this example (with verification of the associated
correctness conditions) may be found in [Traynor and Liu 91].

A development has three parts: an *interface*, a *private part,* and a *body*. The interface
corresponds to the specification of the component, the private part to the design of the
functions specified in the interface. The body defines the implementation, however,
bodies are not part of the PA^{nn}dA-S subset of PA^{nn}dA. The transformational model
of software development is illustrated in figure 3.

Requirements Analysis

Informal   *Problem Analysis*
Informal   *Requirements Specification*

Development

                                          ⇑ *Validation*

Formal   *Requirement Specification*
                        ⇓   ⇑ *Verification*

Formal   *Design Specification*
                        ⇓   ⇑ *Verification*

Formal   *Construction of implementation*
Evolution   ⇓

                Changes in requirements   ⇒   *Re-development* ⇑

Figure 3. A transformational model of software development

The production of the original requirements involves the construction of the interface specification. Development (or refinement) will produce the private part and the body. The latter two are constructed by transformation. Transformations encapsulate or formalise a grain of programming expertise and are selected by the developer and applied by the system with appropriate interactive guidance. The selection and parameterisation of the transformations correspond to design decisions made by the developer.

4.2 The Algebra of Data

Specifications of all objects are given by modeling the required properties with algebraic types. Algebraic specification of data types has been used extensively to model various types of system (for some illustrative examples see [Broy 90], [Breu 91], and [Astesiano et al 90]). The theoretical foundations are well studied [Ehrich and Mahr 85] and algebraic methods provide a powerful toolset for attacking many classes of specification and development problem.

Informally, a *signature* generates a universe of terms (a term algebra or Herbrand Universe). A set of *axioms* over the terms generates a *quotient* algebra from this universe. The axioms can be thought of as partitioning the elements of the term algebra into accessible an inaccessible portions. The specification below gives an algebraic definition of family relationships.

```
package family is

is_father_of:  person × person → boolean;

is_grandfather_of:  person × person → boolean;

is_mother_of: person × person → boolean;

father_of:  person → person;

grandfather_of:  person → person;

mother_of: person  → person;

axiom for all x, y: person =>
        is_father_of(x, x) = false,
        is_mother_of(x, y) -> is_father_of(x, y) = false,
        is_mother_of(x, x) = false,
        is_father_of(x, y) -> is_mother_of(x, y) = false,
        (exists z:person => is_father_of(z, x) -> father_of(x) = z),
        (exists z:person => is_mother_of(z, x) -> mother_of(x) = z),
        (exists z:person => (is_father_of(z, y) or is_mother_of(z, y)) and
                is_father_of(x, z) -> is_grandfather_of(x, y) = true),
        father_of(father_of(x)) = y -> grandfather_of(x) = y,
        father_of(mother(x)) = y -> grandfather_of(x) = y;
end family;
```

Figure 4. Knowledge about family relationships

Notice that the specification leaves out information which may be considered an important in the definition of a family structure. For example, there is no explicit classification of sex; this is an implicit part of the specification, the developer may decide to make this explicit in the process of developing an efficient implementation. Notice also that no specific family is defined. Only the structure of family relationships is given. A specific family unit may be defined by importing the functions defined here into a new package and then using these functions to specify the relationships between individuals of a particular family. Note that the definition of grandfather_of will allow more than one solution.

The parameterisation of the knowledge representation structure given in figure 4 is given below and will be used as the knowledge base for a subsequent example.

```
with family;
package Jones_Clan is
fred, jean, mary, john, phil, tom:person ;
axiom
        father_of(fred) = tom,
        father_of(phil) = fred,
        father_of( mary) = fred,
        father_of( jean) = fred,
        father_of(john) = fred,
        mother_of(phil) = mary,
        father_of(mary) = tom;
end Jones_Clan;
```

Figure 5. An example knowledge base

4.3 The Algebra of Programs

Definition: Algebraic formalisation of programs.

PL is the signature of some programming language defined as an abstract data type, in this case the $PA^{nn}dA$ language itself where PL = {SP, CP}. SP is a set of sorts corresponding to syntactic categories of the language PL and CP is a set of function symbols whose domain and range are members of the set SP.

V is a set of symbols, with associated types from SP, denoting **variables (scheme variables)** .

A **program** is a well-formed formula from the term algebra W[PL].

A **program scheme** is a well-formed formula from W[PL, V]; terms with typed scheme variables.

Definition: Transformation rules as theorems in the semantic domain.

A function F, with some syntactic category as domain and range, is called a **transformation rule** if and only if for all the programs fragments P : P *Impl* F(P) where *Impl* is the implementation relation (defined in Vol I of [Krieg-Brückner and Hoffmann 91]) with respect to the semantics of the language, i.e. P *Impl* P' through some transformation rule or function F if and only if the formula $\forall$ P: P = F(P) is a the theorem in the semantic domain of the language.

Definition: Conditional Transformations.

A **conditional transformation** is a transformation rule for which ∀ P: P = F(P) cannot be shown to be a theorem in the semantic domain of the language. However,
 R(P) -> ∀ P: P = F(P) can be shown to hold. The undischarged portions of the correctness proof become a precondition on the application of the transformation function.

Conditional transformation rules are necessary in the situations where properties of the program fragments, denoted by scheme variables, are necessary to prove the correctness of the transformation. In such situations, lemmas are assumed in the correctness proofs. Such assumptions must be discharged when the transformation is instantiated in context. The lemmas assumed in the correctness proof become the precondition on the transformation.

Constructing terms corresponding to program fragments results in program terms in their *canonical* form. When specifying transformations, the concrete form of the object language is a much more comfortable and efficient form of expression. Note that terms, constructed from using the functions from the algebraic type defining a formalism, will reflect the abstract syntax structure of the formalism being modeled. Defining program transformations using the abstract syntax of the programming language is laborious. In general, it is more comfortable to use the concrete syntax. The resulting specification is also much more readable. In the following example, concrete program fragments are delimited by the brackets ⌈ ⌋.

The example below defines a transformation rule which commutes the arguments of the logical connective, **and**.

```
with pannda_s
package Commute is
comm : Expression → Expression;
axiom for all a, b :Expression =>
     comm( ⌈ a and b⌋ ) = ⌈ b and a⌋;
end Commute;
```

Figure 6. A transformation rule in concrete form

The equivalent canonical form of this transformation is rather lengthy, due to the complexity of the specification language, and is also difficult to read, this provides sufficient motivation for the use of the concrete form in specifications.

The basic approach outlined here is used to construct the inference system used in deducing properties (making inferences) on knowledge bases. Knowledge bases are constructed as outline in section 2.2.

5 THE DEVELOPMENT MODEL

5.1 Specifying an Inference System

The inference system which will be used to illustrate the deduction process, is the default deduction system of the PROSPECTRA methodology. This is used for convenience, other inference methods may be defined and used within the system.

The inference rules of the deduction system are specified in PA^{nn}dA-S. The rules are relatively straightforward and correspond to a deduction system based on intuitionistic first order logic. The inference rule are formulated as goal directed tactics and are derived from Gentzen's Ga3 calculus (see [Gentzen 69], [Schmidt 84], and [Ritchie 88]). Property deductions are constructive and explanations can be retrieved from the residue of the reasoning process.

There are two portions of the inference system. The first manipulates the formulae of first order logic, used to describe the knowledge base (this also include manipulation of the equality predicate). The second component allows the specification of strategies and tactics to guide the deduction system and provides a mechanism for determining inductive properties of a knowledge base.

Deductions are represented by trees. The nodes of the tree are constructed by the application of inference rules while attempting to deduce some property. Figure 7 gives a portion of the specification of the inference system.

```
with pannda_s, term_manipulation;
package Inf_Rules is

ForAllElim: E: Exp × P: Exp :: NotCaptured(P, E) = true ⟶ Exp;
axiom for all E, E1, P : Exp; X: Designator; T: Type_Expression =>
    (E = ⌈ for all X:T => E1 ⌋) -> ForAllElim(E, P) =  Subst(P, X, E1)
    others -> ForAllElim(E, P) = E;
end Inf_Rules;
```

Figure 7. The inference rule for *for all elimination*

In the above definition the function *subst* replaces all occurrences of the variable, X, in expression E1, with the pattern P. An additional restriction, imposed in the domain of the function declaration of ForAllElim, ensures that no variables in the term P are captured by any inner declaration of the expression E. Renaming may be used to resolve this conflict if it arises.

All the inference rules are formulated in this way. These are then transformed to a language called SSL. This is the input language for an environment generator tool called the Cornell Synthesizer Generator (CSG) (see [Reps and Tietlebaum 86]). These rules are then compiled into the transformational development system (which is itself generated using the CSG).

As a result, these rules are available within the transformational development system as transformations. All the inference rules shown in figure 8 are developed in this way. Note that deductions in the inference system are represented as the manipulation of sequents. The formulae on the left of the turnstile are referred to as the antecedent of the sequent. The formula on the right of the turnstile is the consequent. Elimination and Introduction rules apply to the antecedent and consequent respectively.

The deduction system which results from these rules is quite rudimentary. However, given that strategies and tactics can also be defined, the rules here can be thought of as a kernel which is used to build up more complex (composite) inference methods. The inference rules used in the default deduction system are given below.

Immediate Validity $\Gamma, A \vdash A$

Duplication $$\dfrac{\Gamma, A \vdash C}{\Gamma, A, A \vdash C}$$

Rules for Logical Connectives

Connective	Antecedent	Consequent
$\wedge$ (and)	$\dfrac{\Gamma, A \wedge B \vdash C}{\Gamma, A, B \vdash C}$	$\dfrac{\Gamma \vdash A \wedge B}{\Gamma \vdash A \quad \Gamma \vdash B}$
$\vee$ (or)	$\dfrac{\Gamma, A \vee B \vdash C}{\Gamma, A \vdash C \quad \Gamma, B \vdash C}$	$\dfrac{\Gamma \vdash A \vee B}{\Gamma \vdash A} \quad \dfrac{\Gamma \vdash A \vee B}{\Gamma \vdash B}$
$\rightarrow$ (implication)	$\dfrac{\Gamma, A \rightarrow B \vdash C}{\Gamma \vdash A \quad \Gamma \vdash C}$	$\dfrac{\Gamma \vdash A \rightarrow B}{\Gamma, A \vdash B}$
$\neg$ (not)	$\dfrac{\Gamma, \neg A \vdash C}{\Gamma \vdash A}$	$\dfrac{\Gamma \vdash \neg A}{\Gamma, A \vdash contradiction}$
$\forall$ (for all)	$\dfrac{\Gamma, \forall x\, A(x) \vdash C}{\Gamma, A(t) \vdash C}$	$\dfrac{\Gamma \vdash \forall x\, A(x)}{\Gamma \vdash A(x')}$
$\exists$ (exists)	$\dfrac{\Gamma, \exists x\, A(x) \vdash C}{\Gamma, A(x') \vdash C}$	$\dfrac{\Gamma \vdash \exists x\, A(x)}{\Gamma \vdash A(t)}$

Figure 8. The inference rules

The rules are presented in a top own manner, reflecting the way in which they are applied in a deduction. In the rules, t is a term, well selected so as to allow a successful conclusion to the deduction and x' is a free variable, not already used in the deduction. As a simple example of how the above rules are applied (and the result of their application) is given in the following section.

5.2 Analysis of a Knowledge Base by an Inference Method

As an example, take the problem of trying to determine the grandfather of John, using the knowledge base defined in figure 5. Given this knowledge base, figure 9 shows the sequence of deductions which allows us to satisfy the conjecture $\exists$ x:person => grandfather_of(john) = x.

Notice that, in the first few stages of the deduction, some instantiation of the quantified variable, x, is necessary. This may be arbitrary since, at some later stage, the original instantiation may be changed.

```
Proof of <∃ x:person => grandfather_of(john) = x>
1.>> empty |- ∃ x:person => grandfather_of(john) = x          by Exist Intro with <anyone>
2.>> empty |- grandfather_of(john) = anyone                   by adding
           <∀ x, y: person => father_of(father_of(x)) = y → grandfather_of(x) = y>
3.>> ∀ x,y: person => father_of(father_of(x)) = y → grandfather_of(x) = y |-
                 grandfather_of(john) = anyone          by Forall Elim with <john>
4.>> ∀ y: person => father_of(father_of(john)) = y → grandfather_of(john) = y |-
                 grandfather_of(john) = anyone          by Forall Elim with <anyone>
5.>> father_of(father_of(john)) = anyone → grandfather_of(john) = anyone |-
                 grandfather_of(john) = anyone          by Implies Elim
     6.1>> empty |- father_of(father_of(john)) = anyone       by Applying
                                                              <father_of(john)=fred>
     6.2>> empty |- father_of(fred) = anyone                  by Adding
                                                              <father_of(fred) = tom>
     6.3>> father_of(fred) = tom |- father_of(fred) = anyone         by Immediate
                 Not Proven
AND  7.1>> grandfather_of(john) = anyone |- grandfather_of(john) = anyone
                                                              by Immediate
                 Proven
Not Shown
```

Figure 9. Deducing variable instances

Note that, in the deduction, the variable instantiations in steps 1 and 4 may be modified at any point in the deduction. Deduction step 6.3 provides the appropriate instantiation for variables. The 'anonymous' term, anyone, is used as a placeholder for the actual term which provides a solution. The terms in italic font are extracted from the current theory of the knowledge base (the context in which the deduction is carried out).

The above example, with the correct instantiations for variables, is given in figure 10 below.

```
Proof of <∃ x:person => grandfather_of(john) = x>
1.>> empty |- ∃ x:person => grandfather_of(john) = x          by Exist Intro with <tom>
2.>> empty |- grandfather_of(john) = anyone    by adding
              <∀ x, y: person => father_of(father_of(x)) = y → grandfather_of(x) = y>
3.>> ∀ x, y: person => father_of(father_of(x)) = y → grandfather_of(x) = y |-
              grandfather_of(john) = tom          by Forall Elim with <john>
4.>> ∀ y: person => father_of(father_of(john)) = y → grandfather_of(john) = y |-
              grandfather_of(john) = tom          by Forall Elim with <tom>
5.>> father_of(father_of(john)) = tom → grandfather_of(john) = tom |-
              grandfather_of(john) = tom          by Implies Elim
     6.1>> empty |- father_of(father_of(john)) = tom        by Applying
                                                            <father_of(john)=fred>
     6.2>> empty |- father_of(fred) = tom                   by Adding
                                                            <father_of(fred) = tom>
     6.3>> father_of(fred) = tom |- father_of(fred) = tom   by Immediate
              Proven
AND  7.1>> grandfather_of(john) = tom |- grandfather_of(john) = tom
                                                            by Immediate
              Proven
QED
```

Figure 10. The complete deduction

A straight forward strategy could be envisaged which would allow simple deductions like this to be done automatically. For example, the *matching* of the left hand sides of the conjectures in steps 2, 6.1, and 6.2, with the rules in the knowledge base, identifies the correct rules for the subsequent deductions. Similar observations can be made for the other rule applications in the deduction. In addition, the deduction tree provides a *constructive* basis for generating an explanation. Looking at the deduction in a bottom up manner, the justification is given by steps 6.2, 6.1, and 5. The purpose of the other steps in the deduction are for instantiation of variables and for validating the application of rules.

5.3 Other Inference Methods and Strategies

Other inference rules and methods may be easily specified within the system using the language PAnndA-S. This requires that a transformation be defined which manipulates the object terms in a manner consistent with the desired inference system.

For example, the resolution rule [Robinson 65], which is the basis of the Prolog language could be defined. A library of transformations exist which simplifies this task. The libraries already defined for the transformation system include such facilities as unification, pattern matching, rewriting, and substitution. The rewriting, available within the system, may also be used as a simple mechanism for forward or backward chaining through a knowledge base. Specifying strategies is also straightforward. For example, a simple strategy, which would result in the deduction shown in section 3.2

is given in figure 11.

```
with pannda_s, General_trafo, Proof, current_theory;
package solver is

Esolve, solve: Exp x TP_THEORY -> boolean;
axiom for all Q: Exp; Th:TP_THEORY =>Esolve(Q, Th) = solve(⌈ empty |- Q⌋, Th);

axiom for all V,X,Y,Z,Q,Q1,Q2: Exp; Quant: Quantifier; Vx:Designator; Tvar: Type_exp;
       Th:TP_THEORY =>
Immediate(Q) -> solve(Q, Th) = true,
Or_Intro(Q) = ⌈Q1 or Q2⌋ -> solve(Q, Th) = solve(Q1, Th) or solve(Q2, Th),
And_Intro(Q) = ⌈Q1 and Q2⌋ -> solve(Q, Th) = solve(Q1, Th) and solve(Q2, Th),
Or_Elim(Q) = ⌈Q1 and Q2⌋ -> solve(Q, Th) = solve(Q1, Th) and solve(Q2, Th),
Q = ⌈X |- Y ->Z⌋ and Implies_Intro(Q) = Q1 -> solve(Q, Th) = solve(Q1, Th),
Q = ⌈X -> Y |- Z⌋ and Implies_Elim(Q) = ⌈Q1 and Q2⌋ ->
                        solve(Q, Th) = solve(Q1, Th) and solve(Q1, Th),
Q = ⌈Quant Vx:Tvar => X |- Y⌋ and Get_Var_AInst(⌈Quant Vx:Tvar => X ⌋, Q, Th) = V and
       Quant_Elim(Q, V) = Q1) -> solve(Q, Th) = solve(Q1, Th),
Q = ⌈X |- Quant Vx:Tvar => Y⌋ and Get_Var_CInst(⌈Quant Vx:Tvar => Y ⌋, Q, Th) = V and
       Quant_Intro(Q, V) = Q1 -> solve(Q, Th) = solve(Q1, Th),
not Immediate(Q) and Get_Left_Rule(Q, Th) = R and Add_Rule(Q, R) = Q1 ->
                        solve(Q, Th) = solve(Q1, Th),
others -> solve(Q, Th) = false;
end solver;
```

Figure 11. A deduction strategy

Some of the functions used in the definition require explanation. Get_Var_AInst and Get_Var_CInst attempt to instantiate a quantified variable appearing in the antecedent and conclusion respectively. Get_Left_Rule matches the conclusion with the left hand side of a rule in the knowledge base (denoted by Th), and Add_Rule adds this to the current deduction.

This strategy, uses only the rules defined as part of the calculus. Esolve requires, as parameters, the deduction query to be satisfied and the *local theory* of the current specification. The strategy is not as general as it could be. At the expense of some more sophisticated analysis and matching, the strategy could be made very general, and could be used for a large class of deduction problem.

6 AN EXAMPLE

In the following example, a slightly different form of knowledge base is used. Here an inference system may be employed which may be based on the resolution principle. The example illustrates the problem of deducing which sport is being described when various attributes concerning the sport are given as the basis of the deduction. The type framework in which the knowledge base is defined in given in figure 12.

```
package Sports is
type sport is private;
type area is private;
type field is private;

Has_players: sport × natural  → bool;

Has_area: sport × area  → bool;

Has_field_struct: sport × field  → bool;

Uses_ball: sport  → bool;
rect, circ, squr: area;
net, nonet, divnet: field;
end Sports;
```

Figure 12. The type framework

Note that only the definition mechanism and the construction functions are given here. Figure 13 shows the above type system being used to construct a knowledge base which is, essentially, in conjunctive normal form, this is given below.

```
with Sports
package Games is
cricket, squash, badminton, volleyball, basketball, boxing, soccer, tennis: sport;
axiom for all X:sport =>
        Uses_ball(X) and Has_area(X, rect) and Has_players(X,2) and
         Has_field_struct(X,nonet) -> X = squash,
        Uses_ball(X) and Has_area(X, rect) and Has_players(X,22) and
         Has_field_struct(X,nonet) -> X = soccer,
        not Uses_ball(X) and Has_area(X, squr) and Has_players(X,2) and
         Has_field_struct(X,nonet) -> X = boxing,
        Uses_ball(X) and Has_area(X, circ) and
         Has_field_struct(X,nonet) -> X = cricket,
        Uses_ball(X) and Has_area(X, rect) and Has_players(X,12) and
         Has_field_struct(X,divnet) -> X = volleyball,
        not Uses_ball(X) and Has_area(X, rect) and (Has_players(X,2) or
         Has_players(X,4)) and Has_field_struct(X,divnet) -> X = badmington,
        Uses_ball(X) and Has_area(X, rect) and Has_players(X,10) and
         Has_field_struct(X,nonet) -> X = baskeyball,
        Uses_ball(X) and Has_area(X, rect) and (Has_players(X,2) or Has_players(X,4))
            and Has_field_struct(X,divnet) -> X = squash;
end Sports;
```

Figure 13. The knowledge base

Inferences in this knowledge base may be carried out as shown in figure 14. It should

---

Proof of <∃ x:sport => Uses_ball(x) and Has_area(x, rect) and Has_players(x,22) and
Has_field_struct(x, nonet) -> x=x>

1.>> empty |-∃ x:sport => Uses_ball(x) and Has_area(x, rect) and Has_players(x,22) and
Has_field_struct(x, nonet) -> x=x

by Exist Intro with <soccer>

2.>> empty |-A3 and A1 and A0 and A2 -> soccer=soccer   by adding
<∀ x: sport Uses_ball(X) and Has_area(X, rect) and
Has_players(X,22) and Has_field_struct(X,nonet) -> X = soccer>

3.>> ∀ x: sport Uses_ball(X) and Has_area(X, rect) and
Has_players(X,22) and Has_field_struct(X,nonet) -> X = soccer |-
A3 and A1 and A0 and A2 -> soccer=soccer   by Forall Elim with <soccer>

4.>> (A3 and A1 and A0 and A2) -> soccer = soccer |-
(A3 and A1 and A0 and A2) -> soccer = soccer   by implies Intro

5.>>A3 and A1 and A0 and A2 and (A3 and A1 and A0 and A2) -> soccer = soccer
|- soccer=soccer   by Implies Elim

6.>>A3 and A1 and A0 andA2 and soccer=soccer |- soccer=soccer   by immediate
Proven

AND 7.1>> A3 and A1 and A0 and A2 |- A3 and A1 and A0 and A2   by And Intro
7.2>> A3 and A1 and A0 and A2 |- A3   by immediate
Proven

AND 7.3>>A3 and A1 and A0 and A2 |- A1 and A0 and A2   by And Intro
7.4>> A3 and A1 and A0 and A2 |-A1   by immediate
Proven

AND 7.5>> A3 and A1 and A0 and A2 |- A0 and A2   by And Intro
7.6>>A3 and A1 and A0 and A2|- A0   By Immediate
Proven

AND 7.7>>A3 and A1 and A0 and A2|- A2   by immediate
Proven

QED

Figure 14. The deduction

---

be noted, that textual, local, abbreviations can be defined which substantially reduces
the size of the deduction. Given the abbreviations Has_players(soccer, 22) = A0,
Has_area(soccer, rect) = A1, Has_field_struct(soccer, nonet) = A2, and Us-
es_ball(soccer) = A3, the deduction would be presented as in Figure 14.

The initial query is straight forward where facts about the game in question are given
and the existentially quantified variable represents the deduction to be performed.
There are various forms the conjecture may take, but the instantiation of the quantified variable is given by the knowledge base directly. It should be noted that from
step 4 of the deduction onwards, the in-built automatic deduction features derive all
the required deduction steps (independently of any strategy). A strategy is required
to determine the initial instantiations. This strategy would be similar to that shown in
figure 11. It should also be noted, that the immediate validity rule is directly applicable in step 4 of the deduction. If it had been applied here the deduction would be complete. However, in the general case, it is probably desirable to construct as full a deduction as possible, in particular, when explanations are desirable.

7 FURTHER WORK

The work presented in this paper is a description of on-going research. The current thrust is in the development of more sophisticated inference methods within the development environment.   The extensibility of the system allows such activities to be carried out in a convenient and straight-forward manner.

Development histories provide the basic mechanism for generating explanations. They also provide a basis for re-development, abstraction and reuse of concrete developments and deductions.   The properties of the deduction system presented here also offer a flexible framework for the development of deduction strategies (heuristics). More details of the deduction system may be found in [Traynor 92].

The incorporation of weights in the knowledge base, as a means of undertaking inference base on probabilistic reasoning, is a area of interesting future work. Again, the extensibility of the development system makes such experimentation a relatively comfortable activity.

The possible use of the rules of inductive inference which are available in the development environment have only been explored briefly, these methods show promise as a means of constructing generalisations from specific knowledge bases.

A complete formalisation of the transformation development framework is not given here. The detail of such an abstract semantic framework are under construction and preliminary details can be found in [Liu and Traynor 92].   Such a framework is a prerequisite for the formalisation of expert system development within the transformational framework.

8 CONCLUSIONS

The framework outlined here presents a rigorous methodology for the development of expert system *shells* and their associated knowledge bases.   The powerful tools, available as part of the basic transformational environment, also contribute significantly to the effectiveness of the system outlined. Deductions performed within the default deduction system are guaranteed to be correct. However, introducing new inference rules requires the correctness of the inference method to be demonstrated, this point has not been addressed here.

The tools available within the development environment for determining properties of knowledge bases have not been illustrated due to lack of space. However, the consistency and completion mechanisms are important tools in the knowledge engineering phase of expert system construction.   More details of these tools may be found in Vol I and II of [Krieg-Brückner and Hoffmann 91].

9 REFERENCES

[Ada 83] The Ada programming language reference manual. ANSI/MILSTD 1815A, US Dept. of Defence, Goverment Printing Office, 1983.

[Astesiano et al 90] Astesiano, E., Giovani, A., and Reggio, G., Processes as Data Types: Observational Semantics and Logic. Semantics of Systems of Concurrent Processes, Springer LNCS 489, (1990).

[Breu 91] Breu, R. Algebraic Specification techniques in Object-Oriented Programming Environments. Thesis Dissertation, Passau, (1991).

[Broy 91] Broy, M., Some Algebraic and Functional Hocus Pocus with Abracadabra. Information and Software Technology, (1991).

[Ehrich and Mahr 85] Ehrich, H. and Mahr, B. Fundamentals of Algebraic Specification I: Equations and Initial Semantics. Springer (1985).

[Gentzen 69] Gentzen, G.: Investigations into Logical Deduction, In: 'The Collected Papers of Gerhard Gentzen', pages 68-131, North-Holland (1969).

[Krieg-Brückner and Hoffmann 91] Krieg-Brückner, B., Hoffmann, H. (eds.):PROgram development by SPECification and TRAnsformation: Vol. 1: Methodology, Vol. 2: Language Family, Vol. 3: System. PROSPECTRA Reports M.1.1.S3-R-55.2, -56.2, -57.2. Universität Bremen, (1990). (to appear in LNCS).

[Krieg-Brückner 88] Krieg-Brückner, B.: Algebraic Formalisation of Program Development by Transformations. in : Proc. European Symposium On Programming '88, LNCS 300, pages 34-48, (1988).

[Krieg-Brückner et al 91] Krieg-Brückner, B., Karlsen, E., Liu, J., Traynor, O.: The PROSPECTRA Methodology and System: A unified development Framework. In Proc. VDM '91, Springer Verlag, LNCS 552, pages 361-397 (1991).

[Liu and Traynor 92] Liu, J and Traynor, O., A Review of Transformational Development System, Technical Report Universität Bremen, In Preparation.

[Plant 90] Robet T. Plant, On the Verification, Validation, and Testing of Knowledge-Based Systems. , The Journal of Knowledge Engineering, Vol. 3, No. 1, pgs 59-67, 1990.

[Ritchie 88] Ritchie, B.: The Design and Implementation of an Interactive Proof Editor, Ph.D. Thesis, University of Edinburgh, (1988).

[Schmidt 84] Schmidt, D.: A Programming Notation for Tactical Reasoning, Proc. of the 7th Intl. Conf. on Automated Deduction, LNCS 170, Springer Verlag, (1984).

[Traynor 92] Traynor, O., The PROSPECTRA Proof System, in Vol III, Chapter. 4 of [Krieg-Brückner and Hoffmann 91]

[Traynor, Liu 91] Traynor, O., Liu, J., The Development of Correct Programs by Specification and Transformation, in Proc. ICYCS Conference, Beijing, July 1991.

TOWARDS A METHOD FOR
MULTI-AGENT SYSTEM DESIGN

Arturo Ovalle & Catherine Garbay

Groupe SIC (Integrated Cognitive Systems)
Equipe de Reconnaissance des Formes et de Microscopie Quantitative
Laboratoire TIM3 - Institut IMAG
Bât. CERMO - BP 53X - 38041 Grenoble Cedex, FRANCE

Abstract

We describe a method for Multi-Agent System design which is assisted by two original typologies, resulting from the deeper study of knowledge and reasoning. The first typology reflects a formal character while the second reflects a technological character. The purpose of the Formal Typology is the classification and structuring of knowledge and reasoning. The Technological Typology handles the parameters governing the reasoning intrinsic to Multi-Agent technology, not only at the individual level of the agent but also within a group of agents. Possible correspondence between both of these typologies will become concrete by the presentation of the Multi-Agent generator MAPS (Multi-Agent Problem Solver), and the Multi-Agent system KIDS (Knowledge based Image Diagnosis System) devoted to Biomedical Image Interpretation.

Keywords

Second Generation Expert Systems, Multi-Agent System Design, Distributed Artificial Intelligence, Knowledge and Reasoning Modeling, Control, Biomedical Image Interpretation.

1. INTRODUCTION

Among knowledge based systems using artificial intelligence techniques we are particularly interested in the Multi-Agent systems which arise from their second generation (systems using multiple reasoning schemes). The Multi-Agent paradigm results from distributed artificial intelligence approaches and makes it possible to overcome the drawbacks encountered during the resolution of complex problems. The main issue of the Multi-Agent approach involves the distribution of tasks and skills among intelligent entities that co-operate, pooling their knowledge and their expertise to attain an aim (Ferber 88). In this way, not only a multi-modal knowledge representation, and reasoning schemes handling are permitted but also, co-operative problem solving. In addition, a variety of reasoning schemes emerge which corresponds not only to individual behaviour but also to behaviour developed within the group of agents.

However, one of the major difficulties of Multi-Agent approaches results in the risk for the developer of such systems to be rapidly "lost" as a result of the variety of parameters to be handled, which characterizes this technology. It should be noted that there is a remarkable evolution in this technology. But there is a need for conceiving methods which can integrate specificities of Multi-Agent technology.

The aim of the work presented here is thus to propose a method for Multi-Agent system design composed of two essential parts : a Formal Design followed by a Technological Design, which are respectively assisted by a Formal Typology and a Multi-Agent Technological Typology. The Formal Typology for knowledge and reasoning classification permits a synthetic view of elements which are usually presented in an unstructured way. In addition, this typology provides a tool to assist modeling of knowledge and reasoning. The Technological Typology handles the parameters governing the reasoning intrinsic to Multi-Agent technology, and not only at the individual level of the agent but also within a group of agents.

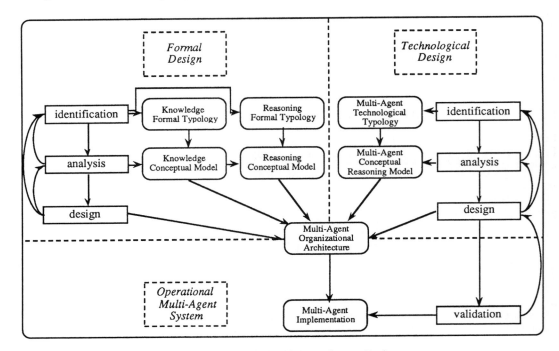

Figure 1 : Method for Multi-Agent System Design :
Formal Design and Technological Design.

A variety of methodologies have been proposed for structuring and analyzing knowledge such as KADS (Breuker 89) or KOD (VOG 88) especially for knowledge acquisition purposes. They are totally independent of a technique or system. KADS methodology assists user to construct several models, including conceptual models of domain knowledge and reasoning, model of the user / system cooperation, model of the functional conception and physical models. In KOD methodology two axes are introduced which define models and paradigms to assist the knowledge acquisition process.The method presented here proposes to bring together knowledge and reasoning formalisation with specific characteristics related to Multi-Agent technology.

The Formal Design and the Technological Design (Fig.1) which comprises our method are respectively presented in parts 2 and 3. Possible matches between Formal Design and Technological Design then become concrete by the presentation of Multi-Agent generator MAPS (Multi-Agent Problem Solver) described in part 4 and the Multi-Agent system KIDS (Knowledge based Image Diagnosis System) described in part 5. The KIDS system is intended for Biomedical Image Interpretation purposes.

2. FORMAL DESIGN

Figure 1 shows the three main steps followed by the Formal Design : knowledge and reasoning identification step (1), knowledge and reasoning model analysis step (2) and Multi-Agent architectural design step (3). The first step uses Formal Typologies for knowledge and reasoning structuring that will be described later. The second step uses a model of knowledge and reasoning obtained from the previous step which is handled by the Multi-Agent system. The third step aims at completing agent skills for each of the agents comprising the Multi-Agent architecture. Feedback is indeed possible between these three steps to complete and enhance the Multi-Agent architecture.

2.1. Formal Typology for Knowledge Structuring

The Formal Typology for knowledge structuring organizes knowledge elements into four axes underlying properties and differences which distinguish each of the classes and sub-classes that have been identified : functional axis, structural axis, level of abstraction axis and domain specific axis. These four axes are described below.

Functional Axis

The functional axis determines a distinction among "figurative" knowledge (objects), "operative" knowledge (actions), "reflexive" knowledge (knowledge about knowledge) and heuristic (knowledge about knowledge handling). Each of these knowledge classes can be distinguished from the others by means of its functional character, useful for medical reasoning modeling. In fact, we have used a task (operative knowledge) oriented modeling approach for cytological expertise modeling (Ovalle 91c). These tasks handle different types of knowledge including descriptive knowledge ("figurative" knowledge) which frequently exhibits an uncertain or imprecise character ("reflexive" knowledge). Finally, it should be noted that this variety of knowledge schemes is finally handled by specific strategies ("heuristic" knowledge).

Figurative Knowledge (or objects) permits the naming and the description of the elements of a problem involving data, facts, hypotheses or even results. Some examples of figurative knowledge handled in cytological diagnosis are the following : a specific image of a specimen, microscopic field, cellular morphology or pathology.

Operative Knowledge (or actions) denotes a procedure or inference rule carried out according to figurative knowledge elements. Operative knowledge can be classified according to the structural axis determined by structural relationships relating the figurative knowledge they handle.

Reflexive Knowledge can be defined as that giving information on the nature of a knowledge element with respect to a specific domain. A figurative or operative knowledge might thus be qualified as vague or imprecise, uncertain, ambiguous, complete or partial, coherent or conflicting, ...(Aussenac 89). The Heuristic knowledge denotes every knowledge element which indicates different the ways and conditions to handle a knowledge element : two types of heuristics can be distinguished depending on the figurative or operative character of the knowledge they handle. Both of them are in fact knowledge about knowledge and imply the expression of a variety of reasoning schemes and they will therefore be examined in this context.

Structural Axis

Structural knowledge can be described as an arrangement of knowledge elements that are related together by different types of associations. Structural axes distinguishes between intrinsic, contextual, compositional, taxonomic and causal knowledge.

Intrinsic Knowledge describes properties related to knowledge. It is required to determine representative properties able to describe, identify and differentiate a special type of knowledge from others. Morphological descriptors such as size, shape, texture, colour, thickness... or malignancy descriptors including grade or state for a tumour may be attached to visual objects in medicine.

Contextual Knowledge permits to focalize or situate an object or an action within a specific context. The same object placed in two different contexts might differently be seen : an object will not display the same apparent size if its neighbourhood involves big or small objects. An action can be relevant or insignificant depending on context. Compositional knowledge describes the simple or complex character of objects and actions. For a specific object it is required to determine whether it is comprised or not of other objects or if it determines in itself an unique undecomposed entity.

Taxonomic Knowledge is every structure that can be described by means of a tree where its nodes are figurative or operative knowledge related by hierarchically specialized relationships. Causal Knowledge describes cause/effect relationships which bring together not only the variables of a system (biological or physical) but also their observed state (malignant or faulty). Taxonomies and causal graphs are essentially used by experts for classifying pathologies in diagnosis formulation (Ovalle 91c).

Level of Abstraction and Specific Domain Axes

It should be noticed that figurative, operative, reflexive and heuristic knowledge types may be distributed among several level of abstractions : in computer vision for example we can distinguish among the following levels : sensorial, perceptual, iconic and semantic. Some of these are highly dependent of a specific domain of application while others are completely independent : already in the computer vision field it is considered that "high" level knowledge is domain dependent while "low" level knowledge is in opposition independent. Figurative knowledge in cytology defines the following three levels of abstraction (Ovalle 91c) : image level, image descriptor level, and interpretation level.

2.2. Formal Typology for reasoning structuring

Formal Typology for knowledge structuring has organized knowledge elements into four axes (§ 2.1) : functional axis, structural axis, level of abstraction axis and domain specific axis. Since the reasoning strongly depends on the type of knowledge elements they handle, these four axes will also determine different types of reasoning. In fact, this organization will help us for reasoning classification and analysis purposes. It should be noticed that elementary reasoning interact to constitute complex reasoning schemes that will be called "hybrid".

A elementary reasoning handles a specific type of knowledge (e.g. "figurative" or "operative"), as defined through the Formal Typology. An example of elementary reasoning is the hierarchical handling of operative knowledges (e.g. an action scheduling), so-called planning.

A hybrid reasoning results from the need to integrate or combine elementary reasonings. A hybrid reasoning thus handles different types of knowledge. Figure 2 illustrates an operative & compositional hybrid reasoning which drive the execution of the main expert tasks that are implied during diagnosis formulation in cytopathology.

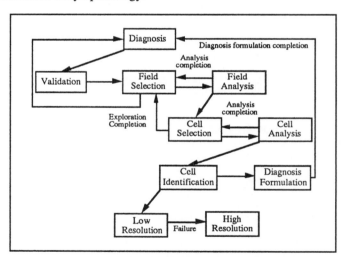

Figure 2 : Operative & compositional hybrid reasoning.

A deeper reflexion on different types of classes and sub-classes for reasoning schemes which compose the Formal Typology can be found in (Ovalle 91c).

3. MULTI-AGENT TECHNOLOGICAL DESIGN

The three main steps followed by the Multi-Agent Formal Design are also used by the Multi-Agent Technological Design (Fig. 1 at the right) : reasoning identification step (1), reasoning model analysis step (2) and Multi-Agent architectural design step (3). The first step uses the Multi-Agent Technological Typology that will be described afterwards. The second step uses a model of reasoning obtained from the previous step and handled by the Multi-Agent system. The third step aims at completing agent skills for each of the agents composing the Multi-Agent architecture. Feedbacks are also possible among steps in the Technological Design in order to complete and enhance the Multi-Agent architecture design.

3.1. Multi-Agent Technological Typology

Multi-Agent reasoning must be examined according to two perspectives, as follows : the perspective of the agent and the perspective of the group of agents (society of agents). Reasoning developed in a society of agents depends on choice made at the individual level (i.e. internal structure of the agents) and within the group of agents level (task and skill distribution modes, communicating protocols and modes, co-operating and organization modes). Parameters composing the Technological Typology which govern individual level reasoning will be described first those which govern reasoning at the group of agent level will be subsequently described.

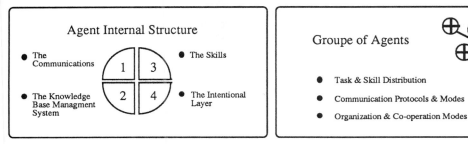

Figure 3 : Multi-Agent Technological Typology through two perspectives :
agent individual level (left side in the figure) and group of agents level (right side in the figure).

The agent

From the individual agent point of view the study of the Agent Internal Structure is made to analyze different types of reasoning developed by the agent. Reasoning from the individual point of view should consider the parameters which depend on the sophistication degree of the agent : communication and reaction possibilities to external events, knowledge base management abilities, problem solving skills and expertise, autonomous degree for making decisions, and knowledge about itself and others.

The *structure of the agent* is thus comprised of four essential parts (Ferber 91) : the first describes the agent as a "communicating" and "reactive" entity ; it is responsible of interactions with others agents and the environment. The second part describes the agent as a "rational" entity ; it determines the control mechanisms that have been given to the agent : planning possibilities and internal task supervision (internal information request, knowledge base updating) and external task supervision (external information request, environment movements, …) ; the third part describes the agent as a "specialist" and is strongly dependent on the application domain. It thus concerns the expertise of the agent, its skill domain, its expertise. Finally, the fourth part describes the agent as an "intentional" entity in which knowledge is included about itself and others. This issue implies the ability of the agent to reason with respect to others, which thus implies the ability of modeling the knowledge of others (beliefs), their abilities and objectives, and also the ability of anticipating their behaviour and action plans (their intentions). These four levels of agent structuring and sophistication are considered below as parameters allowing the definition of our Multi-Agent reasoning Typology from the individual agent perspective.

A deeper study of *reasoning associated with communications* among agents has been made by (Chaib-Draa 90). This author established that information exchange among agents participating in co-operation is vital, not only for local task solving, but also for enhancing the coherence and co-ordination at the group of agents level. The three essential components of communication paradigm should more deeply analyzed for information exchange optimization : information exchange modality, message exchange content (Durfee 85) and finally the protocol to be used. It should be noted that the modes most commonly used for Multi-Agent information exchange are the information sharing (blackboard approach) and message sending modes.

Reasoning associated with Knowledge Base Management implies the control possibilities of the agent such as operational access to the knowledge base, but also task execution, information request decisions and task delegation abilities (explicit requests for action execution). Information searching activated by external request can, in fact, fail since the agent knowledge base may be incomplete : the request for information should be transmited in this case within the agent network. The same case holds for tasks requested of the agent that could not be accomplished by him : these specific tasks should be therefore delegated to other agents.

Reasoning associated to resource handling concerns the agent skills, which are domain dependent. These are described according to the agent expertise : its know-how in a specific domain or, more precisely, criteria used to choose significant objects or actions that will be used for a problem solving step at a given time.

Intentional Reasoning is developed within agents provided with "intentionality". Their reasoning allows agents to analyze their own problem solving abilities, and to decide the best way to handle their abilities. Moreover, they make it possible to reason with respect to their knowledge on others, thus adapting their behaviour with respect to the outside.

The group of agents
Reasoning developed at the group of agents level (society of agents) depends on choices performed within the group of agents on the following three parameters :
- task and skill distribution modes ;
- communication protocols and modes ;
- co-operation and organization modes.

The *task and skill distribution* can be carried out in a modular manner ; the expertise can also be decomposed according to multiple or concurrent points of view. In this last case, it is necessary to assign the agent network new reasoning abilities which could allow it to manage conflicts which result from problem solving performed in concurrence.

Communication protocols establish the means and modes of communication among agents. Two types of Multi-Agent systems can be distinguished depending on whether information exchange is made throughout a common memory or blackboard (implicit communication mechanism) or whether it is performed by message sending (explicit communication mechanism). In the first case, communication reasoning becomes simpler in that agents do not directly communicate with others. The problem of the choice of an "addressee" agent is not considered in this case.

Co-operation and organization modes describe the manner in which a group of agents co-operate for problem solving. This co-operation depends on numerous factors such as agent role assignment or bounded rationality associated to information exchange among agents.

The choice of a co-operation approach such as the "network protocol", for example, implies that extensive reasoning abilities should be assigned to agents not only in order to establish contracts but also to synchronize tasks among agents of the same group. In the "intermediate result exchange" approach, a particular reasoning scheme is handled that focuses on truth maintenance on several agent knowledge bases.

In "local planning" approaches a specific reasoning scheme is used that concerns the local plan generation. In this case, several plans are created for task planning not only at the individual level but also in a co-ordinated manner at the group level. In "organizational" approaches role allocation and assessment of relationships among agents are made a priori by creating an organization adapted to the problem to be solved.

It is obvious that a compromise should be found between choices made within the internal architecture of agents, which constrain local reasoning schemes, and choices made within the group of agent organizations, which constrain the reasoning at more global level. We can moreover observe an inter-dependence between choices adopted for the internal agent structure and choices concerning the group of agents organization.

4. THE MULTI-AGENT GENERATOR MAPS

MAPS (Multi-Agent Problem Solver) is defined as a generic environment dedicated to the design of distributed knowledge-based systems (Baujard 90).

4.1. The Basic Structure of Agents
We first describe the internal architecture of the agents, communication modes, knowledge base management abilities, problem solving skills and expertise, and high level behaviours throughout the Technological Typology described above.

The agent internal architecture
Two classes of agents are involved in MAPS generator, called Knowledge Server (KS) and Knowledge Processor (KP), communicating by message sending (Fig. 4). These agents are responsible for handling descriptive and operative knowledge elements respectively : they thus entail a distribution of knowledge in terms of static and dynamic elements, that permits a balance to be reached between problem modeling and problem solving abilities.

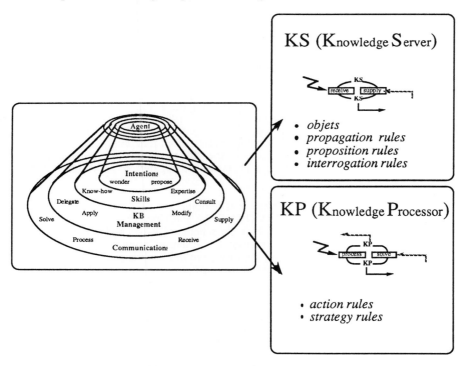

Figure 4 : Agent Model for MAPS generator through Technological Typology :
two types of agents, KS (Knowledge Server) and KP (Knowledge Processor), are instanciated from this Model.

The external layer or *communication layer* describes the social behaviour of an agent, seen as an autonomous agent able to react to external events. Communication is based on a very simple message sending protocol : any request is sent in an explicit way to a specific agent, according to a "command" mode (Hautin 86) in opposition to information sharing mechanism as in the blackboard approach (Läasri 89) (Hayes-Roth, 1985). Four types of messages are used for the information exchange among the MAPS agents : "Receive and Supply" are addressed to KS agents and "Process and Solve" are addressed to KP agents.

The *Knowledge Base Management layer* concerns the classical operations to access the knowledge base, such as consultation or modification of elements (for KS agents) but also task execution and task delegation abilities (for KP agents). Low level operations that are performed by the inference engine, such as production rules filtering and application are also considered as involved in this layer.

The *Skill layer* is determined by the dedicated skills which are specific domain dependent and described by the expertise and know-how of the agent. There are in this layer several rules for object selection (within KS agents) and for action selection (within KP agents) which are applied at a given time in the problem solving.

Intentional layer : high level behaviours
- KS Agents : specific behaviour (or high level reasoning) are developed when external requests "Receive" and "Supply" have been received, as follows :

Receive
(AND   Update
         Propagate
         (OR   (AND   Propose info
                  SEND KP Process info)
         (AND   Interrogate pb
                SEND KP Solve pb)))
	Supply
	(OR Get
	         SEND KP Solve pb
	     (AND Propose info
	               SEND KP Process info)
	     (AND Interrogate pb
	              SEND KP Solve pb)))

Agents thus reason in an autonomous way in the manner best suited to answer the sending request, through their own resources, but also depending on services offered by the KP agents with whom they communicate. As can be seen, in case of a "Receive" request, a first attempt is made to Update the knowledge base, then to search valid information (Propose) and finally to send it outside (Send KP Process). In case of failure at any of these three steps, the KS agent can search for the lacking information (Interrogate), to request it of an outside KP agent (Send KP Solve), and finally to resume the whole Receive cycle. The basic role of a KS agent is the completion and dissemination of knowledge. In case of a Supply request, the element is first of all tentatively obtained (Get call), and then sent back to the caller. In case of failure, the KS agent can try to resume the current unsuccessful solving strategy, by entering a Propose/Interrogate cycle, which is similar to the previous one.

- KP Agents : two methods called "Process" and "Solve" are used here which in turn call the corresponding internal methods (respectively Data-Drive and Goal-Drive). The behaviour of a KP agent may thus be represented by a very simple linear scheme : such an agent may only conclude the success or failure of its activities. The sole processing alternative it might propose in case of failure occurs at the rule selection level. Reasoning abilities have not been assigned to these agents. Such agents involve a set of rules, which may describe any deductive or procedural analysis, and a set of meta-rules driving their selection.

The group of agents
We first describe choices adopted in the Task and Skill Distribution, Communication Protocol and modes, are described below and finally Co-operation & Organization modes.

Task and Skill Distribution
Task and Skill Distribution is made in a modular manner : the notion of conflict or multiple points of view are not considered here. An agent is finally designed as an autonomous entity : it is able to react to a limited number of requests, through a predetermined solving scheme. This scheme determines a behavioural scheme which depends on the current problem being solved, the agent resources to solve problems, but also the possible help that could be given by other agents.

Communication Protocol and modes
Communication among agents is made by a message sending mechanism : any request is sent in an explicit way to a specific agent according to a "command" mode (Hautin 86) in opposition to information sharing mechanism as in the blackboard approach (Läasri 89) (Hayes-Roth, 1985).

Figure 6 shows thus an information exchange among agents performed in a KS & KP "minimal" multi-agent architecture.

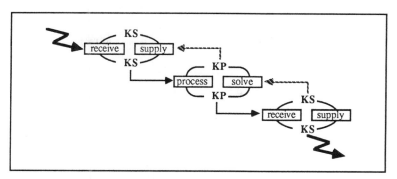

Figure 5 : A KS & KP "minimal" multi-agent architecture.

Co-operation & organization modes
A "minimal" generic architecture for problem solving may thus be defined as involving one KS agent communicating with one KP agent: the KS agent in this case involves both the data and results associated to the problem at hand, while the KP agent involves some problem solving elements. However, a more realistic scheme implies 2 KS agents communicating with one KP agent in order that the data and results be distributed between 2 different agents (Fig. 5).

Such "minimal" generic architecture may in turn be specialized to model complex problems. Distributing static knowledge elements among several KS agents makes it possible to differentiate between them according to their conceptual levels and thus handle them in a dedicated way. Distributing dynamic knowledge elements among several KP agents makes possible to model successive processing steps, but also to point out the presence of high level processing alternatives.

From a dynamic point of view, finally, the functional as well as structural agent features that have been described give rise to powerful problem solving strategies which appear to depend on the resources and competences of the various agents, but not on the individual decision of a centralized control structure.

Flexible prediction/verification strategies can thus be obtained as a local reasoning developed by a specific KP agent (production rule selection through meta-rules), or as a Propose/Interrogate cycle locally produced within a KS agent where initial hypothesis has been produced by an external KP agent. Prediction/verification is thus modelled with a more "operative" character in the first case and with more "figurative" character in the second.

Control cycle chaining : sources of hybrid reasoning
The control cycle chaining resulting from the interaction of KS and KP agents (Fig. 6) determines the control cycle of the MAPS system. It thus alternates between a KS control cycle and a KP control cycle. A specific KS control cycle essentially develops the following two operations : a searching and selection of objects that likely applied, which we call *"local figurative selection"* followed by a searching and selection of tasks (KP agents) also likely applicable called *"global operative selection"*. This last operation insures that control will be transferred to a KP agent.

A specific KP control cycle, on the other hand, generates three operations : a searching and selection of actions likely to be applied, that we call *"local operative selection"* followed by the action application called *"execution"* with associated results, and finally a search and selection of specific representation level (KS agents) called *"global figurative selection"*. Values obtained as a result of an action execution should be used to update a knowledge base of an KS when necessary, which stores figurative knowledge elements.

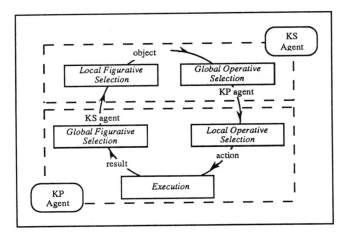

Figure 6 : Control cycle chaining of MAPS agents :
source of figurative & operative hybrid reasoning.

5. THE KIDS MULTI-AGENT SYSTEM

KIDS has been designed under MAPS as a Multi-Agent System (Ovalle 91a) to model the human reasoning approach in cytology. This system handles heterogeneous knowledge such as those described above (figurative, operative, reflexive and heuristic knowledge), involved in cytological specimen exploration. We first describe different knowledge schemes that are handled by the KIDS system through the Formal Typology, and then describe the three analyses steps which determine three different groups of agents.

5.1. The Knowledge
Figurative and operative knowledge which reflect the medical expertise have been distributed within several KS and KP connected in a network (rightmost window in Fig. 7).

Figurative Knowledge
Figurative knowledge describes the set of objects handled at different stages in cytological specimen analysis. These knowledge elements have been distributed within different KS agents not only depending on their specific level of abstraction, but also on existent relationships during problem solving. Here, we can distinguish the specimen image level, the lowest magnification level, the highest magnification level, cellular morphological descriptors level, observed cellular type representation level, and finally the diagnosis formulation level. The following 4 main knowledge representation levels can be determined : the image level, the descriptor level, the identification level, and finally the interpretation level. These levels are in fact vital levels in the understanding of a visual image.

Operative Knowledge
Six main tasks have been modelled in the KIDS system and represented through KP agents (Ovalle 91b). These tasks are listed below : they correspond to different axes of knowledge organization :

    - specimen validation   --> intrinsic axis (description) ;
    - field selection   --> contextual axis (focusing) ;
    - magnification change   --> intrinsic axis ;
    - morphological analysis   --> intrinsic & structural axes (perception & description)
    - cellular identification   --> intrinsic axis
                                   & taxonomic (matching & classification) ;
    - diagnosis interpretation   --> causal & taxonomic axes (deduct & propagation) ;

Reflexive and Heuristic Knowledge

The reflexive knowledge used in the KIDS system describes the uncertain and evolutive character of knowledge inherent in medical diagnosis. The attribute "presence" has thus been introduced to qualify the confidence of each diagnosis hypotheses formulated. The following are the possible values for this attribute : absent, low-probability, uncertain, perhaps, without-doubt and likely. Propagation rules have also introduced the role is truth maintenance verification of current diagnosis hypotheses that haven been produced.

Heuristic knowledge determines local criteria for relevant information selection purposes (fields or cells in particular) or some decision making, such as low/high magnification alternation. This decision making is presently handled in interactive mode : an agreement must in fact be required from an external observer.

5.2. Group of Agent Behaviour

Three essential analysis steps, which determine three different group of agents, can be distinguished in KIDS (Ovalle 91a) : The Specimen Exploration Step or validation and field selection step, the Cell Type Identification Step which concerns a preliminary analysis of morphological descriptors followed by the identification task, and Diagnosis Formulation Step or interpretation step.

Specimen Exploration Step

The *task and skill distribution* for Specimen Exploration Step is the following : Specimen Image Acquisition is driven by KS-Specimen agent, Specimen Exploration is driven by KP-Explore agent and Field Selection is driven by KS-Low-Resolution agent.

The *Group of Agents Behaviour* for this phase can be described as follows : an image of the specimen is acquired by KS-Specimen agent and then transmitted to KP-Explore agent. A particular specimen exploration strategy is implemented in that agent, in the form of a loop which controls the successive sending of fields to KS-Low-Resolution agent. After reception by KS-Low-Resolution, user agreement is requested to know whether analyzing such field is relevant or not, or whether it would need high magnification analysis.

Cell Type Identification Step

The *task and skill distribution* concerning the Cell Type Identification Step is the following : Cellular Morphological Analysis is driven by KP-Analyze agent, Descriptor Computation is driven by KS-Morphology agent, and Cell Type Identification is driven by KP-Identify agent.

The *Group of Agents Behaviour* for this phase can be described as follows : after reception by KP-Analyze agent, the field is segmented and a second loop is implemented, which controls the successive sending of cells to the KS-Morphology agent. The latter is then responsible for collecting relevant morphological information and send it to KP-Identify agent for further identification. It should be observed that user agreement is again requested, to know whether analyzing the current cell is relevant or not. The various cell descriptors are currently requested of the user : the contour of current cell is graphically highlighted for this purpose. Cell type identification is afterwards performed by KP-Identify agent by means of inference rules, based on a cross-correlated table in which cell morphologies are assigned to cell types. Such identification may then be validated or not by the user (activation of KS-Cell-Type interrogation rules). In case of acceptance, a scoring procedure is activated as conclusion part of KS-Cell-Type propagation rule. In the opposite case, the next cell is simply proposed for analysis, i.e. control is sent back to loop 2.

Diagnosis Formulation Step

The *task and skill distribution* for the Diagnosis Formulation Step is the following : Diagnosis Formulation is driven by KP-Interpret agent, and Potential Diagnosis Hypothesis Storing is driven by KS-Diagnosis agent.

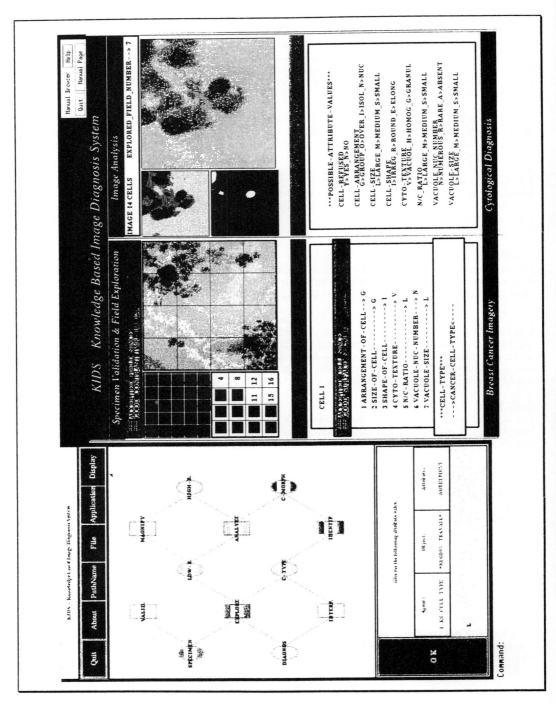

Figure 7 : The KIDS graphical interface (rightmost interaction window) interacting with the MAPS programming environment (leftmost interaction window). Reasoning performed by the Cell Type Identification step is illustrated here : the "cancer" cell type is associated to the 1st cell analyzed within the 7th exploration field.

The *Group of Agents Behaviour* for this phase can be described as follows : the scoring of cell types directly assists the diagnosis formulation that is performed by KP-Interpret and based on a cross-correlated table tying cell types to pathologies.

Proposed diagnosis hypothesis is finally received by KS-Diagnosis agent ; activating propagation rules then entails requesting the user to validate the proposed diagnosis or not. Control is sent back to previous steps even if a satisfactory diagnosis has been obtained. Different behaviour could indeed be developed.

6. CONCLUSION

A method for Multi-Agent system design has been presented which first develops a Multi-Agent Formal Design assisted by two formal typologies that have been shown to be very useful for knowledge and reasoning structuring. The main interest in the use of these Formal Typologies are the following :

- facility for identifying and computer transcribing of several classes of knowledge and reasoning comprised within the expertise to be modelled ;
- comprehension of intrinsic characteristics of reasoning according to the variety of knowledge they handled ;
- potential integration analysis of reasoning not only within the tasks but also when a co-operation between tasks takes place ;
- possibility of a "constructive" design of the system (Chandrasekaran 87) by first integrating simple reasonings schemes and then obtaining complex combinations of reasoning ;

Even though structuring facilities as given by these formal typologies are shown to be useful for knowledge and reasoning modeling, these typologies still remain very general, difficult to understand and can be distant from informatic implementation. In fact, these typologies do not permit direct implementation. A Technological Typology was thus necessary for more efficient handling of the informatic tools but also for defining technological specifications. Moreover, we attempted to produce a thought tool to better understand, if possible, difficulties and requirements of Multi-Agent technology.

There are a variety of advantages in using the Technological Typology proposed above, among which are:
- the definition of general parameters governing reasoning not only at individual level of the agent but also at the group of agents level ;
- the lightening of system design tasks by means of a better understanding of the Multi-Agent Technology ;
- the specification of high level behaviour permitting a general problem solving modeling ;
- the study of MAPS programming environment from a new perspective.

The Multi-Expert generator MAPS has been therefore presented through a new perspective to combine Formal and Technological typologies proposed above. MAPS is in fact a robust software approach which permits not only the integration of different kinds of informatic tools (multi-functional operators, a variety of processing methods, for example) but also it permits the integration of solving strategies and control mechanisms.

During the design of Multi-Agent systems such as KIDS, Formal and Technological typologies which assist our method were satisfactorily complemented. In fact, knowledge and reasoning modeling is facilitated by formal typology which combines informatic transcription and human expertise. Moreover, expertise transfer is facilitated by the alternation between the identification and informatic transcription of diverse knowledge and reasoning schemes. If we look at knowledge and reasoning elements composing the expertise and consider the dedicated abilities of different KIDS agents, they can be identified by means of categories established within Formal and Technological Typologies.

Technological Typology, on the other hand, combine system developer with intrinsic issues characterizing Multi-Agent environments. This typology allows the developer to better handle the Multi-Agent generator MAPS thus reducing system design tasks.

The KIDS system still remains a prototype and has not yet been used in medical practice. Special studies will therefore be devoted to man-machine communication and also to system validation. In fact, even though a multiple window mechanism is used by the KIDS system and permits visualization of results from reasoning made by diverse groups of agents, user dialogue still remains limited and primitive. As for system validation, a special effort will be made to complete knowledge elements that are handled by the system and to integrate new reasoning schemes. Moreover, an additional effort will be devoted to the interactive acquisition of specimen images by interfacing a camera to the microscope. This microscope will be provided with motorized stages that are directly driven by the system which will therefore control the slide exploration. This will allow us to develop a really operational version of the KIDS system.

References

(Aussenac 89) Aussenac, N. : *Conception d'une méthodologie et d'un outil d'acquisition de connaissances expertes*. Thèse de docteur en Informatique, Spécialité : Intelligence Artificielle. Université Paul Sabatier de Toulouse, octobre 1989.

(Baujard 90) Baujard, O. & Garbay, C. : *A programming environment for distributed expert system design*. Expert System Applications, ExpertSys., pp. 27-32.

(Breuker 89) Breuker A. & Wielinga B.J. : *Knowledge acquisition as modelling expertise : The KADS methodology* , Proceedings first European workshop on knowledge acquisition for knowledge-based systems.

(Chaib-Draa 90) Chaib-Draa B. *Contribution à la résolution distribuée de problème : une approche basée sur les états intentionnels*. Thèse de docteur en sciences, spécialité Automatique Industrielle et Humaine. Université de Valenciennes et du Hainaut-Chambrésis, 1990.

(Chandrasekaran 87) Chandrasekaran, B. : *Towards a functional architecture for intelligence based on generic information processing tasks*. Proc. 10th IJCAI pp. 1183-1192. IEEE Computer Society Press, 1987.

(Durfee 85) Durfee E.H., Lesser V.R. et Corkill D.D. *Coherent Coorporation Among Communicating Problem Solving*. Proc. of the Distributed Artificial Intelligent Workshop, pp. 231-276, dec., 1985.

(Ferber 88) Ferber, J. & Ghallab, M. : *Problématique des univers multi-agents intelligents*. Actes des Journées nationales du PRC-GRECO "Intelligence Artificielle", pp 295-320.Teknea., 1988.

(Ferber 91) Ferber J. *Introduction à l'Intelligence Artificielle Distribuée. Dossier : Intelligence Artificielle Distribuée*. Bulletin de l'AFIA, n°6, pp. 16-19, juillet, 1991.

(Hautin 86) Hautin, F. et Vailly, A. : *La coopération entre systèmes experts*, Actes des Journées nationales du PRC-GRECO "Intelligence Artificielle", Cepadues Editions, 1986.

(Hayes-Roth 85) Hayes-Roth, B. *A blackboard model of control*. Artificial Intelligence, vol 26, pp. 251-321, 1985.

(Lâasri 89) Lâasri H. et Maître B.*Organisation du contrôle dans les architectures de blackboard*, RIA 1989, Vol 3 N° 1.

(Ovalle 89)   Ovalle, A., Pesty, S., Seigneurin, D. et Garbay, C. *Développement de Systèmes à Base de Connaissance pour l'Interpretation d'Images Biomédicales*. Tutorial : RFIA. Demi-journée de synthése: Nouvelles perspectives de l'imagérie médicale ; microscopie et macroscopie, de l'analyse à l'interprétation. AFCET-INRIA, 1989.

(Ovalle 91a)   Ovalle, A. et Garbay, C. *KIDS : A Distributed Expert System for Biomedical Image Interpretation*. 12th International Conference on IPMI, pp. 419-433. Colchester et Hawkes (Eds), Springer-Verlag, 1991.

(Ovalle 91b) Ovalle, A. et Garbay, C. *Raisonnement et Contrôle en Univers Multi-Agent : Une Application à l'Interprétation d'Images Biomédicales*, Actes du congrès AFCET-RFIA., pp. 625-633, Lyon, nov. 1991.

(Ovalle 91c)   Ovalle, A.: *Contribution à l'étude du raisonnement en univers multi-agent : KIDS, une application à l'interprétation d'images biomédicales*. Thèse de docteur en Informatique de l'UJF, 1991.

(Smith 80) Smith R.G.*The contract net protocol : high level communication and control in a distributed problem solver*, IEEE Trans Comput, C-29, pp. 1104-1113.

(Vogel 88) Vogel C. : *Génie cognitif*. Paris, Masson, collection science cognitive 1988.

Jigsaw: Configuring knowledge acquisition tools

D. R. PUGH and C. J. PRICE

Department of Computer Science
University of Wales
Aberystwyth
Dyfed
SY23 3DB
United Kingdom

Abstract

This paper describes work on the construction of a configurable knowledge acquisition tool, *Jigsaw*. Unlike automated knowledge acquisition programs such as MORE [Kahn, 1988], MOLE [Eshelman, 1988], and OPAL [Musen, 1989], each of which automates elicitation for just one problem solving method, it is possible to alter *Jigsaw*'s knowledge acquisition strategy to match different problem solving methods.

The work is based upon eliciting knowledge for problem solvers made up from different combinations of generic task (as defined in [Chandrasekaran, 1986] and [Chandrasekaran, 1988]). Each combination of generic tasks defines the functionality of a different problem solving method. However, the eventual aim of this work is that it will be possible to adapt it to a range of different KADS [Schreiber et. al., 1987] interpretation models and thus it will be part of a complete knowledge acquisition methodology.

The paper outlines the requirements for such a knowledge acquisition tool and details the distributed architecture which allows the tool, *Jigsaw*, to achieve the required flexibility to elicit knowledge for such problem solvers. An important part of this flexibility is the way in which *Jigsaw* can be configured to match different types of problem solver. This is described in some detail.

Jigsaw has been used to reproduce the MDX2 [Sticklen, 1987] knowledge base, which was initially constructed by using manual knowledge acquisition techniques. The paper gives a description of how *Jigsaw* elicited this knowledge.

Finally, conclusions are drawn from the work with *Jigsaw* and pointers are given to further work which needs to be carried out.

1 INTRODUCTION

Several of the more useful knowledge acquisition tools address the problem of acquiring knowledge for a single problem solving task. For example, MOLE elicits knowledge for a variant of "heuristic classification" [Clancey, 1985] called "cover and differentiate". The advantage with this type of knowledge acquisition tool is that the questioning of the expert can be tailored to eliciting information specifically required by the problem solving strategy. On the down side, these tools are only useful if the intended knowledge based system can employ the problem solving strategy understood by the tool. Therefore, these tools only cover a very small proportion of the total number of potential knowledge based systems that could be constructed.

KADS on the other hand, a methodology for constructing knowledge based systems, aims to provide the knowledge engineer with a means by which a large number of very different knowledge based systems can be constructed. One of the main aims in KADS is to construct a conceptual model. This model is a description of the expert's knowledge in terms which are independent of a computer implementation.

A knowledge engineer can construct a KADS conceptual model in two ways. The first is to simply build it from scratch, which can be a long and arduous task. The knowledge engineer not only has to collect the domain knowledge, but also has to elicit the inferences, structures of the domain knowledge, and problem solving strategies employed. The second way a conceptual model can be constructed is to select an appropriate problem solving method (called an interpretation model in KADS) from the interpretation model library. This can be then be used as a basis for eliciting the domain knowledge from the expert.

Eliciting knowledge to construct the conceptual model using a predefined problem solving method in KADS is comparable to MOLE eliciting knowledge for its problem solving method of "cover and differentiate"[1]. Therefore, if a knowledge engineer using KADS decided that "cover and differentiate" was the required problem solving method, then MOLE could be used to elicit the knowledge from the expert as opposed to the knowledge engineer performing it manually.

At present, the interpretation library in KADS has around 30 different problem solving methods, and the KADS team acknowledge that further types of problem solving methods need to be constructed for many knowledge based system tasks. If we wished to automate knowledge elicitation within the KADS system, many different knowledge acquisition tools as complex as MOLE would need to be built in order to cover the variety of tasks included in the interpretation model library.

There is possibly an easier solution to this problem. KADS structures its interpretation models by splitting each of the problem solving methods into smaller, more basic, problem

---

[1] The primary difference is that MOLE takes into account that the elicited knowledge must be automatically turned into an executable knowledge based system. KADS expects the knowledge engineer to do this manually at a later stage.

solving chunks. Each interpretation model could be thought of as being made up from a number of simple problem solving methods each of which could be obtained from a central toolset.

It would now be possible to write a knowledge acquisition module for each of these basic problem solving methods and then, when an interpretation model is chosen by the knowledge engineer, these knowledge acquisition modules could be combined to match the structure of the problem solving method described by the interpretation model. This would allow automated elicitation to take place for the chosen interpretation model. Configuring a set of simple knowledge acquisition modules for each interpretation model is much less work than building a whole new knowledge acquisition tool for each interpretation model. Once the knowledge acquisition modules have been configured for a particular interpretation model, this configuration can be stored ready to be used again.

In essence, this is what we have achieved with *Jigsaw*. In order to simplify the experiment, we have used Chandrasekaran's generic tasks as building blocks for a range of problem solving methods. These tasks can be combined in order to construct more comprehensive problem solving methods as are found in the interpretation model library in KADS.

The description of how *Jigsaw* provides configurable knowledge acquisition modules is split into the following main sections:

Requirements for reusable knowledge acquisition. This section discuses the requirements for a tool which is to elicit knowledge for problem solvers made up from a number of generic tasks.

The Jigsaw system. Jigsaw is described in some depth over a number of sections. The description covers the architecture, the information flow within the architecture, and a description of the individual components, including information on how *Jigsaw* is configured to match a particular combination of generic tasks.

Constructing a medical diagnostic system. This section outlines the main stages of eliciting knowledge for the MDX2 knowledge base, and then shows part of the completed knowledge base.

Further work and conclusions. Finally, further work to be performed on *Jigsaw* is outlined and conclusions about the work are made.

2 REQUIREMENTS FOR REUSABLE KNOWLEDGE ACQUISITION
There are three main requirements for a knowledge acquisition tool which is capable of eliciting knowledge for combinations of generic tasks:

1. The knowledge acquisition modules need to be easy to configure to different combinations of generic tasks.

2. The tool must be easy to use. One way this can be achieved is by making the dialogue between the expert and the knowledge acquisition tool as natural as possible.

3. The tool should be able to produce executable code.

The first two of the above requirements suggest that the knowledge acquisition modules should be combined in some form of architecture. This would allow the knowledge engineer to specify to a central point the modules required for each new problem solver. Otherwise the modules would have to be "glued" together each time automated knowledge acquisition is to take place. It would also allow each of the modules to communicate information during the elicitation process, allowing this process to be more fluid.

An architecture designed by Hunt [Hunt, 1990] was used as a basis for the architecture of *Jigsaw*. The next section describes *Jigsaw* in some detail.

3 THE JIGSAW SYSTEM

Jigsaw has been constructed in Pop11 under the Poplog system on Sun workstations.

As can be seen in figure 1, *Jigsaw* consists of a number of components: the *manager*; a communications node; various knowledge acquisition modules; and a datastore for each of the knowledge acquisition modules.

Exact information flow within *Jigsaw* is defined at run time — as *Jigsaw* responds to the answers the expert gives. However, once the expert decides to initiate the knowledge elicitation process, the information flow takes the following basic path:

1. The *manager* asks the expert for some information which will be used to document the system.

2. Depending upon the configuration of the problem solver, the *manager* makes a choice of the first knowledge acquisition module to be called into action. (Because of the way the knowledge engineer defines the configuration, within a separate file, this choice is trivial.)

3. The *manager* sends a message to the *communications node* specifying that the knowledge acquisition module in question is to start eliciting information from the expert.

4. The *communications node* passes this message on to the relevant knowledge acquisition module.

5. The knowledge acquisition module initiates knowledge elicitation. If at any time the knowledge acquisition module is unable to elicit the information needed to define a particular concept within the domain, the knowledge acquisition module:

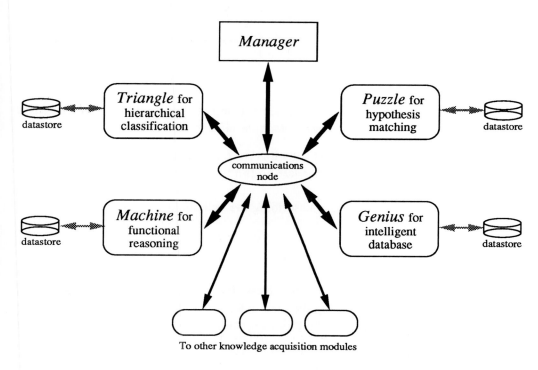

Figure 1: The architecture of Jigsaw

(a) Sends a broadcast message to the *communications node* asking if any knowledge acquisition module is capable of eliciting this particular type of knowledge.

(b) The *communications node* sends this message to each of the knowledge acquisition modules in turn until it receives a reply saying that it managed to elicit the appropriate information, or until every knowledge acquisition module has been visited.

(c) The calling knowledge acquisition module is sent a message from the *communications node* stating the success of the broadcast message.

(d) If no knowledge acquisition module is able to elicit the required knowledge then a warning message is produced for the knowledge engineer. The knowledge engineer will subsequently have to add the required information (obtained from the expert) to the code produced by *Jigsaw*.

(e) The knowledge acquisition module continues eliciting information.

6. When the knowledge acquisition module has completed its elicitation, control reverts back to the *manager* (via the *communications node*).

7. The *manager* calls upon the next knowledge acquisition module asking it to perform its knowledge elicitation until there are no further modules to be called.

The next four sections are devoted to describing the individual components of *Jigsaw* in more detail.

4 THE MANAGER

The *manager* is in charge of the elicitation process. It is responsible for the overall control of problem solving, and for providing the main interface to the expert. It is the *manager* which uses information about how the tasks are configured to decide which knowledge acquisition modules to call and when.

4.1 Configuration

Which knowledge acquisition modules are used, and when, depends upon the configuration of generic tasks in the problem solver.

Figure 2 shows seven example problem solvers constructed from four different generic tasks[2]. *Jigsaw* is capable of performing the knowledge acquisition for each configuration of these generic tasks providing that the correct problem solving structure has been provided for the *manager* by the knowledge engineer. At present this information is defined within a file, which is then read by *Jigsaw*.

---

[2]These are the four tasks that we have been working with.

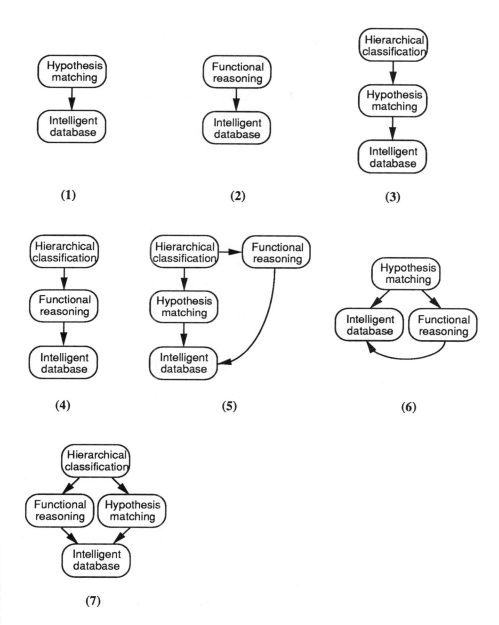

Figure 2: Different problem solvers

Depending upon the structure of the generic tasks in the problem solver, different knowledge acquisition modules will have to be called at different times. The knowledge engineer has to define the order in which to call the knowledge acquisition modules. For the four tasks, *hierarchical classification, hypothesis matching, functional reasoning* and *intelligent database*, defining the order in which they are to be called is straightforward because the generic tasks are strongly inter-related.

For example, it is usual for the *hierarchical classification* task to require another generic task to define how to traverse the hierarchy — either *hypothesis matching* or *functional reasoning*. In this situation, it is *Triangle*'s duty (the knowledge acquisition module for *hierarchical classification*) to call upon the services of the relevant knowledge acquisition module, *Puzzle* or *Machine*, to find this information. Therefore, even though three knowledge acquisition modules are being used, the *manager* has only to call upon the services of *Triangle*, which sorts everything else out.

In combination 7 in figure 2, that used by MDX2, *hierarchical classification* is responsible for asking the knowledge acquisition modules for *functional reasoning* or *hypothesis matching* to perform their task. In turn, they are both responsible for initiating the knowledge acquisition module for the *intelligent database*. The knowledge engineer specifies *hierarchical classification* to the *manager*, and the knowledge acquisition modules work out the rest. *Hierarchical classification* is the *main* generic task in the problem solver.

In figure 2 all the combinations, except for configuration 5, can be described to *Jigsaw* by specifying that the main generic task is the top task in the figure. For configuration 1 it would be *hypothesis matching*, configuration 2 it would be *functional reasoning* and so on. In configuration 5 there are two main tasks — *hierarchical classification* and *functional reasoning*. The results from executing the classification hierarchy are passed to the *functional reasoning* task — *hierarchical classification* is not using *functional reasoning* to solve an intermediate problem, whereas it is in configuration 7.

Another aspect of the configuration process is the specification of available knowledge acquisition modules to the communications node. The communications node is able to utilise this information when knowledge acquisition modules are trying to find a knowledge acquisition module capable of eliciting the information to solve an intermediate problem.

5 THE KNOWELDGE ACQUISITION MODULES
Each knowledge acquisition module is connected to the communications architecture through a similar knowledge acquisition module interface. This section will first look at this interface and then a brief description will be given of the four knowledge acquisition modules which have been implemented.

5.1 The Knowledge Acquisition Interface

The interface provides a means by which each knowledge acquisition module can communicate with other resources — either the *manager* or another knowledge acquisition module. Therefore, to facilitate this cooperation between tasks, each knowledge acquisition module interface has a number of features. These include:

Ability to send messages. A knowledge acquisition module will need to send two different types of message. The first is a message to another named knowledge acquisition module. The second is a broadcast message to all other modules. In each case, the communications mechanism deals with distributing the messages. Therefore, the interface has only to send the relevant information to the communications node.

Ability to receive messages. Various messages will be received by the node from both the *manager* and other knowledge acquisition modules.

Request checking. Each time a message is sent to a knowledge acquisition module interface, it is checked to see if the module is able to deal with the request. This is made possible because the interface has information about what sorts of knowledge the module is capable of eliciting.

Acceptance of failure. If a knowledge acquisition module has failed to perform the knowledge elicitation that the interface undertook on behalf of the module, then other modules must be informed. This information will change depending on the type of message that was received.

5.2 Example Knowledge Acquisition Modules

Each knowledge acquisition module shares a number of similar features. These include:

A datastore. This holds the elicited knowledge in an easily accessible form.

A code producer. This converts the information in the datastore into executable code to be run by the generic task shells.

Each knowledge acquisition module has a different strategy for performing knowledge acquisition. This strategy is targeted to the representation of the generic task for which the knowledge acquisition is being performed. Due to limited space it is not feasible to describe each knowledge elicitation strategy in any detail. A brief description of each is given in order to make the example in section 8 more clear. For a more in-depth description of *Triangle* and *Puzzle* see [Pugh and Price, 1992].

5.3 Triangle

Triangle, the knowledge acquisition module for *hierarchical classification*, has three main aims within its knowledge acquisition strategy. These are:

1. To identify the components of the hierarchy.

    This can be carried out in one of two ways: top down or bottom up.

2. To find the relationships between the different levels within the hierarchy.

    The generic task for *hierarchical classification* requires information on whether child nodes are mutually exclusive, if they are then a path down the hierarchy can only be followed through one child; and if a child has more than one parent node, whether a path through both parents is required for the path to follow through the child.

3. To find information about each node in the hierarchy so that the hierarchy can be traversed correctly.

    For each node in the hierarchy, this involves asking all the other knowledge acquisition modules whether they can find this information. If one of them can, then a link to the information in that other knowledge acquisition module's datastore is sent back to *Triangle*.

5.4 Puzzle

Puzzle, the knowledge acquisition module for *hypothesis matching*, is composed of four different stages. These are:

1. Identify the hypothesis.

    This information will either come from another knowledge acquisition module (which has called upon the services of *Puzzle*); or *Puzzle* will ask the user.

2. Identify how accurate the result defining the probability of the hypothesis is to be.

    The result could range from a simple *yes* or *no*, to a string of nine possible results ranging from *confirmed* to *ruled out*.

3. Identify a list of factors which affect the probability of the hypothesis.

    The factors can be anything which affects the outcome of a hypothesis. Each one can either be a simple variable, or another hypothesis.

4. For every possible result to be returned by the *hypothesis matcher*, find the allowable values of each of the factors.

5.5 Machine

Machine, the knowledge acquisition module for *functional reasoning*, has three stages within its knowledge elicitation process. These are:

1. Decompose the device into its functional components.

   This can be carried out in one of three ways: top down, bottom up, and a mixture of the two. The top down and bottom up methods are similar to those found in *Triangle* (section 5.3).   The mixture of the two methods involves a general top down decomposition first, then finishing with a bottom up description of the specific components. This is very useful when describing large physical devices.

2. Identify the functions of the device and its sub-components.

   For the device and its sub-components ask their individual functions.   This is performed top down.

3. Find out how the device operates in terms of the interaction of the functions of its sub-components.

   Each function is either described in terms of the functions below it in the hierarchy, or in terms of functions that are assumed (for example, Newton's second law).

5.6 Genius

Presently, *Genius*, the knowledge acquisition module for the *intelligent database*, has just two stages. These are:

1. Identify the possible values a variable can take.

2. Identify if the variable has a default value.

The strategy defined for the *intelligent database* is the minimum requirement for being able to use the other tasks. The functionality of this knowledge acquisition module will be expanded at a later date.

6 THE DATASTORES

Each knowledge acquisition module works to construct a datastore of its own type of knowledge. This datastore can be altered in much the same way as a simple database (deletions, updates, and amendments).

The information within the datastore is held in a different representation to that of the generic task code it represents. The reason for this is to make the datastores easier to manage in terms of altering the contents and saving the information to file. To run the information which has been stored, a simple conversion program converts the information in the datastore to the code which implements the generic task represented by that datastore.

7 THE COMMUNICATIONS SYSTEM

The communication mechanism has two main functions. The first is to allow communication between each of the components during knowledge elicitation. The second is to maintain consistency between the individual datastores.

7.1 Communication Between Components

There are three way in which communication between the components of *Jigsaw* can take place. That is communication between *manager* and knowledge acquisition modules and vice versa, and between the knowledge acquisition modules themselves. Messages take one of the following form:

- A direct call to another knowledge acquisition module. This can be the *manager* or a knowledge acquisition module asking another module to execute.

- A broadcast message calling for help. This is directed at any knowledge acquisition module able to deal with the request. This type of message comes from a knowledge acquisition module which knows the type of knowledge which needs to be elicited, but does not know which knowledge acquisition module to call.

- An order for each knowledge acquisition module to perform a certain duty. This type of request comes from the *manager*. An example would be asking each module to store the contents of its datastore in a particular file.

7.2 Consistency Between Individual Datastores

With each knowledge acquisition module having its own datastore, maintaining consistency is an important issue. Each datastore holds information pertaining to an individual generic task, but this does not mean that the information in one datastore can be altered without affecting the other datastores. The reason for this is that the problem solving capabilities of concepts within the domain may be spread over a number of generic tasks. Therefore information is interlinked between datastores. If a change is made in one datastore, then information in another datastore may have to be altered or discarded. This issue has not been addressed in any detail as yet.

One final aspect of the communications mechanism is that it is capable of serving any number of knowledge acquisition modules. New knowledge acquisition modules can be added, and provided that the *communications node* knows where to access the new modules, the modules become an integral part of *Jigsaw*.

8 CONSTRUCTING A MEDICAL DIAGNOSTIC SYSTEM

Due to space limitations it is not possible to give a complete demonstration of how *Jigsaw* elicits knowledge from an expert.   A description will be given of the main steps in constructing one particular knowledge based system. The system in question is MDX2 first written by Sticklen. We have been attempting to reproduce the MDX2 knowledge base using *Jigsaw*.

The structure of the MDX2 knowledge base in terms of generic tasks can be seen in figure 3.

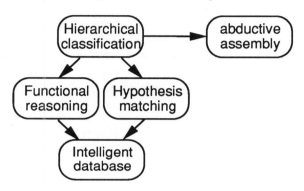

Figure 3: Generic task structure in MDX2

It can be seen that MDX2 includes five different tasks. Two of these tasks are *main* tasks — *hierarchical classification* and *abductive assembly*.

In MDX2, the classification hierarchy is used to limit the number of possible results. Each level of the hierarchy is a specialisation of the level above. The aim of problem solving is to reach the lowest possible level in the hierarchy and hence the most well defined answer. It is possible to follow more than one path through the hierarchy, and when problem solving ceases, *hierarchical classification* returns the most specialised node reached by each path. To allow decisions about which paths to take through the hierarchy, the *hierarchical classification* task can obtain heuristic knowledge in the *hypothesis matcher*; and knowledge obtained from first principles defined within the *functional reasoner*. In MDX2, once the classifier has done this task its results are passed to the *abductive assembler* which finds the best combination of results which describe an answer to the problem.

Currently, we do not have a knowledge acquisition module for the *abductive assembly* generic task, therefore *Jigsaw* only elicits knowledge for the main part of MDX2's problem solving.

The first stage in the construction of MDX2:

1. The knowledge engineer specifies that *hierarchical classification* is the *main* task within the file *Jigsaw* reads (to find out this information).

2. The expert starts the knowledge elicitation session.

3. *Jigsaw* asks the expert a few general questions. These include both the expert's and the knowledge engineer's names.

4. *Jigsaw* then reads the file describing the main generic tasks.

5. The main task is *hierarchical classification* therefore the *manager* calls *Triangle*. This is done via the *communications node*.

Once *Triangle* has received the call from the *Manager* (via the communications mechianism) it starts its own process of querying the expert for information. As this information is entered *Triangle* stores it in its own datastore. Stage two, *Triangle* eliciting knowledge, is as follows:

1. *Triangle* asks the expert the type of elements to be classified. In this case the answer is: *patient_diseases*.

2. It then asks which method of decomposition is to be used to create the hierarchy. The answer is: *Top down*.

3. Working from top to bottom, *Triangle* elicits the *patient_disease* hierarchy. Part of this information can be seen in figure 4.

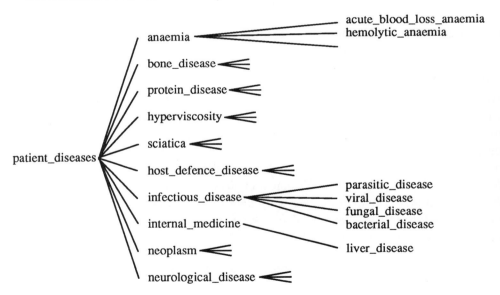

Figure 4: An outline of MDX2's hierarchy as acquired by *Jigsaw*

4. Once the hierarchy has been elicited, *Triangle* examines the hierarchy and asks the expert about some of the relevant relationships between the different levels of the hierarchy. Are child elements mutually exclusive? Do both parents of an element

have to be true for a child to be true? (when a child has more than one parent, in a tangled hierarchy).

Triangle then goes through the whole hierarchy, from top to bottom, finding out information about how to traverse the hierarchy during problem solving. This information comes from either *hypothesis matching* or *functional reasoning*.

Triangle achieves this by putting a broadcast message on the *communications node*. Essentially, this message is a call for help. *Triangle* is unable to elicit this type of knowledge and it is asking other modules if they can. The *communications node* takes the message to each of the other modules in turn, clockwise around the node. Therefore, this message is first sent to the *manager* which looks to see if it has the capabilities of dealing with the request. It does not, and the message is sent to *Puzzle*. *Puzzle* can deal with the request, but does not know if this type of knowledge is required in this case, so it asks the expert. If the expert replies *yes* then *Puzzle* will elicit the required knowledge and send an appropriate message to *Triangle*. *Triangle* will then continue with the next item in the hierarchy. Otherwise the message continues around the communications node. *Genius* cannot elicit this type of knowledge and subsequently ignores the request. *Machine* then receives the message and asks the expert if it can elicit the correct type of knowledge. If it can, it does so. Finally, if the message is returned unanswered to *Triangle* it leaves a stub for the knowledge engineer to fill in at a later date.

Both *Puzzle* and *Machine* elicit knowledge following the outlines given in sections 5.4 and 5.5 respectively. During their knowledge elicitation both call upon the services of *Genius*, to find out information about different variables which have been entered.

8.1 THE KNOWLEDGE BASE
The code which *Jigsaw* produces is very similar to the code used to execute MDX2. Figure 5 shows part of the MDX2-Jigsaw knowledge base. It can be seen that there are two different code constructs. The first is from *Triangle*'s datastore, code for *hierarchical classification*; and the second is from *Puzzle*'s datastore, code for *hypothesis matching*.

9 FURTHER WORK
There are a number of areas where *Jigsaw* could benefit from further work. Areas identified to date include:

Backtracking errors. Currently, *Jigsaw* does not allow its user to alter information once it has been input into the knowledge base. If *Jigsaw* were to be used in earnest then this would have to be overcome. The main challenge is in maintaining consistency between each of the datastores: information in one datastore often references other datastores.

```
(define-classification-specialist patient_disease          ;;; This is the top level in the hierarchy
    (classifier= patient_disease_hierarchy)
    (sub-specialists= anaemia
                      bone_disease
                      protein_disease
                      hyperviscosity
                      sciatica
                      host_defence_disease
                      infectious_disease
                      internal_medicine
                      neoplasm
                      neurological_disease)
    (establish-reject= (judge patient_disease_summary))      ;;; This is where to look for information on how to
    (establish-confidence-vocabulary= usual-9-val)          ;;; traverse the hierarchy
    (establish-threshold= likely)
    (suspend-threshold= unlikely)
    (child-join= exclusive) )
)

(define-classification-specialist internal_medicine         ;;; internal_medicine is a subspecialist of
    (classifier= patient_disease_hierarchy)                  ;;; patient_disease
    (super-specialists= patient_disease)
    (sub-specialists= liver_disease)
    (establish-reject= (judge internal_medicine_summary))
    (establish-confidence-vocabulary= usual-9-val)
    (establish-threshold= very likely)
    (suspend-threshold= likely) )
)

(define-classification-specialist liver_disease             ;;; liver_disease is a subspecialist of
    (classifier= patient_disease_hierarchy)                  ;;; internal_medicine
    (super-specialists= internal_medicine)
    (establish-reject= (judge liver_disease_summary))
    (establish-confidence-vocabulary= usual-9-val)
    (establish-threshold= very likely)
    (suspend-threshold= likely) )
)

(define-recognition-agent liver_disease_summary             ;;; This is the information liver-disease uses
  match-1-recognition-agent                                 ;;; to find out if it is to be part of the path
    (output-confidence-vocabulary= usual-9-val)             ;;; traversing the hierarchy
    (no-match-confidence= unlikely)
    (features= (ask IDABLE  IsoEnzymeIncreaseImagingAbnormality usual-3-val)
               (ask IDABLE  Clinical_generalLab_results usual-3-val)
               (ask IDABLE  History usual-3-val) )
    (patterns= ( (yes yes yes) 3 => very-likely)
                 (yes yes ?) 3 => likely)
                 (yes no yes) 3 => likely)
                 (yes neutral yes) 3 => likely)
                 (yes no ?) 3 => somewhat-likely)
                 (yes neutral ?) 3 => somewhat-likely)
                 (no yes yes) 3 => somewhat-likely)
                 (neutral yes yes) 3 => neutral)
                 (no no yes) 3 => neutral)
                 (neutral yes ?)3 => neutral)
                 (neutral ? yes) 3 => neutral)
                 (neutral ? neutral) 3 => neutral)
                 (no no neutral) 3 => somewhat-unlikely)
                 (neutral ? false) 3 => somewhat-unlikely)
                 (no no no) 3 => unlikely)  ) )
)
```

Figure 5: Part of MDX2-Jigsaw's knowledge base

Iterative refinement of the knowledge base. Knowledge based system construction is an iterative process — continually improving a prototype until both the knowledge engineer and the expert are satisfied with the result. *Jigsaw* should be able to cope not only with adding, deleting and altering information, but also able to alter the structure of the intended knowledge base by adding generic tasks and altering the way that the generic tasks are combined.

Improved user interface. The current interface is textual. Adding some form of graphical interface would provide a means by which the expert could have a better idea of what sort of structures were being created.

Inclusion of domain knowledge. Protege [Musen, 1989] is a tool which constructs an automated knowledge acquisition tool (p-OPAL) by first eliciting domain knowledge. This domain knowledge is used to make the knowledge acquisition tool more effective, because it can ask questions which are related to the domain and therefore more specific in their nature.

This sort of pre-processing, along with some form of graphical interface, would make *Jigsaw* much easier to use.

10 CONCLUSIONS

Work on *Jigsaw* is still in its infancy. Much work is still required in order for it to become a usable tool for constructing knowledge based system. Even so, a number of important conclusions can be drawn from this work.

Jigsaw shows that it is indeed possible to bridge the gap between comprehensive methodologies, which cover many different types of knowledge based system, and automated knowledge acquisition tools which are capable of eliciting detailed domain knowledge. *Jigsaw* is capable of eliciting knowledge for a number of different problem solving methods and, more importantly, it can be expanded to cover more problem solving methods by adding knowledge acquisition modules for other generic tasks.

Providing it is possible to split the interpretation models within KADS into smaller problem solving chunks (similar to generic tasks), which we believe it is, it should be possible to adapt *Jigsaw* to include knowledge acquisition modules for these chunks of data. This would allow *Jigsaw* to automate the elicitation of knowledge for a number of different interpretation models, and hence be part of a complete methodology.

References

[Chandrasekaran, 1986] B. Chandrasekaran. Generic Tasks in Knowledge-based Reasoning: High-level Building Blocks for Expert System Design. *IEEE Expert*, Vol 1, pp. 23–30, Fall 1986.

[Chandrasekaran, 1988] B. Chandrasekaran. Generic Tasks as Building Blocks for Knowledge-based Systems: The Diagnosis and Routine Design Example. In *The Knowledge Engineering Review*, pages 183–210. Cambridge University Press, September 1988.

[Clancey, 1985]   W.J. Clancey. Heuristic Classification. *Artificial Intelligence*, 27(3):289–350, 1985.

[Eshelman, 1988]   L. Eshelman. MOLE: A knowledge-acquisition tool for cover-and-differentiate systems. In S. Marcus, editor, *Automating Knowledge Acquisition for Expert Systems*, pages 37–80. Kluwer Academic Publishers, 1988.

[Hunt, 1990]   J. E. Hunt and C. J. Price. Performing Augmented Model-based Diagnosis. *Presented at the International Symposium on Mathematical and Intelligent Models in System Simulation*, Brussels, September 1990.

[Kahn, 1988]   G. Kahn. MORE: From observing knowledge engineers to automating knowledge acquisition. In S. Marcus, editor, *Automating Knowledge Acquisition for Expert Systems*, pages 7–35. Kluwer Academic Publishers, 1988.

[Musen, 1989]   M. .A. Musen. *Automated Generation of Model Based Knowledge Acquisition Tools*. Research Notes in Artificial Intelligence. London:Pitman, 1989.

[Pugh and Price, 1992] D. R. Pugh and C. J. Price. Acquiring different types of knowledge: A distributed architecture. To be published in *European Knowledge Acquisition Workshop '91*. Springer-Verlag, 1992.

[Schreiber et. al., 1987] G. Schreiber, J. Breuker, B. Bredeweg, and B. Wielinga. Modelling in KBS Development. In *Avingnon '87*, pages 283–296, 1987.

[Sticklen, 1987]   J. Sticklen. MDX2, An Integrated Medical Diagnostic System. *PhD Thesis*, The Ohio State University, 1987.

On the Relationship between Repertory Grid and Term Subsumption Knowledge Structures: Theory, Practice and Tools

MILDRED L G SHAW & BRIAN R GAINES

Knowledge Science Institute
University of Calgary
Calgary, Alberta, Canada T2N 1N4
mildred@cpsc.ucalgary.ca & gaines@cpsc.ucalgary.ca

A number of practical knowledge acquisition methodologies and tools have been based on the elicitation and analysis of repertory grids. These result in frames and rules that are exported to knowledge-based system shells. In the development of repertory grid tools, the original methodology has been greatly extended to encompass the data types required in knowledge-based systems. However, this has been done on a fairly pragmatic basis, and it has not been clear how the resultant knowledge acquisition systems relate to psychological, or computational, theories of knowledge representation. This paper shows that there is a close correspondence between the intensional logics of knowledge, belief and action developed in the personal construct psychology underlying repertory grids, and the intensional logics for term subsumption knowledge representation underlying KL-ONE-like systems. The paper gives an overview of personal construct psychology and its expression as an intensional logic describing the cognitive processes of anticipatory agents, and uses this to survey knowledge acquisition tools deriving from personal construct psychology.

1 PERSONAL CONSTRUCT PSYCHOLOGY

George Kelly was a clinical psychologist who lived between 1905 and 1967, published a two volume work (Kelly, 1955) defining personal construct psychology in 1955, and went on to publish a large number of papers further developing the theory many of which have been issued in collected form (Maher, 1969). Kelly was a keen geometer with experience in navigation and an interest in multi-dimensional geometry. When he came to formalize his theory he took as his model Euclid's *Elements* and axiomatized personal construct psychology as a *fundamental postulate* together with eleven *corollaries*, terming the primitives involved *elements* and *constructs*. Kelly presented his theory as a *geometry of psychological space* (Kelly, 1969), and his conceptual framework is very clear if seen in these terms.

What Kelly achieved through the use of geometry was an intensional logic, one in which predicates are defined in terms of their properties rather than extensionally in terms of those entities that fall under them.   Logics of knowledge and belief are essentially intensional (Hintikka, 1962), and in his time there were no adequate formal foundations for intensional logic.   It was not until 1963 that Hintikka published the model sets formulation that gave intensional logic its *possible worlds* formal foundations (Hintikka, 1963), and hence formal foundations for cognitive science in logical terms only became possible in the late 1960s.   The intensional nature of semantic networks in artificial intelligence was recognized in the late 1970s (Woods, 1975; Brachman, 1977; Shapiro, 1979), and their philosophical and logical structure as cognitive models has been detailed by Zalta (1988).

The dichotomous aspect of constructs is the most significant aspect of the difference between Kelly's constructs and current usage of the term, 'concept.'   His *dichotomy corollary* states this (Kelly, 1955):

"A person's construction system is composed of a finite number of dichotomous constructs." (p.59)

and it is a consequence of the two-sided nature of a distinction represented in the geometry.   That people tend to conceptualize the world in terms of restricted sorts that are then dichotomized is a phenomenon identified in antiquity (Lloyd, 1966) and common across many cultures (Maybury-Lewis and Almagor, 1989).

The taxonomic, abstraction, or subsumption, hierarchy between concepts is recognized in Kelly's *organization corollary* (Kelly, 1955):

"Each person characteristically evolves, for his convenience of anticipating events, a construction system embracing ordinal relationships between constructs." (p.56)

He uses this ordinal relation in the development of the psychology to model the dynamics of change in conceptual systems.   For example, that one has "core constructs" that one is very reluctant to change because of the dependencies that exist within one's constructions.

Kelly's "repertory grid" methodology for eliciting conceptual structures has become a widely used and accepted technique for knowledge elicitation, and has been implemented as a major component of many computer-based knowledge acquisition systems.   A comprehensive computer-based elicitation and analysis system for repertory grids was developed by Shaw with applications mainly in educational, clinical and management studies (Shaw, 1979).   Gaines and Shaw suggested that repertory grids would provide a useful development technique for expert systems (Gaines and Shaw, 1980), and later published a validation study of the elicitation of the BIAIT methodology from accountants and accounting students using computer-based repertory grid elicitation (Shaw and Gaines, 1983).   Boose, in an independent parallel study, reported success in a wide range of industrial expert system developments using computer elicitation of repertory grids (Boose, 1984), and since then many knowledge acquisition systems have incorporated repertory grids as a major elicitation technique (Boose and Bradshaw, 1987; Diederich, Ruhmann and May, 1987; Garg-Janardan and Salvendy, 1987; Shaw and Gaines, 1987; Ford, Cañas, Jones, Stahl, Novak and Adams-Webber, 1990).

The repertory grid methodology has evolved in the light of application experience and now has major differences from that described by Kelly. Shaw took advantage of the processing power and interactivity of computers to introduce on-line analysis and feedback to the person from whom the grid was being elicited (Shaw, 1980). In expert systems terms, this can be seen as highlighting correlations that might be spurious and lead to incorrect rules in later analysis. Shaw and Gaines introduced new forms of analysis of the repertory grid based on fuzzy sets theory (Shaw and Gaines, 1979) which became the basis of rule extraction (Gaines and Shaw, 1986). Boose and Bradshaw made changes to the grid structure introducing hierarchical data structures to cope with more complex domains (Boose and Bradshaw, 1987). Bradshaw, Boose, Covington and Russo showed how many problems that did not seem appropriate to repertory grids could be formulated in terms of them (Bradshaw, Boose, Covington and Russo, 1988).

The original repertory grid methodology was based on only one aspect of Kelly's personal construct psychology, his dichotomy corollary. The standard grid is a flat structure of elements described in terms of dichotomous constructs that does not represent the hierarchical structure of Kelly's organization corollary. Hinkle developed a technique of *laddering*, based on "why" and "how" questions, for investigating ordinal relations between constructs (Hinkle, 1965), and Boose incorporated a laddering tool in ETS (Boose, 1986). However, ordinal relations between constructs were not the primary focus in initial applications of repertory grid tools.

This changed as the second generation toolbench, AQUINAS (Boose and Bradshaw, 1987), was developed in the light of experience with ETS, and hierarchical structures of tasks, experts, elements and constructs were introduced into the data structures and interfaces. It also changed as conceptual induction techniques were used to derive hierarchical concept structures from the rules extracted from repertory grids (Gaines and Shaw, 1992). Recently, the intensional logic underlying the psychological primitives of personal construct psychology has been developed in detail (Gaines, 1990), and this has been used to develop knowledge acquisition tools based on a visual language that corresponds to a formal semantics for semantic nets (Gaines, 1991c). These later developments suggest that personal construct psychology can also provide foundations for tools in which ordinal relations are a primary focus, such as those that use some form of semantic network to build domain and task ontologies directly.

2 THE INTENSIONAL LOGIC OF PERSONAL CONSTRUCT PSYCHOLOGY

Kelly's geometrical model of personal construct psychology may be reformulated as a corresponding intensional logic of knowledge representation. We take his notion of a distinction as primitive and examine how distinctions may relate to each other in psychological space. If one distinction carves out a region that contains that carved out by another then the first distinction may be said to *subsume* the second. If one distinction carves out a region that does not overlap that carved out by another then the first distinction may be said to be *disjoint* to the second. These relations are in themselves sufficient to define an intensional logic of distinctions in that the more complex relations may be composed from them. Extensional considerations may be introduced by noting that, if an element is placed within the region carved out by a distinction, then we may say that the distinction is *asserted* to apply to the element.

The subsumption and disjoint relations may be defined in an algebraic formalism by representing distinctions by bold lower case letters such that a distinction applied to another distinction is concatenated to the right of it. Then the definition above translates as one distinction will be said to *subsume* another if it can always be applied whenever the other can. It can be represented formally as:

$$\text{``b subsumes a''} \qquad \mathbf{a} \rightarrow \mathbf{b} \;\Leftrightarrow\; \vdash \mathbf{xa} \Rightarrow \vdash \mathbf{xb} \qquad\qquad (1)$$

That is, **b** subsumes **a**, if and only if whenever one asserts **xa** one also asserts **xb**. The definition is to be read intensionally in terms of a *commitment* to the way in which distinctions will be made, such that if **a** is made then there is a commitment to **b** being made also. This is why the form $\forall \mathbf{x}$ is avoided—the notion of all the distinctions to which **a** and **b** may be applied is not well-defined.

Subsumption corresponds to increasing generality since the subsuming distinction can be applied to at least as many things as that subsumed. In (1) concept **a** is said to be *subordinate* to concept **b**, and **b** *superordinate* to **a**. Subsumption supports Kelly's organization corollary, and captures his use of the term that one construct subsumes another, and also the use of the same term in knowledge representation, that one concept subsumes another. Subsumption between computational concepts corresponds to the "is-a" relation in knowledge representation schema. The interpretation of subsumption in terms of commitment above corresponds to the definitional form of the "is-a" relation. The computed form of "is-a" requires some further structures which are developed in the next section when primitive and non-primitive concepts are differentiated.

The disjoint relation is definable in similar terms, that one distinction is disjoint with another in that one can never be applied whenever the other can. It can be represented as:

$$\text{``a disjoint b''} \qquad \mathbf{a} \text{---} \mathbf{b} \;\Leftrightarrow\; \vdash \mathbf{xa} \Rightarrow \neg \vdash \mathbf{xb} \qquad\qquad (2)$$

That is, **a** is disjoint with **b**, if and only if whenever one asserts **xa** one does not assert **xb**. The definition is again to be read intensionally in terms of a commitment to the way in which distinctions will be made, such that if **a** is made then there is a commitment to **b** not being made. Disjoint is a symmetric, intransitive relation over distinctions, and supports Kelly's dichotomy corollary and the definition of disjoint concepts in knowledge representation.

It is interesting to note that definition (2) is an asymmetric definition of what is clearly a symmetric relation. Logically, this is possible because the reverse implication can be derived from (2), that is, if one asserts **xb** one cannot assert **xa** because that would imply ¬ ⊢ **xb**. This derivation of symmetry from asymmetry may be logically simple, but it is not semantically trivial. In terms of knowledge representation it corresponds to the essential sequence of definitions: if we define **a** first we cannot define it to be disjoint with **b** because **b** is not yet defined. Psychologically, this asymmetry appears to be related to the empirical asymmetries Adams-Webber has observed in the use of the, apparently symmetric, poles of a construct (Adams-Webber, 1979).

The → and — relations are complementary in establishing four possible binary relations between distinctions, that **a→b**, **b→a**, **a—b**, or none of these. The two subsumption relations can hold together giving an equivalence relation on distinctions. The disjoint relation is incompatible with the subsumption relations, and is *inherited* through subsumption, that is:

$$\textbf{a}—\textbf{b} \text{ and } \textbf{c}→\textbf{a} \Rightarrow \textbf{c}—\textbf{b} \tag{3}$$

3 A VISUAL LANGUAGE FOR THE LOGIC

The arrow and line notion adopted in definitions (1) and (2) translates to a graphical notation defining a *visual language* for the logic (Gaines, 1991c). As shown at the top of Figure 1, Kelly's "construct" in psychological space can be represented by a pair of disjoint concepts corresponding to what he terms the construct "poles," both subsumed by a third concept corresponding to what he terms the "range of convenience." It is this fundamental conceptual unit, or templet that we fit over the world, being a pair of disjoint concepts applied to a restricted domain that characterizes Kelly's use of the logic as a foundation for cognitive psychology. In logical terms, he emphasizes the importance of *opposition* as relative negation applied within a context, rather than absolute negation free of any context. The psychological unit is the triple of concepts in the relation shown rather than the individual concept, or logical predicate, in isolation.

At the center of Figure 1, the abstract components of a concept are given specific instances to exemplify their application. "Evaluable" things may be classified into two disjoint classes, "good" and "bad."

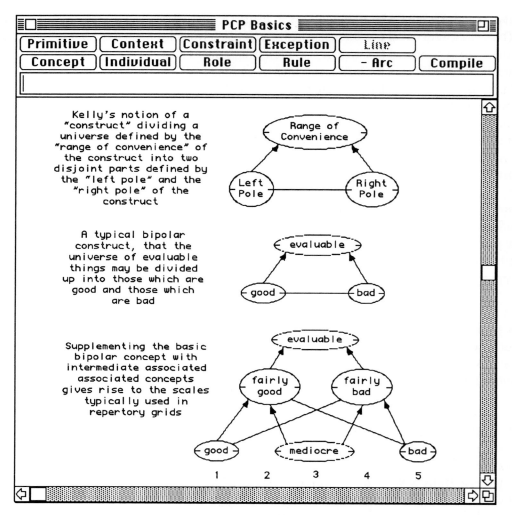

Figure 1 Representation of abstract and specific constructs and scales in a visual language for specifying definitions and assertions in the intensional logic

The emphasis on dichotomous concepts may give the impression that constructs are essentially binary in nature. However, at the bottom of Figure 1 is shown how Kelly's "shades of gray" arise naturally through the addition of related concepts compatible with the original dichotomy. The dichotomy has been split into two such that "bad" is now disjoint both from "good" and "fairly good", and "good" is now disjoint from both "bad" and "fairly bad." "Mediocre" has been added as an additional concept intermediate between "good" and "bad", defined as "fairly good" and "fairly bad." In tools such as the repertory grid these intermediate concepts are represented on a numeric scale as shown under the bottom structure of Figure 1.

The structures in Figure 1 are simple semantic networks in the style of KL-ONE (Brachman and Schmolze, 1985) or KRS (Gaines, 1991a), but they have well-defined logical semantics as defined above, and also strong psychological foundations in personal construct psychology. There is an analogy between the visual language and the representation of chemical structures as atoms and bonds. Distinctions are the atomic primitives in personal construct psychology, and further constructions may be seen as complex 'molecules' formed by distinctions joined through subsumption and disjoint 'bonds.' For example, the complex structure at the bottom of Figure 1 may be seen as the composition of two of the basic construct structures shown at the top. Figure 2 illustrates this with an example developed later in the paper.

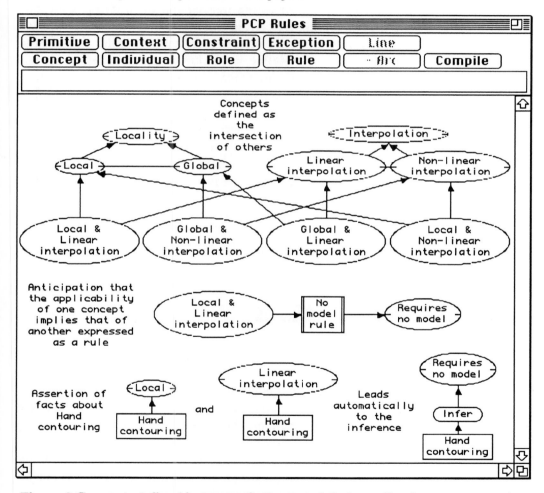

Figure 2 Concepts defined in terms of others, and their application to representing anticipations as rules supporting inference

Multiple constructs in psychological space correspond to multiple axes of reference, and the planes representing their distinctions and ranges of convenience intersect to define regions of the space corresponding to conjunction, composition and multiple inheritance in the logic as shown at the top of Figure 2. This also illustrates an important distinction between the concepts defined by basic distinctions and those defined by intersections. The former are said to be *primitive concepts* and the latter non-primitive, or computed, concepts. In the visual language primitive concepts are distinguished by having a small internal horizontal line at their left and right edges. A primitive concept is incompletely defined in that we have complete freedom of choice as to where to place an element relative to the regions defining its distinction. However, no such freedom exists for non-primitive concepts since they are defined as the intersection of primitive concepts. Logically, we have to *assert* that a primitive concept applies to an element, whereas we can either assert that a non-primitive applies or *recognize* that it applies through the previous assertion of the primitives that define it. In knowledge representation this recognition is termed *classification* (Borgida, Brachman, McGuiness and Resnick, 1989).

The definition of subsumption in (1) applies to non-primitive concepts, but it is no longer a matter of direct commitment but rather of derivation from the composition of commitments for concepts defining the intersection. The "is-a" relation for non-primitive concepts is computable rather than definable—the commitment to their definition in terms of their structure entails a commitment to a derived, rather than a defined, "is-a" relation. Confusion about these two forms of concept, and associated "is-a" relations, caused problems in early developments of semantic nets (Brachman, 1983).

Kelly's theory of anticipation is based on attaching significance to such recognizable intersections:

> "What one predicts is not a fully fleshed-out event, but simply the common intersect of a set of properties" (Kelly, 1955)

The logic remains intensional because there is no implication that elements have already been construed within the intersections. The attachment of an anticipation to the intersect corresponds to a commitment to place an element that falls in this intersect in the region defined by the pole of some other construct also. In logic this is a *material implication* rather than an entailment in that it is not necessitated by the way in which the distinctions are defined but is instead an auxiliary commitment or *rule*. Rules allow a cognitive system to be anticipatory in containing structures which from one set of distinctions made about an event will imply that others should be made leading to prediction or action. Rules play a similar role in computational systems in generating recommendations for decision or action. Overtly modeling the conceptual system of an expert as such a structure is a basis for emulating the expert's performance in a knowledge-based system.

As shown in Figure 2, Kelly's model of anticipation is represented in the visual language by an additional primitive, a rectangle with vertical bars, representing material implication or a rule.   The rule in the center applies to a spatial mapping techniques example used later in this paper.   It has the premise that if a technique is "Local" and involves "Linear interpolation" then the conclusion is that it is "Requires no model."   At the bottom right of Figure 2, an individual "Hand contouring", represented in the visual language as a rectangle, is asserted to be "Local" and "Linear interpolation," represented by arrows from the individual to these concepts.   When the entire knowledge structure of concept definitions, rules and assertions, is then compiled and run through the inference engine, the graph output is that shown at the bottom right of Figure 2.   Hand contouring has been inferred to require no model.

The logic based on Kelly's axiomatic presentation of personal construct psychology, and the visual language representing it, both extend to support the additional features normal in term subsumption knowledge representation systems, such as attributes and relations, or "roles" as they have been termed generically (Brachman and Schmolze, 1985), rules with exceptions (Gaines, 1991b), and contexts (Sowa, 1984).   Figures 1 and 2 have been presented in a graphing tool, KDraw, that provides a fully operational semantics for the input and output of knowledge structures in the visual language, and further illustrations of its application are given later.

4 THE REPERTORY GRID

Kelly introduces the "role repertory grid" (Kelly, 1955) as a means for investigating a person's conceptual structure relevant to inter-personal relations by having them classify a set of people significant to them in terms of elicited personal constructs.   Figure 3 shows the general form of a repertory grid and its relation to the conceptual structures already discussed.   If one takes a particular concept somewhere in the lattice, and a set of individuals asserted to fall under that concept, then the properties defining the concept generate distinctions about the individuals falling under that concept.   These distinctions form the rows of a matrix, the individuals form the columns, and the constraints applying to a particular individual relative to a particular distinction form the values in the matrix.

In simple applications of the repertory grid these constraints are taken to be the values of the individuals on the roles corresponding to the distinctions.   However, it is apparent from Figure 3 that concepts subordinate to those defining the scope of the grid may also be used as if they were individuals, and these may be expected to have more general constraints than single values.   Hence in extended repertory grid elicitation, such as that of AQUINAS (Boose and Bradshaw, 1987) the 'values' in the matrix can in themselves be complex constraints.

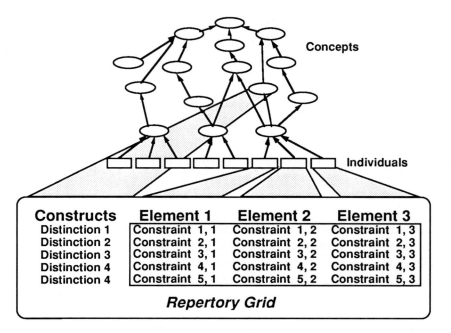

Figure 3 The repertory grid as a matrix of concepts, individuals and constraints

Requires no model	5	5	4	1	3	1	4	4	5	2	5	Requires model
Interval data	5	1	1	1	4	4	1	1	1	1	1	Nominal data
Non-polynomial	5	5	1	1	1	1	5	1	5	1	5	Polynomial
Global	1	1	3	4	4	4	5	2	1	4	1	Local
Intuitive	4	4	5	3	2	1	5	4	5	3	5	Mathematical
Requires spatial search	5	5	2	1	2	3	5	5	5	3	5	Does not require spatial search
Discontinuous	5	5	4	2	1	3	5	5	5	5	5	Continuous
Does not honour data	5	5	2	3	1	2	4	4	5	2	1	Honours data
Linear interpolation	5	5	2	2	3	1	5	5	5	5	5	Non-linear interpolation
Difficult to understand	2	4	1	4	4	5	1	2	1	4	1	Easily understood
Few points	1	3	1	5	3	1	3	2	1	4	2	Many points
Does not consider non-spatial attributes	2	2	2	2	3	3	1	1	2	1	5	Considers non-spatial attributes

Vector trend surface analysis
Negative exponential surface
Most predictable surface
Double Fourier series
Bicubic splines
Hand contouring
Proximal mapping
Distance weighted averaging
Kriging
Trend surface analysis
Probability mapping

Figure 4 A repertory grid about spatial mapping techniques

Figure 4 shows a basic repertory grid elicited from a geographer about spatial mapping techniques. The mapping techniques used as elements are listed as column names at the bottom. The poles of the constructs elicited are listed on the left and the right as row names. The ratings of the mapping techniques along the dimensions of the constructs form the body of the grid. Figure 5 shows the constructs defined in Figure 4 exported to KDraw in the format of Figure 1. The tool used for the elicitation and analysis of grids, KSS0, also allows them to be exported to KDraw and shells such as NEXPERT and BABYLON, as attribute-value structures rather than conceptual primitives.

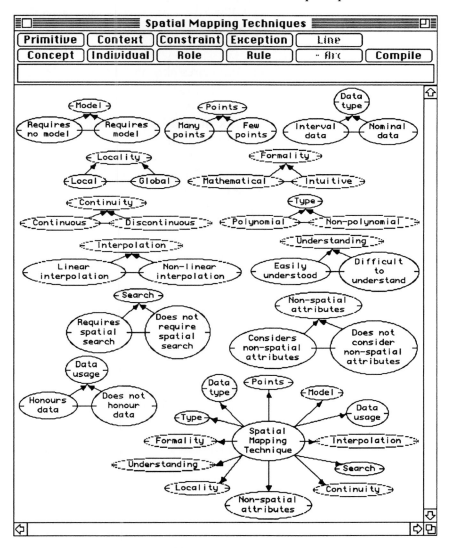

Figure 5 Spatial mapping techniques domain represented in the visual language

The psychological function of the repertory grid is to provide a technique for building the conceptual structure without direct elicitation of concepts and their structures and relationships. The assumption is that it may be easier for a person to provide exemplary individuals in the domain of interest, and then to state in fairly concrete terms how they would distinguish them in terms of properties relevant to the purpose of eliciting the grid. In terms of the intensional logic of the concept structure, the extensional specification of how concepts apply to individuals is clearly inadequate to fully specify the concept structure. However, the structure must be consistent with its model and hence it is possible through suitable analysis techniques to approximate the structure from the extensional data, as is discussed in the next section.

5 CONCEPTUAL CLUSTERING
In analyzing repertory grid data, distance measures play an important role in conceptual clustering and induction. In terms of the logic and visual language, there is a natural construction of a distance between two concepts, x and y, as shown on the left of Figure 6. Let u be some minimal upper bound of x and y subsuming both of them, and l some maximal lower bound subsumed by both of them, and U be the extension of u, and L the extension of l over some universe of individuals. If x and y are identical so will be U and L, whereas if they are disjoint L will be empty. Hence a natural distance measure is the number of individuals that are in U but not L:

$$\text{``}x \text{ distance } y\text{''} \qquad d(x, y) = CU - CL \qquad (4)$$

where CU and CL are the cardinalities of U and L respectively. This measure satisfies the triangle inequality and can be normalized by dividing by its maximum possible value, CU. It is clearly dependent on the universe of individuals involved, but this is appropriate to measuring concept distance in an extensional context. Intensional concept "distance" independent of context is reflected in the relational structures already developed.

The distance measure defined readily extends to dichotomous constructs through the comparison of poles as shown on the right of Figure 6:

$$\text{``}b\text{—}c \text{ distance } d\text{—}e\text{''} \qquad d(b\text{—}c, d\text{—}e) = CA - CF - CG \qquad (5)$$

This measure is a count of the numbers of individuals that fall under the opposite pole of the other construct. Note that it is not invariant if one construct is reversed. This construction generalizes to scales with more than three points. If these scales are numbered linearly it computes a "city block" distance measure—which is precisely that used in construct clustering algorithms such as FOCUS (Shaw, 1980). These distance measures enable natural clusters to be seen that may be grouped as part of a coherent concept, for example, in that they are all contributors to an evaluative dimension.

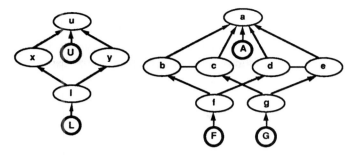

Figure 6 Calculation of distance measures between concepts and between constructs

For example, Figure 7 shows a FOCUS analysis of the grid of Figure 4 in which the distance measure defined in (5) has been used to develop two matrices of inter-element and inter-construct distances. The sets of elements and constructs have then each been sorted to re-order the grid in such a way that similar elements and similar constructs are close together. Thus, near the bottom of the construct clusters, it can be seen that the dimension "Discontinuous—Continuous" is used very similarly to "Requires spatial search—Does not require spatial search", and that both of these relate closely to "Linear interpolation—Non-linear interpolation." Similarly near the top of the element clusters, "Probability matching", "Most predictable surface" and "Trend Surface Analysis" are construed as closely related techniques with very few distinctions between them.

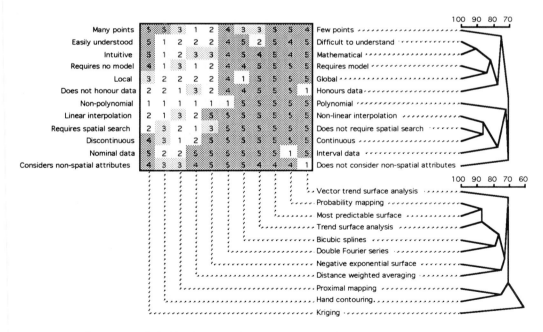

Figure 7 FOCUS hierarchical clustering of spatial mapping grid

6 RULE INDUCTION

The measures used in the induction of a rule linking to concepts are also readily derived as shown in Figure 8. CX is the number of anticipations made by concept x as the left hand side of a rule, and CL is the number which are correct. Thus, the measures of the validity of inducing the rule, $x \rightarrow \rightarrow y$, are:

"prior probability of y" $\quad\quad\quad p(y) = CY/CU \quad\quad\quad\quad\quad\quad\quad\quad\quad$ (6)

"probability correct $x \rightarrow \rightarrow y$" $\quad\quad p(x \rightarrow \rightarrow y) = CL/CX \quad\quad\quad\quad\quad\quad\quad$ (7)

"probability by chance $x \rightarrow \rightarrow y$" $\quad c(x \rightarrow \rightarrow y) = I_{p(y)}(CX-CL, CL+1) \quad\quad$ (8)

where I is the incomplete beta function summing a binomial distribution tail.

These measures are precisely those used by Induct (Gaines, 1989) in inducing rules from datasets. In the application to repertory grids Induct searches for potential rules whereby a target predicate may be deduced from some of the others, and constrains the search to rules whereby the probability that they arise by chance is less than some prescribed threshold. The basic search techniques have been well documented by Cendrowska (Cendrowska, 1987) but for practical applications they need to be controlled by these probabilistic measures, and also to be extended to generate rules with exceptions as these are both more compact and more in accordance with human practice (Gaines, 1991b).

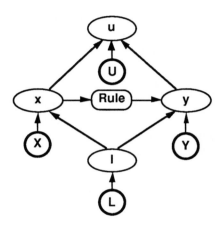

Figure 8 Induction of rules between concepts

To illustrate rule induction from repertory grids, Figure 9 shows an Induct analysis of the grid of Figure 4 in an attempt to determine the rules underlying the use of the term "model," which was a major source of conceptual and terminological difference between experts in the studies from which this data is drawn (Shaw and Gaines, 1989).

Points=Many points -> Model=Requires no model 100% 7.44%
Locality=Local & Interpolation=Linear interpolation -> Model=Requires no model 100% 7.44%
Data type=Interval data & Type=Non-polynomial & Locality=Local -> Model=Requires no model 100% 7.44%
Data type=Interval data & Type=Non-polynomial & Understanding=Easily understood -> Model=Requires no model 100% 7.44%
Formality=Mathematical -> Model=Requires model 100% 4.23%
Search=Does not require spatial search -> Model=Requires model 100% 6.64%
Understanding=Difficult to understand -> Model=Requires model 100% 6.64%

Figure 9 Induct analysis of spatial mapping data

The first percentage at the end of each rule is the *probability correct* as defined in (7), and the second is the *probability by chance*, or statistical significance, as defined in (8). Figure 10 shows these rules exported from KSS0 to KDraw. The frame definition of Figure 5 and the rules of Figure 10, both derived from the grid of Figure 4, may be edited within KDraw and then exported to a knowledge-based system shell as an operational knowledge structure. Practical system development involves the derivation of such structures for the different sub-domains involved, together with the addition of rules that export inferences from one sub-domain to another.

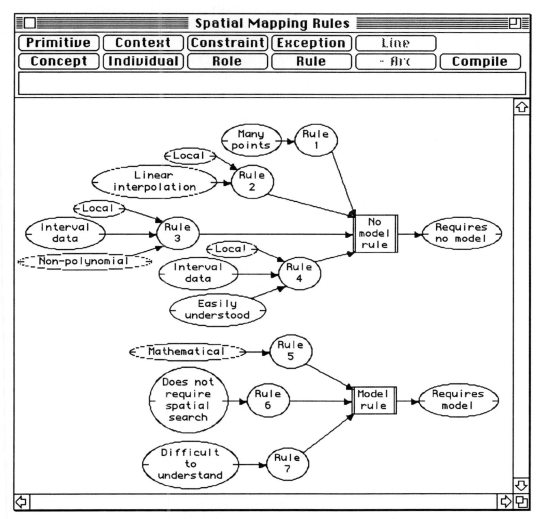

Figure 10 Rules about which techniques require a model represented in the visual language

7 USING REPERTORY GRIDS

The use of the repertory grid to elicit concept structures involves a variety of psychological and analytical techniques, including:

1. Careful definition of the purpose of the elicitation and the appropriate sub-domain to be considered. Maintaining this context so that the purpose and domain do not tacitly change during elicitation is also very important.

2. Choice of exemplary individuals that characterize the relevant features of a domain. This choice is very important and is a major focus of attention in both tool design and application. Fortunately, experts often find it natural to discuss a domain in terms of stereotypical cases, but much care is required to elicit a full range of stereotypes adequate to characterize a domain.

3. Various techniques may be used for initial element elicitation including interviews, protocol analysis, brainstorming with groups of experts, and keyword extraction from relevant textual material (Shaw and Gaines, 1987; Shaw and Woodward, 1990).

4. Online analysis of the interim conceptual structures may be used to detect closely related distinctions and use this to request information on potential stereotypes that might specifically reduce the closeness of the distinctions (Shaw, 1980).

5. The elicitation of some initial distinctions may again derive from interviews, protocols, brainstorming and text analysis.

6. When no prior information is available, triadic elicitation in which a randomly selected set of three individuals is presented with a request to state in what way are two alike and differ from the third can be effective.

7. Online analysis of the interim conceptual structures may be used to detect closely related individuals and use this to request information on potential distinctions that might specifically reduce the closeness of the individuals (Shaw, 1980).

8. The conceptual structure can be developed through various forms of hierarchical and spatial cluster analysis such as FOCUS (Shaw, 1980) and principal components analysis (Slater, 1976, 1977).

9. Rule induction may be used both to derive potential implications between concepts and also, since the premise of a rule is itself a concept, to develop non-primitive concepts and their subsumption relations (Gaines and Shaw, 1992).

10. Direct elicitation of the concept structure may be mixed with indirect development of the grid (Boose and Bradshaw, 1987; Gaines and Shaw, 1990).

8 CONCLUSIONS

Personal construct psychology is a theory of individual and group psychological and social processes that has been used extensively in knowledge acquisition research to model the cognitive processes of human experts. The psychology has the advantage of taking a constructivist position appropriate to the modeling of specialist human knowledge but basing this on a positivist scientific position that characterizes human conceptual structures in axiomatic terms that translate directly to computational form.

The repertory grid knowledge elicitation methodology is directly derived from personal construct psychology. In its original form, this methodology was based primarily on the notion of dichotomous constructs and did not encompass the ordinal relations between them captured in semantic net elicitation. However, it has been extended in successive tools developed for applied knowledge acquisition and tested in a wide variety of applications.

This paper has given an overview of personal construct psychology and its expression as an intensional logic describing the cognitive processes of anticipatory agents. A theoretical framework has been developed and shown to provide logical foundations for personal construct psychology and computational knowledge representation schema. The framework is generated from the single primitive of "making a distinction." It has been used to provide cognitive and logical foundations for existing knowledge acquisition tools and techniques, and for the design of integrated knowledge acquisition systems.

ACKNOWLEDGMENTS
Financial assistance for this work has been made available by the Natural Sciences and Engineering Research Council of Canada. We are grateful to many colleagues for discussions over the years that have influenced the research described in this paper, in particular John Boose, Jeff Bradshaw, Marc Linster, Alain Rappaport, Nigel Waters, Brian Woodward and colleagues at the Knowledge Acquisition Workshops world-wide.

REFERENCES
Adams-Webber, J.R. (1979). **Personal Construct Theory: Concepts and Applications**. Chichester, UK, Wiley.

Boose, J.H. (1984). Personal construct theory and the transfer of human expertise. **Proceedings AAAI-84**. pp.27-33. California, American Association for Artificial Intelligence.

Boose, J.H. (1986). **Expertise Transfer for Expert Systems**. Amsterdam, Elsevier.

Boose, J.H. and Bradshaw, J.M. (1987). Expertise transfer and complex problems: using AQUINAS as a knowledge acquisition workbench for knowledge-based systems. **International Journal of Man-Machine Studies 26** 3-28.

Borgida, A., Brachman, R.J., McGuiness, D.L. and Resnick, L.A. (1989). CLASSIC: a structural data model for objects. **Proceedings of 1989 SIGMOD Conference on the Management of Data**. pp.58-67. New York, ACM Press.

Brachman, R.J. (1977). What's in a concept: structural foundations for semantic nets. **International Journal of Man-Machine Studies 9** 127-152.

Brachman, R.J. (1983). What IS-A is and isn't. **IEEE Computer 16**(10) 30-36.

Brachman, R.J. and Schmolze, J. (1985). An overview of the KL-ONE knowledge representation system. **Cognitive Science 9**(2) 171-216.

Bradshaw, J.M., Boose, J.H., Covington, S.P. and Russo, P.J. (1988). How to do with grids what people say you can't. **Proceedings of the Third AAAI Knowledge Acquisition for Knowledge-Based Systems Workshop**. pp.3-1-3-15. Banff, University of Calgary.

Cendrowska, J. (1987). An algorithm for inducing modular rules. **International Journal of Man-Machine Studies 27**(4) 349-370.

Diederich, J., Ruhmann, I. and May, M. (1987). KRITON: A knowledge acquisition tool for expert systems. **International Journal of Man-Machine Studies 26**(1) 29-40.

Ford, K.M., Cañas, A., Jones, J., Stahl, H., Novak, J. and Adams-Webber, J. (1990). ICONKAT: an integrated constructivist knowledge acquisition tool. **Knowledge Acquisition 3**(2) 215-236.

Gaines, B.R. (1989). An ounce of knowledge is worth a ton of data: quantitative studies of the trade-off between expertise and data based on statistically well-founded empirical induction. **Proceedings of the Sixth International Workshop on Machine Learning**. pp.156-159. San Mateo, California, Morgan Kaufmann.

Gaines, B.R. (1991a). Empirical investigations of knowledge representation servers: Design issues and applications experience with KRS. **ACM SIGART Bulletin 2**(3) 45-56.

Gaines, B.R. (1991b). Integrating rules in term subsumption knowledge representation servers. **AAAI'91: Proceedings of the Ninth National Conference on Artificial Intelligence**. pp.458-463. Menlo Park, California, AAAI Press/MIT Press.

Gaines, B.R. (1991c). An interactive visual language for term subsumption visual languages. **IJCAI'91: Proceedings of the Twelfth International Joint Conference on Artificial Intelligence**. pp.817-823. San Mateo, California, Morgan Kaufmann.

Gaines, B.R. and Shaw, M.L.G. (1980). New directions in the analysis and interactive elicitation of personal construct systems. **International Journal Man-Machine Studies 13** 81-116.

Gaines, B.R. and Shaw, M.L.G. (1986). Induction of inference rules for expert systems. **Fuzzy Sets and Systems 18**(3) 315-328.

Gaines, B.R. and Shaw, M.L.G. (1992). Integrated knowledge acquisition architectures. **Journal for Intelligent Information Systems 1**(1) to appear.

Gaines, B.R. & Shaw, M.L.G. (1990). Cognitive and logical foundations of knowledge acquisition. **Proceedings of the Fifth AAAI Knowledge Acquisition for Knowledge-Based Systems Workshop**. pp.9-1-9-24. Banff, Canada, University of Calgary.

Garg-Janardan, C. and Salvendy, G. (1987). A conceptual framework for knowledge elicitation. **International Journal of Man-Machine Studies 26**(4) 521-531.

Hinkle, D.N. (1965). The change of personal constructs from the viewpoint of a theory of implications. Ohio State University.

Hintikka, J. (1962). **Knowledge and Belief**. Ithaca, New York, Cornell University Press.

Hintikka, J. (1963). The modes of modality. **Acta Philosophica Fennica 16** 65-81.

Kelly, G.A. (1955). **The Psychology of Personal Constructs**. New York, Norton.

Kelly, G.A. (1969). A mathematical approach to psychology. **Clinical Psychology and Personality: The Selected Papers of George Kelly**. pp.94-113. New York, Wiley.

Lloyd, G.E.R. (1966). **Polarity and Analogy**. Cambridge, Cambridge University Press.

Maher, B., Ed. (1969). **Clinical Psychology and Personality: The Selected Papers of George Kelly**. New York, Wiley.

Maybury-Lewis, D. and Almagor, U., Ed. (1989). **The Attraction of Opposites**. Ann Arbor, University of Michigan Press.

Shapiro, S.C. (1979). The SNePS semantic network processing system. **Associative Networks: Representation and Use of Knowledge by Computers**. pp.179-203. New York, Academic Press.

Shaw, M.L.G. (1979). Conversational heuristics for enhancing personal understanding of the world. **General Systems Research: A Science, A Methodology, A Technology**. pp.270-277. Louisville, Kentucky, Society for General Systems Research.

Shaw, M.L.G. (1980). **On Becoming A Personal Scientist: Interactive Computer Elicitation of Personal Models Of The World**. London, Academic Press.

Shaw, M.L.G. and Gaines, B.R. (1979). Externalizing the personal world: computer aids to epistemology. **Improving the Human Condition: Quality and Stability in Social Systems**. pp.136-145. Louisville, Kentucky, Society for General Systems Research.

Shaw, M.L.G. and Gaines, B.R. (1983). A computer aid to knowledge engineering. **Proceedings of British Computer Society Conference on Expert Systems**. pp.263-271. Cambridge, British Computer Society.

Shaw, M.L.G. and Gaines, B.R. (1987). KITTEN: Knowledge initiation & transfer tools for experts and novices. **International Journal of Man-Machine Studies 27**(3) 251-280.

Shaw, M.L.G. and Gaines, B.R. (1989). A methodology for recognizing conflict, correspondence, consensus and contrast in a knowledge acquisition system. **Knowledge Acquisition 1**(4) 341-363.

Shaw, M.L.G. and Woodward, B. (1990). Mental models in the knowledge acquisition process. **Knowledge Acquisition 2**(3) 179-206.

Slater, P., Ed. (1976). **Dimensions of Intrapersonal Space: Vol. 1**. London, John Wiley.

Slater, P., Ed. (1977). **Dimensions of Intrapersonal Space: Vol. 2**. London, John Wiley.

Sowa, J.F. (1984). **Conceptual Structures: Information Processing in Mind and Machine**. Reading, Massachusetts, Adison-Wesley.

Woods, W.A. (1975). What's in a link: Foundations for semantic networks. **Representation and Understanding: Studies in Cognitive Science**. pp.35-82. New York, Academic Press.

Zalta, E.N. (1988). **Intensional Logic and the Metaphysics of Intentionality**. Cambridge, Massachusetts, MIT Press.

STRATEGY MAZE: An On-line Tool for Supporting Management of the Knowledge Acquisition Process

Nora Y L YUE & Benita COX

The Management School, Imperial College of Science, Technology & Medicine,
53 Prince's Gate, Exhibition Road, London SW7 2PG, ENGLAND

ABSTRACT

This paper describes an on-line system which serves to support the management of the Knowledge Acquisition Process. Research on Knowledge Acquisition has tended to focus on the difficulties encountered in the elicitation of cognitive processes from the human expert with less emphasis being placed on the specific difficulties encountered in the management of Knowledge-Based Systems projects. The results of empirical research undertaken by the authors identified the need for improved rigour in the management of the Knowledge Acquisition Process [Yue & Cox, 1991, 1992a,b]. The Strategy Maze is the implementation of these results.

The goal of the Strategy Maze is to reduce and prevent risks to Knowledge Acquisition projects through improved management. The Strategy Maze identifies those management issues which must be addressed at the planning and implementation stages of the project if risk is to be minimised. The system consists of three levels: the *Scoping Level* which is designed to reduce and prevent those risks arising from the lack of clear project definition; the *Requirements Analysis Level* which provides a comprehensive checklist of the tasks and activities which need addressing prior to implementation of the project; and the *Implementation Level* which assists in the reduction and prevention of potential project risks during the implementation, monitoring, and control stages of the project.

1 INTRODUCTION

Knowledge-Based Systems (KBS) differ from conventional computer systems in their degree of dependence upon the elicitation, representation and emulation of human knowledge. This dependence on the particular *'cognitive components'* of systems design has resulted in a class of problems and difficulties specific to the building of KBS systems. These problems are different and frequently more complex than those associated with traditional software engineering design. As a consequence, current literature on Knowledge Acquisition (KA) has tended to focus on the difficulties encountered in the elicitation of cognitive processes from the human expert, and hence, the associated technical difficulties encountered in building such systems. Less emphasis has been placed on the specific difficulties encountered in the management of KBS projects.

This emphasis on KA is reflected in current model-based KA tools, such as KADS [Breuker & Wielinga (1987); Breuker et al (1987); Wielinga et al (1991)] and KEATS [Motta et al, 1986; 1988], which provide model-based support for the KA process, but do not directly address or provide support for the management aspects of the KA process. The results of empirical research undertaken by the authors identified the need for improved rigour in the management of the KA process [Yue & Cox, 1991, 1992a,b]. The Strategy Maze represents the integration and analysis of the these research results with existing literature. Whilst it is acknowledged that it is not possible to provide a single methodology applicable to all KA scenarios, it is the purpose of this paper to provide guidelines based on our research findings of the most pertinent management attributes for consideration. In particular, the following work are integrated with our empirical research results: Stammers R, Carey M S and Astley J A (1990) on task analysis; Laufmann S C, DeVaney D M and Whiting M A (1990) on the source of knowledge; Scott A C, Clayton J E and Gibson E L (1991) on development time estimation, case characteristics definition, interview preparation, and formation of conceptual model; Meyer M and Booker J (1991) on the selection of question areas and questions; Kirman B (1990) on human reliability assessment; and Parker M F (1990) on project status reporting, project reviews, project change control and project completion.

KBS systems have somewhat different architectures from conventional software systems. This difference requires a managerial approach specific to the development of KBS systems, and in particular, to the KA process. KBS development life cycle is very similar to a conventional software development life cycle at the *requirements analysis* stage. However, at the *requirements specification* stage, there are more significant differences, particularly during the analysis phase. The managerial analysis performed in the Strategy Maze is a detail process which not only involves requirement analysis, but also specifically towards knowledge acquisition, and it is in this area that the methodology of the Strategy Maze differs most significantly from conventional methodologies. In fact, KBS and conventional methodologies share greater similarities towards the implementation end of the development spectrum, and then separate again during the post-implementation phases. Because the Requirements Analysis Level of the Strategy Maze differs the most from conventional systems development, particular attention has been specifically placed and emphasised on this level of analysis. Subsequent phases such as implementation and maintenance are quite similar to their conventional counterparts and therefore, only the managerial aspects of the activities in these phases are covered. The Strategy Maze integrates traditional approaches to conventional software project management process with managerial requirements specific to KA projects. It integrates the "*requirements analysis*", "*requirements specification*", and "*maintenance*" phases of conventional software development life cycle together with other component phases specific to the KA process into an on-line tool for supporting management of KA projects.

2 OVERVIEW OF THE STRATEGY MAZE

The Strategy Maze is designed to reflect the traditional management functions of planning, organising, staffing, directing and controlling, and their application to the KA process. In particular, it focuses on the planning procedures associated with the KA process.

The goal of the Strategy Maze is to reduce, minimise, and prevent risks to KA projects through improved management by means of assessing the completeness of the managerial planning activities. The subject of risk management in traditional software engineering project has been extensively discussed [Boehm (1981, 1989); Deutsch (1981)]. This paper addresses risk management in the context of KA projects.

The system has been designed to assist the knowledge engineer in the following areas:

* *Risk Management*
  - reduce and prevent potential project risks;
  - prioritise potential project risks;
  - facilitate risk management planning;
  - assist in risk monitoring.

* *Project Scheduling*
  - schedule the stages of the KA project;
  - facilitate time management of the KA project;
  - prevent unrealistic time scheduling.

* *Project Milestone Management*
  - define individual milestone checkpoints;
  - track the project's progress;
  - monitor and control project reviews.

* *Uncertainty Management*
  - minimise uncertainties in areas within each project milestone;
  - prevent changes to project requirements.

* Critical Success Activities Management
- identify critical success activities at crucial stages of the project;
- ensure major critical success activities are carried out.

The high risk managerial planning activities identified from the empirical research are group into sets of components according to their importance and expected time of execution in the KA process. The managerial activities to be carried out can broadly be divided into three distinctive groups:

(i) managerial activities aimed at reducing and preventing potential project risks arising from the lack of clear project definition;

(ii) high risk managerial activities which need to be accomplished prior to implementation of the project; and

(iii) managerial activities aimed at reducing and preventing potential project risks during the implementation, monitoring, and control stages of the project.

The Strategy Maze is designed to identify those management issues in these three broad groups. Hence, the system consists of three main programs each representing one of the three levels of analysis (figure 1):

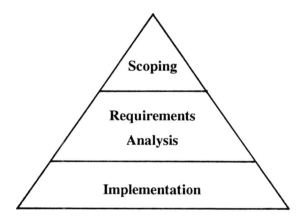

Figure 1: The Three Levels of Analysis in Strategy Maze

Each of these levels represents an important phase in the KA project and consists of a series of components which constitute the architectural framework of the Strategy Maze as shown in figure 2.

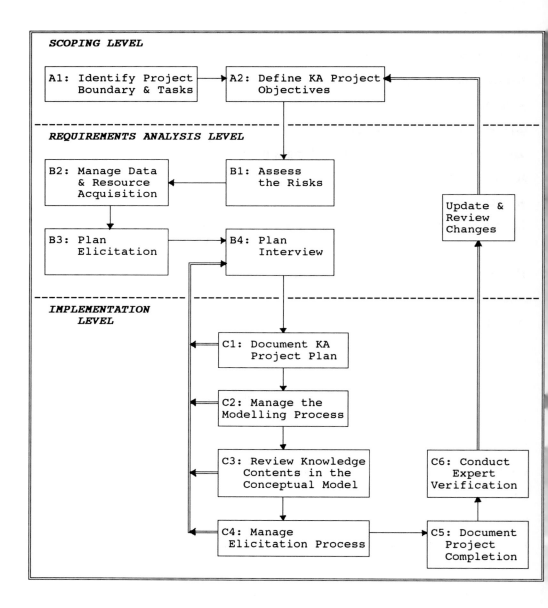

Figure 2: <u>Architectural Framework of the Strategy Maze</u>

The three levels have been designed to assist in risk management, project scheduling, project milestone management, uncertainty management, and critical success activities management. The aim of each level is shown below:

I Scoping Level - designed to reduce and prevent high potential project risks arising from the lack of clear project definition. Figure 3 shows the sub-level components within the Scoping Level. The Scoping Level assists in reducing, minimising, and preventing risks associated with:

- project specification/identification/assessment;
- ill-defined project objectives;
- incomplete identification of or changes in project scope;
- ill-defined project boundary and domain characteristics;
- incomplete identification of major tasks and subtasks;
- lack of determination and identification of critical success factors.

II Requirements Analysis Level - designed to reduce and prevent potential project risks associated with tasks and activities which need addressing prior to implementation of the project. Figures 4 and 5 show the sub-level components within the Requirements Analysis Level. The Requirements Analysis Level assists in reducing, minimising, and preventing risks associated with:

- unrealistic estimation of project costs and budgets;
- shortfalls in essential project personnel;
- inappropriate operating environment;
- ill-managed knowledge sources;
- unrealistic project schedules;
- lack of planning and organisation of elicitation;
- inadequate planning and organisation of interviews.

III Implementation Level - designed to reduce and prevent potential project risks during the implementation, monitoring, and control stages of the project. Figures 6 and 7 show the sub-level components within the Implementation Level. The Implementation Level assists in reducing, minimising, and preventing risk associated with:

- lack of documentation of project plan;
- incomplete project progress record at each milestone;
- undelivered project status reporting;
- inadequate project reviews;
- lack of continuous knowledge-base assessment;
- continuing stream of requirement changes;
- incomplete project documention;
- lack of expert verification and evaluation;

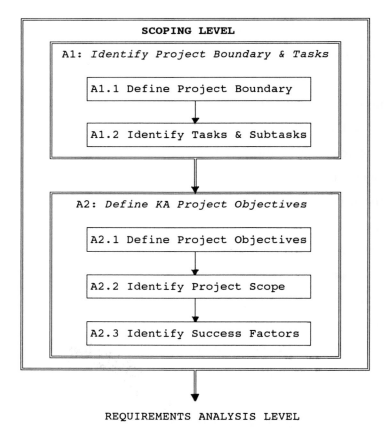

Figure 3: Sub-Level Components within Scoping Level

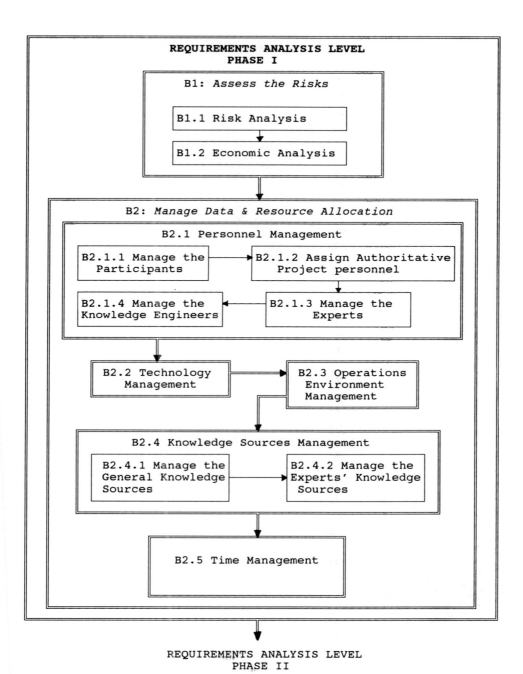

Figure 4: <u>Sub-Level Components within Requirements Analysis Level Phase I</u>

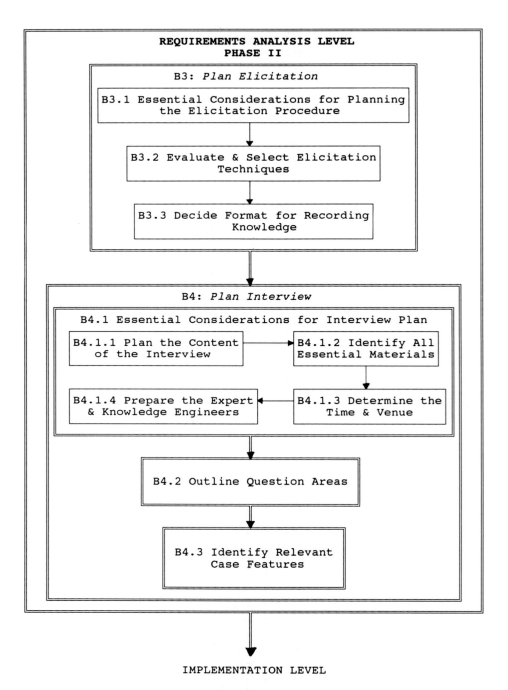

Figure 5: <u>Sub-Level Components within Requirements Analysis Level Phase II</u>

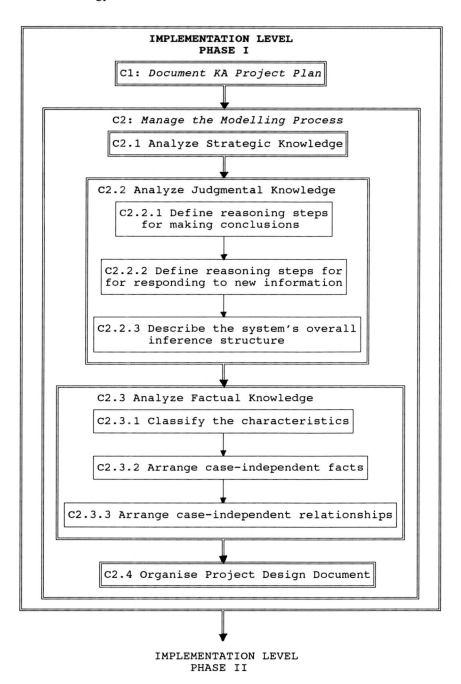

Figure 6: <u>Sub-Level Components within Implementation Level Phase I</u>

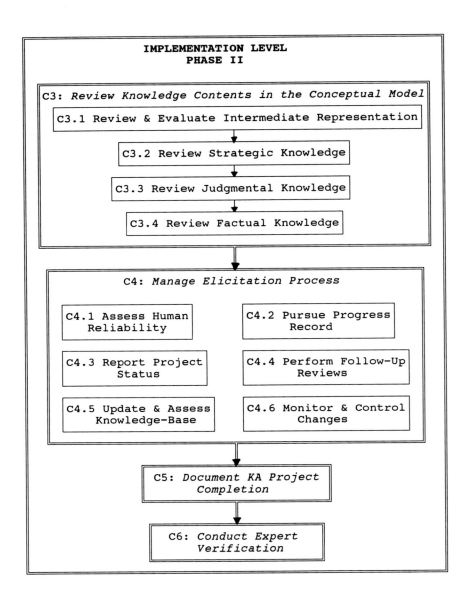

Figure 7: <u>Sub-Level Components within Implementation Level Phase II</u>

3 ASSESSMENT OF THE STRATEGY MAZE

The Strategy Maze is based on a collection and synthesis of "*issues*". An issue is a statement representing a managerial task or activity. Each is designed to reduce and prevent potential project risks by identifying tasks and subtasks necessary to ensure rigour in the management activities associated with the KA project.

Each of the three levels is divided into several sub-level components, each consisting of a number of issues (examples of issues for the three levels are shown in figures 8,9,10). The user indicates his *orientation* to each issue (i.e. the degree to which he feels he has successfully addressed that particular issue). These orientations are then scored on a five level scale ranging from strong positive to strong negative indicating the strength of his conviction. An example of a scoring table is shown in figure 11.

```
A2.1 Define Project Objectives
■ Define the project's purpose or goals.
■ Determine the objectives of the project from the knowledge
  engineer's perspective.
■ Determine the objectives of the project from the expert's
  perspective.
■ Determine whether the objective is to collect the experts'
  answers or their problem-solving processes.
■ Determine if the project assumptions and constraints are well
  formed, realistic, and defensible.
■ Determine and set out milestones for the project.
■ Assess the users' requirements.
■ Emphasise the importance of giving proper consideration to end
  user requirements during product development.
■ Identify the deliverables from the project.
```

Figure 8: Examples of Management Issues within Scoping Level

B2.4.1 **Manage the General Knowledge Sources**
- Identify all knowledge sources or supporting documents.
- Assess the magnitude of the information required.
- Determine the level of complexity of knowledge required.
- Determine the nature of the knowledge.
- Determine whether the knowledge is resident in individual experts or is a community involvement.
- Determine the accessibility to the knowledge.
- Compare the relative quantities of problem-solving knowledge with that of domain-specific data involved in the project.
- Determine the familiarity of elicitor with domain knowledge.

Figure 9: <u>Examples of Management Issues within Requirements Analysis Level</u>

C2.1 **Analyze Strategic Knowledge**
- Identify the high-level steps the system should perform.
- Draw a flow chart to illustrate the order in which the system should perform these high-level steps.
- Define the conditions under which the system should perform each high-level step.
- Subdivide any high-level step that consists of more than a small number of input, reasoning, and output actions.
- Define as many levels of substeps as required.
- Define the objectives of each substep.
- Identify the information that should be available to the system before it undertakes the step.
- Describe the sequence of input, reasoning, and output actions that should be performed in the step.

Figure 10: <u>Examples of Management Issues within Implementation Level</u>

```
┌─────────────────────────────────────────────────────────┐
│╔═══════════════════════════════════════════════════════╗│
│║            ASSIGN INDICATION   LEVEL                   ║│
│║  Please assign an indication level for this           ║│
│║  issue with its own orientation and strength:         ║│
│║                                                       ║│
│║     Strong Positive Indication          [   ]         ║│
│║     Weak Positive Indication            [   ]         ║│
│║     Neutral/Inconclusive Indication     [   ]         ║│
│║     Weak Negative Indication            [   ]         ║│
│║     Strong Negative Indication          [   ]         ║│
│╚═══════════════════════════════════════════════════════╝│
└─────────────────────────────────────────────────────────┘
```

Figure 11: <u>Scoring Table</u>

4 EVALUATION & INTERPRETATION OF RESULTS

The Strategy Maze interprets and analyses the inputs by assessing the total counts for each of the indication levels (Strong Positive to Strong Negative) together with the degree of importance of the individual groups of issues for the KA project according to the weightings assigned to them.

The users' responses are assessed at the completion of each level, minimum targets are set which the user must attain before he is recommended to progress to the next level. These *targets* constitute the issues in each level, each issue successfully addressed is assigned a *count*. The total number of *counts* for each indication level is given in an indication score table as shown in figure 12 below.

```
┌─────────────────────────────────────────────────────────┐
│╔═══════════════════════════════════════════════════════╗│
│║            INDICATION SCORE TABLE                     ║│
│║      The total number of indication scores           ║│
│║      obtained for each indication level are          ║│
│║      shown as follows:                               ║│
│║                                                       ║│
│║  No. of Strong Positive Indications        [   ]      ║│
│║  No. of Weak Positive Indications          [   ]      ║│
│║  No. of Neutral/Inconclusive Indications   [   ]      ║│
│║  No. of Weak Negative Indications          [   ]      ║│
│║  No. of Strong Negative Indications        [   ]      ║│
│╚═══════════════════════════════════════════════════════╝│
└─────────────────────────────────────────────────────────┘
```

Figure 12: <u>Indication Score Table</u>

Weights are assigned to each of the sub-level components. The value of these weights are set according to the weights of the perceived risks identified from previous research which each sub-level component is designed to reduce and prevent. These perceived risks are weighted in accordance with their associated factors and criteria which influences the management of the KA process as identified from research [Yue & Cox, 1991, 1992a,b] Thus, the three main levels (Scoping Level, Requirements Analysis Level and Implementation Level) have been designed and arranged according to the weights assigned to their associated sub-level components.

Analysis is performed at the completion of each level after the total number of counts for each indication level is completed in the scoring table. The underlying assumption in the interpretation of these total counts is that the potential project risk is related to the level of completeness of the managerial activities that has been undertaken. The following shows the general guidelines on the recommendations resulted from the Scoping Level analysis:

> * If the user has scored over ten percent of all issues with strong negative indicators regardless of the percentage or strength of other issues, this signifies that too high a percentage of highly relevant issues have not been sufficiently well addressed. The user is strongly recommended to reconsider these issues again before proceeding to the Requirements Analysis Level.

> * If the user has scored over twenty percent of all issues with negative indicators regardless of its strength, this again signifies that too high a percentage of highly relevant issues have not been sufficiently well addressed. This user is strongly advised to reconsider these issues again before proceeding to the Requirements Analysis Level.

> * If the user has scored over fifty percent of all issues with neutral or inconclusive indicators, it indicates that there is a high degree of uncertainty or potential risk to the project since neutral indicators identify areas where adequate information is lacking. The user is advised to reconsider these issues again before proceeding to the Requirements Analysis Level.

> * If the user has positively scored over fifty percent and negatively scored under twenty percent of all issues regardless of their strength, this indicates that the user has adequately gathered the majority of important information and satisfied the minimum requirements for this level. The user is advised to proceed to the Requirements Analysis Level.

* If the user has scored less than fifty percent of all issues with positive indicators, less than twenty percent of all issues with negative indicators, and less than fifty percent of all issues with neutral or inconclusive indicators, this shows that the majority of all the issues were either negatively or neutrally addressed. This indicates that although there are no significant areas where important information is lacking, uncertainty and risk of failure of the project would be further reduced by addressing these issues. The user is advised to reconsider those negatively and neutrally addressed issues again before proceeding to the Requirements Analysis Level.

The recommended general guidelines given in the Strategy Maze are, therefore, based upon the percentages scored for each indication level for each level of analysis. There are minimum targets with fixed percentages which the user must attain before he is advised to progress to the next level. The choice of these fixed percentages was arbitrary and based on the author's perceived importance of each of the levels according to the weights assigned to each of their associated sub-level component. The following gives a summary of the minimum targets set for each level of analysis:

For **Scoping Level**, the user must score:
under 10% of all the issues **strong negatively,**
under 20% of all the issues **negatively,**
under 50% of all the issues **neutrally,** and
over 50% of all the issues **positively.**

For **Requirements Analysis Level Phase I**, the user must score:
under 10% of all the issues **strong negatively,**
under 20% of all the issues **negatively,**
under 50% of all the issues **neutrally,** and
over 50% of all the issues **positively.**

For **Requirements Analysis Level Phase II**, the user must score:
under 20% of all the issues **strong negatively,**
under 40% of all the issues **negatively,**
under 50% of all the issues **neutrally,** and
over 50% of all the issues **positively.**

For **Implementation Level**, the user must score:
under 25% of all the issues **strong negatively,**
under 40% of all the issues **negatively,**
under 50% of all the issues **neutrally,** and
over 50% of all the issues **positively.**

These recommendations are based on different weights assigned to all components of the framework as explained previously.

5 CONCLUSION

This paper has described an on-line system, the Strategy Maze, developed in response to the need for a structured method for improved rigour in the management of the Knowledge Acquisition process as reported by knowledge engineers. It is aimed at reducing, minimising, and preventing potential project risk through improved management. The Strategy Maze consists of three levels of analysis each of which contains several sub-level components. For each sub-level component, those management issues that are critical and important to the potential success of the Knowledge Acquisition project, and which ultimately will directly affect and improve the quality of the knowledge base have been identified. The system captures the user's response, scores the analysis automatically, and offers recommendations.

The Strategy Maze is intended to be used so that outcomes from the managerial activities can be recorded and justified. A limitation of this system is the depth and breadth of information required to be entered by the user in order for the analysis to be performed. It is acknowledged that the answers to some of the questions raised cannot be known until the Knowledge Acquisition project is in progress. However, the intent is not always to derive precise responses, but to highlight and raise awareness of potential problem areas.

The Strategy Maze provides a foundation upon which knowledge engineers can plan the management of future elicitation sessions by generating permanent documentation and justification of the assessment task and results. It highlights critical management issues in the planning and implementation stages of Knowledge Acquisition projects, enabling knowledge engineers and development staff to address these issues before they become major problems or risks to the project. Thus, the system can contribute significantly to successful Knowledge Acquisition projects. The Strategy Maze is currently under evaluation and review. Early analysis of results has been positive. In addition, the system may be incorporated into knowledge acquisition systems within future knowledge-based systems environments. The Strategy Maze is expected to further evolve to better accommodate the managerial needs of knowledge engineers, enabling them to address these issues prior to and during the Knowledge Acquisition Process.

REFERENCES

[Boehm, 1981] Boehm B W. *Software Engineering Economics*. Prentice-Hall, Englewood Cliffs, N.J., 1981.

[Boehm, 1989] Boehm B W. *Software Risk Management*. IEEE Computer Society Press, 1989.

[Breuker and Wielinga, 1987] Breuker J A and Wielinga B J. "Knowledge acquisition as modelling expertise: the KADS methodology". *Proceedings of the first European Workshop on Knowledge Acquisition for Knowledge-Based Systems*, Reading: Reading University, section B1, UK, 2-3 September 1987.

[Breuker et al., 1987] Breuker J, Wielinga B, Someren M, de Hoog R, Schreiber G, de Greef P, Bredeweg B, Wielemaker J and Billault J-P. "Model-driven knowledge acquisition: interpretation models". Deliverable task A1, *Esprit Project 1098*, Amsterdam: University of Amsterdam, 1987.

[Deutsch, 1981] Deutsch M S. "Software Project Verification and Validation", *Computer*, **14**(4), pp.54-70, 1981.

[Kirwan, 1990] Kirwan B. "Human Reliability Assessment" in *Evaluation of Human Work*, J R Wilson and E N Corlett (Editors), Taylor & Francis Ltd., pp.706-754, 1990.

[Laufmann et al., 1990] Laufmann S C, DeVaney D M and Whiting M A. "A Methodology for Evaluating Potential KBS Applications". *IEEE Expert*, Volume 5, Number 6, pp.43-66, December 1990.

[Meyer and Booker, 1991] Meyer M and Booker J. "Selecting Question Areas and Questions" in *Eliciting and Analyzing Expert Judgement*. Academic Press, pp.55-67. 1991.

[Motta et al., 1986] Motta E, Eisenstadt M, West M, Pitman K and Evertsz R. "KEATS: The knowledge engineer's assistant *(Alvey Project IKBS/20)*". *Final Project Report, HCRL Technical Report No. 20, December 1986*. Milton Keynes, UK: Human Cognition Research Laboratory, The Open University, 1986.

[Motta et al., 1988] Motta E, Eisenstadt M, Pitman K and West M. "Support for knowledge acquisition in the knowledge engineer's assistant". *HCRL Technical Report No. 30, January 1988*. Milton Keynes, UK: Human Cognition Research Laboratory, The Open University; also published in *Expert Systems*, Vol. 5, No. 1, pp.6-28, 1988.

[Parker, 1990] Parker M F. "Managing Successful Applications" in *Managing Information Systems for Profit*, T Lincoln (Editor), Wiley Series in Information Systems, pp.180-183, 1990.

[Scott et al., 1991] Scott A C, Clayton J E and Gibson E L. *A Practical Guide to Knowledge Acquisition*, Addison Wesley, 1991.

[Stammers et al., 1990] Stammers R B, Carey M S and Astley J A. "Task Analysis" in *Evaluation of Human Work*, J R Wilson and E N Corlett (Editors), Taylor & Francis Ltd., pp.134-160, 1990.

[Wielinga et al., 1991] Wielinga B J, Schreiber A The, Breuker J A. "KADS: A Modelling Approach to Knowledge Engineering". *Esprit Project P5248 KADS-II*, An Advanced and Comprehensive Methodology for Integrated KBS Development, Amsterdam, 1991.

[Yue and Cox, 1991] Yue N Y L and Cox B. "Towards a Clearer Definition of Requirements for the Enhancement of the Knowledge Acquisition Process". *Proceedings of the Australian Workshop on Knowledge Acquisition for Knowledge-Based Systems*, Pokolbin, (Uni. of Sydney),pp.185-201, August 20-23, 1991.

[Yue and Cox, 1992a] Yue N Y L and Cox B. "MAFKAP: A Management Framework for the Knowledge Acquisition Process". *Proceedings of the Fifth International Symposium on Knowledge Engineering*, Seville, Spain, October 5-9, 1992.

[Yue and Cox, 1992b] Yue N Y L and Cox B. "Towards a framework for the Management of Knowledge Acquisition: MAFKAP". *Proceedings of the Second Japanese Knowledge Acquisition for Knowledge-Based Systems Workshop: JKAW92*, Kobe and Hatoyama, Japan, November 9-13, 1992.

Concurrent Engineering using Collaborating Truth Maintenance Systems

C.J.HINDE & A.D.BRAY

Dept. Computer Studies
University of Technology
Loughborough
Leics LE11 3TU.

1 ABSTRACT

The truth maintained blackboard model of problem solving as used in the Loughborough University Manufacturing Planner had supported collaboration between experts which were closely linked to the management system. On realistic problems the size of the assumption bases produced by the system and the overall size of the blackboard combined to impair the performance of the system. This model of design supported the collaboration of experts around a central blackboard. Clearly collaboration is a necessary condition for concurrent decision making and so the basic framework for collaboration is preserved in this model.

The Design to Product management system within which the Planner had to operate had a central "Tool Manager" through which all communication was routed. In order to implement a model of simultaneous engineering and also to support collaborative work using this model a multiple context design system is useful, if not essential. Our model extends this by distributing the control between the various expert agents where each agent treats the others as knowledge sources to its own private blackboard. All interaction between agents is done using a common communication protocol which is capable of exchanging contextual information necessary to separate contexts in the Assumption based Truth Maintenance System (de Kleer 84) environment. The hierarchical model of control by a central tool manager has been replaced by a heterarchical model of distributed control. The agents are configured using a single line inheritance scheme which endows each agent with its required knowledge and also allows it to declare its functionality to its colleagues. Because the systems are distributed the assumption bases can be kept much smaller as the private reasoning leading to a particular consequence from a set of premises is hidden from the agents colleagues who are only aware that a particular set of choices result from a set of premises.

2 CONCURRENT ENGINEERING

The particular problem area we have been concerned with is the design of a suitable architecture with which to support concurrent engineering. Engineering design, and in fact design of many sorts has proceeded with a statement of requirements followed by a "design" phase where the designer produces a specification of a form which will fulfil the functional requirements of the "user". This is then passed to the production engineer who designs a method of manufacture which will produce the specified form in the most economic manner often using the machinery available but sometimes by designing special purpose machinery. Typically the requirements specification will only seek to specify that which is known to be producible and the design phase will similarly consider the requirements of production. Concurrent engineering will take into account all aspects which may influence a decision at the time that decision is to be made.

The "Design to Product" Alvey demonstrator (Burrow 89, Burrow & Hinde 90) went some way towards the concept of concurrent engineering but concentrated more on isolated elements of problem solving (Hinde et al. 89,Millington 90) within an overall integrating framework (Burrow & Hinde 90) rather than to apply the concepts of concurrent engineering throughout the project.

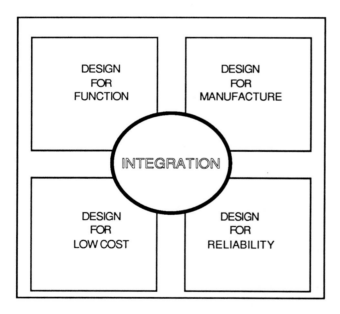

Figure 1. The central concept behind concurrent engineering is integration.

The central organising concept (Figure 1) was that of an "Information Management System" to represent the developing design and a "Tool manager" to manage communications between the various components of the "Design to Product" system. All communication was routed through the Tool Manager" and all information made available to the tools was kept in the "Information Management System". The elements of the "Information Management System" were of various kinds including geometrical objects, process plans etc. Two of the components of the "Design to Product" system were based on de Kleer's Assumption Based Truth Maintenance ideas (de Kleer 84) although their use of the ATMS was in some respects different. The two elements which were based on truth maintenance system were the Edinburgh Designer System (Millington et al. 90) and the Loughborough University Manufacturing Planner (Hinde et al. 89). The components of the "Design to Product" system are represented by the squares however the "Information Management System" and the "Tool Manager" are encompassed in the central "Integration" circle.

3 BASIC ARCHITECTURE

The work done at Loughborough is based on a Truth Maintained Blackboard system (Engelmore & Morgan 88). This works around the concept of a number of experts collaborating around a common blackboard, moderated by a manager. All communication between experts and intermediate results are stored in this area. The multiple context nature of the blackboard allows inconsistent environments to be developed, which allow the system and the operator to follow up more than one idea concurrently, in much the way that humans tend to work.

The TMS works around the concept of a blackboard containing entries. Entries given to the blackboard by users as specifications or requirements are in the form of assumptions, with associated ratings which specify how feasible or desirable the assumptions are felt to be. When an expert or calculating engine takes a number of entries and produces a result from it, then this result is called a consequence of those entries, and the list of assumptions that led to the consequence is called the assumption base. Assumptions are initial defeasible entries, whereas initial indefeasible entries are facts. In the Loughborough system an expert can derive a consequence in two key ways; necessarily and possibly. A necessary assumption is one where the assumption base could only lead to that result through processing by the expert, and a possible assumption is one where more than one outcome is possible even if there is only one outcome delivered by the expert. The expert must also specify how feasible any outcome of a possible result is, to give it a ranking compared to other possible consequences of that assumption base. All the truth maintained agents in our system are Assumption Based in that each entry can stand without reference to its derivation path, only the assumptions which underpin its validity are needed.

In order to understand the problems that are found later in the paper, it may help to have an idea of the internal representation used in the ATMS. This should give a feel for the amount of data that may need to be stored when many assumptions are used to solve a large problem. The format of the entries is:

(tag, entry, assumption bases)

tag is a unique tag to distinguish entries from one another and to provide a reference for
   building assumption bases.

entry is the actual entry.

assumption bases are the lists of assumptions which underpin the entry, or justify it.

The statement:

{[], user, possible, [a=1]} would result in the following entry being made:

(1, a = 1, [[1]])   This is a self justifying assumption. The reading of this is that "a=1" is
true if entry 1 is true, i.e. if "a=1" is true. It stands on its own but may be contradicted.

(2, b = 0, [[2]])   This is also self justifying.

(3, c = -4, [[3]])

(4, a*x^2 + b*x + c = 0, [[4]])

These may be presented to an algebraic equation solver which could deliver, as possible
answers, the two entries "x=2" & "x=-2".

(5, x = -2, [[1, 2, 3, 4, 5]]) This is a partially self justifying assumption,i.e. a possible
derivation of entries 1-4.

(6, x = 2, [[1, 2, 3, 4, 6]])   As is this.

(7, x > 0, [[7]])   This eliminates the entry "x=-2" from any environment containing
assumption 7.

(0, false, ([[0],[1,2,3,4,5,6],[1,2,3,4,5,7]]) This is the entry that declares 5 and 6 are
inconsistent in the context of 1,2,3 & 4 etc. If we were able to state that 5 & 6 are inconsistent
in all possible worlds then the assumption base of our false entry would be
[[0],[5,6],[1,2,3,4,5,7]]. This results in shorter assumption bases.

The protocol used in the "Design to Product" tool manager routed everything through a central
controller which potentially caused bottlenecks. By distributing the message passing around the
agents we encourage point to point contact but by means of the collection of agents into a
project we also control which agents are allowed to talk to one another. The other fundamental

difference which must be emphasised is the fact that each element is a central controller for all other elements and so we have a heterarchy instead of a hierarchy.

4 TOLERANCES

We were keen at the end of "Design to Product" to explore concurrent engineering further and studied the ideas of economic tolerances using the Taguchi system (Taguchi et al. 89). Briefly the Taguchi system relates required tolerances, costs of not achieving those tolerances denoted as failure costs, process tolerances and process costs together so that expensive high tolerance processes are not used to produce low value goods. The required tolerances for the product are specified as part of the functional specification and these may be performance tolerances as well as dimensional tolerances. If the product is a high value product then it would be expensive to produce a product which did not meet those tolerances, such a product would be a jet engine turbine blade, and so a process delivering a very close tolerance would be used possibly costing a large amount of money. Manufacturing processes tend to deliver tolerances according to a distribution and so we associate a probability that a particular process can meet the particular required tolerance. We may use more expensive processes to reduce the incidence of failure, however this must be offset against the cost of the process versus the cost of failure.

Although we can specify the required functional tolerances before selecting the processes used to manufacture a product we cannot select the tolerances to manufacture to unless we already know the cost of those processes, and we cannot know the costs of those processes until we know what those processes are. This particular problem exemplifies all the problems of concurrent engineering and requires circular or iterative logic to overcome them. The manufacturing tolerances cannot be selected until the costs of the processes are known, the costs of the processes cannot be known until the processes have been selected and the processes cannot be selected until the tolerances have been determined, figure 2 illustrates this.

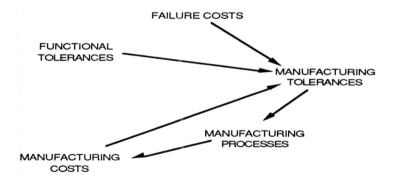

Figure 2. The relationship between costs, manufacturing tolerances and selection of processes.

One of the traditional ways round this problem of assigning tolerances to components is to use default tolerances on the entire component and to assign closer tolerances where necessary. These higher tolerances are assigned using expert knowledge and by consulting the organisation's book of tolerances. Other ways include assigning the same tolerance to all parts of the component in order to reduce the number of tolerances that must be specified. This can be wasteful leading to over engineered products costing too much to manufacture.

The book of tolerances will contain commercially useful information and is based on past experience of manufacturing similar products. By keeping the justifications which lead to the assignment of dimensions and tolerances this book can be updated and the context within which various tolerance assignments are made is preserved.

In order to make progress in this circular argument we need to make assumptions, the first simplifying assumption is that the manufacturing tolerances will not exceed the required tolerances, in other words we will not deliberately make something outside the required tolerances, or make something which costs more to make than we can sell it for. This assumption gives us an outer envelope of tolerances such that any process which delivers a tolerance distribution outside cannot possibly be economic. As our management system is a multiple context blackboard system we are then able to make a set of assumptions about the processes which are possible, and also the relationships between the processes (Bray et al. 92). The relationship between the form of the product and the manufacturing processes also needs to be determined and there will typically be many such alternative relationships; again we are able to assume a wide range of interpretations in this (Herbert et al. 90) because of our use of a TMS. Again the use of a single context message passing system which stores results and not their contexts precludes this multiple context refinement strategy.

Having made our initial assumptions about sets of possible processes we are now able to calculate the effect of the tolerances delivered by those processes and therefore the functional tolerances implied by those processes. The cost of manufacture can now be ascertained and the manufacturing tolerances associated with those costs be calculated, these are invariably closer than the initial sets of tolerances and so some sets of processes can be eliminated. Interestingly a close toleranced product that can actually be manufactured by the system is much easier to deal with than an easily made product as there are fewer sets of feasible processes.

The interaction between the functional requirements and manufacturing processes introduces various problems not only concerned with meeting the functional requirements as initially specified but also in modifying those requirements in the light of further knowledge of what can be manufactured. It would be possible, and the Design to Product demonstrator explored this path, to design and build an expert system which would determine at the design stage whether or not a particular product could be manufactured however this system should also offer constructive criticism of the form chosen rather than just give a yes/no answer; the critic/modifier pair is popular idea in rule induction systems (Bundy 85). In order for this to be effected the modifier needs to have some idea of the initial requirements, often a change in the nominal value and achievable tolerances of one parameter will require changes in the nominal values and required tolerances of other parameters, we are constrained in any realistic system to consider both the functional requirements and the manufacturing capabilities simultaneously.

This interaction is illustrated easily by considering the manufacture of a hole where there are only a limited set of drill bits. If we have a tolerance assigned to the volume of the hole to be drilled then we have a relationship between the diameter of the hole, its depth and its volume. We may assign a preferred depth to the hole and then derive a diameter consistent with our functional requirements only to find the required diameter cannot be manufactured with a simple drilling operation. By assigning a set of suitably close drills we can derive a set of diameters and depths, each diameter associated with a particular depth satisfying the required volume. The design form is therefore modified by considerations of manufacture.

The technology we have used is one solution to the problem of providing software systems to support concurrent engineering however the use of a single blackboard based truth maintenance system becomes unwieldy as the entries can attract very many assumptions, we have found several hundred assumptions attached to some entries towards the end of a session. Clearly although the idea of an ATMS allows multiple contexts to be explored it can carry with it a high computational cost.

The use of a standard for communicating design tools as employed in the final phase of "Design to Product" (Burrow & Hinde 90) and becoming popular eliminates the large assumption bases as they have no relevance to the essentially single context system which is the outside world of the design tools. It would also be unreasonable to insist that all components of an engineering design system could cope with the assumption bases and operate in multiple contexts. We therefore also have to be able to integrate single context systems into our design environment.

We have two problems now, the first problem is that we wish to operate in a multiple context environment and not all the components of our system can necessarily maintain multiple contexts; secondly if they could we would soon find the cost of maintaining those assumption bases becoming prohibitive.

5 THE SOLUTION
In using our system we have noticed that in many problem solving situations various different paths lead to the same conclusion. The entry corresponding to that final conclusion then

contains several assumption bases corresponding to the different chains of reasons which gave rise to that conclusion, this is so even when we are very careful to make sure that every entry on the blackboard is unique. The chain of reasons, or justification path, leading to a conclusion may then be of the form in figure 3.

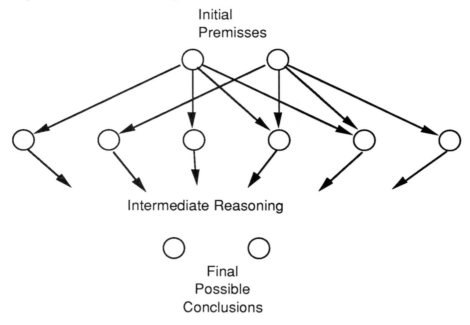

Figure 3. showing a reason graph justifying two final possible conclusions from a set of initial premises. The intermediate reasoning may be quite complex.

We are using the notation and language associated with Justification based Truth Maintenance systems (Doyle 79) as even though each entry stands alone supported only by its basic assumptions it is the reasoning path that has lead to those assumptions.

The agent requiring the statement that two final possible conclusions may be derived from the set of initial premises does not need to know how those two conclusions were arrived at but merely that they are possible consequences. The situation in figure 3 would have several possibly large assumption bases tagged on to the final possible conclusions corresponding to and as a result of the intermediate reasoning. Only if the intermediate reasoning was a chain of necessary consequences would the final assumption bases be relatively small.

Representing the derivation of the final conclusions as a direct possible consequence of the initial set of consequences we arrive at figure 4.

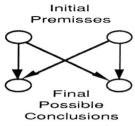

Figure 4. Showing the reduced chain of reasons derived from figure 3.

The preceding argument has focused strongly on the relationship of the consequences to the initial premises via the justifications used to produce those consequences. The external message passing protocol must necessarily focus on what consequences can be drawn from what premises and cannot know the set of assumptions required to fully support the conclusions. In that sense the outside message passing system is acting as a Justification based Truth Maintenance system but the major disadvantage of using such a system, namely long justification paths, is eliminated as each message contains only short paths. Only if all the justifications were placed together would we find the system becoming unmanageable. We have a mixture of two technologies, ATMS and JTMS, taking advantage of both when appropriate.

6 MESSAGE PASSING PROTOCOL

The form of most messages between elements of the system are of the form:

Starting with these premises (P1,P2,..) can you derive something of the form (R1,R2,..) where P1, P2 are instantiated and R1,R2 are patterns giving some goal direction. The reply will state whether the result is a possible result or a necessary result introducing modality into the system.

The system passes messages from element to element in the following basic forms:

{preconditions, source, modality, source_result_patterns}

This is the form used to ask a question from an element, the requesting agent sends a message to another element which has declared its ability to answer such questions, in that it will make declaration of the form:

{precondition_patterns, self, self_result_patterns}

meaning that given a set of preconditions matching precondition_patterns self is prepared to produce something which matches self_result_patterns.

The questioner instantiates precondition_patterns to suitable values and may also partially instantiate result_patterns in which case this will restrict the ability of self to answer but also give self a better idea of what source is looking for.

self will send a message back to source with all the fields instantiated and also adding a modality field which will tell the receiver the status of the results, in the form:

{preconditions, self, modality, results}

For example an algebraic equation solver might be posed the following question from an interested agent. 'user' is an agent who simply make statements which they may or may not be able to justify.

{[], user, possible, [a = 1,b = 0,c = -4,a*x^2 + b*x + c = 0]}

means that "with no preconditions user states that it is possible that a = 1,b = 0,c = -4,a*x^2 + b*x + c = 0 are conjointly true".

Another way of stating almost the same thing is to use the modality necessary:

{[], user, necessary, [a = 1,b = 0,c = -4,a*x^2 + b*x + c = 0]}

meaning that "with no preconditions user is prepared to assert that it is necessary that a = 1,b = 0,c = -4,a*x^2 + b*x + c = 0 are conjointly true".

This now has the status of being universally true and has no preconditions attached to it, if anything whatsoever contradicts this statement then the contradictory statement is inconsistent with all possible worlds (necessary) leading from the empty set of preconditions and is therefore false or wrong.

The algebraic equation solver could take this information, and produce the following pair of statements:

{[a*x^2 + b*x + c = 0, a = 1, b = 0, c = -4], user, possible,[x = -2] }
{[a*x^2 + b*x + c = 0, a = 1, b = 0, c = -4], user, possible, [x = 2] }

Clearly, these assumptions are inconsistent, but at the moment each is equally valid. If we add the assumption:

{[], user, necessary, x > 0 }

$x = -2$ is not consistent with this information, and so any environment based on this new assumption must base its work upon $x = 2$ and not $x = -2$. As we made the statement "$x > 0$" necessarily true with no preconditions then the alternative value "$x=-2$" cannot exist in any possible world as it contradicts a statement which is true in all worlds. "$x = -2$" would still be a valid entry if we had made the statement:

{[], user, possible, x > 0 }

and may be of use in other contexts should we require them. Within an ATMS there is no reason to dispose of $x = -2$ or consider it to be redundant only because it is inconsistent with one possible view, however if x>0 were made a necessary fact and not an assumption, then we there would be no justification for keeping x=-2, and it would be lost.

Our communications protocol between elements of the system requires that each element be able to return not only the answer to a question but also the question itself, this ensures that any sub system capable of maintaining several contexts can insert the new fact into the correct context and can do so without creating an excessively large assumption base. We are therefore operating a need-to-know information system, if an explanation is required for any reason it is straightforward to request the complete justification path.

For example we may request an algebraic equation solver to start with $a*x^2 + b*x + c = 0$ and request an answer of the form:

x=?.

In a conventional single context system the algebraic equation solver might reply with:

x=2

which is a possible answer given suitable values for the coefficients. What we have hidden here is the work done by the algebraic equation solver in determining suitable coefficients and determining actual values for a, b and c. Clearly x=2 is always a possible answer but it is also possibly the least helpful of all.

The answer "x=2" could be transmitted around the system as

{[],possible,[x=2]}

meaning "with no preconditions a possible answer is **x=2**".

A much more helpful answer enabling the receiver to reconstruct the assumption bases would be

{[a*x^2 + b*x + c = 0],possible,[x=2]}

meaning "a possible solution to a*x^2 + b*x + c = 0 is x=2".

We are stating that x=2 is a possible solution to the quadratic equation as given however the equation solving system will have obtained values for a,b and c but has not been required to deliver the values and so can only give a possible answer. The set of answers in this case could be of the form:

{[a*x^2 + b*x + c = 0],possible,[x=2]}
{[a*x^2 + b*x + c = 0],possible,[x=-2]}

depending upon the various values of a,b and c whereas the second case would give us the contexts within which x could take on the various possible values.

We gain in representational efficiency in almost all cases, in our earlier example it was clear from how easily and quickly the assumption bases increase in size, however this result could be passed on to another agent as:

{[a*x^2 + b*x + c = 0],possible,[x=2]}
{[a*x^2 + b*x + c = 0],possible,[x=-2]}

and restored as truth maintained entities within that agent as

(1,[a*x^2 + b*x + c = 0], [[1]]).
(2,[x=2],[[1,2]]).
(3,[x=-2],[[1,3]]).

demonstrating a large economy of representation.

So far we have demonstrated how separation of truth maintenance systems may be achieved by delivering the essential justifications of consequences but eliminating much of the intermediate reasoning. The intermediate course of transmitting minimal justifications based on the belief that each subsystem can be relied on to produce reliable results but keeping sufficient contextual information for the subsequent reasoning to be justified allows both multiple context reasoning throughout the system and economical representation. This generally makes a substantial difference to the representation of a problem provided the paths branch out and subsequently come together. If the problem is partitioned to minimise inter agent communication, much the way as we would select entities in an entity relationship analysis (Chen 76) or select objects in an object oriented system (Booch 90) then we achieve the economy of representation outlined.

7 DECENTRALISATION

The method of organising such a system of collaborating truth maintenance systems as a set of objects is typically through a centralised message handler as in SmallTalk (Goldberg 84) and the

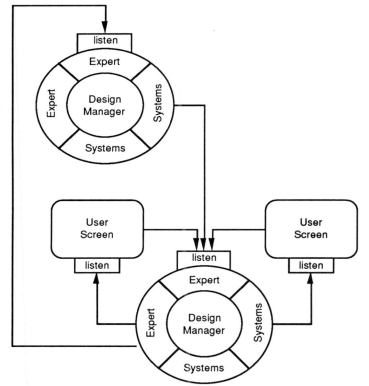

Figure 5. The system elements collaborate in a heterarchical fashion with no central control, this shows the presence of users integrated into the system having declared their interests to their collaborators and become part of the group as equal partners.

Design to Product Tool Manager (Burrow 89, Burrow & Hinde 90). Each of the elements in our system is based on a truth maintained architecture and is derived from the LUMP manufacturing planning system (Hinde et al. 89). Each element of this sort is therefore capable of acting as a central organising system treating all other agents as contributory engines that make bids to the blackboard manager for information and deliver justified entries to the truth maintained blackboard. Each element is also an object in the sense that it has an encapsulated data space which is truth maintained and responds to messages from other agents which see themselves as the centre of their own particular universe. The system can either be regarded as one with no centralised control or one with several centralised controllers, each blackboard can be independently scheduled and the flow of information round the system is essentially asynchronous. The elements all contain a management system and are extended by adding various knowledge sources to give tightly coupled computing ability or adding a standard communications interface to communicate with other system elements. Figure 5 shows a collection of elements, some computer based, but others as humans participating in the overall problem solving process as partners in a heterarchy. We introduce here the concept of a "problem centred" system rather than "human centred" or "computer centred" system. The users are assumed to be able to "keep their options open" and as such may be viewed as multiple context systems and as rational agents would therefore be "Truth Maintained".

As each element is "fired up" it announces its presence and functionality to other members of its "project" which it is designed to communicate with and they will then be able to ask it questions as and when required. The only concession to centralisation is a table containing the sets of declared functionality which each member, as it joins, will consult to be able to use correctly the already existing members of the project community.

8 COLLABORATION BETWEEN PROJECTS

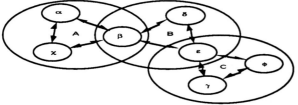

Figure 6. Projects are denoted by capital English letter whereas agents are denoted by small Greek letters. Agent α in project A may communicate with agent γ in project C by passing requests first to agent β in project B, who then passes the request to agent ϵ in project C who then finally makes a request to agent γ.

Each element of a collection of collaborating truth maintenance systems may be a member of one or more projects, a project is a collection of collaborating elements which have agreed to share resources by becoming members of a project community. Project communities may intersect and share agents which may declare a different functionality to each project thereby acting as a gateway between them. The gateway agents will tend to declare a wide ranging functionality and pass requests to other more specific members for consideration.

9 CONFIGURATION

All truth maintained agents within the system contain a private ATMS blackboard system and the basic means to interact with one another and so there is a common kernel to all agents. A particular set of "skills" may be attached to this kernel by loading various calculating engines to specialise the agent to its particular task. Although not all elements require the same set of skills most require the ability to solve simple algebraic equations and so there are other larger kernels which can form the basis of even larger agents. The line of inheritance takes on properties which allow the agent to perform various tasks and there is no barring or preclusion involved in the configuration stage (Touretzky 86). Although the inheritance is single line the possibility of one of the calculating engines delivering the wrong results contradicting results delivered by another engine is real, as it is with any large scale system, but causes no actual problems due to the multiple context nature of the system. Contradiction by one engine of another's results merely results in separate contexts being formed and so we are able to build in redundancy if required and to run two or more engines in parallel given they may implement different problem solving strategies. The freedom to contradict results allows two or more human users to work simultaneously on the same problem in different ways. Although we explicitly have single line inheritance the potential duplication of functionality means we have to cope with the problems of multiple inheritance, the use of an ATMS circumvents any serious problems.

10 SUMMARY

The paper has outlined some of the problems associated with concurrent engineering, notably the requirement that each element of the concurrent system has available not only the results of its computations but also a range of results which would generally be justified. A prototype system which takes parametrised geometrical forms and attaches manufacturing plans to them using the Taguchi system of quality engineering has been developed and implemented. This system has been separated into several sub systems responsible for various aspects of the overall problem solving demonstrating the increase in efficiency brought about by partitioning the problem.

11 REFERENCES

Booch, G., 1986, Object-Oriented Development, IEEE Trans. on Software Eng., Vol. SE12 No 2 Feb. 1986, pp. 211-221.

Bray, A.D., Hinde, C.J., Herbert, P.J., Temple, D.M. & Round, D. 1992, Multiple Context Planning within a Truth Maintenance System, Knowledge Based Systems, in press.

Bundy, A., Silver, B. and Plummer, D., 1985, An analytical comparison of some rule learning programs. Artificial Intelligence, Vol. 27, 1985, pp. 137-181.

Burrow, L.D., 1989, The Design to Product Alvey Demonstrator. I.C.L. Technical Journal, Vol.6 No. 3.

Burrow, L.D., & Hinde, C.J., 1990, Integrated Information Systems for Design and Manufacture, Business Benefits of Expert Systems, sponsored by the S.G.E.S., Sept. 1990.

Chen, P.P., 1976, The Entity-Relationship Model - Toward a Unified View of Data, ACM Trans. on Database Systems, Vol. 1, No. 1 March 1976, pp. 9-36.

Goldberg, A., 1984, SmallTalk-80: The Interactive Programming Environment , Addison-Wesley.

de Kleer, J., 1984, Choices without backtracking. Proceedings of the Conference of the American Association for Artificial Intelligence.

de Kleer, J., 1986a, An Assumption-based TMS. Artificial Intelligence Journal, Vol. 28, pp. 127-162.

de Kleer, J., 1986b, Extending the ATMS, Artificial Intelligence 28, pp. 163-196.

de Kleer, J., 1986c, Problem solving with the ATMS, Artificial Intelligence 28, pp. 197-224.

Doyle, J., 1979, A Truth Maintenance System, Artificial Intelligence Journal , Vol. 12, pp. 231-272.

Engelmore, R. & Morgan, A., 1988, Blackboard Systems, Addison-Wesley, London.

Herbert, P.J., Hinde, C.J., Bray, A.D., Launders, V.A., Round, D. & Temple, D.M., 1990, Feature Recognition Within a Truth Maintained Process Planning Environment, I.J.C.I.M. 3 No 2. Taylor & Francis.

Millington, K., 1990, Edinburgh Designer System. Business Benefits of Expert Systems, sponsored by the S.G.E.S., Sept. 1990.

Hinde, C.J., Bray, A.D., Herbert, P.J., Launders,V.A. & Round, D., 1989, A Truth Maintenance Approach to Process Planning. in ed. Rzevski, G., 1989, Artificial Intelligence in Manufacturing, Computational Mechanics Publications: Southampton Boston Springer-Verlag: Berlin Heidelberg New York London Paris Tokyo.pp 171-188.

Taguchi, G., Elsayed, E.A. & Hsian, G.T., 1989, Quality Engineering in Production Systems, McGraw-Hill.

Touretzky, D.S., 1986, The Mathematics of Inheritance Systems, Pitman Publishing Ltd., London.

OCKHAM'S RAZOR AS A GARDENING TOOL

Simplifying Discrimination Trees by Entropy MiniMax

Richard S. Forsyth,
　　　　Department of Mathematical Sciences
　　　　University of the West of England
　　　　Coldharbour Lane
　　　　BRISTOL　　BS16 1QY
　　　　+44 (0)272-656261
　　　　email: rs_forsyth@uk.ac.brispoly.cv

"Pruning is done to prevent over-crowding, for the health of the plant, to open up the lower branches to the light and to create space." -- Ashley Stephenson, The Garden Planner (1981).

Abstract: Discrimination or Classification Trees are a popular form of knowledge representation, and have even been used as the basis for expert systems. One reason for their popularity is that efficient algorithms exist for inducing such trees automatically from sample data (Brieman et al., 1984; Quinlan, 1986). However, it is widely recognized among machine-learning researchers that trees derived from noisy or inconclusive data sets tend to be over-complex. This unnecessary complexity renders them hard to interpret and typically degrades their performance on unseen test cases. The present paper introduces a measure of tree quality, and an associated tree pruning technique, based on the minimum-message-length (MML) criterion (Wallace & Freeman, 1987; Wolff, 1991). Empirical trials with a variety of data sets indicate that it achieves greater than 80% reduction in tree size, coupled with a slight improvement in accuracy in classifying unseen test cases, thus comparing favourably with alternative simplification strategies. Moreover, it is simpler that previously published pruning techniques, even those based on the MML principle such as that of Quinlan & Rivest (1989).

Keywords: Machine Learning, Data Compression, Inductive Inference, Information Theory, Entropy Minimax, Classification Algorithms, Discrimination Trees.

1. INTRODUCTION

One reason for the popularity of discrimination trees (also known as decision trees) for representing knowledge is that they are relatively easy to understand. The example tree in Figure 1, for discriminating between aquatic and non-aquatic species of animal, should illustrate this point.

[Figure 1 -- Aquatic versus Non-Aquatic Animals.]

Another reason for the popularity of such trees is that several induction algorithms exist for generating them from example data. Of these, the best known is Quinlan's ID3 (Quinlan, 1979) which is one of the most popular machine-learning algorithms. However, when applied to noisy data it tends to generate large, complex discrimination trees that fit the training instances well but generalize poorly to unseen cases. This problem (not unique to ID3) has been called "the cancerous problem of contrivedness" (Christensen, 1980) but is more usually known as <u>overfitting</u>.

To reduce the risk of overfitting, modern versions of ID3, and similar algorithms, generally incorporate <u>tree-pruning</u> or simplification mechanisms. Simplification can be achieved either by halting the tree-growing process early (<u>pre-pruning</u>) or by growing the tree to its full extent and then cutting off branches which cover too few training instances to be statistically reliable (<u>post-pruning</u>). It is generally found that post-pruning is preferable to pre-pruning (Niblett, 1987), since it partly compensates for the fact that the ID3 algorithm does no explicit look-ahead.

Several different methods of post-pruning have been proposed.

Brieman et al. (1984) have developed a technique known as cost-complexity pruning which attempts to find a near-optimal compromise between the complexity of the decision tree and its accuracy by using the statistical technique of cross-validation (Stone, 1977). It is a practically effective but computationally very expensive technique.

Niblett (1987) has investigated ways of minimizing the expected classification error-rate of a decision tree on future cases, without reference to the complexity of the tree. This entails using a more realistic error estimate, the Laplacian error estimate, than that provided by resubstitution of the training data. It normally also leads to a simplification of the fully grown tree.

Quinlan (1986, 1987) has compared several statistically based pruning methods, as well as a method which involves translating the decision tree into a set of production rules.

Most of these methods have been found to give better predictive results on noisy data sets than using the unmodified ID3 algorithm; thus, in pragmatic terms, the problem of overfitted decision trees can be regarded as solved. Nevertheless, recent work in this area (e.g. Quinlan & Rivest, 1989) continues in an attempt to find tree pruning methods with a sounder theoretical basis.

2. LEARNING AS DATA COMPRESSION

This approach draws on a long tradition in cognitive science which emphasizes the principle of information economy, an idea that was fashionable a generation ago (e.g. Quastler, 1956; Attneave, 1959; Edwards, 1964) but which subsequently fell from favour.

Recently, however, this idea has been revived as the minimum-message-length (MML) criterion (Rissanen, 1987; Wallace & Freeman, 1987; Cheeseman, 1990). This paper uses the related terminology of Wolff (1982, 1988) who used essentially the same principle as the basis of a grammatical induction program called SNPR. A key feature of SNPR is that it is able to correct overgeneralized rules without the need for explicit error-correcting feedback in the form of counter-examples because it is always seeking the most economical description of its input data.

Briefly, Wolff's system seeks the most efficient grammar for describing a body of text. The efficiency of a grammar (e_g) with reference to a particular text corpus is:

$$e_g = (s_r - s_c) / s_g \qquad [1]$$

where s_r is the size, in bits, of the raw text, s_c is the size, in bits, of the text after encoding by the grammar and s_g is the size of the grammar itself, again measured in bits.

Learning a grammar is thus viewed as a data-compression task. Given two grammars of equal size the one which achieves greater compression when applied to the training text is preferred. Likewise, given two grammars capable of making equivalent savings by encoding the training data, the smaller is preferred. (For further elaboration of these ideas, see Wolff, 1991.)

3. A METHOD OF TREE-COMPRESSION

The present study approaches the tree-simplification problem in a similar manner, by treating it as a data-description task in which the discrimination tree plays a role analogous to the grammar in Wolff's system. The objective is then to find the tree that allows greatest compression of the training data relative to its own size.

In order to quantify this objective, a measure of tree quality is needed which takes into account both the complexity of the tree and of the savings it achieves in encoding the training data. Information theory (Shannon & Weaver, 1949) is used here as the basis for such a measure which, for computational convenience, is expressed as a cost to be minimized rather than a figure of merit to be maximized.

3.1 A Measure of Tree-Quality

The cost of a tree is computed as the sum of the costs attached to all its leaf nodes:

$$\text{cost(Tree)} = \Sigma \, \text{cost(node}_i) \qquad [2].$$

The cost of each leaf node has two components, the cost attributable to the node itself and the cost of the subset of training cases it classifies (assuming optimal encoding):

$$\text{cost(node}_i) = d_i + e_i * n_i \qquad\qquad [3]$$

where

    d_i is the depth of the node concerned, i.e. the number of steps down
              from the root of the tree;
    e_i is the average entropy of the outcome data at that node;
    n_i is the number of cases sorted to that node.

The depth of a node (d_i) provides a good measure of its cost because the tree-pruning program described herein (TREEMIN) at present deals only with binary decision trees. Hence to reach a node at depth d implies that d binary choices have been made. This one-off cost is incurred by having that node in the (notional) alphabet of symbols used to encode the training data and is set against any savings that can be achieved by using that node to compress the data.

The second component of the cost function

$$e_i * n_i$$

uses standard information-theoretic principles (Abramson, 1963) to calculate the cost, in bits, of an optimal Huffman coding of the outcome data from the frequencies positive and negative instances that reach node_i.

Once again, use is made of the fact that TREEMIN deals only with two-choice outcomes (though extension to multiple categories poses no problem in principle) so that

$$e_i = -(p*\log(p) + (1-p)*\log(1-p)) \qquad\qquad [4]$$

where p is the proportion of positive instances falling into node_i and logarithms are to the base 2. (Note that $0*\log(0)$ is defined to equal 0.)

To sum up, the tree is viewed as an encoding scheme and its cost computed as the sum of its own size plus the size of the encoded outcome data. Both the size of the tree and the size of the encoded data are measured in a 'common currency', namely information-theoretic bits.

3.2 A Tree Optimization Procedure

Given a suitable cost measure, the tree optimization procedure becomes relatively straightforward.

The TREEMIN program reads in an unpruned tree and assigns a static value to every node, including non-terminal nodes. This is calculated from formula [3] by treating each node as if it were a leaf node.

Then a dynamic value is assigned to each node by summing the best values of its subnodes (i.e. the lesser of their static or dynamic values) using a recursive procedure. Leaf nodes have no subnodes, so their dynamic values are equal to their static values.

Next the program scans the tree, seeking non-terminal nodes whose static values are less than or equal to their dynamic values. Such nodes are made into leaf nodes by cutting off their descendant branches, as these descendants do not improve the quality of the tree. (Note: as presently implemented, the program never allows deletion of the root node.) Finally the pruned tree is printed out in a suitable format.

The tree produced by this procedure is an optimal abbreviation of the original tree (with respect to the cost function employed). It does not follow, however, that it is the optimum tree obtainable from the same data, since TREEMIN, like most such programs, does not attempt to rearrange the order of nodes.

4. EMPIRICAL TRIALS

TREEMIN has been tested empirically by comparing its results with three other commonly used methods of tree-pruning on a number of test data sets. These data sets are briefly described below.

4.1 Test Data-Sets

1. QUIN : This is an artificial data-set designed to model a task in which only probabilistic classification is possible and which contains disjunctions. It is effectively the same as Quinlan's "Prob-Disj" data-set (Quinlan, 1987) and consists of ten random binary variables (v1 to v10). The outcome (Y or N) or each case is assigned according to the conditional expression:
>   IF v1 & v2 & v3
>   OR v4 & v5 & v6
>   OR v7 & v8 & v9
>   THEN outcome = Y (prob=0.9), outcome = N (prob=0.1)
>   ELSE outcome = Y (prob=0.1), outcome = N (prob=0.9).

One attribute, v10, is irrelevant. A training set of 400 cases and a test-set of 200 cases were generated.

2. RAND : This is simply a random data set containing twelve random binary variables plus a target variable which is 1 in approximately 50% of the cases and 0 in the other 50%. A training set of 255 instances and a test set of 100 training instances were used.

3. DIGIDAT : This example is essentially the same as that used by Brieman et al. (1984) as a test case. Each data record is generated by simulating a faulty Liquid Crystal Display in which digits are displayed by setting bars on or off. There are seven bars, each of which can be on or off. A training file of 359 examples and a test set of 642 examples was used, in which every bar had a 0.1 probability of being in error -- either on when it should have been off or vice versa. In addition, four spurious fields, containing purely random data, were included with each case. Here the binary decision task given to the tree-growing program was to distinguish 8's and 9's from the other numerals.

4. ZOOBASE : The fourth data-set contains details of 101 animal species. Each is described in terms of 18 attributes such as the number of legs it has and whether it gives milk to its young. The data was randomly split into a training set of 51 records and a test set containing the remaining 50 cases. The learning task for the system was to induce a rule for distinguishing aquatic from land-living creatures. This data has been more fully described elsewhere (Forsyth, 1990).

5. CARDIAC : The fifth data-set was taken from Afifi & Azen (1979). It describes 113 critically ill patients brought into a hospital in Los Angeles. Attributes measured for each patient on admission include systolic pressure, mean arterial pressure, heart rate and shock-type (a categorical variable). Here the classification task is to discriminate the patients who survived from those that died. For the present trial this data was randomly divided into a training set of 69 cases and a test set of 44 cases.

6. GRANDEE : The sixth data-set contained details of the horses taking part in the Grand National steeplechase (held at Liverpool every year) in the years 1987 to 1992 inclusive. Each horse was described in terms of a number of variables, such as betting odds, age, longest winning distance, weight carried etc. Only the first 24 horses in racecard order were included, as horses lower down the handicap very rarely finish in the first four. This data was divided chronologically rather than randomly: the years 1987 to 1989 formed a training set of 72 cases; the years 1990 to 1992 formed the test set, also of 72 cases. The objective here was to form a tree that would distinguish horses that completed the course from those that failed to finish. (70 of the 144 horses in the total data-set did manage to finish the course.)

7. MELANOMA : The final data-set was obtained from Frenchay Hospital, Bristol, as part of a long-term study of patients with Melanoma, a dangerous form of skin cancer that has become increasingly prevalent in Britain in recent years. Details of 307 patients were used for the present trial, measured on such variables as age-at-presentation, sex, thickness of tumour, site of tumour and so on. The objective here was to find a tree that would distinguish patients who were still alive five years after surgery from those that died within five years. Training was done on a random subset of 199 cases and testing on the remaining 108.

4.2 Results

On each data-set, the basic ID3 algorithm was used to produce an unpruned discrimination tree, then four different simplification strategies were employed.

Method 1 : Prune backwards from leaf nodes till a node is reached such that the Chi-squared statistic (Siegel & Castellan, 1988) at that node has a probability of less than 0.05 under the null hypothesis -- i.e. prune backwards to the 95% confidence level.

Method 2 : As Method 1 but pruning back till the value of Chi-squared has a probability of less than 0.01 -- i.e. prune back to the 99% confidence level.

Method 3 : Prune the tree as described in section 3.2 but using the Laplacian error-rate as the quantity to be minimized (rather than coding cost). In two-outcome tasks, the Laplacian error rate (Le_i) of a node (assuming prior ignorance in a Bayesian sense) is

$$Le_i = (1 + min(y,n)) / (y + n + 2) \qquad [5]$$

where y is the number of positive exemplars and n the number of negative exemplars found at that node.

Method 4 : Prune the tree to minimize the overall coding cost as described in sections 3.1 and 3.2 (MinCost pruning).

[Table 1 -- Number of Leaf Nodes.]

Data Set	Original Tree	95% C.I.	99% C.I.	Laplace	MinCost
QUIN	50	19	12	40	10
RAND	68	7	2	62	3
DIGIDAT	37	9	6	12	7
ZOOBASE	6	3	3	3	3
CARDIAC	11	4	3	10	4
GRANDEE	10	4	2	6	4
MELANOMA	26	16	7	22	7
Sums :	208	62	35	155	38
Saving %	0	70.19	83.17	25.48	81.73

Table 1 shows the sizes of the decision trees produced on each of the four data sets by the various methods. Clearly all the pruning methods do reduce the number of terminal nodes.

Table 2 lists the percentage error rates obtained when using the pruned and unpruned trees on the corresponding test data. Percentage error rate is a simple but reasonably sensitive index of predictive accuracy.

The figures show that simplification is **not** normally bought at the expense of accuracy.

[Table 2 -- Percentage Error Rates on Unseen Data.]

Data Set	Original Tree	95% C.I.	99% C.I.	Laplace	MinCost
QUIN	16.5	18.5	15.5	15.5	16.5
RAND	55	47	47	55	43
DIGIDAT	15.11	11.68	11.68	12.3	11.68
ZOOBASE	16	14	14	14	14
CARDIAC	25	29.55	29.55	25	29.55
GRANDEE	38.89	34.72	40.28	38.89	34.72
MELANOMA	40.74	41.67	37.04	42.59	35.19
Mean :	29.61	28.16	27.86	29.04	26.38

Clearly all the pruning methods tested achieve significant simplifications coupled, on the whole, with improved classification accuracy on unseen data. This agrees with the findings of earlier studies (e.g. Clark & Niblett, 1987; Quinlan, 1987).

Benchmarking exercises such as the present one can never be conclusive, but these figures do suggest that:

(1) the MinCost method is a viable methods of tree simplification; and
(2) the Laplacian error estimate, at least in its basic form, gives poor results.

5. CONCLUSIONS

The BitCost measure used by TREEMIN is based on a very simple model of descriptive parsimony. Essentially it states that a leaf node in a decision tree can only justify its existence if the number of bits required to specify that node is balanced by an equivalent reduction in the number of bits required to specify the outcome data which arrive at that node.

Given its simplicity, the performance of this model on test data is quite impressive. The empirical results on these medium-sized data sets are consistent with the view that minimizing this measure of coding cost (as proposed in sections 3.1 and 3.2) gives decision trees that are at least as good as, and possibly better than, pruning to the 99% confidence level. This lends support, at least indirectly, to Wolff's SP theory (Wolff, 1991) from which our model was derived.

A notable coup for the MinCost method was its performance on the random data set. In theory, optimal pruning should leave only a single node, the root, with this data. MinCost pruning reduced this tree from 68 to 3 leaf nodes (one more than pruning to the 99% confidence level). However, its performance in classifying the test data was actually better than chance and better than that of the other methods. The explanation for this seems to be that it managed to exploit a minor flaw in the random number generator used to create the data. One could hardly ask for more from an inductive technique than that it should find a hidden regularity that is not even supposed to exist.

5.1 Advantages of MinCost Pruning

TREEMIN's method of tree pruning appears to have certain advantages over previously published techniques.

    1. It is easy to compute.

    2. It uses all the data (unlike cross-validation, which requires splitting the full dataset into two or more sets).

    3. It does not need any 'fiddle factors' such as coefficients weighting tree-size against error-rate, or even the setting of an arbitrary conventional significance level (e.g. 5% versus 1% significance level).

    4. It does not depend on any assumptions from sampling theory such as Gaussian noise distribution nor does it attempt to estimate population parameters such as mean or standard deviation.

    5. It does not depend on anyone's skill at encoding an **actual** tree, but rather uses an ideal or limit-case measure of tree-size.

In the first and last points above the present work differs from recent work based on the MML (Minimum Message Length) principle, e.g. that of Quinlan & Rivest (1989).

Although set within a data-compression context and inspired in particular by Wolff's work on information economy, TREEMIN effectively performs a different size-vs-fit trade-off from other similar systems. Rather than explicitly balancing the cost of sending the tree down some imaginary communication channel against the information gained about the dependent variable by using that tree, TREEMIN implicitly balances the cost of the information used about the independent variables (in feature space) against the information gained about the dependent variable.

5.2 Discussion

This paper has presented an information theoretic model (the MinCost model) and an associated quality function (the BitCost measure) for the task of decision-tree simplification. The results of using the model and its associated quality measure on several test problems are promising enough to warrant further investigation.

As has been pointed out:

"the predictive promise of a [tree] depends on the apparent error-rate of the tree and on the size of the tree. These criteria work in opposite directions, and the problem is that there is no obvious a priori method of establishing the correct trade-off between them." (Watkins, 1987.)

Most previous methods of establishing the complexity-versus-accuracy trade-off have indeed been somewhat ad hoc, but it is the contention of the present paper that -- by setting the induction task within an entropy-minimaxing framework -- a rational measure of tree quality can be obtained using information theory.

If this contention is correct, we are not confined merely to the pruning of decision trees. We can easily apply a similar logic to the pruning of regression trees. Indeed a general quality measure would apply to other formalisms (such as production rules) created by other algorithms (such as simulated annealing).

For example, it should be possible to adapt this approach to another of the guises in which the complexity-vs-accuracy trade-off crops up, namely the problem of correctly 'sizing' a neural network. It would be especially interesting to attempt to apply the MinCost model to the Upstart Algorithm (Frean, 1990), which dynamically extends a network of Perceptron-type linear threshold units as learning proceeds, resulting in a hierarchical structure rather like an ID3 decision tree.

Undoubtedly the MinCost model is not the last word on this subject, but it does represent a modest contribution to the ongoing philosophical debate on induction, since it provides a practical implementation of the principle of scientific parsimony known as Ockham's Razor, in honour of the 14th-century philosopher William of Ockham, who stated that entities should not be multiplied without need.

A modern enunciation of this principle is Wittgenstein's dictum that:

"the procedure of induction consists in accepting as true the simplest law that can be reconciled with our experiences" (Wittgenstein, 1961).

Though widely accepted, this maxim is somewhat ill-defined. Philosophers of science have argued at length over the meanings of its two key terms: (a) simplicity and (b) compatibility with the facts (Popper, 1959, 1980; Katz, 1962). One merit of the present work is that it provides a relatively straighforward operational measure of these two key terms, within the framework of information theory.

Acknowledgements

Part of the development of TREEMIN, and associated software, was supported by the UK Transport and Road Research Laboratory under contract ref. BIX-516. The author would also like to express thanks to Bridget Broggio, David Clarke, Dave Elliman, James Higgs, Dean McKenzie, Gerry Wolff and Richard Wright for helpful comments and suggestions.

References

Abramson, N. (1963) -- Information theory and coding: McGraw-Hill, New York.

Afifi, A.A. & Azen, S.P. (1979) -- Statistical analysis: a computer oriented approach, 2nd ed.: Academic Press, New York.

Attneave, F. (1959) -- Applications of information theory to psychology: Holt, New York.

Brieman, L., Friedman, J.H., Olshen, R.A. & Stone, C.J. (1984) -- Classification and regression trees: Wadsworth, Calif.

Cheeseman, P. (1990) -- The minimum message length criterion. In J. Shrager & P. Langley (eds.) Computational models of scientific discovery & theory formation: Morgan Kaufmann, San Mateo, CA.

Christensen, R. (1980) -- Entropy minimax sourcebook, vol 3: Entropy Ltd., Lincoln, Mass.

Clark, P. & Niblett, T. (1987) -- Induction in noisy domains. In: I. Bratko & N. Lavrac (eds.) Progress in machine learning: Sigma Technical Press, Wilmslow, Cheshire, pp. 11-30.

Edwards, E. (1964) -- Information transmission: Chapman & Hall Ltd., London.

Forsyth, R.S. (1990) -- Neural learning algorithms: some empirical trials: Proc. 3rd Int. Conf. on neural nets & their applications (Neuro-Nîmes-90): EC2, Nanterre, pp. 301-317.

Frean, M. (1990) -- The Upstart algorithm: a method for constructing & training feedforward neural networks: Neural Computation, 2, pp. 198-209.

Katz, J.J. (1962) -- The problem of induction and its solution: Univ. Chicago Press, Illinois.

Niblett, T. (1987) -- Constructing decision trees in noisy domains. In: I. Bratko & N. Lavrac (eds.) Progress in machine learning: Sigma Technical Press, Wilmslow, Cheshire, pp. 67-78.

Popper, K.R. (1959, 1980) -- The logic of scientific discovery: Hutchinson, London. (1st German edition, 1935.)

Quastler, H. (1956) -- Information theory in psychology: Free Press of Glencoe, New York.

Quinlan, J.R. (1979) -- Discovering rules by induction from large collections of examples. In: D. Michie (ed.) Expert systems in the micro-electronic age: Edinburgh University Press, pp. 168-201.

Quinlan, J.R. (1986) -- Induction of decision trees: Machine learning, 1, pp. 81-106.

Quinlan, J.R. (1987) -- Simplifying decision trees: Int. J. man-machine studies, 27, pp. 221-234.

Quinlan, J.R. & Rivest, R.L. (1989) -- Inferring decision trees using the minimum description length principle: Information & Computation, 80, pp. 227-248.

Rissanen, J. (1987) -- Stochastic complexity: J. Royal Statistical Soc. (B), 49, 3, pp. 223-239.

Shannon, C. & Weaver, W. (1949) -- The mathematical theory of communication: U. Illinois Press, Urbana.

Siegel, S. & Casetllan, N.J. (1988) -- Nonparametric Statistics, 2nd ed.: McGraw-Hill, New York.

Stephenson, A. (1981) -- The garden planner: Book Club Associates, London.

Stone, M. (1977) -- Cross-validation: a review: Math. operationforsch. statist. ser. statist., 9, pp. 127-139.

Wallace, C.S. & Freeman, P.R. (1987) -- Estimation and inference by compact coding: J. Royal Statistical Soc. (B), 49, pp. 240-265.

Watkins, C.J.C.H. (1987) -- Combining cross-validation and search. In: I. Bratko & N. Lavrac (eds.) Progress in machine learning: Sigma Technical Press, Wilmslow, pp. 79-87.

Wittgenstein, L. (1961) -- Tractatus logico-philosophicus: Routledge & Kegan Paul Ltd., London (tr. by Pears & McGuinness).

Wolff, J.G. (1982) -- Language acquisition, data compression and generalization: Language & communication, 2(1), pp. 57-89.

Wolff, J,G. (1988) -- Learning syntax and meanings through optimization and distributional analysis. In: Y. Levy, I.M. Schlessinger & M.D.S. Braine (eds.) Categories and processes in language acquisition: Lawrence Erlbaum, New York, pp. 179-215.

Wolff, J.G. (1991) -- Towards a theory of cognition and computing: Ellis Horwood, Chichester.

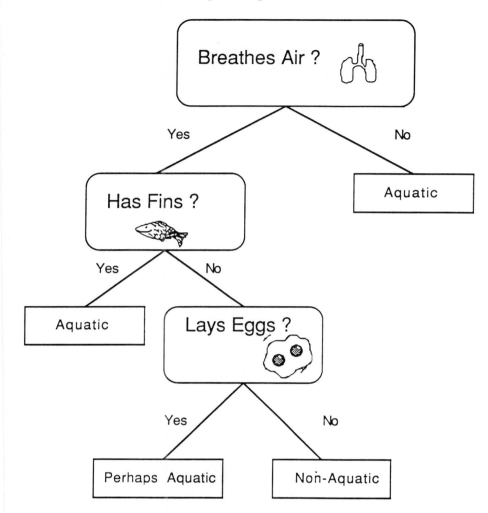

Figure 1 -- Example Decision Tree :
Aquatic versus Non-Aquatic
Animals.

A Designer's Consultant

J.W. Brahan, B. Farley, R.A. Orchard, A. Parent, C.S. Phan

Institute for Information Technology
National Research Council
Ottawa Canada K1A 0R6
jack@ai.iit.nrc.ca

Abstract

Most expert systems perform a task on behalf of the user. The task usually involves gathering and analyzing data, and recommending or initiating the appropriate action. However, expert systems can also play an important role in showing the user how to perform a task. In this role, the expert system provides support until it eventually becomes of decreasing importance as its knowledge base is transferred to the user. This category includes Help Systems, Coaching Systems, and Tutorial Systems. In this paper, we discuss the development of an Intelligent Advisor combining the three functions in a system to assist the user in acquiring and refining the knowledge required to carry out a design task. The combined system provides a means of introducing a training facility as an integral part of the work environment. The primary goal of our project is the creation of a system in which the generic advisor components are identified along with the methodology required to adapt them to specific applications. The conceptual modelling phase of database design was chosen as the application domain to develop the system and to demonstrate feasibility. An initial prototype has been implemented, which illustrates the operation of the system in each of the three modes as applied to database modelling. The technology is currently being extended to a second application domain.

1 Introduction

ERMA (Entity-Relationship Modelling Advisor) is a knowledge-based system that serves as a consultant to the user of a computer-based design tool, providing advice as required. While most expert systems carry out a task on behalf of the user, ERMA shows the user how to perform a task. Its underlying goal is to transfer to the user those parts of its knowledge base that respond to needs identified from user questions and user problems encountered in interacting with the design tool. It provides support until it eventually becomes of decreased importance as its knowledge

NRCC33234

is transferred. Common types of systems that are concerned with knowledge transfer
are Help Systems (Breuker, 1990), Coaching Systems (Burton and Brown, 1979),
and Tutorial Systems (Clancey, 1986). In this paper, we address the topic of an
Intelligent Advisor, that combines these three functions to support the acquisition
of knowledge adapted to the needs of the individual user. ERMA was developed
within the framework of an Intelligent Advisor Project that involved the collaboration
of the National Research Council, Laval University, the University of Leeds, and
Systemoid Ltée[1]. The primary goal of this project was the creation of a system
in which the generic advisor components are identified along with the methodology
required to adapt them to specific applications. The conceptual modelling phase of
database design was chosen as the application domain and an initial prototype has
been implemented to demonstrate feasibility.

2 System Functionality

The Intelligent Advisor serves as an interface between the user and an interactive
computer system. It is aimed primarily at facilitating use of those systems, such as
engineering design tools, where knowledge of the application domain is a prerequisite
to using the tool effectively. This knowledge is not part of the tool, but is expertise
that the user must bring to the interaction. The Intelligent Advisor is intended
to serve users who possess skill levels in the application domain that extend from
neophyte to experienced user. Three main functions are provided. In a reactive
mode, the Advisor provides help in response to the user's questions. The help that
is given must be directly related to the user's indicated need and must be effective
in helping the user get on with the task at hand. In a proactive mode, the Advisor
observes the user's interaction with the system and offers advice aimed at helping
the user achieve his or her desired goals more effectively. The third role is that of
a tutor. Using an apprenticeship-based approach, the tutor uses pre-solved design
cases and builds on the reactive and proactive functionalities to introduce the user to
the domain concepts and design methodology necessary to apply the design tool.

3 Knowledge Acquisition

Development of an Advisor with the desired functionality requires knowledge of the
application domain. It also requires a knowledge of the communication protocols
governing the interchange between a user and an advisor. For example: what types
of questions are asked by the user? what answers are given by an expert advisor?
what is the nature of the dialogue that takes place between user and advisor to
clarify questions and answers? To address the requirement for knowledge governing
the communication protocols, a series of simulations were run. User and expert were
placed in separate rooms. The user was assigned the task of producing a conceptual

---

[1]Succeeded by CSA Recherche Ltée

data model using the Silverrun-ERM design tool (Modell, 1989). The user was shown how to use the design tool and how to communicate with the expert through his workstation. He was instructed to ask questions when in difficulty or in doubt and to express his thoughts aloud so that they could be recorded. The expert advisor could observe the user's conceptual model on a reproduction of the user's screen and could communicate with the user via his terminal. Six subjects participated in the study. Four had little or no formal training and little or no relevant experience in data modelling. Two subjects were experienced data modellers. The task consisted of designing a conceptual data model for an Unsatisfactory Condition Report (UCR) Management System for use within the Department of National Defence. (The UCR is a formal report used to record problems with materiel and related procedural matters.) An initial, incomplete model was given to the user to make the task easier.

A process adapted from Dialogue Game Theory was applied to analyze the collected protocols (Levin and Moore, 1977). A classification scheme was based on the analysis of a single subject representative of the primary target users of the system: an analyst with little formal training and limited experience in conceptual data modelling but a good knowledge of the application domain. The approach was developed and applied to the first subject in collaboration with the Computer-Based Learning Unit at the University of Leeds and subsequently completed at the National Research Council using the data from the five remaining subjects. Results of the analysis provided question and response typologies on which the reactive help function of the Advisor is based. The protocol analysis has identified 12 types of questions that a user might ask. The examples presented in Table 1 are drawn from the entity-relationship modelling domain. However, the question types are believed to be sufficiently general to apply to any design application involving concepts, objects associated with those concepts, and actions or tasks to manipulate the concepts and objects.

4 The Design Tool

For the simulation experiment, a commercial CASE tool, Silverrun-ERM was used. This is a graphics tool designed for the preparation of the conceptual design of a database based on the entity-relationship model. The tool is essentially a mechanism for creating a dictionary of objects to be defined and manipulated through a graphics interface. It was provided by Systemoid Ltd. who also made the modifications to the tool necessary to link it to the NRC program that provided the communication between the user and advisor in the simulation. However, the complete communication support required between the CASE tool and Advisor could not be accurately defined early in the project. With the constraints on changes to a commercial software product, it was decided that a CASE tool emulator would have to be built to achieve the necessary flexibility. The HyperNeWS system (van Hoff, 1989), which was used for the Advisor interface, incorporated a fairly powerful drawing tool. This provided a convenient mechanism for development of the required CASE tool emulator.

Table 1. Types of Questions

Question Type	Description	Example
1. General Elaboration	Request for information on a concept of the design domain or the domain to which it is applied. The expected answer is a description of the concept tailored according to the system's assessment of the user's knowledge.	Tell me about entities.
2. Specific Elaboration	Request for information on a specific aspect of a concept	What is the purpose of cardinalities
3. Validation of the Current Model	Request to check that an object in the user's design is valid. i.e. Does the object fulfil the purpose of its conceptual type? Does its value reflect the user's intended meaning?	Check the validity of the minimum cardinality between the entity *professor* and the relationship *teach*.
4. Validation of a Future Model	Request to check the validity of a proposed action to modify the current model, such as creating a new object or changing a value.	Should I create the relationship *registration*?
5. Validation of a Future Model — Alternative actions	Request to be told which of two different actions would be more appropriate.	Should I assign the attribute *date* to the entity *course* or to the relationship *registration*?
6. Enablement — Decision about taking an action	Request for information on the conditions and/or rules that determine if a given action should be carried out.	How do I decide if I should create an entity?
7. Enablement — Decision about taking alternative actions	Request for information on the conditions and/or rules that determine which of two different actions should be carried out.	How do I decide whether I should create an entity or create a relationship?
8. Enablement — Decision about names and values	Request for information on the conditions and/or rules that govern the value to which an attribute is set or the name that should be assigned an object.	How do I decide on the value of the maximum cardinality of a link between an entity and a relationship? How do I decide on the name of an entity?
9. Enablement — Decision about time of an action	Request for information on the conditions and/or rules that determine when a given action should be carried out.	When should I set the cardinalities?
10. Enablement — Performing an action	Request for information on the conditions and/or rules that govern the execution of a given action.	How can I represent the triple *professor – teaches – courses*?
11. Value Assignment	Request to be told the value that should be assigned an attribute of a given object.	What value should I give to the minimum cardinality of the link between the entity *professor* and the relationship *teaches*?
12. Knowledge Base Content Query	Request for information on the contents of the knowledge base in terms of concepts, tasks, or constraints.	Give me a list of all concepts that apply to entity-relationship modelling.

5 System Architecture

The system, illustrated in Figure 1, consists of three primary modules corresponding to the three Advisor functions: Proactive Help, Reactive Help, and Tutorial. These primary modules are supported by the Design Knowledge Base and two data modules: the Data Model and the User Model. The Data Model, which is maintained by a session monitor within the Advisor-side Interface unit, represents the conceptual model design that is being created by the user. The User Model, which is maintained by the User Modeller, provides an estimate of the user's knowledge of conceptual modelling tasks and concepts.

Communication between the Advisor and the computer-based design tool is through the Advisor-Tool Interface. It consists of two components: the Tool-Side Interface and the Advisor-Side Interface. The Tool-Side Interface transmits the user's operations on the design tool to the Advisor and forwards requests from the Advisor to the design tool. The Advisor-Side Interface monitors the user design operations in order to maintain an internal copy of the data model created by the user. When a user operation is identified, this module sends a message to the System Scheduler to be forwarded to other modules of the Advisor for appropriate actions. The Scheduler coordinates the invocation of the Tutor, the Help Modules, and the User Modeller in response to user operations. Interactions between the user and the Advisor are through the User Interface Module.

The prototype Advisor is implemented in Common Lisp on a Sun SPARCstation using HyperNeWS 1.4 for the graphics interface. Currently under consideration is the transfer of the implementation to a PC platform and the X-Window environment.

6 Knowledge Representation

The knowledge that is used by the Proactive Help Module for constraint checking and rule or plan detection is primarily of a procedural nature, as is the knowledge used by the Tutorial Module. However, the knowledge used by the Reactive Help Module for answer generation is primarily of a declarative nature. Moreover, in order for the answerer to manipulate the static knowledge in an effective and efficient manner, the knowledge elements need to be structured and linked by various kinds of relations to form semantic networks. Given these mixed requirements, a frame-based representation offers many advantages. Knowledge elements can be structured easily with frames and they can be linked by relations to form networks. Procedural knowledge can be conveniently coded as slot values to be executed by external interpreters. The Advisor frame representation is implemented in Common Lisp. Each frame is a data structure consisting of a set of slots and a set of values for each slot. There are two types of slots. Attribute slots are used to store descriptive information. Relation slots are used to define linkage between frames. The frame system allows demons to be

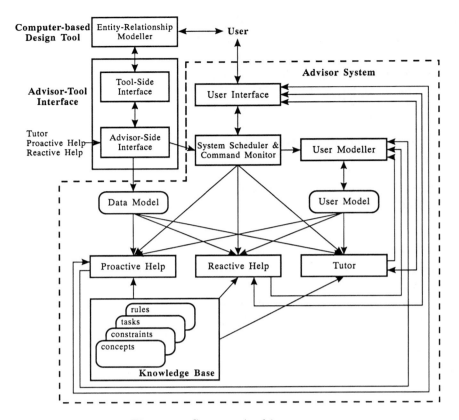

Figure 1: System Architecture

defined and attached to slots to take appropriate action when the value of the slot is changed.

The relation feature of the frame system permits the establishment of inheritance hierarchies through which information about an ancestor is inherited by its descendants if the information is not defined locally in the descendant frames. In the Advisor knowledge base, this feature is used, for example, to establish specialization and generalization relations between concepts. Any relation can be defined to have an inverse relation. This feature is used throughout the Advisor's knowledge base and the inverse linkages are automatically created and maintained by the system.

Four types of knowledge elements are identified: concepts, constraints, tasks, and rules of good practice. Concepts are generally referred to as the *what is* type knowledge. They are the basic elements of knowledge that one has to understand in order to perform a design task effectively. Examples of concepts are entity, relationship, and cardinality. Constraints, in general, are conditions that must be satisfied or validated during various stages of a design process. Three types of constraints are identified:

value constraints, constituent constraints, and validity constraints. *The maximum cardinality must be greater than zero* is an example of value constraint type. Tasks are design steps to achieve specific goals. For example, *creating entity-set* is a task, or design step, with its obvious goal of creating an entity set. A task can be primitive or composite. A primitive task is one that requires no other tasks to achieve its goal. This collection of tasks corresponds to the set of the primitive design operations such as creating entity-set, making attribute link. A composite task, on the other hand, is one that consists of some group of tasks to be carried out in a certain order to achieve the intended goal. Rules of good practice are the heuristics that an expert uses to achieve a better design or to do his or her design more efficiently. *Cardinalities should be defined immediately after an entity relation link is made* is an example of a rule of good practice.

7 User Model

The User Model provides information relating to the user's knowledge of the application domain based on the history of his or her interaction with the system. Its purpose is to support the adaptation of the system's response and interventions towards matching the requirements of the individual user. Data are gathered as the user performs tasks using the design tool, requests help, and violates design constraints. The content of the user model as implemented in the prototype is based on the analysis of the dialogue protocols gathered during the previously described simulation experiments. Each answer or dialogue episode was described in relation to a set of variables relevant to the experts choice of content and organization. The variables found to be of significance include the following:

- User beliefs in respect to concepts and tasks.

- Previous questions asked by the user.

- Results of requests to validate the user's conceptual data model.

- History of the user's constraint violations.

Information from the User Model is used to identify different answering strategies and different factors within the strategies and to control the presentation of guidance information in the Tutorial Module. The value of the user model, however, remains to be proven and this will be a key topic in the evaluation of the prototype.

In considering the role of the User Model, it is to be noted that a strong emphasis has been placed on user initiative in providing for adaptation to individual user requirements. An embedded hypertext facility provides for adaptability but with control in the hands of the user. Information generated by the system in the form of answers to questions, reports of constraint violations, and tutorial information provides links to related information within the knowledge base. By selecting any of the items identified in bold font in text generated by the advisor, the user can obtain additional information.

8 The Reactive Help Module (Question Answering)

Design of the Reactive Help Module or Question-Answering Module is based on the results of the protocol analyzes described previously. The user composes a question via menu. By pressing the *Question Button*, the user gains access to the menu containing the different question types in the form of introductory question statements. After the user selects the question type, the corresponding menus for completing the question are presented in sequence, with the appropriate choices of concepts and tasks. In some cases, the user will be required to type the name of an object or to pick an object from the model displayed in the design window. Once a question has been completed and confirmed with the *Confirm Button* the answer is displayed. The menu content is either predetermined or generated at run time. Our current goal is to move as far as possible towards generating all menus at run time. This feature allows the knowledge base to be built incrementally. Any addition or deletion of knowledge elements will be reflected dynamically in the menus without changing the question generating procedures.

The answers generated by the Advisor depend on several factors: the local need (question type, topic, and source), the user's level of knowledge, the local context, etc. The form of the answers and to a certain extent their content have been identified from the protocol analysis. Our approach to the implementation of the question-answering module has been derived from that taken at the University of Leeds in the EUROHELP project based on the use of rhetorical predicates (Hartley *et al.*, 1990). Associated with each question type is an answer type or *answer frame*, consisting of a sequence of functions or *predicates* that set the directions for retrieving the content of, structuring, and uttering the answer. In this way, answers are constructed from pieces of information found in the knowledge base through the use of content predicates with structure determined by organizational and instantiation predicates. We have augmented this with a knowledge expansion facility in the answer based on a hypertext mechanism.

Of the 12 question types identified, 4 have been implemented to date in our initial prototype. These are: general elaboration, specific elaboration, validation of current model, and validation of future model. Work is currently underway on the development of tools to facilitate the implementation of the remaining question types and the extension of the knowledge base.

9 Proactive Help

The Proactive Help Module provides a coaching function. It monitors the user's interaction with the design tool and intervenes with suggestions to assist in attaining the intended goal. When a change is detected in the conceptual model that the user is designing, a situation recognizer is called into play. This serves as a first focusing step in checking for nonconformance to rules and for violation of constraints. In the current prototype, the number of situations that have been identified is limited. First, we have the set of primitive design operations. This includes operators such as creation of a new entity and modification of the cardinality of an entity-relation link. In addition to these primitive design operators, several status points are identified as recognizable situations. These include: *end of session, a few steps after creation of an entity*, and *a few steps after the creation of an entity-relation link*. Rules and constraints are checked when any of these situations is encountered. For example, the rule stating that an identifier should be specified immediately after the creation of an entity will be checked at the situation: *a few steps after entity creation*.

The situation recognizer invokes a constraint and rule check which detects any constraint violations, subsequent corrections, and rule nonconformities. Results are passed to the User Modeller for updating the User Model and to the Intervener, which generates advice to the user as appropriate.

10 Tutorial Module

The Tutorial Module provides a means whereby the neophyte can be introduced to the domain knowledge necessary to apply the design tool. It has been designed using apprenticeship learning as the basic model (Collins *et al.*, 1986). This approach emphasizes the acquisition of skills directly related to the accomplishment of meaningful tasks. Abstract concepts are only introduced as they are required to explain a given task. The student is guided through a set of examples that illustrate application of the target skill set. In the initial exposure, tasks are executed and explained by the system. As the student is exposed to the skills, responsibility for executing the tasks is gradually handed over until the student is capable of carrying out the tasks with little or no interaction from the Tutorial Module. Course content consists of a set of solved design problems. In each of these, the design process is defined by an initial state, which is the statement of the problem to be solved, a final state, which is the solution, and a number of intermediate states that represent the steps in solving the problem. Each of these states has a situation description, identification of the applicable design concepts, the decision to be made based on the methodology that is being followed, and the action to be taken. If the User Model indicates no evidence that the user knows the applicable concepts, the Tutor will execute the task, provide an explanation of the action and the concepts involved, and provide an update to the user model as appropriate. Once a concept has been explained, the next time a task is encountered based on that concept, the student will be given the opportunity to carry out the task. At any point the student can ask for a hint and if still incapable of executing the task can request the system to do so. It is important to note that the Tutor is embedded in the Advisor environment giving the student full access to the two other modules or modes of operation. At any time, the student can enter the reactive help mode to ask a question. All actions by the student that change the design model are processed by the Proactive Help module which provides warning of any constraint or rule violation.

During initial development of the tutorial module, one tutorial case was prepared and manually incorporated in the system. However, the potential was recognized for the use of the system to interact with the expert in the creation of tutorial cases through a role-reversal approach. In this mode, the system acts as the student while the expert carries out a design exercise using the CASE tool. At each step in the design, the system prompts the expert for the required supporting information. Once the case is completed, the system analyzes the steps and identifies the solution paths that are permitted by the design methodology. The solution set is then presented to the expert for verification. Two cases have been prepared using this facility. The results clearly indicate that it offers a cost-effective means for creating tutorial cases and a tool that can be used by the expert in a natural mode of interaction.

11 Conclusion

Our goal in this project is the development of Advisor technology that will assist the user of an interactive computer-based design tool to acquire and apply the knowledge necessary to make effective use of that tool. The Advisor must be capable of being integrated in the work environment as a transparent facility that does not interfere with a user who only wants to consult the Advisor occasionally. By combining the functions Coach, Help, and Tutor with a hypertext knowledge expansion facility, we have created an environment that demonstrates a natural means of knowledge transfer consistent with the information workstation environment. It allows the user to participate actively as an intelligent agent, in the control of the process. Facilities incorporated in the Advisor support the economical creation of tutorial cases by the domain expert and a practical means of adapting the system to particular application needs.

Feasibility has been demonstrated with a limited prototype developed for the conceptual data modelling domain. Application to a second domain has been initiated in a project to develop an Advisor for use in the siting of navigational beacon antennas at airports.

Acknowledgements

We are indebted to our many colleagues who participated in the Intelligent Advisor Project, which resulted in the system described in this paper. We are particularly grateful to Roger Hartley, Andrew Cole, Rachel Pilkington, Colin Tattersall, and Qassim Hasson, of the University of Leeds, for their contribution to the question-answering facility and to the formulation of the initial project proposal; to Marie-Michèle Boulet of Laval University, who contributed a large part of the domain knowledge and an early Advisor implementation; to Philippe Duchastel, for the early studies that lead to the tutorial design; to Daniel Pascot who suggested the application domain, provided the Silverrun CASE tool and advice regarding conceptual design techniques; to André Laurendeau, who organized the subjects for the simulation experiments and developed the first tutorial case; to Philippe Davidson, who implemented the initial version of the tutorial module; to Xueming Huang, who implemented the case acquisition module; and to François Vernadat, who provided advice at many critical stages in the project.

References

Breuker J. (ed) (1990). EUROHELP: Developing Intelligent Help Systems. ESPRIT Project Report, University of Amsterdam, Department of Social Science Informatics, Amsterdam.

Burton R.R and Brown J.S. (1979). An investigation of computer coaching for informal learning activities. International Journal of Man-Machine Studies, 20, 21-23.

Clancey W.J. (1986) Intelligent Tutoring Systems: A Tutorial Survey. Stanford University, Stanford CA. Report No. STAN-CS-87-1174.

Collins A., Brown J.S. and Newman S.E. (1986). Cognitive Apprenticeship: Teaching the Craft of Reading, Writing and Mathematics. BBN Laboratories Incorporated, Cambridge MA. Technical Report No. 6459.

Hartley J.R., Pilkington R., Tait K. and Tattersall C. (1990). Question interpretation and answering. in J. Breuker (editor). EUROHELP: Developing Intelligent Help Systems.

Levin J.A. and Moore J.A. (1977). Dialogue Games: Meta-communication structures for natural language interaction. Cognitive Science, 1(14).

Modell, H. (1989). Six CASE products for the Macintosh. Computer Language, 6(6), 111-131.

van Hoff, A.A. (1989). HyperNeWS 1.3 User Manual. The Turing Institute, Glasgow.

Fairness of Attribute Selection
In Probabilistic Induction

A.P. White and W.Z. Liu

Computer Centre
University of Birmingham
Birmingham B15 2TT

Abstract. In this paper, the problem of obtaining unbiased attribute selection in probabilistic induction is described. This problem is one which is at present only poorly appreciated by those working in the field and has still not been satisfactorily solved. It is shown that the method of binary splitting of attributes goes only part of the way towards removing bias and that some further compensation mechanism is required to remove it completely. Work which takes steps in the direction of finding such a compensation mechanism is described in detail.

1 Introduction

Automatic induction algorithms have a history which can be traced back to Hunt's concept learning systems (Hunt et al., 1966). Later developments include AQ11 (Michalski & Larson, 1978) and ID3 (Quinlan, 1979). The extension of this type of technique to the task of induction under uncertainty is characterised by algorithms such as AQ15 (Michalski et al., 1986) and C4 (Quinlan, 1986). Other programs, developed specifically to deal with noisy domains include CART (Breiman et al., 1984) and early versions of Predictor (White 1985, 1987; White & Liu, 1990). A recent review of inductive techniques may be found in Liu & White (1991). However, efforts to develop these systems have uncovered a problem which is at present only poorly appreciated by those working in the field and has still not been satisfactorily solved.

The principle behind automatic induction should, by now, be well known. Briefly, the idea involves using a suitable inductive algorithm to operate on a set of training cases (i.e. examples) in order to generate rules for dealing with similar cases which might arise in future. If required, the derived rules can be subsequently incorporated into an expert system.

In general, attributes in the training set may be categorized into two types: discrete attributes and continuous attributes. An attribute is discrete if it takes values in a finite set. Discrete attributes can be further divided into two types:

categorical and ordered discrete attributes. Categorical attributes are those whose values have no natural ordering and ordered discrete attributes are those whose values can be naturally ordered. An attribute is called continuous if its measured values are real numbers. For example, in medical data, age and blood pressure are continuous attributes, while blood type and sex are categorical attributes and social class (as measured on a five-point scale) is an ordered discrete attribute.

Discrete attributes may have different numbers of values, i.e. their degree of discreteness differs. The number of possible distinct values that a discrete attribute may take is called its "arity". Continuous attributes, on the other hand, may take values from an infinite set. These differences between attributes pose a serious problem for attribute selection.

2   Discrete Attributes

During the process of building the medical diagnostic system ASSISTANT (Kononenko et al., 1984), it was found that discrete attributes with more values were often being chosen by the algorithm in preference to more relevant attributes with fewer values when the transmitted information criterion, H_T, was used. This problem was also identified by Hart (1985). She pointed out that the more distinct values an attribute can take, the more likely it is to *appear* to discriminate well by chance. Thus, those discrete attributes with high arity have an "unfair advantage" over those having fewer values. This empirical finding has been proved theoretically by Quinlan (1988). A simple example may clarify the argument. Suppose we wish to compare the informativeness (i.e. the discrimination power) of two discrete attributes of different arity, e.g. sex (two values) and blood type (four values), in a subject domain with k classes. The technique of attribute selection by using transmitted information runs into the difficulty that the two values of H_T are not directly comparable because they have been derived from tables with different numbers of cells (one contingency table has $k - 1$ degrees of freedom, while the other has $3(k - 1)$). (It should be noted that this *particular* problem does not occur if the χ^2 test statistic is used. Although χ^2 values with different numbers of degrees of freedom are not themselves directly comparable, the χ^2 *probability*, however, can take into account, via the degrees of freedom parameter, the number of attribute values for each attribute).

One naive remedy that allows transmitted information to be used was suggested by Kononenko et al. (1984). This requires that all tests have only two outcomes. Instead of having one branch for each possible value of an attribute in the decision tree, values of the attribute are divided into two subsets and the inductive algorithm builds only binary branches, one for each subset of values. In order to decide how to split the values of the attribute into two subsets, all possible binary partitions are considered. The one which gives the highest value for H_T is considered the best way to split that attribute and this maximum value of H_T is used to represent the discrimination power of that attribute on class. Quinlan believed that the H_T values worked out in this way can fairly measure the informativeness of attributes. He declared (Quinlan, 1988):

> If all tests must be binary, there can be no bias in favour of attributes with large numbers of values and so the objective has certainly been achieved.

In fact, this statement is not true. The method just described does not provided a complete solution to the problem. There is another aspect to the difficulty. Simply having the same shape of $k \times 2$ contingency table by binary splitting those attributes with high arity into two subsets does not root out the bias towards those attributes with more values. Consider a categorical attribute with m different values. It is obvious that there are $2^{m-1} - 1$ ways of splitting the m values into two subsets and that a value of H_T can be calculated for each of these. The maximum of these $2^{m-1} - 1$ quantities is then used to represent the discrimination power of the attribute. This is obviously misleading because true binary attributes, such as sex, only have one possible way of splitting. This criticism also applies to the technique of using the χ^2 test as a selection criterion. If we denote the best χ^2 value by $\chi^2_{\max}$, experiments with binary splitting of random variables show that the resulting distribution of $\chi^2_{\max}$ is strongly dependent on the number of values of the attribute under consideration. For attribute selection to be unbiased, some further compensation is needed to overcome the bias towards those attributes with more values.

Although the remedy implemented in ASSISTANT was incomplete, it did reduce the bias towards high-arity attributes because, at least, all contingency tables from which H_T was derived were of the same dimension. This is consistent with the report of Kononenko et al. that smaller decision trees with an improved classification performance have been built in this way.

Other methods of overcoming the problem posed by attributes with different numbers of values have been attempted by several researchers. Kononenko et al. (1984) also tried to reduce the bias towards those attributes with more values by normalizing H_T by dividing it by the logarithm of the number of values of attributes. The results achieved with this method were not satisfactory because very important attributes with large numbers of values were then discriminated against. Quinlan (1988) suggested an alternative method by using the gain ratio (i.e. the ratio of information gain H_T to attribute information H_A), as an attribute selection criterion, instead of H_T. However, this criterion is not fair either. Consider the following 2×3 contingency table, in which rows represent classes and columns represent attribute values:

	a_1	a_2	a_3	
C_1	10	20	5	35
C_2	2	4	9	15
	12	24	14	50

and another slightly different one:

	a_1	a_2	a_3	
C_1	15	15	5	35
C_2	3	3	9	15
	18	18	14	50

Intuitively, we know the discrimination power of the attributes in these two tables are the same. If the gain ratio is to be a fair criterion of attribute selection, then we would expect them to have the same magnitude of gain ratio. However, they have different values of gain ratio, 0.0989 and 0.0952 respectively. This is obviously misleading. Furthermore, if we consider the following contingency table:

	a_1	a_2	a_3	
C_1	16	14	5	35
C_2	3	3	9	15
	19	17	14	50

which is derived from the second table by introducing more association between attribute and class. The gain ratio of the attribute in this table, 0.0955, is still less than that in the first table. Thus, the gain ratio criterion unfairly favours those attributes with smaller attribute information H_A. Unlike this criterion, other measures such as the χ^2 or H_T can detect that the attributes in the first two tables are of the same discrimination power and that the attribute in the third table is more informative than those in the first two tables.

3 Continuous Attributes and Optimal Splitting

Based on the discussion so far, the χ^2 probability seems to be a better criterion for attribute selection since other measures, such as H_T and its variants, have at least one of the following disadvantages:

- Their distribution under the null hypothesis is unknown. Thus, a stopping rule is impossible to implement.

- They favour those attributes with more distinct values.

However, the method of simply using the χ^2 probability alone also presents some problems. First of all, having one branch for each possible value is infeasible because a discrete attribute may have a great number of values and, furthermore, continuous attributes may take values from an infinite set of values. Also, values of continuous attributes of future cases may not exist in cases of the training set at all, making it impossible for the derived decision tree to classify such cases. Secondly, continuous attributes give contingency tables which are too big for the χ^2 test.

These contingency tables may have too many cells with low expected values, rendering the chi-square distribution a poor approximation to the actual distribution of the χ^2 test statistic. The worst case is when attributes are completely continuous so that the frequency counts in the cells of the contingency tables are all 0 or 1.

One solution to the problems described above is to use the technique of optimal splitting (i.e. binary splitting in the optimal place). The technique is to work entirely with binary trees. All attributes which are not originally binary are converted into "pseudo-binary" attributes by the technique of optimal splitting. Its use in dealing with discrete attributes has been discussed by Kononenko et al. (1984) and was described in the previous section. Continuous attributes can be dealt with in a similar way. This involves splitting the initial attribute between every possible pair of adjacent values (in a sense of numerical order) to yield a number of derived binary variables which replace the original non-binary attributes. If the original attribute has m distinct values present in the training set, this would mean generating $m-1$ binary variables. The best of these $m-1$ variables, as judged by the criterion for attribute selection (i.e. the χ^2 test), then becomes the pseudo-binary attribute which is used in place of the original attribute. In more detail, each of the $m-1$ derived variables is cross-tabulated against class for all the cases at the node under consideration and a χ^2 value is calculated for each of them. The variable with the largest χ^2 (denoted by $\chi^2_{\max}$) is chosen as the pseudo-binary attribute to represent the original attribute. Perhaps it should be mentioned that this technique leaves open the possibility that a multi-valued attribute may legitimately be branched on more than once (at different cutting points) in the same path of the decision tree.

As regards the method of binary splitting, Quinlan (1988) pointed out two undesirable side-effects. First, it could lead to unintelligible decision trees with unrelated attribute values being grouped together and multiple tests on the same attribute in the same path. Secondly, a discrete attribute with m values has $2^{m-1}-1$ different ways of splitting the m values into two subsets. This is not a problem if m is small, but the approach would appear infeasible for an attribute with many values.

Let us consider these criticisms in more detail. Different types of attribute should be dealt with in different ways. Categorical attributes do not have any natural ordering on their values. For this reason, it is essential to consider all possible binary combinations of values in order to decide where to split an attribute. On the other hand, ordered discrete attributes can be treated in the same manner as continuous ones, as described above. Thus, for ordered attributes, there will be no grouping of unrelated values. This approach would appear to answer Quinlan's first objection.

The next point is that of unintelligible trees resulting from branching more than once on the same attribute in the same path. This criticism seems too strong. Paths with this property may not correspond to the sort of production rules that a human expert would provide but they are nevertheless *intelligible*.

The final point relates to the combinatorial explosion of $2^{m-1} - 1$ as m increases. Mathematically, this must be admitted. However, for most practical examples, this would not appear to be a problem. It is usually the case that categorical attributes take only a small number of possible values — rarely more than four.

At first sight, optimal splitting seems to be a very satisfactory solution to the problem posed by attributes having different numbers of values because each attribute is converted into a binary one, which makes all the derived attributes have the same base of $k \times 2$ contingency tables (where k is the number of classes at the node under consideration). However, as mentioned before, this does not provides a complete solution to the problem. Instead, it raises the difficulty of requiring further compensation for taking the maximum χ^2 value from different numbers of candidates. The necessity for further compensation is not appreciated by most researchers in the area of automatic induction. None of the work cited previously addresses this problem, which is addressed below.

4   Compensating χ^2_{max}

As mentioned in the previous section, the optimal splitting technique gives unfair advantage to pseudo-binary attributes (in comparison with true binary attributes) during attribute selection. This makes it necessary to build a further compensation function for taking the maximum χ^2 value, χ^2_{max}, from different numbers of possible candidates, in order to make all χ^2_{max} values directly comparable.

Another aspect of the problem is the implementation of a stopping rule, which is based on a statistical significance test. In the case of optimal splitting, the test will not have the same *actual* significance level for pseudo-binary attributes derived from attributes of different numbers of distinct values. This is because the test is applied to χ^2_{max} rather than a straightforward χ^2 value. Under the null hypothesis of no association between attribute and class, the χ^2 statistic is approximately distributed as chi-square with $k - 1$ degrees of freedom (where k is the number of classes) but χ^2_{max} will not be distributed in this way and its c.d.f. (cumulative distribution function) is not known. Ideally, if a compensation function can be found to reduce bias towards non-binary attributes, then the statistical significance test which can be applied to χ^2 values of true binary attributes can also be applied legitimately to compensated χ^2_{max} values of non-binary attributes which have been subjected to optimal splitting.

5   Simulating the Behaviour of $\chi^2_{\max}$ with Ordered Attributes

5.1   Aims

Because of the intractable problems involved in finding a satisfactory theoretical formulation for the behaviour of $\chi^2_{\max}$, it was decided to investigate (using Monte Carlo simulation techniques) the behaviour of $\chi^2_{\max}$ under the null hypothesis of no association between attribute and class. As with the χ^2 values, we are interested in the upper percentage points of the c.d.f. (cumulative distribution function) for $\chi^2_{\max}$. For any given significance level α (e.g. 0.05), if we can establish a function for the expected value of $\chi^2_{\max}$ (under the null hypothesis), with N', the number of splitting points, as one of its parameters, then a stopping rule can be implemented. This function can be regarded as a baseline. Any attribute with a $\chi^2_{\max}$ value above the baseline is considered to be significantly associated with class. If none of the $\chi^2_{\max}$ values is found to exceed the baseline, then the whole branching process stops. As regards the problem of attribute selection, if we can obtain the various probabilities of the $\chi^2_{\max}$ values of these significant attributes, through a similar function to that of the baseline, then we can simply select that attribute (from those significant ones) whose value for $\chi^2_{\max}$ has the most extreme probability, i.e. the one with the least probability of occurring by chance, given no actual association with class.

5.2   Method

In the experiment, a continuous attribute and a vector of classes were randomly generated for n cases so that there was no inherent association between class and attribute. Two classes were simulated, the most frequent class with probability p. In order to investigate the behaviour of $\chi^2_{\max}$ as a function of the number of splitting points, (N'), of the attribute, this latter parameter was assumed to take a number of different values ranging from 2 to $n - 1$, in approximately equal logarithmic steps. These splitting points were arranged so that, as far as possible, the resulting intervals contained equal numbers of scores.

The sample size, n, was varied systematically in approximately equal logarithmic steps from 21 to 2001. Six different class probability ratios were used, with the probability of the most frequent class ranging from 0.5 to 0.95. For each combination of parameters, 500 simulation trials were performed, yielding 500 values of $\chi^2_{\max}$. The required upper percentage points of the c.d.f. for $\chi^2_{\max}$ were then estimated from these data and summarised as a series of 42 tables.

5.3   Results

Shortage of space precludes the display of these tables. However, two points were immediately evident from casual inspection. Firstly, the results for $\chi^2_{\max}$ did not seem to be very reliable, i.e. the standard errors for estimating this statistic were obviously high. (This is hardly surprising. Maxima tend not to be well behaved and are consequently difficult to estimate accurately). Secondly, the prevalence of ties in the values for $\chi^2_{\max}$ was very noticeable. Brief examination suggested that these tended to occur more frequently for small values of n or when the upper percentage point was close to unity.

However, some systematic tendencies were discernible in the data. For example, there was a clear tendency for $\chi^2_{\max}$ to increase with N' and also with $p(C_1)$. Dependence on n was less clear.

5.4   Regression Analysis

The foregoing remarks indicate that there is little point in trying to fit a smooth multi-parameter function for estimating $\chi^2_{\max}$ in terms of the upper percentage point, N', n and $p(C_1)$. However, we should bear in mind that, at any given node (during the path-generating process), the number of cases and the class probabilities will be the same for all attributes and the significance level, α will have been decided as a parameter for the entire path-generation process. For this reason, it was decided to examine the dependence of $\chi^2_{\max}$ on N' only.

Close inspection of the data suggested that, for any particular combination of parameter values for n, α and p, $\chi^2_{\max}$ increases linearly with $\log(N')$. Thus, the estimated upper percentage point $(1 - \alpha)$ for $\chi^2_{\max}$, denoted by $est(\chi^2_{\alpha,\max})$ will be given by an equation of the form:

$$est(\chi^2_{\alpha,\max}) = a + b\log(N') \tag{1}$$

For a true binary attribute, there is only one possible way of splitting, i.e. $N' = 1$. In this case, $est(\chi^2_{\alpha,\max})$ is actually χ^2_α. Thus, the intercept, a, is χ^2_α with $k - 1$ degrees of freedom (where k is the number of classes), i.e. the upper percentage point of the c.d.f. for chi-square corresponding to a significance level of α. It is only the slope, b, that needs to be estimated empirically. Thus we arrive at the following equation:

$$est(\chi^2_{\alpha,\max}) = \chi^2_{\alpha,k-1} + b\log(N') \tag{2}$$

This relationship was investigated formally by using least squares regression techniques to find the slopes for each combination of parameter values. The method used was to fit a model with no intercept and to determine the intercept separately from theoretical considerations (described above).

5.5   Discussion

There are basically two matters to be considered – the stopping rule and the attribute selection problem. As indicated previously, at any given node, n and $p(C_1)$ are the same for all attributes (provided that the number of missing values is small) and α has been fixed. This means that a compensation function for N' can be determined by performing a Monte Carlo simulation, in situ, at each node. This should provide a consistent stopping rule.

The problem of attribute selection is more difficult. An earlier idea proposed by White & Liu (1990) was to regard Equation (2) as a baseline for attribute selection and to select that attribute whose value for χ^2_{max} exceeds the relevant baseline by the largest amount. The branching process is terminated when none of the χ^2_{max} values is found to exceed the baseline.

Initially, this approach seemed to work well. Unfortunately, the regression results displayed in the previous section show that this method is badly flawed. In the proposed solution, the χ^2_{max} functions in $\log(N')$ are assumed to be parallel. However, the results obtained for the slopes indicated clearly that this assumption cannot be maintained. There is a marked tendency for the slopes to increase with increasing percentage value and also with class probability. Also, these increases interact positively, i.e. the rate of increase with class probability is itself greater for high percentage values.

These results mean that the attribute with the greatest distance from the stopping rule baseline is not necessarily the one with the χ^2_{max} value of most extreme probability. Figure 1 gives an illustrative counter-example. In this figure, attribute A_2 has a larger distance from the the baseline than attribute A_1. According to the original idea, attribute A_2 should have preference for selection over attribute A_1. This is not correct because A_1 is the attribute with the χ^2_{max} value of more extreme probability.

This criticism does not apply to the stopping rule because, for any given α, the slope, b, can always be properly estimated by Monte Carlo simulations. In attribute selection, it is impossible to estimate the slope, b, because the probabilities, α, of the χ^2_{max} values of various attributes are unknown. In fact, these probabilities are the very features of the attributes that we wish to compare with each other in order to select the attribute with the χ^2_{max} value of the most extreme probability. One possible way to get rid of this problem is to establish a function, f, of the slope, b, with α as one of its parameters:

$$b = f(\alpha, \ldots)$$

Then Equation (2) could be re-expressed as follows:

$$est(\chi^2_{\alpha,max}) = \chi^2_{\alpha,k-1} + f(\alpha, \ldots)\log(N') \tag{3}$$

Unfortunately, fitting such a function seems difficult and pointless for the following reasons:

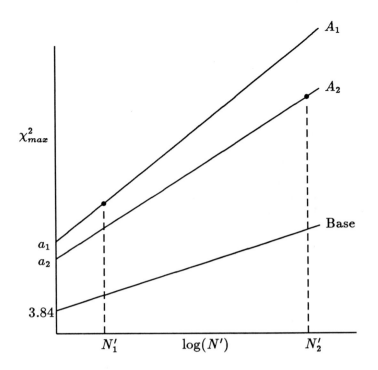

Figure 1: Attribute selection with multiple compensation functions.

- As described above, slopes of $\chi^2_{\max}$ for different percentage points are different.

- Slopes differ considerably and do not seem to be estimated reliably. This is really not surprising because maxima drawn from any distribution tend to have large standard errors.

- Slopes depend on too many parameters. It seems that they depend on both the α and $p(C_1)$. There is a suspicion that they may also depend on n.

As a result, it seems impossible to implement a suitable compensation function for attribute selection, using $\chi^2_{\max}$. It is worth mentioning that another problem with the Monte Carlo simulation technique is that it is very clumsy and time-consuming. At every step of the branching process, it is necessary perform the simulation because those parameters such as the number of cases n, class probability $p(C_1)$ and number of splitting points N' may change after case partitioning. Strictly speaking, it is necessary to perform a simulation *for each attribute* at each node! Clearly, a more efficient procedure is required.

6   The Use of χ^2_{mean}

Let us consider again, the technique of optimal splitting, described in Section 3. An ordered attribute with m distinct values, has $(m-1)$ possible splitting points. Splitting at each of these points yields $(m-1)$ χ^2 values. It seems reasonable to suppose that the best place to split the attribute is at the point which gives the largest value of χ^2 (denoted by χ^2_{max}). The approach described in the previous section, was to use this χ^2_{max} value to represent the discrimination power of the original attribute and then try to compensate for attributes with different numbers of distinct values. However, from the discussion in the previous section, this approach seems infeasible. Now that the use of χ^2_{max} causes intractable problems, using the mean (denoted by χ^2_{mean}) of these $(m-1)$ χ^2 values to represent the discrimination power of the original attribute becomes a natural choice to try, because of the fact that the standard error of the mean should be substantially smaller than that of the maximum.

A small experiment with genuine data indicated that, when real association between class and attributes was present, χ^2_{mean} behaved much like χ^2_{max} in selecting the important attributes. This gave reassurance concerning the viability of this approach and so further simulation experiments were undertaken to establish which parameters were important in determining the values for χ^2_{mean} in the upper percentage points of its distribution.

Further simulation experiments were conducted to investigate the influence of various parameters on the upper percentage points of χ^2_{mean} under the null hypothesis, i.e. when no association between class and attribute was present. Shortage of space precludes the detailed description of these experiments. For this reason, a summary is presented below. Particularly important points are dealt with in more detail.

1. χ^2_{max} and χ^2_{mean} were compared in an experiment which used two equi- probable classes and three different sample sizes, n, of an ordered attribute drawn from a uniform distribution. A range of values for N' (number of splitting points) was employed. The results indicated that, whereas χ^2_{max} increased monotonically with N', χ^2_{mean} was much less influenced by this parameter and appeared to decrease to an asymptotic value as N' became large. Furthermore, although the dependence of χ^2_{max} on n was quite weak, the relationship between χ^2_{mean} and n was weaker still.

2. The effect of class probability, n and N' on χ^2_{mean} were investigated. As before, an ordered attribute drawn from a uniform distribution was employed. Best subset regression techniques showed that neither class probability nor n had any discernible effect on the upper percentage points for χ^2_{mean}. For a given upper percentage point, the only parameter of importance was the reciprocal of N', which accounted for approximately 87% of the variance of χ^2_{mean} for both the 90th. and 95th. percentiles.

These results show a pleasing simplicity. They indicate that most of the variance of χ^2_{mean} can be accounted for in terms of a simple function of a single variable. The implications of this are that it should be possible to implement a stopping rule for χ^2_{mean}, which does not involve performing Monte Carlo simulations at each node. Instead, for any given significance level, termination thresholds could be decided in advance for each of the attributes, yielding considerable improvements in computational efficiency.

7   Simulating the Behaviour of χ^2_{mean} with Different Attribute Distributions

Another experiment was undertaken for two principal reasons. Firstly, it was thought desirable to investigate the effects of attribute distribution on the behaviour of χ^2_{mean}, in case some allowance needs to be made for attributes drawn from different distributions. Secondly, as the previous experiment gave such encouraging results for expressing χ^2_{mean} in terms of the reciprocal of N', it was decided to try to extend the model to include some function of α, in order to fit a surface to *all* the upper percentage points of χ^2_{mean}. A third, subsidiary, aim for the experiment was to check again that the number of cases, n, was not an important parameter as regards influence on χ^2_{mean}. The method used in this experiment was similar to that described earlier except that the class probability was fixed at 0.5 and two different attribute distributions were used – uniform and normal.

Preliminary inspection of the results showed that the data from the two distributions differed, so it was decided to deal with each separately. Statistical analysis focused on the top ten percentage points of the χ^2_{mean} distribution. Trial fitting of various combinations of these variables for the data obtained from the normally distributed attributes, revealed that a bivariate linear function in $\log(\alpha)$ and $\frac{1}{N'}$ accounted for an adjusted R^2 of 85.3%. However, this fit was improved by the inclusion of a product term of these two variables, giving an adjusted R^2 of 93.2%. A similar approach with the data from the uniformly distributed attributes showed that the corresponding bivariate linear function accounted for an adjusted R^2 of 92.4% and that adding the product term increased this figure to 95.9%. On the basis of these results, it was decided not to include any further parameters.

On the whole, these results seemed satisfactory. However, examination of the residuals revealed a small number of excessively large residuals. Such occurrences did not appear for every combination of parameter values but, when they were present, they were always associated with the most extreme α values. This feature is not due to a poor choice of function but is actually caused by a phenomenon which requires some explanation. Firstly, because of the nature of the data, the χ^2_{mean} values are correlated and hence large residuals will tend to cluster together. Secondly, the standard errors of estimate of the upper percentage points are inversely related to α. Thirdly, the sampling distribution of these parameters becomes more and more highly skewed as α decreases. These factors work together with the result that, as α becomes more extreme, the estimates become increasingly unreliable and subject to large positive error.

For this reason, the regressions were performed again, using robust regression techniques. The two resulting equations were:

$$est(\chi^2_{\alpha,\text{mean}}) = 0.547 - 0.512\log(\alpha) - \frac{1.401}{N'} - \frac{1.079\log(\alpha)}{N'} \tag{4}$$

for the normal case and:

$$est(\chi^2_{\alpha,\text{mean}}) = 0.036 - 0.820\log(\alpha) - \frac{0.980}{N'} - \frac{0.792\log(\alpha)}{N'} \tag{5}$$

for the uniform.

As a final check, these empirical functions were used to estimate χ^2 values for three upper percentage points, namely the 95th., 99th. and 99.9th. These were calculated to be 3.89, 6.48 and 10.19 respectively, for the uniform distribution and 3.91, 6.47 and 10.14 for the normal. These compare favourably with the theoretical values of 3.84, 6.64 and 10.83. For both distributions, the estimates are very good for the first two points and even for the 99.9th. point, the error is less than ten per cent.

In summary, these results seem most satisfactory. They indicate that a quadratic surface can be used to fit the upper percentage points of the χ^2_{mean} distribution, when this statistic is derived from a normally or uniformly distributed attribute by the binary splitting process, described earlier. Such a surface could not have been fitted if the χ^2_{max} statistic had been used. However, it must be noted that the function coefficients do depend on the attribute distribution used.

8   Simulating the Behaviour of χ^2_{mean} with Categorical Attributes

As mentioned earlier, a categorical attribute with n_c distinct values has $2^{n_c-1} - 1$ different ways of binary splitting, while an ordered attribute only has $n-1$ splitting points. It has already been shown in the previous section that a quadratic surface can be used to fit the upper percentage points of χ^2_{mean} for ordered attributes. The first purpose of this experiment was to check that, under the null hypothesis of no association between attribute and class, χ^2_{mean} behaves in a comparable manner for categorical attributes to that shown in previous sections for continuous attributes. The second purpose was to investigate the importance of class probability and number of cases, n, on the behaviour of χ^2_{mean}.

The method used in this experiment was similar to that used previously. Two classes were considered and six level of class probability were employed. Number of cases, n, was varied in eight approximately equal logarithmic steps. The simulated attribute was drawn from a discrete uniform distribution. Thus, the categories were arranged to be of equal size, on average. Since binary categorical attributes can only be split in one way, they can be treated in the same manner as ordered attributes. Thus, they were excluded from this experiment. Number of categories, n_c, was varied from 3 to 8. Consequently, the number of splitting points, N'_c, ranged from 3 to 127.

As before, statistical analysis focused on the top ten percentage points of the χ^2_{mean} distribution and the same statistical methods were used. However, there was an additional difficulty with this experiment. For the earlier experiments with ordered attributes, it was shown that quadratic functions in $\log(\alpha)$ and the reciprocal of N' provided good approximations for the upper percentage points of χ^2_{mean}. With categorical attributes, it is not immediately obvious whether the counterpart of N' is N'_c or $n_c - 1$. In the case of ordered attributes, the number of splitting points is one less than the number of categories. On the other hand, when categorical attributes are used, it is not clear whether it is the number of splitting points or the number of categories (less one) which is important. The best quadratic function was actually a "mixture" of the two ideas and involved $\log(\alpha)$, the reciprocal of N'_c and the product of $\log(\alpha)$ and the reciprocal of $n_c - 1$. This was a rather untidy result but this function did produce an adjusted R^2 of 96.0%. More importantly, however, the function produced better estimates for known upper percentage points of χ^2 than any other quadratic function and was preferred on these grounds. Just as with the ordered attributes, neither n nor class probability were found to be important. By employing robust regression, the following equation was obtained:

$$est(\chi^2_{\alpha,\text{mean}}) = 0.855 - 0.164 \log(\alpha) - \frac{1.847}{N'_c} - \frac{1.497 \log(\alpha)}{n_c - 1} \tag{6}$$

The corresponding estimated χ^2 values for the 95th., 99th. and 99.9th. upper percentage points were 3.98, 6.66 and 10.48 respectively. These were felt to be satisfactorily close to the theoretical values of 3.84, 6.64 and 10.83. Again, these results seem quite satisfactory. They indicate that a quadratic surface can be used to fit the upper percentage points of the χ^2_{mean} distribution, when this statistic is derived from a categorical attribute by taking all possible binary combinations of categories.

9 The Application of Compensation Functions

The various simulation experiments reported earlier, strongly support the idea that it is possible to find reasonable approximations for the upper percentage points of χ^2_{mean}, when this statistic has been derived by cross-tabulating class and pseudo-binary attribute, as described earlier. This means that it is possible to derive a small set of compensation functions which can be used to control the processes of attribute selection and branching termination, in a way which is statistically acceptable.

The compensation functions could be used like this. At each node in the branch under consideration, that attribute with the smallest *compensated* χ^2_{mean} probability is selected for branching on, provided that it is less than the stopping rule threshold. Obviously, different compensation functions need to be used for different attribute, according to their type and distribution. In principle, this would appear to offer an empirical solution to the problem of fairness of attribute selection that was mentioned earlier. Of course, some further work is needed with categorical attributes, in order to investigate the behaviour of χ^2_{mean} in those circumstances in which the categories do not have equal probability.

Perhaps one of the most exciting ideas comes from considering the application of these techniques in the more simple circumstances where all the attributes are ordered and truly continuous, i.e. where there are no tied values in the observations. Under these conditions, this approach constitutes a method for conducting a form of non-parametric discriminant analysis. It is obvious that the classification results of the method will be invariant over any monotonic transformation of any of the attributes. Thus, the method could be of importance to those dealing with ordinal data.

When attribute values are grouped, the technique does not work quite as neatly. At present, the best that can be done under these circumstances, is to identify which distribution type best approximates each attribute and apply to each attribute the appropriate compensation function. However, another interesting idea is to attempt to parameterise the shape of the distribution in some way that can be incorporated into a more general compensation function. Work is continuing along these lines.

References

Breiman, L., Friedman, J.H., Olshen, R.A. & Stone, C.J. (1984). *Classification and Regression Trees*. Belmont: Wadsworth.

Hart, A.E. (1985). Experience in the use of an inductive system in knowledge engineering. In *Research and Development in Expert Systems*, edited by M.A. Bramer, pp. 117-126. Cambridge: Cambridge University Press.

Hunt, E.B., Marin, J. & Stone, P.J. (1966). *Experiments in Induction*. New York: Academic Press.

Kononenko, I., Bratko, I. & Roskar, E. (1984). Experiments in automatic learning of medical diagnostic rules. *Technical Report*. Jozef Stefan Institute, Ljubjana, Yugoslavia.

Liu, W.Z. and White, A.P. (1991). A review of inductive learning. In *Research and*

Development in Expert Systems **VIII**, edited by I.M. Graham and R.W. Milne, pp. 112-126. Cambridge: Cambridge University Press.

Michalski, R.S. and Larson, J.B. (1978). Selection of most representative training examples and incremental generation of VL_1 hypotheses: the underlying methodology and the descriptions of programs ESEL and AQ11. *Report* No. **867**, Department of Computer Science, University of Illinois, Urbana, Illinois.

Michalski, R.S., Mozetic, I., Hong, J. & Lavrac, N. (1986). The multi-purpose incremental learning system AQ15 and its testing applications to three medical domains. In *Proceedings of the AAAI Conference* (Philadelphia).

Quinlan, J.R. (1979). Discovering rules by induction from large collections of examples. In *Expert Systems in the Micro-Electronic Age,* edited by D. Michie, pp. 168-201. Edinburgh: Edinburgh University Press.

Quinlan, J.R. (1988). Decision trees and multi-valued attributes. *Machine Intelligence*, **11**, 305-318.

Quinlan, J.R., Compton, P., Horn, K.A. & Lazarus, L. (1986). Inductive knowledge acquisition: a case study. *Technical Report* 86.4, School of Computing Science, New South Wales Institute of Technology.

White, A.P. (1985). PREDICTOR: An alternative approach to uncertain inference in expert systems. In *Proceedings of the Ninth International Joint Conference on Artificial Intelligence* (Los Angeles, 1985), edited by A. Joshi, vol. 1, pp. 328-330. Los Altos: Morgan Kaufmann.

White, A.P. (1987). Probabilistic induction by dynamic path generation in virtual trees. In *Research and Development in Expert Systems* **III**, edited by M.A. Bramer, pp. 35-46. Cambridge: Cambridge University Press.

White, A.P. & Liu, W.Z. (1990). Probabilistic induction by dynamic path generation for continuous attributes. In *Research and Development in Expert Systems* **VII**, edited by T.R. Addis and R.M. Muir, pp. 285-296. Cambridge: Cambridge University Press.

An Application of Case-Based Expert System Technology to Dynamic Job-Shop Scheduling

A. BEZIRGAN

Institute for Automation, Technical University Vienna
Treitlstraße 3 / 183 / 1, A-1040 Vienna, Austria
Tel.: 00 43 - 1 - 588 01 - 81 84, Fax: 00 43 - 1 - 56 32 60
e-mail: aberziga@email.tuwien.ac.at

ABSTRACT

This paper describes the structure and components of a case-based scheduler named CBS-1 which is being created to demonstrate the feasibility and utility of case-based reasoning (CBR) for dynamic job-shop scheduling problems. The paper describes the characteristics of a specific real-world scheduling task used in the work on CBS-1, identifies major problems to consider, and gives arguments for and against the application of CBR. The functions of the components of the system are illustrated by examples. Finally, some existing case-based schedulers are compared with CBS-1.

1 INTRODUCTION

Scheduling is the allocation of resources, like machines or human power, to operations over time to achieve certain goals. In job-shop scheduling the goals to be achieved are the processing or production of discrete parts in several steps each requiring several different resources. Dynamic scheduling is scheduling simultaneously with the execution of the processes that are affected by the created schedules.

In the Interuniversitary Centre for CIM (IUCCIM) in Vienna the production process for remote controlled toy cars is used to demonstrate the main ideas in CIM. In this context the problem of scheduling incoming orders for toy cars into the ongoing production process arises. There are several reasons for the complexity of such a scheduling task.

- There is a combinatorial explosion of the number of possible schedules (which must be checked for feasibility) in each problem dimension such as the number of machines and operations. This makes it necessary to use implicit representations of the search space instead of enumerative representations.

- There are a number of constraints which a valid schedule must satisfy such as due dates and constraints concerning operation sequences. Interactions of these constraints make scheduling decisions difficult.

- Scheduling decisions very often depend on context. This makes it difficult to write down an explicit goal function. What is good in one context can be bad in another.

- Dynamic scheduling involves reacting in time to changes in the environment.

On the other hand, in a CIM environment there is an abundance of information of various kinds available in machine readable form. Orders, prices, inventory lists, and production process logs can be stored over a long period of time. These informations represent a repository of valuable real-world experience. Today, the main user of such experience is the human scheduler, who utilises it to perform dynamic scheduling manually.

This abundance of information and its use through human schedulers is a pointer to the applicability and utility of CBR. The availability of cases is a prerequisite for the applicability of CBR (see Kolodner and Riesbeck (1989)). Reasoning from cases does not involve exploring the whole search space. Thus the problem of combinatorial explosion is avoided. One strength of CBR lies in its ability to deal with context dependent information. Thus constraint interaction and context dependency can be modelled efficiently in a case-based system. On the other hand, CBR is not well suited for optimisation problems since it does not explore the whole search space. However, the impact of this weakness becomes smaller in a real-time environment in which a timely solution is often better than a perfect solution that misses deadlines. Further, CBR is usually faster than enumerative methods. Thus after weighing advantages and disadvantages against each other, CBR seems to have the characteristics needed for a reasoning method to be suitable for dynamic scheduling tasks.

The CBS-1 (Case-Based Scheduler One) project represents an attempt to demonstrate the feasibility and utility of CBR for dynamic job-shop scheduling problems by creating a CBR system for scheduling orders for toy cars in the IUCCIM. The next section introduces the toy car production process in some detail. After that the architecture and the components of CBS-1 are described.

2   TOY CAR PRODUCTION AT THE IUCCIM

The main products of the IUCCIM factory at this time are the remote controlled toy car (Ferrari Testarossa) and its parts. It is planned to allow custom designed parts to be produced in future. About 30 of the 60 parts needed for the complete Ferrari are produced in the IUCCIM factory. The other parts are delivered by other companies. The latter parts are only needed in the final assembly stage of the production process and are usually stored in sufficient amounts in the factory. Orders are accepted for whole cars or parts. An order usually specifies the ordered part, a production deadline, an amount, quality criteria, such as the surface quality of a part, and some other requirements such as the colour of the car. Orders may arrive at any time and are to be scheduled as soon as possible. Orders also have priorities.

There is a total of 12 machines including laser cutting tools, turning machines, and drills. Each machine is capable of performing several operations. We assume that a machine cannot perform two or more operations simultaneously. Although generally one operation can be performed by more than one machine, the quality of the result of the operation and its execution time depend on the machine on which the operation is performed. For each part there is a fixed set of alternative process plans. In the process plans the average machine preparation durations and operation execution durations are given as exact times though they may vary in real-world operation.

The IUCCIM factory is used for courses in CIM, for product demonstrations, and as a platform for trying out research ideas in CIM related technology. CBS-1 is an instance of the latter category.

3 THE CASE-BASED SCHEDULER CBS-1

Figure 1 shows the structure of CBS-1. The central knowledge store in CBS-1 is the case base. The case base contains information on machines, products, processing operations, process plans, orders, and the current status of the factory. It also contains historical information on these items, i.e. a log of the temporal development of the factory. Scheduling decisions made earlier are also kept in the case base and make up the cases in CBS-1. These pieces of information are all linked together and build a semantic net organised around a time-line. The most important linking elements in this net are the so called justification structures. These structures use a rich causal vocabulary to describe the relations between states and events that led to a particular scheduling decision. For example, such a justification structure could state that an inferior machine B was used for a certain operation since machine A which would be used otherwise was out of order.

The case base manager keeps the information in the case base about the current state of the factory up-to-date. This is done by monitoring information on the success or failure of processing steps (schedule execution report, SER) delivered by the underlying process control system. It also updates predictions about the future state of the factory by inserting newly created schedules into the case base. Since the case base can become quite large, the case base manager also realises a "forgetting" function, which removes information no longer needed, not used often, or not used for a long time.

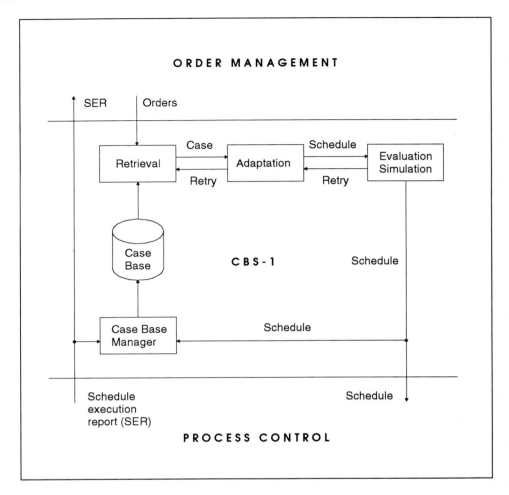

Figure 1: The structure of CBS-1

Given a new order and the knowledge structures mentioned above the retrieval component retrieves a set of similar previous cases from the case base. The most similar case is
then passed on to the adaptation component. Similarity is judged by several means. First,
superficial features of orders, e.g. kinds of parts ordered, amount ordered, and time
remaining to due date, hint to relevant cases. Second, constraints on orders represent a
further hint. Orders with comparable constraints, such as a certain required maximum
production duration, are considered more similar than others. Third, similarity of the
current status of the factory and its state during a previous case points to further relevant
cases. If machine A has a breakdown now and it had a breakdown in a previous case then
these cases are somewhat similar. Fourth, similarity is assessed by analysing the current

causal configuration and comparing it with the justification structures in the case base. If two operations are known to require the same bottleneck resource then a similar case may be retrieved by searching for the causal configuration "scheduling of operation A on machine B made scheduling operation C on machine B impossible".

The adaptation component is a rule-based system for manipulating the most similar previous case to create a schedule for the current orders. To do so it utilises the justification structure of the old case, analyses the old solution and the differences between the old and the new orders. Rules map the above pieces of information to functions. These functions are applied to the solution in the old case to obtain a schedule for the new orders. For example, if the justification structure in an old case states that a certain machine M had to be used because M is fast and the due dates were tight, then the adaptation component can check if these conditions are valid for the new order and if not, select another machine which may be slower but also cheaper in operation. Another simple adaptation would involve using a machine other than the one mentioned in the old case if the new order has higher quality requirements that cannot be met by that machine.

Although the adaptation component proposes new schedules by making plausible and rational changes to old feasible schedules, the proposed schedules cannot be guaranteed to be feasible. Hence a simulator is used to evaluate the feasibility of the proposed schedules. Each of the three stages, namely retrieval, adaptation, and evaluation may signal the previous stage the need for an alternative input if the current input does not lead to success. If the evaluation signals unfeasibility of the proposed schedule, alternative adaptation strategies may be tried. If adaptation signals inadaptability, retrieval can deliver the next most similar case. If retrieval cannot find similar cases it signals this to the order manager. There is an upper limit to this retrial mechanism. If this limit is reached without generating a feasible schedule the order manager is informed. Note also that CBS-1 cannot process any orders for which the retrieval component cannot find a similar case. If all goes well, a schedule is passed on to process control for execution.

4 CASES

One can imagine several different definitions of the term *case* in a job-shop scheduling environment. First, a case can be a record of information related to a single scheduling decision, e.g. which process plan to select for a certain ordered part or which machine to use for a certain operation. This definition of *case* is related to the constraint satisfaction problem view of scheduling (see for example Fox and Sadeh (1990)) and makes many connections between cases in the case base necessary. These connections represent the dependencies of scheduling decision on each other. Second, cases can be memory packages containing information involved in scheduling a certain order, i.e. a case contains a log of all relevant activities in the factory from the time of arrival of an order until the ordered product leaves the factory. Since the scheduling of incoming orders is influenced by the schedules of earlier and later orders, cases are once again strongly interconnected.

We could also try to define cases from a more resource centred point of view rather than from the order based view above. However, no matter how one defines cases, strong interactions between them are inevitable. This is a consequence of the strong dependency of scheduling decisions on each other, on context, and on problem constraints, and is to be seen as an intrinsic characteristic of job-shop scheduling problems. Thus it seems that the goal of defining tightly coupled units capturing global scheduling information (cases) which are loosely interconnected (in the case base) is infeasible in this context. Therefore cases are taken to be sets of related pieces of information having to do with the scheduling of a certain order and connected with pointers. These sets have fuzzy (i.e. unsharp) and floating (i.e. changing with time) boundaries.

4.1 Problem Descriptions

The problem description in a case consists of information on *goals*, on *constraints on goals*, and on *the problem environment*. The main goal is the generation of a schedule for a new order. Figure 2 shows a sample order. Orders may specify vague values for certain fields, such as *very fast* for *speed*. These can be interpreted as soft constraints which can be relaxed to a certain extent to obtain a feasible schedule.

```
Order no.: 3412
Customer name: Mr. Henry        Customer importance: very important
Part: Ferrari Testarossa        Amount: 5
Order date: 13.6.1992 8:00      Due date: 13.8.1992 12:00 ± 5 h
Colour: red                     Speed: very fast
Wheels: standard                Remote control range: short
...
```

Figure 2: A sample order

Constraints describe restrictions on the kinds of solutions to be generated, e.g. cost or quality requirements. The different types of constraints which can be specified here are much like in the ISIS system (see Fox (1987)). Some constraints are introduced by the production company, e.g. maximal allowed production cost, earliest/latest start date, earliest/latest finish date, wish to minimize stores, and order priorities. There are also constraints which are derived by a pre-processor from an order and the current state of the factory. Figure 3 shows a possible constraint list for the above order. The language used in expressing constraints must be a restricted language since retrieval and adaptation must be able to check equality and subsumption relations between constraints which would be infeasible if, for example, unrestricted first order predicate calculus expressions were allowed. For the following demonstrations simple feature lists are used.

```
┌─────────────────────────────────────────────────────────────────────────┐
│  Order no.: 3412                        max. prod. costs: AS 1000,00 / piece │
│  earliest finish: 12.8.1992 12:00   priority: high (important customer)      │
│  ...                                                                        │
└─────────────────────────────────────────────────────────────────────────┘
```

Figure 3: Constraints

An internal model of the factory and its current status make up the problem environment. This model is kept as part of the case base and updated when necessary, e.g. when events like machine breakdown occur. Thus it does not have to be specified explicitly in every problem description. The information managed in this context is the same information that a Gantt-Diagram conveys. Figure 4 shows the status information for a machine.

```
┌─────────────────────────────────────────────────────────────────────────┐
│  Machine no.: 12                    Name: Hueller Hille                     │
│    Schedule:                                                                │
│      ...                                                                    │
│      13.6.1992 10:00-12:00:         Order 3407; Plan 2; Op. 3               │
│      13.6.1992 12:00-16:00:         Order 3314; Plan 1; Op. 1               │
│      13.6.1992 16:00-18:00:         Maintenance                            │
│      13.6.1992 18:00-22:00:         Order 3408; Plan 1; Op. 6               │
│      ...                                                                    │
└─────────────────────────────────────────────────────────────────────────┘
```

Figure 4: Schedule for a sample machine

4.2 Solutions

The solution consists of an assignment of resources to operations over time. This represents a prediction of the development of the activities in the factory. The output of the system is an event-driven schedule and a set of commands to machines and personnel ensuring the execution of the schedule. The system also produces a prediction of the temporal development of the production process. A line of the form "13.6.1992 12:00-16:00: Order 3314; Plan 1; Op. 1" in Figure 4 represents a part of such a prediction. The event-driven schedule consists of rules of the form "if 1 x part1 and 1 x part2 and 2 x part3 are available then assemble them to part21".

4.3 Justification Structures

For each scheduling decision a case also contains a justification structure that gives reasons for this decision. In justification structures a causal vocabulary is used which facilitates adapting previous schedules. This vocabulary makes it possible to express causal dependencies like "scheduling operation O_1 of plan 1 for order no. 1243 on machine 15 at 16.6.1992 9:00-15:00 made scheduling operation O_2 of plan 2 for order no. 1423 on machine 15 on 16.6.1992 impossible" (see figure 5). This way relations of scheduling decisions and constraints which were important in a certain decision process can be recorded. The language of causal configurations contains relations like "A enables B", "A causes B", "A disables B", "A is a side-effect of B", "A is the desired effect of B".

Machine no.: 15   Name: Collet Minor
Schedule:

    ...
    16.6.1992 00:00-09:00:   idle
    16.6.1992 09:00-15:00:   Order 1243; Plan 1; O_1
    16.6.1992 15:00-24:00:   idle

    ...

O_1 needs machine 15 for 6 hours. O_1 indivisible.
O_2 needs machine 15 for 10 hours. O_2 indivisible.

Figure 5: A conflict situation

The justification structures build causal links between problems encountered in scheduling an order and their solutions. In the above example one possible solution could be to start O_1 an hour later. This would make it possible to schedule O_2 between 00:00 and 10:00. This solution would be recorded in the case base linked to the problem and to the justification structure. Furthermore, the justification structures are generalised to build causal problem classes. These classes improve the connectivity of the case base as will be seen in retrieval. The above justification could be generalised to the class: The side-effect of one scheduling decision leads to the infeasibility of a later scheduling task.

5 RETRIEVAL

When a new order arrives the retrieval component searches the case base for a previous order that is most similar to the current one. The methods for assessing similarity have already been mentioned. In CBR we try not to retrieve cases that cannot be adapted. Thus similarity is judged by the ease of adapting an old solution to become a solution to the new problem. This means that the definition of similarity - and hence retrieval - depends crucially on the capabilities of the adaptation component. The most similar old order is not found by comparing all old orders to the new one but by exploiting the semantic net to get from one similar case (case sharing one or more constraints or other features with the new order) to another.

For example, given a new order we can easily retrieve all previous orders for the same product. This is possible since all cases have pointers to the descriptions of the products produced as well as to the plans used. The associated cases are similar to the new order in the sense that they deal with the same product. Using further constraints on quality or quantity we can further differentiate between these cases. Following other links we can get to further cases which may be of use. For example, having decided to use a certain plan we can take a look at previous usages of that plan and the problems that were encountered then. Further, using some deeper features such as constraint looseness may help in retrieving more useful cases. Finally, the adaptation component is not bound to use one case in generating a new schedule. It can as well use several cases, one in solving each specific scheduling decision problem. In the following, adaptation from a single case is assumed.

The following example shall demonstrate the utility of justification structures in retrieval. Suppose that the order shown in figure 6 is received. Suppose further that to satisfy the order only one machine and one operation is needed, namely machine 32. Figure 6 also shows the schedule for machine 32 representing the current status of the factory. This causal configuration (infeasible scheduling task, side-effect of a previous scheduling decision being responsible) could then lead - through utilisation of the justification structures in the case base - to a reminding of the case related to figure 5. Thus the system could try to use the same strategy of moving the hindering operation slightly to get a larger block of idle time to schedule the new order.

```
Order no.: 3442
Customer name: Mr. Mayer        Customer importance: important
Part: base-plate                Amount: 100
Order date: 16.6.1992 8:00      Due date: 16.6.1992 18:00
...
-----------------------------------------------------------------------
Needed: Plan 1, Op. 1 ⇒ Machine 32 for 8 hours
-----------------------------------------------------------------------
Machine no.: 32                 Name: EMCO
Schedule:
    ...
    16.6.1992 08:00-09:00:      idle
    16.6.1992 09:00-11:00:      Order 3489; Plan 1; Op. 2
    16.6.1992 11:00-18:00:      idle
    ...
```

Figure 6: A new order and current machine status

The system could have other remindings too, such as that of a case in which the same problem was solved by splitting up the order in two parts, scheduling one part before the hindering operation and the other after it. This solution is worse than the previous one, because the duration of the operation will increase due to the doubled machine preparation time. Nevertheless, this approach could lead to a feasible schedule, too. At the present time no notion of optimality is supported in our system. The point is, that remindings using justification structures helped a lot in solving the scheduling problem.

After the most similar old order is selected adaptation is performed. The result of the adaptation is a new case including a solution to the new problem. Next it is checked either the new solution satisfies all constraints. If it does, we are done. Else either the next similar old order is tried or a soft constraint is relaxed. If after several adaptation tries no solution is found then the system is unable to deal with the given problem and the user must be consulted. For example, the adapted unsuccessful solutions may be presented to the user or he may be requested to relax some hard constraints.

6 ADAPTATION

The justification structures in the case base play a central role in adaptation. They make it possible to alter old cases in a *plausible and rational* manner. Justification structures associated with retrieved cases indicate conditions under which the solution was adequate in the past. For the example in figure 6, the adaptation component would check the applicability of the retrieved problem solution strategy (that was to slightly reschedule the hindering operation) by checking the validity of the conditions that led to the past solution. These conditions are available through justification structures. Such conditions would be that both the old (Order 3489; Plan 1; Op. 2) and the new (Order 3442; Plan 1; Op. 1) operations be indivisible and that the sum of the idle times of the required machine in the relevant time interval be greater than the total duration of the new operation. If the strategy is applicable then a suitable rate for shifting the hindering operation must be calculated, the operation must be rescheduled, and the new order must be scheduled. If the strategy is not applicable then another strategy is searched. If such a strategy is found, the adaptation tries to fit it to the new situation. Otherwise either the problem is infeasible or lies beyond the capabilities of the system.

7 CONCLUSIONS

CBS-1 is not the first system to attack scheduling tasks with CBR methods. Hennesy and Hinkle (1991), Barletta and Hennessy (1989), and Mark (1989) report of a system called Clavier which performs autoclave management and which shall schedule several autoclave ovens in a real-world environment. However, Clavier does not operate in the domain of dynamic job-shop scheduling and deals only with a small and special set of machines. Miyashita and Sycara (1992) introduce work on the CABINS system which operates in a domain comparable to the one of CBS-1. However, CABINS is concerned with the interactive repair of schedules and not with automatic schedule generation. Inserting a system like CABINS between CBS-1 and production control could lead to a more powerful scheduler capable of dealing with a richer set of scheduling problems. Future work on CBS-1 will include the implementation of the system and its evaluation in real-world environment. A further goal is to broaden the class of scheduling problems that can be handled.

REFERENCES

R. Barletta, D. Hennessy, *Case Adaptation in Autoclave Layout Design*, in Proc. Case-Based Reasoning Workshop, Morgan Kaufmann Pub., Inc., 1989, p. 203-207.

A. Bezirgan, *Case-Based Reasoning Systems*, Technical Report, Christian Doppler Laboratory for Expert Systems, Vienna, 1992, forthcoming

M. S. Fox, *Constraint-Directed Search: A Case Study of Job-Shop Scheduling*, Morgan Kaufmann Pub., Inc., 1987, 184 p.

M. S. Fox, N. Sadeh, *Why is Scheduling Difficult? A CSP Perspective*, in Proceedings ECAI 90, 1990, p. 754-767

D. Hennesy, D. Hinkle, *Initial Results from Clavier: A Case-Based Autoclave Loading Assistant*, in Proc. Case-Based Reasoning Workshop, Morgan Kaufmann Pub., Inc., 1991, p. 225-232.

J. Kolodner, C. Riesbeck, *Case-Based Reasoning*, Tutorial MA2 at the IJCAI-89, 1989

W. Mark, *Case-Based Reasoning for Autoclave Management*, in Proceedings Case-Based Reasoning Workshop, Morgan Kaufmann Pub., Inc., 1989, p. 176-180

K. Miyashita, K. Sycara, *CABINS: Case-Based Interactive Scheduler*, in Working Notes, AAAI Spring Symposium Series, Symposium: Practical Approaches to Scheduling and Planning, 1992, p. 47-51.

C. K. Riesbeck, R. C. Schank, *Inside Case-Based Reasoning*, Lawrence Erlbaum Associates, Pub., 1989, 423 p.

Neural Network Design via LP

James P. Ignizio §

and Wonjang Baek †

§ **University of Virginia**
† **Mississippi State University**

1 INTRODUCTION

Examples of the pattern classification problem (known variously as: pattern recognition, discriminant analysis, and pattern grouping) are widespread. In general such problems involve the need to assign objects to various groups, or classes, and include such applications as: (i) the assignment of production items to either defective or non-defective classes as based upon the results of tests performed on each part, (ii) the assignment of personnel to jobs as based upon their test scores and/or physical attributes, (iii) the assignment of an object detected by radar to either a friendly or unfriendly category, (iv) the categorization of investment opportunities into those that are attractive and those that are not, and so on. Early (scientific) efforts to model and solve the pattern classification problem utilized, for the most part, statistical approaches. In turn, these approaches usually rely upon the somewhat restrictive assumptions of multivariate normal distributions and certain types of (and conditions on) covariance matrices. More recent attempts have employed expert systems, linear programming (LP) and, in particular, neural networks. In this paper, we describe the development of an approach that *combines* linear programming (specifically, traditional linear programming and/or linear goal programming [Ignizio, 1982]) with neural networks, wherein the combined technique is itself monitored and controlled by an expert systems interface.

More specifically, we describe the use of expert systems and linear programming in the *simultaneous* design and training of neural networks for the pattern classification problem. While a relative handful of other investigators have recently proposed linear programming for neural network design and training, the approach proposed here differs from earlier concepts in that it:

- reduces, if not eliminates the somewhat *ad hoc* and heuristic nature of earlier approaches
- substantially reduces both the number and size of the linear programming models that need to be solved
- resolves, in a systematic fashion, the determination of the actual types of network processing elements — and thus permits ultimate, actual hardware replication

- resolves certain limitations (and/or open questions) of earlier approaches (e.g., for objects with ambiguous classifications)
- allows for a greater variety of performance measures, as well as for *multicriteria* performance measures
- permits a systematic means for the conduct of meaningful and accurate sensitivity analyses

2   BACKGROUND

Pattern classification has evolved from a primarily *ad hoc*, purely judgmental process to one that is now relatively scientific and systematic. However, the most rigorous of the conventional approaches to pattern classification utilize statistically-based methods (e.g., Fisher's Linear Discriminant function) that are subject to a variety of restrictive assumptions — assumptions that often are simply not defensible in real world application. This has led to efforts dedicated toward the development of more robust and/or improved methods — most recently through the use of neural network classifiers. However, there are certain significant drawbacks to the neural network concept — and these limitations have led to increased interest in alternative approaches, including *renewed* interest in the use of linear programming (LP) as either a pattern classifier (i.e., by itself) or as a means to more efficiently design and train neural network classifiers. In the past few years, considerable progress has been made in this area through the efforts of a number of investigators, and particularly through the contributions of Bennett and Mangasarian [1990], and Roy and Mukhopadhyay [1991]. However, while these approaches have shown considerable promise, they have certain shortcomings that we believe that we have been able to overcome, or at least mitigate, in the approach to be discussed.

We describe, in this paper, an *improved* LP-based approach for the *simultaneous* design (i.e., architecture specification) and training of neural networks for pattern classification. More specifically, this approach involves:

1.   The development of a totally algorithmic approach to the design and training of neural network classifiers. (Existing approaches require the use of various heuristic, judgmental and *ad hoc* procedures in the conduct of their methodology — as will be discussed in more detail in the following section.)
2.   A *substantial* reduction in both the size and number of LP models to be solved (i.e., in comparison to existing LP-based methods) — by means of: (i) the concepts of *foreign object masking* and *supermasking*, and (ii) other constraint reduction techniques that are specifically designed to take advantage of the peculiar nature of the forms of LP models encountered in the pattern classification problem.
3.   The development of a means for the elimination or mitigation of certain limitations of alternative LP-based approaches. In particular, the problem of ambiguous classifications (i.e., instances in which an object to be classified either falls within the boundaries of two or more classes or falls outside the boundaries of all existing classes) is addressed and resolved.

4.   The coordination and oversight of the entire process by means of an intelligent interface. More specifically, we use an expert system to access the data, form the associated LP models, evaluate the intermediate results, and finally list the architecture and parameters of the neural network for pattern classification.

3   OVERVIEW OF ALTERNATIVE METHODS

Since there exists extensive literature on the more conventional approaches to pattern classification — and of their advantages and disadvantages — there is no need to reiterate that material. Instead, in this section we very briefly describe the characteristics of the relatively few earlier methods of pattern classification using linear programming — focusing then on the two most recent and promising of these. Evidently, one of the earliest (if not the earliest) proposals for the use of LP in pattern classification was due to Mangasarian [1965]. This was followed — in the 1980s — by a number of proposals for various enhancements and extensions [Freed and Glover, 1981]. However, until recently, the use of LP in pattern classification was considered as a strictly "stand alone" concept. This perspective was changed with the proposal, by Bennett and Mangasarian [1991], to transform the results of the LP approach into an equivalent and *predetermined* neural network (i.e., a network in which the complete architecture *and* all link weights are known).

3.1 The Methods of Bennett and Mangasarian and of Roy *et al*

In essence, the work of Bennett and Mangasarian resulted in an approach to simultaneously train and design a feed-foward neural network. In comparing their approach to conventional backpropagation, it was noted that the Bennett and Mangasarian method had a number of significant advantages, including: the automatic determination of the number of hidden units, 100% correctness on the training set, substantially faster training, and the elimination of parameters (e.g., as in the case of backpropagation in which such values are both judgmental and sensitive) from the approach. The method has been dubbed the Multisurface Method, or MSM. It was shown that pattern classification could be accomplished via the solution of a sequence of LP models, resulting in the separation of the various classes by *piecewise-linear surfaces* — with convergence in polynomial time. Bennett and Mangasarian then proposed "a novel representation of the MSM classifier as a trained feed-forward neural network."

Bennett and Mangasarian have compared the performance of their approach (although not in hardware form and only, evidently, on a limited number of examples) with that of backpropagation (BP) for a number of test cases. Details with regard to this comparison may be found in the reference [Bennett and Mangasarian, 1990]; however, the result was that the MSM method required *much* less training time, achieved 100% correctness on the training set — and similar correctness (i.e., as compared with BP) on the test set, and utilized a similar number of nodes in the hidden layer. Yet another very important advantage of the MSM approach is that all operations are on linear models (i.e., linear programs) and thus a global optimal solution is assured. On the other hand, the training of conventional neural networks (e.g., backpropagation networks) is typically accomplished by means of nonlinear search, and thus there is always the likelihood of becoming stuck at a local optimal solution — and in fact a solution that may not even be feasible.

More recently, Roy and Mukhopadhyay [1991] have proposed and evaluated (again, on but a few examples) an approach similar to the Bennett and Mangasarian MSM method. However, there is at least one significant difference between the two concepts. Specifically, Roy's method incorporates *quadratic* separating surfaces — while still retaining linear models (i.e., LP models). This is because a quadratic (or any polynomial) function is linear in terms of its coefficients — and the variables (i.e., the class test scores) are always known in the pattern classification problem.

Roy's method involves the development, via the solution of a sequence of LP models, of a set of "masks." These masks, in turn, are simply quadratic functions whose coefficients have been determined via the solution of the LP models. However, essential to this approach is the need for some method of *clustering* — plus some *ad hoc* approach to the identification and elimination of data points that are assumed to be "outliers." In narrative form we may describe Roy's method as follows:

- We first attempt to "weed out" the outliers for every class under consideration. Roy proposes to accomplish this by means of cluster analysis.
- Clustering is accomplished via some heuristic cluster algorithm — such as k-means clustering. In essence, in the initial phase a number of clusters are developed and any of these which contain less than some arbitrary number of objects is considered to be an outlier — and these data (i.e., all of the objects in the associated cluster) are then dropped from consideration. The result of this phase is an *initial* set of clusters for all of the elements in each class.
- For the remaining clusters, and starting with the first class, we attempt to find a mask (i.e., quadratic function) that serves to separate this class from all others. This is to be accomplished via the solution of a set of LP models (where such models may involve up to as many constraints as there are objects, of all classes, to be classified). If a feasible LP is developed, then complete separation has been achieved.
- If complete separation is possible, we then move on to the next class. However, if complete separation is not possible (denoted by an infeasible LP), we must break up the sample patterns in the infeasible clusters into smaller clusters using, once again, a clustering analysis procedure. This procedure is repeated until complete separation is achieved and all necessary masks for the class have been developed. We then move to the next class and repeat the process.
- The final result of Roy's method (as with that of Bennett and Mangasarian) is the development of all the information necessary to establish a *trained* neural network for pattern classification.

While we certainly consider the methods of Bennett and Mangasarian, or Roy *et al*, to be significant contributions, we still felt that significant improvement was possible. For example, Bennett and Mangasarian's method involves the development of a piecewise-linear boundary and we have found (as should be intuitively obvious) that this requires the solution of a large number of LP models if complete accuracy is to be achieved. In other words, separation can only be accomplished via nonlinear surfaces and the approximation of such surfaces, by piece-wise linear approximations, can be a tedious process.

Roy's method uses quadratic (or, if desired, any polynomial) surfaces and thus alleviates what we consider to be one disadvantage of the method of Bennett and Mangasarian. However, Roy's method is not without drawbacks. One of the most prominent of these is the fact that there is a repeated need for cluster analysis — and any clusters so derived are a function of the particular (*heuristic*) cluster analysis method employed. As such, the successful implementation of Roy's method requires — we believe — a substantial amount of art, judgement, and experience. Further, the final solution obtained by Roy's method is dependent upon the order in which the classes are considered, the specific clustering algorithm used, and the judgement of the user (e.g., as to when to consider points to be outliers). Consequently, for the same problem, different individuals can develop different solutions and different network structures. Another drawback of the method is that the LP models that must be solved are frequently of large size. In fact, such models often have as many (or nearly as many) rows as there are objects *of all classes*. Consider, for example, a rather modest-size problem with five classes and roughly 100 objects per class in the training set. The solution of this problem via Roy's method would require the frequent solution of LP models with about 500 constraints per model.

3.2 A Comparison with Our Method
Before addressing the details of the approach that we propose, let us compare our concept with that of both Bennett/Mangasarian and Roy. Specifically, our method:

- never requires the solution of any LP model of size greater than ($m_k + F_k$) rows by (j) variables; where m_k is the number of objects in class k, j is the number of scores (i.e., features, or attributes), and F_k is the number of foreign objects within the supermask of class k (typically, a small number). (Thus, for the five class, 100 training objects/class example stated above, our method would never require the solution of an LP exceeding roughly 100 constraints while that of Roy would require the solution of models with 500 constraints. *And, by taking advantage of the peculiar structure of LP models for pattern classification, we are able to even further reduce the sizes of these models.*)
- employs a strictly algorithmic, systematic procedure that avoids heuristic and/or *ad hoc*, judgmental methods (e.g., such as clustering analysis and/or outlier deletion) and thus will develop results that may be replicated.
- utilizes, as does Roy's method, nonlinear separation surfaces and thus avoids the need for less efficient piece-wise linear surfaces.
- is, like the method of Bennett/Mangasarian or Roy, completely nonparametric and results in all of the information needed to construct a fully-trained neural network classifier.
- Further, the method that we have developed addresses, directly, a number of issues that have not been addressed in the earlier, alternative concepts. These include:
  - specific hardware design and implementation considerations

- efficient classification of "ambiguous" objects (i.e., those new objects that either do not lie within any existing boundaries *or* that lie within the regions claimed by two or more classes)
- the adaptation of LP-based sensitivity analysis for the sensitivity analysis of the resultant classifier

4 OVERVIEW OF *MOST*

The method that we have developed is denoted as the "Method of Supermasking and Trimming," or the MOST procedure. In order to best explain the MOST approach, consider a set of training data for objects associated with a problem of pattern classification. As may be noted in either Table 1 or Figure 1, there are 12 objects in class A and 8 in class B (the method is not limited to just the two-class problem as it proceeds in an identical fashion for any number of classes). Each object happens to be associated with two attributes (i.e., score 1 and score 2) and the values for these attributes are listed in the second and third columns of the table. Thus, our goal is to find a means to develop class boundaries that may then be used to classify any future objects that are encountered (i.e., into class A or B). Note that in Figure 1 the black boxes represent the class A objects and the circles represent those of class B. Clearly, linear separation is not possible and neither is it obvious as to whether or not those objects of class B (i.e., b1, b2, and b3) that appear to fall "within" class A are "outliers." (In fact, we may assume here that they are not and thus, if discarded, this decision would result in the development of less efficient boundaries.)

TABLE 1. Illustrative Training Set Data

Training Object	Score 1 $[x_{i,1,k}]$	Score 2 $[x_{i,2,k}]$	Object class
a1	0.2	0.5	A
a2	0.2	0.8	A
a3	0.3	0.4	A
a4	0.3	0.7	A
a5	0.4	0.3	A
a6	0.4	0.9	A
a7	0.5	0.3	A
a8	0.5	0.8	A
a9	0.6	0.4	A
a10	0.6	0.6	A
a11	0.6	0.7	A
a12	0.7	0.5	A
b1	0.4	0.5	B
b2	0.4	0.6	B
b3	0.5	0.5	B
b4	0.6	0.9	B
b5	0.7	0.8	B
b6	0.7	0.9	B
b7	0.8	0.7	B
b8	0.8	0.8	B

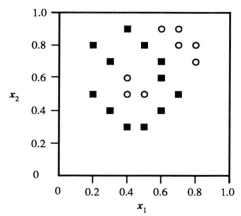

x_2

x_1

FIGURE 1. Graph of Training Set

The specific algorithm for the conduct of MOST (i.e., the Baek and Ignizio algorithm) is provided in the Appendix to this paper. Here, we simply illustrate its application on the training set listed previously.

We shall use the following notation throughout the remainder of the discussion:

$x_{i,j,k}$ = represents the score, on attribute j, of the ith object of class k (e.g, in Table 1, the score of object "a2" on test 2 may be denoted as $x_{2,1,1}$)

$i = 1, 2,\ldots, m;$ $\qquad j = 1, 2,\ldots, n;$ $\qquad k = 1, 2,\ldots, K$

We may — analogous to the masking concept proposed by Roy — employ a quadratic function to represent our *nonlinear* separating hypersurfaces, where this function is denoted as m(**x**), or the *masking function*. Thus, the mask boundary defined by m(**x**) = 0 may be represented as a hyperquadric — such as a hyperellipsoid.

In the two-dimensional case (i.e., just two attributes), the form taken on by the masking function is simply:

$$m(\mathbf{x}) = v_1 x_{i,1,k}{}^2 + v_2 x_{i,2,k}{}^2 + v_3 x_{i,1,k} x_{i,2,k} + v_4 x_{i,1,k} + v_5 x_{i,2,k} + v_6$$
where v_t = the weight to be assigned to term t of the quadratic function

Since the attribute scores (i.e., the values of the x's) are known, the masking function itself becomes simply a *linear* function of the unknown weights (the v's).

Given a set of training data, we proceed by first selecting all training data points associated with a specific class (e.g., class *r*). From this data, we form an associated LP model — and solve this model. The solution of the model provides us with the *supermask* for the class under consideration. In general, the LP model *for a supermask* is given as:

$$\text{minimize} \quad \sum_{i \in \mathbf{P}_r} \rho_i$$

subject to:

$$s_r(\mathbf{x}) - \rho_i = 0 \quad i \in \mathbf{P}_r,$$
$$v_1 = -1,$$
$$\rho_i \geq 0 \quad i \in \mathbf{P}_r,$$

where: $\mathbf{P}_r$ = the set of object indices associated with class r

ρ_i = deviation of any object of class r outside the boundaries of the supermask

$s_r(\mathbf{x})$ is the quadratic masking function for which the coefficients (i.e., the v_i's) are to be determined and is of the form as presented previously by m($\mathbf{x}$)

The solution of the above model will provide us with the coefficients of a *quadratic* expression. We term such a function a *supermask* and it always encompasses, within its boundaries, *all of the training data points of the specific class under consideration.* And this supermask concept is one of the new features of our approach — and a feature permitting, we believe, far more efficient classification. (It may also be noted that our supermasking concept completely eliminates the need for the repeated clustering analysis as employed in Roy's method.)

For our example, the LP model for determining the supermask of class A is given by:

$$\text{minimize } \rho_1+\rho_2+\rho_3+\rho_4+\rho_5+\rho_6+\rho_7+\rho_8+\rho_9+\rho_{10}+\rho_{11}+\rho_{12}$$

subject to:

$$0.04v_1+0.25v_2+0.10v_3+0.20v_4+0.50v_5+v_6-\rho_1=0$$
$$0.04v_1+0.64v_2+0.16v_3+0.20v_4+0.80v_5+v_6-\rho_2=0$$
$$0.09v_1+0.16v_2+0.12v_3+0.30v_4+0.40v_5+v_6-\rho_3=0$$
$$0.09v_1+0.49v_2+0.21v_3+0.30v_4+0.70v_5+v_6-\rho_4=0$$
$$0.16v_1+0.09v_2+0.12v_3+0.40v_4+0.30v_5+v_6-\rho_5=0$$
$$0.16v_1+0.81v_2+0.36v_3+0.40v_4+0.90v_5+v_6-\rho_6=0$$
$$0.25v_1+0.09v_2+0.15v_3+0.50v_4+0.30v_5+v_6-\rho_7=0$$
$$0.25v_1+0.64v_2+0.40v_3+0.50v_4+0.80v_5+v_6-\rho_8=0$$
$$0.36v_1+0.16v_2+0.24v_3+0.60v_4+0.40v_5+v_6-\rho_9=0$$
$$0.36v_1+0.36v_2+0.36v_3+0.60v_4+0.60v_5+v_6-\rho_{10}=0$$
$$0.36v_1+0.49v_2+0.42v_3+0.60v_4+0.70v_5+v_6-\rho_{11}=0$$
$$0.49v_1+0.25v_2+0.35v_3+0.70v_4+0.50v_5+v_6-\rho_{12}=0$$

$$v_1=-1 \text{ and } v_2,v_3,...,v_6 \text{ unrestricted}$$
$$\rho_i \geq 0 \quad i=1,2,...,12$$

Solving this LP model, we obtain the following values for the supermask:

$$v_1 = -1, \quad v_2 = -0.75, \quad v_3 = -0.375, \quad v_4 = 1.0875, \quad v_5 = 1.05, \quad v_6 = -0.4775.$$

Therefore, the supermask for the objects of class A is defined by:

$$-x_1^2 - 0.75x_2^2 - 0.375x_1x_2 + 1.0875x_1 + 1.05x_2 - 0.4775 \geq 0.$$

It is possible that a supermask may encompass objects of another class or classes — points we designate as *foreign objects*. If so, we must form one or more additional LP models so as to determine the *masks* of these foreign objects. In our example, the supermask function listed above will encompass 3 foreign objects: b1, b2, and b3. Thus, we develop a mask for these foreign objects. In general, the LP model to be solved for the determination of foreign object masks is given as:

$$\text{minimize} \quad \sum_{i \in A^{(u)}} \eta_i$$

subject to:

$$m_{r,u}(\mathbf{x}) \le 0 \quad i \in \mathbf{P}_r,$$

$$m_{r,u}(\mathbf{x}) + \eta_i - \rho_i = 0 \quad i \in A^{(u)},$$

$$\sum_{i \in A^{(u)}} \rho_i = 1,$$

$$\eta_i, \rho_i \ge 0 \quad i \in A^{(u)},$$

where: $m_{r,u}(\mathbf{x})$ represents the uth foreign object mask of class r

$A^{(u)}$ = the set of indices of all foreign objects prior to the development of the uth foreign object mask

η_i = the deviation variable associated with the ith foreign object

For our particular example, the LP model associated with the 3 foreign objects is given by:

$$\text{minimize} \quad \eta_1 + \eta_2 + \eta_3$$

subject to:

$$0.04v_1 + 0.25v_2 + 0.10v_3 + 0.20v_4 + 0.50v_5 + v_6 \le 0$$
$$0.04v_1 + 0.64v_2 + 0.16v_3 + 0.20v_4 + 0.80v_5 + v_6 \le 0$$
$$0.09v_1 + 0.16v_2 + 0.12v_3 + 0.30v_4 + 0.40v_5 + v_6 \le 0$$
$$0.09v_1 + 0.49v_2 + 0.21v_3 + 0.30v_4 + 0.70v_5 + v_6 \le 0$$
$$0.16v_1 + 0.09v_2 + 0.12v_3 + 0.40v_4 + 0.30v_5 + v_6 \le 0$$
$$0.16v_1 + 0.81v_2 + 0.36v_3 + 0.40v_4 + 0.90v_5 + v_6 \le 0$$
$$0.25v_1 + 0.09v_2 + 0.15v_3 + 0.50v_4 + 0.30v_5 + v_6 \le 0$$
$$0.25v_1 + 0.64v_2 + 0.40v_3 + 0.50v_4 + 0.80v_5 + v_6 \le 0$$
$$0.36v_1 + 0.16v_2 + 0.24v_3 + 0.60v_4 + 0.40v_5 + v_6 \le 0$$
$$0.36v_1 + 0.36v_2 + 0.36v_3 + 0.60v_4 + 0.60v_5 + v_6 \le 0$$
$$0.36v_1 + 0.49v_2 + 0.42v_3 + 0.60v_4 + 0.70v_5 + v_6 \le 0$$
$$0.49v_1 + 0.25v_2 + 0.35v_3 + 0.70v_4 + 0.50v_5 + v_6 \le 0$$
$$0.16v_1 + 0.25v_2 + 0.20v_3 + 0.40v_4 + 0.50v_5 + v_6 + \eta_1 - \rho_1 = 0$$
$$0.16v_1 + 0.36v_2 + 0.24v_3 + 0.40v_4 + 0.60v_5 + v_6 + \eta_2 - \rho_2 = 0$$
$$0.25v_1 + 0.25v_2 + 0.25v_3 + 0.50v_4 + 0.50v_5 + v_6 + \eta_3 - \rho_3 = 0$$
$$\rho_1 + \rho_2 + \rho_3 = 1$$
$$\eta_i, \rho_i \ge 0 \qquad i = 1,2,3$$
$$v_t \quad (t = 1,2,\ldots,6) \text{ unrestricted}$$

The solution of this latest LP model is given as:

$$\eta_1 = \eta_2 = \eta_3 = 0;$$

$$v_1 = -7.1429, \quad v_2 = -28.5714, \quad v_3 = 0, \quad v_4 = 6.4286, \quad v_5 = 28.5714, \quad v_6 = -8.1429.$$

Using these results, we may define the mask for the three foreign objects within the supermask of class A by the following function:

$$-7.1429x_1^2 - 28.5714x_2^2 + 6.4286x_1 + 28.5714x_2 - 8.1429 \geq 0.$$

Since $\eta_1 = \eta_2 = \eta_3 = 0$, all foreign objects are masked. We may then plot the supermask and the single associated foreign mask for class A — as depicted in Figure 2.

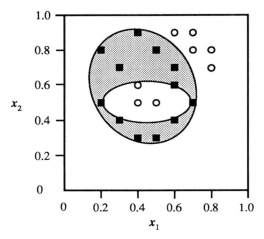

FIGURE 2. Supermask and Foreign Objects Mask for Class A

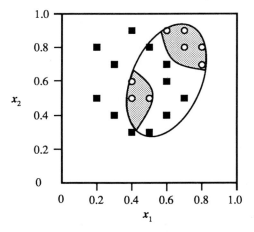

FIGURE 3. Supermask and Foreign Objects Mask for Class B

Any object within the boundaries of the supermask *and not* within a foreign mask may be considered to be of the same class as that associated with the supermask. The procedure is repeated for all remaining classes under consideration. The results for class B are depicted in Figure 3. There, the supermask is the ellipse encompassing all objects of class B and the foreign object mask is the unshaded region within the supermask of class B.

Once we have solved our series of LP models so as develop the supermasks and associated foreign object masks, we may then establish the associated neural network representation. Such a representation, in general form, is depicted in Figure 4.

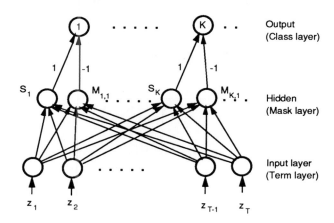

FIGURE 4: Neural Network Representation — General Form

The number of nodes in the output layer is equal to the number of classes. The number of nodes in the input layer is equal to the number of terms in the quadratic expression used to define the supermask or foreign object mask, and is denoted as T. The number of hidden layer nodes is equal to the number of supermasks and masks that had to be developed so as to define the boundaries of each class. Note further that:

- S_k represents the supermask node for class k (k = 1, 2,..., K)
- $M_{k,u}$ is the uth foreign object mask node associated with the supermask for class k
- z_t represents the input signal presented to the first layer node associated with the tth term of the quadratic function employed in the analysis

Finally, the weights on the various branches are determined as follows:

- The branch weight from input node t to a supermask (or mask) node of the hidden layer is given by the coefficient of the tth term of the quadratic function for that supermask (or mask).
- The branch weight from the hidden layer node associated with a supermask to an output layer node is given a value of +1.
- The branch weight from the hidden layer node associated with a foreign object mask to an output layer node is given a value of -1.

Returning to our numerical example, we may construct the associated (and trained) neural network using the results of the solution of our LP models. This network is depicted in Figure 5. Note that, in this figure, only the weights associated with the two supermasks have been specified in order to reduce the complexity of the drawing.

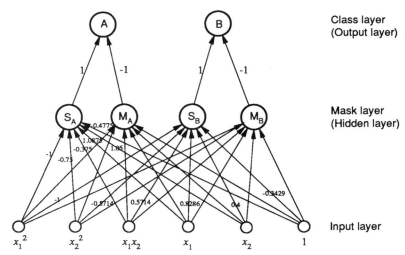

FIGURE 5. The Associated Neural Network for Table 1

For sake of discussion, assume that a new object is to be classed and has scores of 0.45, 0.55. Using the above neural net, classification is achieved. First, the scores will be transmitted to the input layer of the network. This will cause nodes M_A and S_B to be activated. This is because the object's scores fall within both the foreign mask of A *and* the supermask of B. The resultant activation of node M_A will assure that the output layer node A will be turned off while the activation of node S_B will cause output layer node B to be turned on. On the other hand, consider a new object with scores of 0.6, 0.5. It should be clear that such a data point will lie within both the foreign mask of A as well as the foreign mask of B — and would seem to then be assigned to neither class. However, in such "ambiguous" cases, we have refined the network so as to incorporate "maximum selector" layers (e.g, such as those advocated by Lippman [1987]) that serve to associate such data points to their "nearest" (in whatever sense desired) class.

4.1 Additional Enhancements

While the approach as proposed above is, we believe, already a substantial improvement over existing methods, there are still a number of additional enhancements that we are presently investigating. As we noted above, our concept of supermasking accomplishes two things: (i) it eliminates any need for cluster analysis (as used in Roy's method), and (ii) it serves to substantially reduce the size of the LP models that need to be solved. However, we can even further reduce these LP models by taking advantage of the specific nature of the LP models that are used to represent supermasking or masking construction. Here, we note but four examples of such model size reduction and/or exploitation.

First, it appears to almost always be possible (and relatively easy) to further reduce the size of the LP models employed for the determination of supermasks. This is because that the binding constraints in such models are those associated with objects closest to the exterior of the supermask boundaries. For example, in Figure 2 it may be noted that the object at coordinates 0.3 and 0.7 lies in the interior of the supermask and plays no role in the construction of that mask. In real world problems, with real world data, the occurrence of these "interior" elements is even more typical. Thus, we are examining methods for identifying and eliminating such objects (and thus their associated constraints) from the supermasking phase. One simplistic — but seemingly effective — way to accomplish this is to eliminate those objects closest to the centroid determined by all of the objects of the class for which the supermask is to be determined.

The second concept is similar to that noted above. However, here we note that it appears to be almost always possible (and, again, relatively easy) to further reduce the size of the LP models employed for the determination of foreign object masks. Here, we note that the objects associated with the mask, and "far" from the centroid of the foreign objects appear to seldom play a role in the determination of the foreign object mask.

Finally, in a typical LP model for supermasking and foreign object masking, the number of variables is generally far less than the number of rows. Since it is well known that the number of pivots required to solve an LP is a function of the number of rows, it would appear that the solution of the dual of these LP models should be considered.

5 THE EXPERT SYSTEM INTERFACE

While the primary thrust of both our method and this paper has been that of the integration of LP and neural networks, we have found that this integration could be facilitated by means of an expert systems interface. In fact, such an approach amounts to the use of intelligent interfacing [Ignizio, 1991]. Thus, our total concept involves the use of an expert system for the access of the data (i.e., training set) and the automatic transformation of this data into the LP models utilized in the algorithm. Further, the expert system analyzes the output of the LP problem solver so as to decide on the next step (e.g., if the object function value for the LP of a foreign object mask is zero-valued, we proceed to the next supermask — and if not, a new LP must be solved) and, finally, once all supermasks and foreign object masks have been constructed, the expert system uses that information to determine the architecture and branch weights of the associated neural network classifier. In addition to all of this, we are investigating the employment of the expert systems interface in the conduct and interpretation of the sensitivity analysis of the resulting network.

6 EMPIRICAL RESULTS

We have applied the MOST approach to a variety of problems, many of which have appeared in the literature on either pattern classification via statistical methods or in papers on the use of neural networks. In addition, a number of other training sets were synthesized. The results achieved thus far have been excellent. In all cases we are able to guarantee 100% accuracy of classification of the training set data while, at the same time, we retain the ability to generalize (i.e., by means of the maximum selector layers discussed earlier). More specifically, we are able to either surpass or, at the worst, duplicate the classification accuracy results achieved by either Bennett and Mangasarian, or Roy and Mukhopadhyay, while employing considerably smaller LP models. We intend, however, to continue this investigation and we hope to summarize the results obtained in a paper to follow.

7   SUMMARY AND CONCLUSIONS

The MOST method extends the notions presented in earlier works on the application of LP to neural network design and training. In particular, the results obtained by such methods (i.e., in pattern classification) may be, at the least, duplicated while employing smaller LP models and, typically, fewer iterations. Two of the most important new features of our approach is that of the employment of supermasks and reduction (trimming) of the size of the LP models in employed — leading to the name given the approach: MOST, for method of supermasking and trimming. In addition, we have incorporated the concept of generalization in our associated network structure.

8   REFERENCES

Bennett, K.P. and Mangasarian, O.L. (July 1990). "Neural Network Training via Linear Programming," Computer Sciences Technical Report #948, University of Wisconsin – Madison.

Freed, N. and Glover, F. (1981). "Simple But Powerful Goal Programming Models for Discriminant Problems," *European Journal of Operational Research*, 7, 44-66.

Ignizio, J. P. (1982). *Linear Programming in Single and Multiple Objective Systems*, Englewood Cliffs, New Jersey: Prentice-Hall.

Ignizio, J. P. (1991). *An Introduction to Expert Systems*, New York: McGraw-Hill.

Lippman, R.P. (April 1987). "An Introduction to Computing with Neural Nets," *IEEE ASSP Magazine*, 4-22.

Mangasarian, O. L. (1965). "Linear and Nonlinear Separation of Patterns by Linear Programming," *Operations Research*, *13*, 444-452.

Roy, A. and Mukhopadhyay, S. (1991). "Pattern Classification Using Linear Programming," *ORSA Journal on Computing*, *3* (1), 66-80.

9   APPENDIX: BAEK AND IGNIZIO ALGORITHM

It is assumed that we are provided with a training set consisting of K classes of objects. Further, we shall represent the set of indices associated with the objects of class r by $\mathbf{P}_r$.
1.   Set $r=1$, where r is the index associated with the class of objects presently under consideration.
2.   *Establishment of a Supermask*: To obtain the supermask of class r, denoted as $s_r(\mathbf{x})$, solve the following LP model

$$\text{minimize} \quad \sum_{i \in \mathbf{P}_r} \rho_i$$

subject to:

$$s_r(\mathbf{x}) - \rho_i = 0 \quad i \in \mathbf{P}_r,$$

$$v_1 = -1,$$

$$\rho_i \geq 0 \quad i \in \mathbf{P}_r, \tag{A.1}$$

where $s_r(\mathbf{x})$ is the quadratic *supermasking* function for which the coefficients (i.e., the v_i's) are to be determined.

3.　　*Identification of Foreign Objects*: Let $\mathbf{A}$ be the set of indices for those objects within the supermask of class r and which do not belong to class r, as defined by:

$$\mathbf{A} = \left\{ i \mid s_r(\mathbf{x}) \geq 0 \text{ and } i \in \left(\bigcup_{\substack{k=1 \\ k \neq r}}^{K} \mathbf{P}_k \right) \right\}. \tag{A.2}$$

(a)　　Set $u=1$, $\mathbf{A}^{(1)} = \mathbf{A}$.

(b)　　*Construction of Foreign Object Mask*: To obtain the uth foreign object mask of class r, denoted as $m_{r,u}(\mathbf{x})$, solve the following LP model

$$\text{minimize} \quad \sum_{i \in \mathbf{A}^{(u)}} \eta_i$$

subject to:

$$m_{r,u}(\mathbf{x}) \leq 0 \quad i \in \mathbf{P}_r,$$

$$m_{r,u}(\mathbf{x}) + \eta_i - \rho_i = 0 \quad i \in \mathbf{A}^{(u)},$$

$$\sum_{i \in \mathbf{A}^{(u)}} \rho_i = 1,$$

$$\eta_i, \rho_i \geq 0 \quad i \in \mathbf{A}^{(u)}, \tag{A.3}$$

where $m_{r,u}(\mathbf{x})$ is the quadratic masking function for which the coefficients are to be determined.

(c)　　If the LP model of (A.3) has the solution of $\sum \eta_i = 0$, go to step 4. Otherwise, proceed to step 3d, below.

(d)　　Identify the unseparated objects of the set $\mathbf{A}$ by

$$\mathbf{A}^{(u+1)} = \{ i \mid \eta_i > 0 \}. \tag{A.5}$$

Set $u=u+1$ and go to step 3.b.

4.　　If $r=K$, stop. Otherwise, set $r=r+1$ and return to step 2.

KEshell2:
An Intelligent Learning Data Base System

XINDONG WU

Department of Artificial Intelligence
University of Edinburgh
80 South Bridge. Edinburgh EH1 1HN, UK

Email: xindongw@castle.ed.ac.uk

Abstract

An intelligent learning data base (ILDB) system is an integrated learning system which implements automatic knowledge acquisition from data bases by providing formalisms for 1) translation of standard data base information into a form suitable for use by its induction engines, 2) using induction techniques to produce knowledge from data bases, and 3) interpreting the knowledge produced efficiently to solve users' problems. Although a lot of work on knowledge acquisition from data bases has been done, the requirements for building practical learning systems to learn from conventional data bases are still far away for existing systems to reach. A crucial requirement is more efficient learning algorithms as realistic data bases are usually fairly large. Based on *KEshell. dBASE3* and the low-order polynomial induction algorithm HCV. this paper presents a knowledge engineering shell. *KEshell2.* which implements the 3 phases of automatic knowledge acquisition from data bases in an integral way.

1   INTRODUCTION

Over the past twenty years data base research has evolved technologies that are now widely used in almost every computing and scientific field. However, many new advanced applications including computer-aided design (CAD), computer-aided manufacturing (CAM). computer-aided software engineering (CASE). image processing. and office automation (OA) have revealed that traditional data base management systems (DBMSs) are inadequate, especially on the following cases [Wu 90b]:

1

- Conventional data base technology has laid particular stress on dealing with large amounts of persistent and highly structured data efficiently and using transactions for concurrency control and recovery. For some applications like CAD/CAM [Wu 92c] where the data schemata need to vary frequently, new data models are needed.

- In some applications like geographical data and image data, the semantic relationships among data need to be represented as well as the data itself. Conventional data models in data base technology cannot support any representation facility for complex semantic information.

- Traditional data base technology can only support facilities for processing data. Along with the developments of other subjects, like decision science and AI, more and more applications need facilities for supporting both data and knowledge management.

That is why integrating AI technology into data base technology, called IDB (intelligent data base) research, has been identified [Brodie 88] as one of the research frontiers of data base technology and has become a popular research topic all over the world. The current research of IDB centers on five themes, i.e., object-oriented data base systems; deductive data base systems; expert data base systems; intelligent man-machine interfaces which include the design of meaningful operation interfaces and of friendly natural-language interfaces; and recursive query optimization. The knowledge bases (which contain deductive rules and/or semantic information such as the conceptual hierarchy among data) in existing IDB systems can only be built up by hand with known technology. Knowledge acquisition in IDB systems has become a central and difficult problem in IDB research. Research in this area is expected to lead to significant progress in the whole data base field.

Broadly speaking, all kinds of attribute-based learning algorithms can be adapted to extract knowledge from data bases. It is not difficult to add an induction engine to an existing data base system in an *ad hoc* way (such as [Cai *et al.* 91] and [Ke *et al.* 91]) to implement rule induction from data bases or design some specific engines to learn from domain-specific data sets (e.g., [Blum 82]). However, when we integrate machine learning (ML) techniques into data base systems, we must face many problems [Quinlan 89] such as:

- The knowledge learned needs to be tested and/or used back in the integrated IDB systems. This implies more expressive representations for both data (e.g., tuples in relational data bases, which represent instances of a problem domain) and knowledge (e.g., rules in a rule-based system, which can be used to solve users' problems in the domain) and deduction/inference mechanisms are needed.

- More efficient induction algorithms are needed. The algorithms should be capable of being applied to realistic data bases, e.g., $\geq 10^6$ relational tuples. This needs the algorithms to be more efficient than existing ones. Exponential or even medium-order polynomial complexity will not be of practical use.

- Another problem is how to balance ML facilities and other functions in the IDB systems, particularly when is the proper time to trigger the ML facilities.

The first and the third problems both relate how to couple ML facilities with data base and knowledge base technology in IDB systems. This is the main difficulty in developing practical IDB systems. However, the second problem concerning low-order polynomial time induction algorithms is the crucial requirement for knowledge acquisition from data bases. Although a lot of work (e.g., [Cai *et al.* 91], [Ke *et al.* 91] and various induction algorithms [Wu 92b]) has been done, the requirements above for knowledge acquisition from realistic data bases are still far away for existing systems to reach and no existing systems have been reported to be able to integrate ML techniques with both data base and knowledge base technology effectively.

Meanwhile, although some commercial successes have been found in existing learning systems, there are limitations on current ML techniques for both research and applications. Existing knowledge acquisition tools (such as [Mowforth 86, Boose and Gaines 88, Marcus 88]) have concentrated on building knowledge bases for expert systems and designing various learning algorithms. As data base technology has found wide applications in various fields, it will surely generate significant effect on ML research if we can couple them well. Therefore, research on knowledge acquisition from data bases can be viewed as an important frontier for both data base and ML technology [Wu 92b].

In this paper, we will describe an integrated learning system, *KEshell2*, which couples ML techniques with both data base and knowledge base technology. It provides mechanisms for 1) translating relational data base information into a unified representation which integrates data and knowledge, 2) using induction techniques to extract rules from data bases, and 3) interpreting the rules produced to solve users' problems. We define a system which has mechanisms to do all of these 3 phases of work as *an intelligent learning data base system* (ILDB). With an ILDB system, one can, for example, produce 100 or 200 conjunctive rules for 50 diseases from a million medical cases of the 50 diseases. Then, the ILDB system can use the rules in 2 different ways: keeping these rules instead of the original cases because the original cases might take a large space; and using these rules to diagnose new cases.

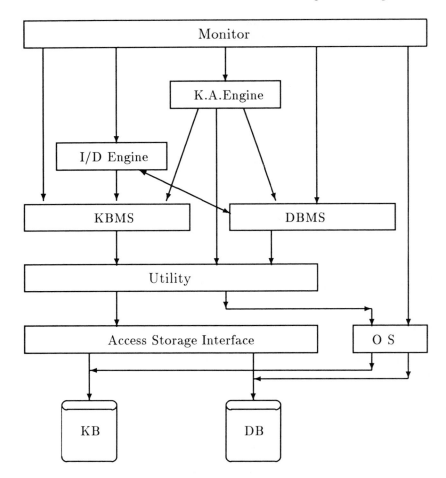

Figure 1: The System Structure of *KEshell2*

2   SYSTEM STRUCTURE

Figure 1 shows the system structure of *KEshell2*, the improved version of *KEshell* [Wu 90a, Wu 91b] with the knowledge acquisition engine, K.A. Engine, which implements induction from data bases, and the data base management subsystem, DBMS, based on *dBASE3* being integrated.

In the diagram, Monitor is a man-machine interface which exchanges information with users in form of pull-down menus. I/D Engine is an inference and deduction engine based on the inference engine of *KEshell*. KBMS and DBMS are facilities adopted mainly from *KEshell* and *dBASE3* respectively to support knowledge base and data base management functions. Utility contains a set of common procedures that are shared by K.A. Engine,

KBMS and DBMS. Access Storage Interface is composed of the basic knowledge/data operators. DB and KB denote data bases and knowledge bases respectively and OS indicates operating system facilities. For the implementation of *KEshell2*, the operating system used was PC-DOS, referred to as DOS hereafter.

2.1   Monitor

The Monitor module in *KEshell2* accepts users' operational commands and calls corresponding functional modules in the system.

There are five options in its main menu: 1. KBMS; 2. I/D Engine; 3. K.A. Engine; 4. DBMS; and 5. DOS with their second-level menus being as follows.

- KBMS: 1. Build a Knowledge Base, 2. Adapt Knowledge, 3. Find Cycles, 4. Sort a Knowledge Base, 5. List Rule Schemata, 6. List Concrete Rules, 7. Edit a KB File, and 8. Clear Working Memory.

- I/D Engine: 1. Forward Chaining, 2. Backward Chaining, 3. Deduction, 4. Knowledge Trace, 5. Clear Evidence, and 6. Adapt Facts.

- K.A. Engine: 1. Semantic Information, 2. Rule Induction by HCV, and 3. Rule Induction by ID3.

- DBMS: 1. Enter dBASE3, and 2. List a Relation.

- DOS: 0. Enter PC-DOS, 1. Load a KB File, 2. Save Knowledge, 3. Directory, 4. Print, 5. Copy, 6. Delete, 7. Rename, 8. Time, 9. Date, 10. List Facts, 11. Adapt Facts, 12. Save Working Memory, 13. Edit a Text File, 14. List a DOS File, and 15. Quit.

The functions of most of the second-level submodules are just what their names have said.

2.2   KBMS

The KBMS module in *KEshell2* is adopted from the *KEshell* system [Wu 90a, Wu 91b]. It supports facilities for interactively building, adapting and displaying knowledge bases, checking for semantic inconsistencies including dead cycles [Wu *et al.* 90a], sorting knowledge bases into partial order to implement linear forward chaining [Wu 91a] and editing knowledge base files.

2.3   DBMS

The DBMS module in *KEshell2* is based on *dBASE3*, a commercial relational data base management system. Users can do conventional data base
operations by simply entering *dBASE3*. However, a new function, *List a
Relation*, is developed here to translate *dBASE3* files into the Prolog-based
representation [Wu 92e] which will be described in Section 3.

2.4   I/D Engine

All the submodules except Deduction in I/D Engine are taken from *KEshell*.
The Deduction submodule which will be described in Section 5 is designed
to interpret the rules produced by the K.A. Engine to solve users' problems.

2.5   K.A. Engine

There are three submodules in the K.A. Engine in *KEshell2*: 1) Semantic
Information, which is a simplified implementation of the approach to generation of semantic networks from relational data base schemata [Wu *et al.* 91],
2) Rule Induction by HCV, which implements the HCV algorithm designed
by the author [Wu 92a, Wu 92d], and 3) Rule Induction by ID3, which implements the well-known ID3 induction algorithm [Quinlan 86]. The second,
Rule Induction by HCV, and the first, Semantic Information, are the core
of the *KEshell2* system. We will describe them in detail in Section 4 and
Section 3 respectively.

3   TRANSLATION OF DATA BASE INFORMATION

3.1   The Prolog-based Representation

Semantic information in the real world includes four different categories:

- descriptive knowledge about entities,

- inherent laws and constraints between attributes or fields in entities,

- relationships among entities which can be further divided into six types
  [Wu *et al.* 90b][1], i.e., hierarchy, fellow member, attribute, role, causal-

---

[1]In order to give a more precise semantic classification, it is possible to divide one or
more of the relationship types here into greater detail. The completeness of a semantic
model can only be defined in terms of specific applications. We cannot say whether all
the relationships here are necessary for every application. Neither can we say they are
complete. However, as we have shown in [Wu 92e], they do exist in the real world.

ity and logical implication, and

- dependency types in the relationships between entities.

The E-R model is one of the most successful methods of formulating useful abstract models in the conceptual structure design of data bases and the key design aid for conventional data bases implemented under a wide variety of commercially available systems [Kazic *et al.* 90]. By focusing on the entities and their relationships, it structures the way designers approach the problem of creating extensible data bases. However, there are two substantial problems here. One is that transforming an E-R model into a relational model during the logical design of data bases results in loss of some semantic information that exists in the E-R model. In other words, the entities and relationships are not distinguished in the relational data model. It is impossible for the relational data model to describe the changes of relationship(s) and other entities caused by an entity in an E-R model. For example, *age* is an important factor for counting an employee's *salary* in many British institutions. However, we cannot explicitly express whether the employee's salary will increase according to the change of his/her age in the relational data model. The other problem is that the E-R model itself is insufficient in expressing complex semantic information as its relationship types, such as one to many and many to many, are too simple to describe explicitly semantic features of the relationships between entities and within entities themselves. For example, different types of relationships, such as logical implication and conceptual inheritance, cannot be expressed in the E-R model.

The E-R model and the relational data model are successful in those applications where only the ability to deal with large amounts of persistent and fixed-format data efficiently is needed. For new applications, such as those mentioned in the introductions, new representation models are in demand. Object-oriented data models are a new generation of extended data models, based on the relational data model. However, object-oriented models are themselves data models although some systems (e.g., POSTGRES [Cattell *et al.* 91]) have included rule processing facilities. Data management, object management and knowledge management are three different dimensions of problem solving techniques. They would all be needed in some complex applications. Knowledge management entails the ability to represent, acquire and enforce a collection of expertise which is part of the semantics of an application. Such expertise describes integrity constraints among data in the application as well as allowing the derivation of data which is usually called virtual data contrasting to the real data stored in the data base(s). The task of knowledge management is a key motivation of deductive data bases research.

To implement both data base and knowledge base management in a single system, we have designed a Prolog-based representation in *KEshell2* with an emphasis on expressing the semantic information which cannot be represented in the relational data model or the E-R model. The following is a summary of the thirteen predicates in the Prolog-based representation. Detailed descriptions and examples of these predicates can be found in [Wu 92e].

$$relation(RelationName, FieldList, Tuples) \tag{1}$$
$$field(RelationName, FieldName, Type) \tag{2}$$
$$is-assoc(Relation) \tag{3}$$
$$assoc-entity(Relation, EntityList, AssocTypeList) \tag{4}$$
$$assoc-type(Relation, AssocType) \tag{5}$$
$$label(Entity, Relation, Label) \tag{6}$$
$$schema(Relation, CauseEntityList, ResultEntity), \tag{7}$$
$$body-left(Relation, No, CauseOrResultEntity, Attri, RelSym, Value), \tag{8}$$
$$body-right(Relation, No, ResultEntity, Attri, Value) \tag{9}$$
$$constraint1(Relation, Attribute, RelSym, Value) \tag{10}$$
$$constraint2(Relation, MappingType) \tag{11}$$
$$constraint3(Relation, Attribute, OuterVariableList, ConstraintString) \tag{12}$$
$$function((Relation, Attribute), (Rel, Attri)List, Function) \tag{13}$$

Predicates (1) and (2) explicitly describe both relational schemata and tuples. Predicate (3) distinguishes relationships from entities. Predicate (4) describes an entity-relationship association in the E-R model. Predicates (5) and (6) identify the semantic type of each relationship and each entity's semantic role in each relationship. Predicates (7), (8) and (9) represent rules in the form of "rule schema + rule body" [Wu 90a, Wu 91b]. Predicates (10), (11) and (12) describe three kinds of constraints knowledge: the integrity of attributes in each relation in the relational data model, the dependency type of each relationship, and the constraint relationship between an attribute in a relation and outer variables. Finally, Predicate (13) describes the regularities of the attributes themselves.

The thirteen predicates here can explicitly represent all the information that can be expressed in the E-R model (i.e., entities, relationships and constraints). Also, the representation binds the actual data, data schemata and semantic constraints together in an explicit way as against the characteristic [Nieme *et al.* 91] of the current deductive data bases that only actual data is represented explicitly in logic while the data schema is implicitly described in form of predicates and thus the disadvantages of the normal way to model relational data bases in Prolog have been eliminated.

3.2   Translation of dBASE3 Files into the Prolog-based Representation

The *List a Relation* submodule in DBMS reads and translates relational data bases in the form of dBASE3 files into the predicates in the Prolog-based representation outlined in Section 3.1.

Table 1: Relational Schema in GOLF.DBF

FIELD	TYPE	WIDTH
ORDER	numeric	2
OUTLOOK	string	8
TEMPERATURE	string	4
HUMIDITY	string	6
WINDY	string	5
DECISION	string	10

Table 2: Tuples in GOLF.DBF

ORDER	OUTLOOK	TEMPERATURE	HUMIDITY	WINDY	DECISION
1	rain	hot	high	true	Don't Play
2	rain	cool	normal	true	Don't Play
3	overcast	hot	high	true	Play
4	overcast	mild	normal	false	Play
5	rain	hot	high	false	Play
6	overcast	cool	normal	true	Play
7	sunny	hot	normal	true	Don't Play
8	sunny	mild	high	true	Don't Play
9	sunny	mild	normal	false	Play
10	rain	cool	normal	false	Play
11	rain	hot	high	false	Play
12	sunny	hot	high	false	Don't Play
13	sunny	cool	normal	false	Don't Play
14	rain	mild	normal	true	Don't Play

For example, GOLF (adapted from [Quinlan 86]) is a sample dBASE3 file. The relational schema and tuples included in the file are listed in Tables 1 and 2 respectively. The corresponding predicates translated by *List a Relation* are given below.

```
relation("GOLF",
["ORDER","OUTLOOK","TEMPERATURE","HUMIDITY",
    "WINDY","DECISION"],
[tuple("1", rain, hot, high, true, "Don't Play"),
tuple("2", rain, cool, normal, true, "Don't Play"),
tuple("3", overcast, hot, high, true, "Play"),
tuple("4", overcast, mild, normal, false, "Play"),
tuple("5", rain, hot, high, false, "Play"),
tuple("6", overcast, cool, normal, true, "Play"),
tuple("7", sunny, hot, normal, true, "Don't Play"),
tuple("8", sunny, mild, high, true, "Don't Play"),
tuple("9", sunny, mild, normal, false, "Play"),
tuple("10", rain, cool, normal, false, "Play"),
tuple("11", rain, hot, high, false, "Play"),
tuple("12", sunny, hot, high, false, "Don't Play"),
tuple("13", sunny, cool, normal, false, "Don't Play"
tuple("14", rain, mild, normal, true, "Don't Play"])
field("GOLF", "ORDER", integer)
field("GOLF", "OUTLOOK", string)
field("GOLF", "TEMPERATURE", string)
field("GOLF", "HUMIDITY", string)
field("GOLF", "WINDY", string)
field("GOLF", "DECISION", string)
```

3.3   Semantic Information Acquisition

The theme of *KEshell2* is the provision of mechanisms for extracting knowledge from data bases. It has not been expected to provide a meaningful operation interface which can detect semantic errors in users' questions by using complex semantic information rather than simply supporting answers or 'no solution'. Therefore, only deductive knowledge which can be used to trigger induction engines are acquired in the Semantic Information submodule.

Simplified from the approach that generates semantic networks from relational data base schemata [Wu *et al.* 91], the Semantic Information submodule in the K.A. Engine works according to the following steps.

1. Find all relations in the working directory, which can be set or changed by the Directory submodule in the DOS module;

2. Ask the user to identify which of the relations is a relationship and of either causality or logical implication type;

3. Read the schema in the identified relation and ask the user to describe the causality structure between the fields in the schema; and

4. Read the tuples in the relation and translate them into executable forms for induction.

The following is an example run of this submodule on the GOLF file shown in Tables 1 and 2. The sentences with K: at the beginning are generated by *KEshell2* and those with M: are input of the user.

K: All the relations in the current working memory have been detected are:
K: DISEASE, GOLF, MONK1, MONK2, MONK3
K: Please indicate which of them is a relationship AND
K: of either causality or logical implication type:
M: GOLF
K: Now, please identify the semantic labels of attributes
K: in the relationship:
K: (All the fields in the GOLF relationship are
K: ORDER, OUTLOOK, TEMPERATURE, HUMIDITY, WINDY, DECISION)
K: The result field:
M: DECISION
K: and the condition fields:
M: OUTLOOK, TEMPERATURE, HUMIDITY, WINDY
K: O.K. The logic structure is:
K: IF OUTLOOK, TEMPERATURE, HUMIDITY, WINDY then DECISION
K: Would you like to induce rules from your current data base now?
M: N

If 'Y'(yes), this submodule will automatically call the Rule Induction by HCV submodule.

4 INDUCTION FROM DATA BASES

4.1 A Survey of Induction Algorithms

Machine learning is a major subfield of artificial intelligence. It has been seen as a feasible way of avoiding the knowledge bottleneck problem in knowledge-based systems development. Research on ML has concentrated in the main on inducing rules from unordered sets of examples, especially attribute-based induction, a formalism where examples are described in terms of a fixed collection of attributes. The learning systems in commercial use today are only inductive ones. Among various induction algorithms [Wu 92b], the three typical families are: the generalization-specialization strategy based AQ-like family including the version space (candidate elimination) and Focussing algorithms, the decision-tree method based ID3-like family, and the extension matrix approach based family.

AQ11 [Michalski *et al.* 78] and ID3 [Quinlan 86] are the two most widespread algorithms in ML. They are respectively representatives of the AQ-like family and the decision-tree method based family. Although AQ11 has been improved on its capacities of noise (including poor description) handling, incremental induction, decreasing rule complexity under noise environments, and constructive induction in its successors such as CN2 [Clark *et al.* 89], AQ15 [Michalski *et al.* 86], and AQ17 [Bloedorn *et al.* 91], and ID3 has been improved on its capacities of decision trees binarization, processing real-valued attributes, incremental induction, gain ratio heuristic for selecting tests, post-pruning of decision trees, and converting decision trees into production rules in its descendants such as NewId [Boswell 90], ID5R [Utgoff 89] and C4.5 (personal communication with Ross Quinlan, May 28, 1992), the ideas developed in AQ11 and ID3 are still the core of the 2 families of algorithms.

However, a new family of inductive algorithms based on the extension matrix approach has been proposed recently. Some experiment has shown [Hong *et al.* 86] that an AE1 algorithm of this family is faster than AQ11 in some cases. We will show below that the new HCV algorithm of this family designed in *KEshell2* has some significant features in time complexity and rule compactness. Since the AQ11 algorithm has been shown [O'Rorke 82] to be more expensive in both the cost of rule production and the complexity of rules produced than the ID3 algorithm, we will compare HCV with only ID3.

4.2   The HCV Induction Algorithm

Let a be the number of attributes $\{X_1, ..., X_a\}$ in an example space, n be $\mid NE \mid = \mid \{e_1^-, ..., e_n^-\} \mid$ where e_i^- $(i = 1, ..., n)$ is the i-th negative example and NE is the set of negative examples, p be $\mid PE \mid = \mid \{e_1^+, ..., e_p^+\} \mid$ where e_i^+ $(i = 1, ..., p)$ is the i-th positive example and PE is the set of positive examples, and $NEM = \{e_1^-, ..., e_n^-\}^T = (r_{ij})_{n*a}$ where T stands for the transpose of a matrix. The *extension matrix* of the k-th $(k = 1, ..., p)$ positive example $e_k^+ = (v_{1k}^+, ..., v_{ak}^+)$ against NE is defined as

$$EM_k = (r_{ij_k})_{n*a}$$

where

$$r_{ij_k} = \begin{cases} * & when \; v_{j_k}^+ = NEM_{ij} \\ NEM_{ij} & when \; v_{j_k}^+ \neq NEM_{ij} \end{cases}$$

and '$*$' denotes a dead element which can not be used to distinguish the positive example from negative examples.

A set of n nondead elements r_{ij_i} $(i \in \{1, ..., n\}, j_i \in \{1, ..., a\})$ that come from the n different i rows of EM_k is called a *path* in EM_k. The path corresponds to the following conjunctive *formula*

$$L = \bigwedge_{i=1}^{n} [X_{j_i} \neq r_{ij_i}]$$

which covers e_k^+ against NE. Each $[X_{j_i} \neq r_{ij_i}]$ here is a selector in variable-valued logic [Michalski 75].

When there exists at least one common path in $EM_{i_1}, ..., EM_{i_k}$ of a positive example set $\{e_{i_1}^+, ..., e_{i_k}^+\}$ against NE, the positive example set is called an *intersecting group* and a formula which corresponds to a common path covers all the intersecting group against NE.

There are two striking optimization problems in the extension matrix approach:

- The minimum formula (MFL) problem: Generating a conjunctive formula that covers a positive example or an intersecting group of positive examples against NE and has the minimum number of different conjunctive selectors.

- The minimum cover (MCV) problem: Seeking a cover which covers all positive examples in PE against NE and has the minimum number of conjunctive formulae with each conjunctive formula being as short as possible.

As the extension matrix EM_k of each positive example e_k^+ against NE contains all such paths that each correspond to a conjunctive formula of e_k^+ against NE and an optimal cover of PE against NE is such a minimum set of formulae that is a logical combination of all the formulae from every EM_k $(k = 1, ..., p)$, both MFL and MCV problems have been proved to be NP-hard [Hong 85]. [Hong 85] proposes two heuristic strategies in AE1: starting search from the columns with the most nondead elements; and simplifying redundance by deductive inference rules in mathematical logic. However, as shown in [Wu 92d], the first heuristic can easily lose optimal solutions in some cases and the second one is still NP-hard in time complexity.

The basic idea for the HCV algorithm is to partition PE into p' $(p' \leq p)$ intersecting groups first; call the heuristic algorithm HFL, which is designed to find a heuristic conjunctive formula (Hfl) which corresponds to a path in an extension matrix or a common path in all the extension matrixes of an intersecting group of positive examples, to find a Hfl for each intersecting group; then finally give the covering formula by logically ORing all the Hfl's.

Four strategies are adopted in the HFL algorithm:

1. The *fast* strategy. In an extension matrix $EM_k = (r_{ij})_{n*a}$, if there is no dead element in a (say j) column, then $[X_j \neq r_j]$ where $r_j = \vee_{i=1}^{a} r_{ij}$ is chosen as the one selector cover for EM_k.

2. The *precedence* strategy. When a r_{ij} in column j is the only nondead element of a row i in an extension matrix $EM_k = (r_{ij})_{n*a}$, the selector $[X_j \neq r_j]$ where $r_j = \vee_{i=1}^{a} r_{ij}$ is called an inevitable selector and thus is chosen with top precedence.

3. The *elimination* strategy. When each appearance of some nondead element in the j_1-th column of some row is always coupled with another nondead element in the j_2-th column of the same row in an extension matrix $EM_k = (r_{ij})_{n*a}$, $[X_{j_1} \neq r_{j_1}]$ where $r_{j_1} = \vee_{i=1}^{a} r_{ij_1}$ is called an eliminable selector and thus eliminated by selector $[X_{j_2} \neq r_{j_2}]$ where $r_{j_2} = \vee_{i=1}^{a} r_{ij_2}$.

4. The *least-frequency* strategy. When all inevitable selectors have been chosen and all eliminable selectors have been excluded but all the selectors chosen have not yet covered all the rows in an extension matrix, exclude a least-frequency selector which has least nondead elements in its corresponding column in the extension matrix.

The first three strategies are complete, which means if there exists one or more shortest conjunctive formulae in an extension matrix they will find it, while the fourth strategy is a sensible heuristic because choosing a column with fewer nondead elements means more columns thus more selectors may be involved in connecting a path.

The time complexity for HCV is $O(pna^3 + p^2na)$ [Wu 92b] and there are 2 theorems below concerning its correctness and performance.

Theorem 1. The formula generated by HCV covers all the positive examples against negative examples in a given example set.

Theorem 2. If there exists at least one conjunctive cover in a given training example set, the formula produced by HCV must be a conjunctive one.

4.3   An Example Run

Taking the data set in Table 2 as an example, the Rule Induction by HCV submodule in the K.A. Engine produces five rules:

if [OUTLOOK=overcast] then [DECISION=Play],

if [WINDY=false] & [OUTLOOK=rain] then [DECISION=Play],

if [TEMPERATURE=mild] & [WINDY=false] then [DECISION=Play],

if [OUTLOOK=[sunny,rain]] & [WINDY=true] then [DECISION=Don't Play], and

if [OUTLOOK=sunny] & [TEMPERATURE=[cool,hot]] then [DECISION=Don't Play].

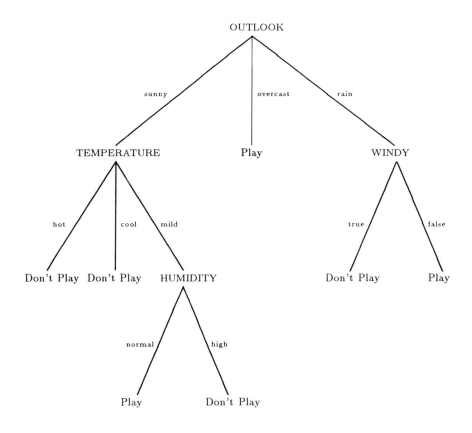

Figure 2: A decision tree for GOLF.

Meanwhile, the decision tree generated by ID3 in the Rule Induction by ID3 submodule for the same example set is shown in Figure 2 which is equivalent to the following decision rules:

if *OUTLOOK=overcast* then *Play*;

if *OUTLOOK=rain* & *WINDY=true* then *Don't Play*;

if *OUTLOOK=rain* & *WINDY=false* then *Play*;

if *OUTLOOK=sunny* & *TEMPERATURE = hot* then *Don't Play*;

if *OUTLOOK=sunny* & *TEMPERATURE = cool* then *Don't Play*;

if *OUTLOOK=sunny* & *TEMPERATURE = mild* & *HUMIDITY=normal* then *Play*; and

if *OUTLOOK=sunny* & *TEMPERATURE = mild* & *HUMIDITY=high* then *Don't Play*.

4.4   A Comparison with HCV and ID3

The reason for using decision trees rather than rules, such as the variable-valued logic rules adopted in AQ11 and HCV, is said by [Jackson 90] to be that the ID3-like algorithms are comparatively simpler than other learning algorithms. From the time complexity of HCV, we can say that the argument is now no longer convincing. Although the information theoretic heuristic (the entropy measure) in ID3 is by no means complete, ID3 needs to examine all possible candidate attributes and their values to choose one attribute at each non-leaf node of its decision trees and thus its time complexity is still expensive [Utgoff 89]. In HCV, although all of the *fast, precedence* and *elimination* strategies are complete, which means if there exists one or more shortest conjunctive formulae in an extension matrix they will not lose it, the *fast* strategy can choose an optimal attribute as soon as it finds the attribute without any attention to other attributes and the *precedence* strategy can choose an inevitable attribute by examining only the values of a row in an extension matrix. High efficiency has been seen as an important requirement for knowledge discovery and exponential or even medium-order polynomial complexity will not be of practical use [Quinlan 89] in realistic data bases. Therefore, the first significant advantage of the HCV algorithm is its low-order polynomial time. It supports a reasonable solution to the NP-hard problem in the extension matrix approach for inductive learning.

With respect to rule compactness, different values of the same attribute (either symbolic or numerical) which take on only positive examples can be easily grouped into a selector in the variable-valued logic. In ID3, once an attribute is selected, all arcs labeled by values that attribute takes must be expanded. This can still make the number of branches (paths) large since at each arc only one value can be labeled, and resulting paths might be longer than those actually needed because, by the time specific concepts (leaves on the decision tree) are developed, irrelevant variables may have been introduced. All of the four strategies in HFL and the partitioning technique in HCV are designed to reduce the number of selectors. For those problems where the *fast, precedence* and *elimination* strategies are enough to produce their final formulae, we can guarantee that the formulae are optimal. From Theorem 2, if there exists at least one conjunctive cover in a given training example set for positive examples against negative examples, the formula produced by HCV must be a conjunctive one. However, the information theoretic heuristic in ID3 is not complete, which means it is not guaranteed to find the simplest decision tree that characterizes the given training instances. From the example set given above and various experiments on different sized data sets including the MONK's problems [Thrun *et al.* 91], the rules produced by HCV are always more compact in terms of the numbers of conjunctive rules and conjunctions than the decision trees or their equivalent decision rules produced by ID3. So, the compactness of rules in HCV is its second advantage. However, the *least-frequency* strategy is still heuristic. We cannot guarantee the rules produced by HCV must be more compact than the decision trees generated by ID3 in all cases.

Also, the rules in the form of variable-valued logic produced in HCV are similar to that adopted in AQ11, which is said [O'Rorke 82] to be the advantage of AQ11 over ID3.

5 INTERPRETING RULES TO SOLVE USERS' PROBLEMS

The Deduction submodule in the I/D Engine is designed to classify examples according to the rules produced by the Rule Induction by HCV submodule. It is actually a data-driven forward chaining engine.

Taking the rules produced by HCV in Section 4.3 as an example, the following is an example run of the Deduction submodule.

    K: The rules (Hfl's) in the working memory are:
    K: if [OUTLOOK=overcast] then [DECISION=Play]
    K: if [WINDY=false] & [OUTLOOK=rain] then [DECISION=Play]
    K: if [TEMPERATURE=mild] & [WINDY=false] then [DECISION=Play]
    K: Please input your example in form of <field/attribute>=<value>:
    M: OUTLOOK=rain, TEMPERATURE=hot, HUMIDITY=normal, WINDY=false
    K: According to the 2nd hfl, (i.e.,
    K: if [WINDY=false] & [OUTLOOK=rain] then [DECISION=Play]
    K:), the deduction result is: Play.

6 CONCLUSIONS

Knowledge acquisition from data bases has been worked over by researchers in several disciplines including AI and data bases for 20 years and is still an important research frontier for both machine learning and data base technology [Wu 92b]. Although a lot of work has been done and some commercial learning packages are available already, existing work has concentrated on the following 4 aspects: 1) building knowledge bases for expert systems, 2) designing various learning algorithms; 3) adding an induction engine to an existing data base system in an *ad hoc* way to implement rule induction from data bases; and 4) designing a specific engine to learn from a domain-specific data set. As we have described, *KEshell2* is an integrated knowledge engineering shell which couples machine learning techniques with both data base and knowledge base technology. It has provided mechanisms for 1) translating *dBASE3* files into the Prolog-based representation which integrates data and knowledge, 2) using induction techniques to extract knowledge from data bases, and 3) interpreting the knowledge produced to solve users' problems. Although there are still some limitations on the current *KEshell2* for putting it into large applications due to it being implemented on PC machines, all the functions and capacities shown in *KEshell2* have demonstrated that the target of building practical intelligent data base systems to implement automatic knowledge acquisition from data bases is no longer difficult or elusive. *KEshell2* is the first ILDB system reported to date which implements the whole three phases of automatic knowledge acquisition from data bases in an integral way.

Acknowledgements

The work presented in this paper was supported in part by the National Natural Science Foundation of China under Grant No. 68975025 when the author was the grant holder and designer of the 68975025 project and is supported in part by the ORS Award of the United Kingdom and the University of Edinburgh Research Scholarship. The author would like to thank Dave Robertson, Robert Rae and Peter Ross for their valuable comments and advice.

References

[Bloedorn *et al.* 91] E. Bloedorn, R.S. Michalski, and J. Wnek, AQ17 - A Multistrategy Constructive Learning System, *Reports of Machine Learning and Inference Laboratory*, Center for Artificial Intelligence, George Mason University, 1991.

[Blum 82] R.L. Blum, Discovery, Confirmation, and Incorporation of Causal Relationships from a Large Time-Oriented Clinical Data Base - The RX Project, *Computers and Biomedical Research*, **15**(1982), 2: 164–187.

[Boose and Gaines 88] J.H. Boose and B.R. Gaines (Eds.), *Knowledge Acquisition Tools for Expert Systems*, Academic Press, 1988.

[Boswell 90] R. Boswell, Manual for NewID version 6.1, *TI/P2154/RAB/4/2.5*, The Turing Institute, Glasgow, 1990.

[Brodie 88] M.L. Brodie, Future Intelligent Information Systems: The Combination of Artificial Intelligence and Data Base Technology, *Readings in Artificial Intelligence and Data Bases*, 1988.

[Cai *et al.* 91] Y. Cai, N. Cercone and J. Han, Learning in Relational Databases: An Attribute-Oriented Approach, *Computational Intelligence*, **7**(1991), 3: 119–132.

[Cattell *et al.* 91] R.G.G. Cattell *et al.*, Next Generation Database Systems, *Communications of the ACM* (special section), Vol. **34**, No. 10, 1991.

[Clark *et al.* 89] P. Clark and T. Niblett, The CN2 Induction Algorithm, *Machine Learning*, **3**(1989), 261–283.

[Hong 85] J. Hong, AE1: An Extension Matrix Approximate Method for the General Covering Problem, *International Journal of Computer and Information Sciences*, **14**(1985), 6:421–437.

[Hong *et al.* 86] J.R. Hong, R.S. Michalski and C. Uhrik, An Extension Matrix Approach to the General Covering Problem, *Applications of Artificial Intelligence I*, J. Gilmore (Ed.), *Proceedings of SPIE 635*, Orlando, Florida, USA, 1986.

[Jackson 90] P. Jackson, *Introduction to Expert Systems*, Second Edition, Addison-Wesley, 1990.

[Kazic *et al.* 90] T. Kazic, E. Lusk, R. Olson, R. Overbeek and S. Tuecke, Prototyping Databases in Prolog, *The Practice of Prolog*, L.S. Sterling (Ed.), The MIT Press, 1990, 1–29.

[Ke *et al.* 91] M. Ke and M. Ali, A Knowledge-Directed Induction Methodology for Intelligent Database Systems, *International Journal of Expert Systems*, **4**(1991), 1: 71–115.

[Marcus 88] S. Marcus (Ed.), *Automating Knowledge Acquisition for Expert Systems*, Kluwer Academic Publishers, 1988.

[Michalski 75] R.S. Michalski, Variable-Valued Logic and Its Applications to Pattern Recognition and Machine Learning, *Computer Science and Multiple-Valued Logic Theory and Applications*, D.C. Rine (Ed.), Amsterdam: North-Holland, 1975, 506–534.

[Michalski *et al.* 78] R.S. Michalski and J. Larson, Selection of Most Representative Training Examples and Incremental Generation of VL1 Hypothesis: the Underlying Methodology and Description of Programs ESEL and AQ11, *Tech. Report UIUCDCS-R-78-867*, Dept. of Computer Science, Univ. of Illinois at Champaign–Urbana, 1978.

[Michalski *et al.* 86] R. Michalski, I. Mozetic, J. Hong and N. Lavrac, The AQ15 Inductive Learning System: An Overview and Experiments, *Proceedings of IMAL 1986*, Universite de Paris-Sud, Orsay, 1986.

[Mowforth 86] P. Mowforth, Some Applications with Inductive Expert Systems Shells, *TIOP-86-002*, The Turing Institute, Glasgow, 1986.

[Nieme *et al.* 91] T. Nieme and K. Järvelin, Prolog-Based Meta Rules for Relational Database Representation and Manipulation, *IEEE Transactions on Software Engineering*, **17**(1991), 8: 762–788.

[O'Rorke 82] P. O'Rorke, A Comparative Study of Inductive Learning Systems AQ11P and ID3 Using a Chess End-Game Test Problem, *ISG 82-2*, Computer Science Department, University of Illinois at Urbana-Champaign, 1982.

[Quinlan 86] J.R. Quinlan, Induction of Decision Trees, *Machine Learning*, **1**(1986), 81–106.

[Quinlan 89] J.R. Quinlan, Requirements for Knowledge Discovery in Data Bases, *Proceedings of IJCAI-89 Workshop on Knowledge Discovery in Data Bases*, Detroit, USA, 1989, xiv.

[Thrun *et al.* 91] S.B. Thrun, *et al.*, The MONK's Problems – A Performance Comparison of Different Learning Algorithms, *CMU-CS-91-197*, School of Computer Science, Carnegie Mellon University, 1991.

[Utgoff 89] P.E. Utgoff, Incremental Induction of Decision Trees, *Machine Learning*, 4(1989), 161–186.

[Wu 90a] X. Wu, *Constructing Expert Systems*, Hefei: Press of the University of Science and Technology of China, China, 1990.

[Wu 90b] X. Wu, A Study on Intelligent Data Base Techniques, *Proceedings of the First Chinese Joint Conference on Artificial Intelligence*, Jilin, China, 1990, 23–30.

[Wu 91a] X. Wu, A Linear Forward Reasoning Algorithm Based on Knowledge Sorting, *Chinese Science Bulletin*, Chinese edition: **36**(1991), 3: 230–232; English edition: **36**(1991), 18: 1574–1577.

[Wu 91b] X. Wu, *KEshell*: A "Rule Skeleton + Rule Body" Based Knowledge Engineering Shell, *Applications of Artificial Intelligence IX* (Proceedings of SPIE 1468), M.M. Trivedi (Ed.), SPIE Society, Bellingham, USA, 1991, 632–639.

[Wu 92a] X. Wu, Optimization Problems in Extension Matrixes, *Science in China*, Series A, Chinese edition: **35**(1992), 2: 200–207; English edition, **35**(1992), 3: 363–373.

[Wu 92b] X. Wu, Inductive Learning: Algorithms and Frontiers, *Artificial Intelligence Review*, **6**(1992): in press.

[Wu 92c] X. Wu, A Frame Based Architecture for Information Integration in CIMS, *Journal of Computer Science and Technology*, **7**(1992): in press.

[Wu 92d] X. Wu, HCV: A Heuristic Covering Algorithm for Extension Matrix Approach, *DAI Research Paper No. 578*, Department of Artificial Intelligence, University of Edinburgh, 1992.

[Wu 92e] X. Wu, A Prolog-Based Representation for Integrating Knowledge and Data, *DAI Research Paper No. 580*, Dept. of Artificial Intelligence, Univ. of Edinburgh, 1992.

[Wu *et al.* 90a] X. Wu and L. Fan, A Cycle Recognition Algorithm for Reasoning Networks, *Journal of Applied Sciences* (in Chinese), **8**(1990), 349–353.

[Wu *et al.* 90b] X. Wu and D. Zhang, A Study of Knowledge Types, *Tech. Report NNSFC-HUT-CS-68975025-90-1*, Hefei University of Technology, 1990; *Journal of Systems Engineering* (in Chinese), accepted, to appear.

[Wu *et al.* 91] X. Wu and D. Zhang, An Approach to Generation of Semantic Network from Relational Data Base Schema, *Chinese Science Bulletin*, Chinese edition: **35**(1990), 21: 1674–1676; English edition: **36**(1991), 14: 1222–1225.

Approaches to Self-Explanation and System Visibility in the Context of Application Tasks.

G.A. Ringland, H.R. Chappel, S.C. Lambert, M.D. Wilson & G.J. Doe

SERC Rutherford Appleton Laboratory.
Chilton, Didcot, OXON. OX11 OQX.
United Kingdom.

ABSTRACT

The degree to which users understand and accept advice from Knowledge-Based Systems can be increased through explanation. However, different application tasks and different sets of users place diverse requirements on an explanation component of a Knowledge-Based System. Thus, the degree of portability of explanation components between applications is reduced. This paper discusses the aspects of explanation that change between application tasks and those that are required for any satisfactory explanation. The requirements placed on Knowledge-based Systems resulting from explanatory capabilities raises implications for the structure and contents of the knowledge-base and the visibility of the system. The discussion is illustrated by four Knowledge-Based System projects.

1. INTRODUCTION

An important feature of knowledge-based systems compared to other information-providing systems is that the knowledge on which they are based is represented explicitly in the system rather than hidden in the design of the system, or represented implicitly in an algorithm. The knowledge can therefore be used not only to solve the problem for which the knowledge-based system was built, but also to show the user what knowledge is used to solve the problem and hence go some way to explain the system's behaviour. However, whilst the explicitness of the knowledge makes it possible to provide some explanatory capability, it does not necessarily mean that the system is capable of producing every explanation required by its users. Some explanations require further reasoning and knowledge to retrieve and act on the knowledge already present in the knowledge-based system.

There are many reasons to add explanation to a knowledge-based system, for example:
1) To justify the system's conclusions to the user (e.g. because the user is sceptical);
2) To help users understand the application and how the conclusion is reached (e.g. because they are learning how to perform the task);

3) To allow the user to discover how changes in conditions produce different conclusions; (e.g. because the user wants to see what change would produce a preferred conclusion); 4) To allow knowledge engineers to understand the reasoning of a system (e.g. for debugging or maintenance purposes).

If these explanations are successful then they will have various beneficial consequences: user confidence in the system is increased; user-training is improved and their understanding of the problem solving process increased; the conclusions of the system are more satisfactory to the user; and the reliability of the system is improved. However, this highlights that there are different purposes and users of explanations even without considering differences arising between applications tasks. The explanation that satisfies the user in each of the cases mentioned above could be different. Even if the explanation-users in (1) and (4) both want to follow the system's reasoning, the terms used in the explanation and the justifications used need to be more system/code-oriented in (4) and more domain-oriented in (1). In (2) the explanation user does not necessarily know whether the system's conclusion is acceptable or how the conclusion should have been reached and so will require a fuller explanation than the explanation user in (1). The explanation user in (3) may ask the system hypothetical questions about other conclusions that may have been reached rather than explanations about the conclusion that has been reached.

2. ADDITIONS TO A KNOWLEDGE-BASED SYSTEM FOR EXPLANATION

The Knowledge Engineering group at the Rutherford Appleton Laboratory (RAL) has been involved in several projects which incorporate explanation in various forms. The projects illustrate the requirements needed for explanation in knowledge-based systems and they are presented in sections 3-6 as case studies. From these projects, three components of explanation in knowledge-based systems can be identified: system visibility; explanation generation; and tailoring of explanations. These three components are introduced below:

(a) System visibility is the property of a system of making its structure, contents and behaviour accessible to a user. It is dependent on there being a structure to the system in the first place, and thereby can be seen to be partly achieved through the design principles on which the system was built. However it is also dependent on the means by which the structure, contents and reasoning are communicated to the user, and so is affected by the interface and user support facilities of the system.

(b) Explanation generation goes a step further than system visibility, it involves reasoning about the structure, contents and behaviour of the system so that it can communicate information to the user about the way it works or the knowledge it holds. It therefore involves additional inferences or knowledge to those that were needed to reach the system's conclusion. The additional reasoning may not be any more than just creating a trace of how the system reached its conclusion or why it needs a certain fact, such as that used in MYCIN (Wallis and Shortliffe, 1984). Despite this relative simplicity it was found that 70% of doctors who followed advice from a MYCIN-like system when an explanation was provided would otherwise have ignored it (Wyatt, 1987). Alternatively, the additional reasoning may involve complex hypothetical reasoning about how other conclusions may have been reached, or meta-knowledge about the way that the system reasons.

(c) Successful communication of an explanation requires the user to understand the information from the system, but not all users will necessarily understand the same explanation. Also, for the explanation to be useful requires it to be relevant to the user's purpose, but different applications and different users of the system will require explanations for different purposes. Therefore the user and the user's reason for needing an explanation must be taken into account when generating an explanation. Where a system has multiple users and/or the system is used for multiple tasks, successful explanation requires the explanation to be tailored to the current user or the current task.

The following case studies illustrate these aspects of explanation.

3. AN EXAMPLE OF SYSTEM VISIBILITY: THE WATER DISTRIBUTION EXPERT SYSTEM

A knowledge-based system is being developed by the Knowledge Engineering Group at RAL which demonstrates system visibility: The Water Distribution Expert System is a three year project funded by a consortium of UK water supply companies to develop an advanced knowledge-based system for the water supply industry. The project is coordinated by the Water Research Centre (WRc). The project for eight Water Companies (Anglian, Mid Kent, North West, Thames, Three Valleys, Southern, Wessex and Yorkshire) commenced in September 1989.

The Water Distribution Expert System has an advanced architecture combining model-based reasoning about the water supply network with several components of heuristic reasoning. The model-based reasoning allows events on a water supply and distribution system to be simulated at a level of abstraction at which domain experts explain their reasoning. A number of heuristics act on the simulation to make the user aware of significant events that happen during the simulation. A further module detects problems on the supply system and suggests remedial actions to the user, and the user can use the model-based simulation to try out these actions or actions of their own.

It was found that users did not necessarily require explanations for the remedial actions suggested by the expert system, because they could simulate the effects of performing these actions using the model-based reasoning in the expert system and see for themselves whether they would work or which actions were preferable. However, what users wanted was confirmation that the model-based reasoning was acting in a realistic way to reflect the behaviour of the real supply system. To satisfy this requirement, the system was designed with a large amount of system visibility so that the model-based reasoning and the contents of the model were always accessible to the user.

The Expert System simulates the behaviour of the real supply system using supply system model. The initial state of the supply system model represents a certain state of the real supply system. When the Expert System runs one step forward, the supply system model changes to the state in which the real supply system would be 30 minutes after the previous state represented, taking only seconds for the Expert System to do. The contents of the model are made accessible to the user through a graphical interface representing a schematic of the actual supply system. At each simulated half hour step, the graphical interface reflects the state of the internal supply system model. Each object in the graphical interface gives graphical feedback as to whether it is currently in a normal or abnormal state. In addition, each object can be selected to give a pop-up which shows the condition of that object. For example, the pop-up of a pump shows the size of the pump, whether it is on or off, broken or working, working automatically or having its normal behaviour overridden, 'on-manual'. The user is able to change the state of the supply system through these pop-ups to reflect actions that would be performed on the real supply system.

The accessibility of the dynamic behaviour of the model is achieved through a running commentary about important events that are happening in the supply system model during the simulation, e.g. Reservoir levels dropping too quickly. The choice of what event is important is selected by a knowledge-base developed from domain expertise. In this way, the user is kept informed of the salient behaviour of the supply system model during the simulation without being overloaded by detail of every parameter.

The essence of the system visibility here is that there is a simple graphical representation of the contents of the system model that is open to inspection to reveal the state of the supply system model, and a textual output that gives the user an understanding of the dynamic behaviour of the supply system model. Thus the system model is made visible through the interface. This gives users confidence in the Expert System's advice because the user can ensure that the advice is based on a believable representation of the supply system and its behaviour. What can be generalised from this example to other applications, such as those involving model-based reasoning, is the means for achieving system visibility: the design principles on which the system was made understandable to the user.

4. EXPLANATIONS IN MMI^2

MMI^2 is a five year research project drawing on 60 man years of effort that started in January 1989 with funding from the CEC under the Esprit initiative[1]. The objective of the project is to develop a highly interactive interface which will allow users to interact with knowledge based systems through co-operative multi-modal dialogues. Users are able to interact with the system by using a command language, natural languages (English, French and Spanish), by mouse gestures, or by graphics with direct manipulation. Advanced dialogue management controls user/system initiative, appropriate response mode, context driven interpretation, etc. The demonstration domain for the interface is local area computer network design and analysis (Wilson et al 1991).

4. 1 Explanation Generation

RAL have been investigating explanation within the MMI^2 project and relating it more globally to the knowledge requirements for explanation in KBS development. Rich explanation capabilities require more knowledge to be made explicit than that needed for the system to perform its task. The aim of work in MMI^2 is to identify what knowledge is needed for explanation for a specific application and identify a methodology for obtaining it during the knowledge acquisition phase of system development. The work uses KADS as a basis for describing the knowledge-modelling required.

To understand what there is to explain for an application task, it is necessary to look at the tasks that the system and user are performing within the whole application task. The knowledge that the users require to perform their part of the tasks and to understand the results of the system's tasks is the knowledge that the system potentially needs to explain. The word "potentially" is used because user may to a greater or lesser extent already have the knowledge required. Therefore the explanation presented needs to take into account the knowledge already known by the user.

The system's tasks in MMI^2 are: to turn the user's informal requirements into a formal specification of the network; to discover incompleteness in the user's informal requirements; to synthesize a design based on the requirements; and finally to describe the design to the user. The user's tasks are to express their informal requirements for the network to the system; resolve problems if the system cannot change these into a consistent formal specification; to analyse the design to see if it is acceptable; and to find a solution in terms of changes to the requirements if the design is not acceptable. Consequently, the knowledge that the user needs within the whole system-user task in MMI^2 is:

---

1. The consortium undertaking the project consists of BIM (Belgium), Intelligent Software Solutions (Spain), University of Leeds (UK), Ecole des Mines de Saint-Etienne (France), SERC/RAL (UK), ADR/CRISS (France), INRIA (France).

1) The mental model of the problem. Included here is the user's knowledge of the domain and their informal requirements and constraints on their network design problem. (This knowledge is needed for users to be able to describe their requirements; to find a solution to problems in producing the formal specification; and to be able to decide whether the design model is a satisfactory solution).

2) The complete detailed design model resulting from a synthesis operation on the formal specification. Understanding the detailed design model will also involve the user's knowledge of the domain.

3) The system's problem solving strategy used to perform the design. (Needed either to learn how to perform the whole network design task or to be able to find a solution if the design produced is unsatisfactory).

4) The system's interface and the limitations on the dialogue: for successful communication where the system's task relies on information from the user, or vice versa.

Dialogues with the MMI^2 system can be seen to be either performing some subtask within the overall system-user task of designing a network, or providing information to the user as explanation. The purpose of the explanation is to enable the user to understand and perform the subtasks involved in the application. Therefore the knowledge that is to be explained to the user is the knowledge that the user needs for the tasks but does not already have, or knowledge required to correct errors and inconsistencies in the knowledge already possessed by the user.

Currently, the user can obtain a wide variety of explanations about the domain itself and the design model that is created by the system, adding to the knowledge identified in (1) and (2) above. The knowledge is represented explicitly in the Network Design Expert System or in the other components of the interface because the system needs it to perform the design, allowing the user to interrogate the system with respect to the classes and instances of objects in the application domain and the relation between them. The interface also contains meta-knowledge about the application and the interface itself which allows the user to ask questions about the expert system, the interface or the requirements for the problem specification. This provides the user with some of the knowledge identified in (1) and (4). The mechanism by which explanations can be given is the same as by which any input of the user is dealt with in the system, although extra reasoning facilities are needed to amplify the answer into a more cooperative one if it was only going to be "yes" or "no". Some examples of explanations from MMI^2 are given:

For (1): The mental model of the domain, informal requirements and constraints on the design solution

> *User:* <in Command mode> help WORKSTATION
> *System:* A workstation is a subtype of computer, and a supertype of apollo and hp_station and microvax_station and sun.

> *User*: <in graphical mode: selects a horizontal shaft>
> *User:* <in natural language> Is using thin cable possible in this shaft?
> *System*: Yes. Using thin cable is possible in any shaft. Thick cable may not be used in horizontal shafts.

> *User:* What are the requirements?
> *System:* <Lists requirements to make a network design>

For (2): The detailed design model

> *User:* Which machines are in which rooms?
> *System:* <Displays a table of rooms and locations>

> *User:* What are the departmentalisation problems?
> *System:* There are no departmentalisation problems.

For (4): The system's interface and limitations of the system

> *User:* Add a workstation to the network.
> *System:* I am sorry.
> The location and type of the workstation cmr98 are underspecified. Adding a workstation requires specification of location and type.
> What is the type of the workstation cmr98?

> *User:* What is the task of the system?
> *System*: computer network design

> *User:* <in Command mode> help bananas
> *System:* I am sorry, but "bananas" is unknown to the system.

In order to answer questions about (3), how the system's performs the application task, further knowledge and inference capabilities must be added to the system. The system should be able to help the user understand how a particular design was made, how designs are made in general, and how changing the initial requirements of the network results in different designs. Because of the natural language interface, the user is able to express questions of this nature, e.g. "Why does the design include thick cable?", "How is the backbone designed?", "Do I have to give this requirement now?", and work is on-going in adding these explanation facilities. Here, additions to the Network Design Expert System are needed to make the knowledge more explicit and accessible. This will enable the states reached by the expert system in synthesizing the design, and the process by which transitions between states occur to become available to an explanation generating component that produces an explanation of the design task for the user.

4. 2 Tailored Output: MMI^2

A further aspect of explanation is explored in the MMI^2 system: that of tailoring the generated explanations, as suggested by McKeown (1985), according to who the user is, what task is being performed and the dialogue context. If explanation can be described as adding to and correcting bodies of knowledge the user has for performing specific tasks, then these bodies of knowledge will not have the same content for all users, they will change throughout the dialogue, and the knowledge needed will be different for different tasks. For these reasons the system's explanations in MMI^2 are tailored by knowledge about the user, the current task and the dialogue context. This knowledge comes from an embedded user-modelling component; a component that detects the user's current task; and a model of the dialogue context respectively.

The overall aim is to tailor the output so that the knowledge being given is pertinent to the current user at this time for the task they are performing. The explanation is then assured to be useful because it is adding to or correcting a body of knowledge that the current user needs to perform a task or to understand a system task. Tailoring of the output occurs in several ways: the system avoids telling the user domain knowledge it believes the user already knows; information that has already been told to the user in the dialogue is told in an abbreviated form on subsequent tellings; different types of user have different levels of detail or content in their explanation; graphical responses that can be shown as tables or graphs are chosen and designed to suit the user's current task and to correspond to the user's preferences and type; system questions are postponed if the user is at the stage of the task where requirements are being given to avoid taking the user's initiative.

5. GRAPHICAL EXPLANATIONS: PARALFEX

The Paralfex project, a research project conducted by the Knowledge Engineering Group at RAL under the Alvey programme, ran for three years until April 1989. The aims of Paralfex were to develop an effective graphical explanation system, to investigate methods for enhancing the modifiability, extendability and transformability of knowledge bases, and to investigate problem solving strategies.

A Source of Finance Adviser was constructed from existing knowledge acquisition transcripts that advises a user on the feasibility of different sources of finance. The knowledge-base was built on the principle that knowledge should be represented as explicitly as possible—not only heuristics but also strategic, structural and support knowledge (Ringland 1986). The advantages of analysing the knowledge base in these terms is that the graphical interface can then employ different forms of presentation for different types of knowledge, the user can be given control of the consultation by separating out the control knowledge, and knowledge reuse becomes possible (both within a domain and across domains). For a fuller description see Lambert and Ringland (1990).

The system advises on the feasibility of different sources of finance depending on a number of contributing factors. The users in this case represented a company which was seeking finance. The users were not interested in an explanation about the system's use of strategic knowledge - they were not trying to learn how to do the task that the system was performing. The explanation they wanted was about how other conclusions could have been reached. The reason for this was that some of the user's figures represented preferences rather than actual values and so they wanted to see what effect changing such value would have on the options for finance possible to them (Lambert and Ringland, 1986). Their question might include:

> "Would the option be viable if this figure was altered?"
> "What was the constraining factor in ruling out this option?"
> "Why are current assets relevant here?"

The system decides between six options representing different sources of finance. At any time, the relative merit of each of the options is represented as a probability figure. To show the user a comparison of the current values of the different options, a "probability meter" is displayed for each option, giving a marker between 0 and 1 representing the probability value of an option. As the consultation proceeds, the probability values are updated. Thus some of the users questions are answered because they can see at a glance which options are looking promising and which are not.

To answer hypothetical questions about what factors need to change in order to make an option viable, the user can expand the probability meter to show how the contributing factors lead to the probability value. The expanded display takes the form of a second rank of meters showing the beliefs in the assertions corresponding to the contributing factors. The user can see which one is constraining the belief in the option as a whole. The contributing factors can themselves be expanded to show the assertions or numerical quantities on which they depend. To show how changing a value affects the system, the user can enter a new value and watch it propagate through the part of the net on display, changing the system's relative belief in assertions. These graphical responses can be seen as an example of system visibility, allowing the user to understand the structural knowledge of the knowledge base: the nature of the entities in the knowledge-base and the existence and significance of links between them as described by Clancey (1983).

To explain the dependency of an option on a contributing factor, each time a quantity is expanded to show what it depends upon, a textual explanation is displayed, explaining the relationship. The knowledge made visible here is the domain knowledge on which the relationships between the entities in the knowledge-base is based. Finally, justifications and typical values of the domain knowledge can be shown graphically and textually, making support knowledge (which justifies the domain knowledge) visible to the user.

The purpose of explanation in this application was identified as being to allow users to understand how different conclusions could have been reached. To fulfil this purpose, the graphical representation of the system's state and reasoning implicitly anticipates and answers the questions of interest to the user without the user having to explicitly formulate the questions. The interface helps the user not just understand why the system's conclusion was reached, but also answer hypothetical questions about how other conclusions may be reached. Explanation is achieved by system visibility through graphical and textual representations of both the static and dynamic aspects of the knowledge-base. This requires knowledge to be made explicit in the knowledge base and for it to be structured, and for the graphical and textual representation of the knowledge to reflect that structure.

6. INTERACTIVE SELF-EXPLANATION ENGINE: I-SEE

I-SEE is a project that will be starting in 1992 with funding from the CEC under the ESPRIT initiative[1]. The goal of the project is to develop foundations on which "Self-Explaining Systems" may be built. The idea behind such systems is to make their reasoning and output understandable to their users. I-SEE will be applicable to various domains and various markets, but will be initially applied to two visible and self-explaining systems; a sewage plant monitoring system and a pollution monitoring system, and also create generic tools to build such systems.

I-SEE will concentrate on the two aspects of making systems understandable to users discussed above: visibility and explanation. Visibility will relate to the system design, the user interface, the relation between the interface and the system design, and user-support facilities such as help facilities and on-line access to information about the system. Explanation will include both dynamic explanation generation and tailoring of the system output according to the current user, and the user's task, taking note of the purpose of explanation for the application. It will therefore attempt to include all of the aspects of explanation mentioned above in order to provide rich self-explaining systems. In doing so, the distinction between general principles required for all applications and specific application-dependent features will be clarified.

7. CONCLUSIONS

Several systems have been described which try to provide explanations for three of the four purposes identified in the introduction:

(1) The Water Distribution Expert System justified the system's conclusions to the user via the visibility of the model-based reasoning.

---

1. The consortium undertaking the project are: SYSECA, (France); British Maritime Technology (UK); Lyonnaise des Eaux Dumez (France); BIM (Belgium); SERC/RAL (UK); Conservatoire National des Arts et Metiers (France)

(2) The MMI^2 demonstrator tries to help different types of users understand more about Computer Network design and aims to explain how the design task is performed, through explanation generation and tailoring of the explanations produced.

(3) The Source of Finance Adviser allows the user to discover how changes in conditions produce different conclusions through system visibility of the changing contents of the knowledge-base as the consultation proceeds, and through pre-stored explanations of domain and support knowledge.

The fourth reason for explanation: to allow knowledge engineers to understand the reasoning of a system is already provided in many expert system shells through rule-tracing. A good example of explanation of this type through system visibility and explanation generation is the Transparent Rule Interpreter described by Domingue (1988).

The case studies described have illustrated that successful designing of explanation capabilities for a given application rely on first knowing the purpose of explanation for this users of the application. Knowing this will elucidate which aspect of the knowledge-based system needs to be made understandable to the user. Explanation cannot be achieved without an explicit representation of that aspect. If explanation is to be achieved through system visibility, the relevant aspect of the system is simply made accessible to the user. Where explanation is achieved through generating an explanation, knowledge about this aspect is required, such as what the function of it is, what relations it holds with other knowledge, what role it played in the system's conclusion, etc. This meta-knowledge is used in generating the explanation. For both of these types of explanation the knowledge-base requires explicitness and structure, but for explanation generation further knowledge is required than that needed to reach the system's conclusion. In other words, meta-knowledge of some aspect of the application. The knowledge needed in order to be able to tailor explanations for the current user, or the current task again needs knowledge in addition to that required for the system to reach its conclusion. Here the knowledge required is about the end-users of the system and about the reasons they require explanation and needs to be acquired during system development.

There is a great deal of generality in the concept of system visibility since it is achieved through design principles and so can be applied to many applications, although the instantiation of the design and the user interfaces through which it is accessed will be application-dependent. Explanation generation and tailoring of explanations is more application-dependent because further knowledge is required in addition to that used for the application task. However, what can be made general is the method by which explanations are generated or tailored. A further advance would be to develop a methodology for identifying the additional knowledge required for explanation during system development.

8. REFERENCES

Clancey, W.J. (1983) The epistemology of a rule-based expert system: a framework for explanation. *Artificial Intelligence*, 20(3), pp215-251.

Domingue J. (1989) TRI: The Transparent Rule Interpreter. In B.Kelly and A.L. Rector (Eds.) *Research and Development in Expert Systems V*, Cambridge: Cambridge University Press, pp126-138.

Lambert S.C. and Ringland G.A. (1987) An approach to Question-Answering and explanation in an Expert Consulting System. In *Proceedings of the Second Workshop of the Alvey Knowledge Based System Club Explanation Special Interest Group*, (University of Surrey, January 8-9th 1987), pp164-168.

Lambert, S.C. and Ringland, G.A.,(1990) "Knowledge representation and interfaces in financial expert systems", In *Proceedings UK IT 1990*, IEE:London pp.434-441.

Lambert, S.C., Ringland, G.A. & Chappel, H.R. (1990) The Development of a Knowledge-based System for the Water Supply Industry. In *IAKE'90: Second Annual Conference of the International Association of Knowledge Engineers*, (San Fransisco, October 3rd-5th 1990). Systemsware Corporations: Rockville, USA, pp323-330.

McKeown K.R. (1985) Tailoring Explanations for the User. In *Proceedings of the Ninth International Joint Conference on Artificial Intelligence*, (Los Angeles, California), pp794-798.

Ringland G.A. (1986) PARALFEX - Research into Expert Systems in the Financial Sector. In *Proceedings of the Alvey IKBS Expert Systems Theme Workshop on Explanation*, (University of Surrey, 20-21 March 1986), IEE:Hitchin, pp132-135.

Wallis, J.W. and Shortliffe, E.H. (1984) Customized explanations using causal knowledge. In *Rule-Based Expert Systems: The MYCIN Experiments of the Stanford Heuristic Programming Project*, Chapter 20, pp317-388, Addison-Wesley Publishing Company.

Wilson, M.D., Sedlock, D., Binot J-L, Falzon, P. (1991) An Architecture For Multimodal Dialogue. In M.M. Taylor, F. Neel & D.G. Bouwhuis (eds.) *Proceedings of the Second Venaco Workshop on Multi-Modal Dialogue*, (Acquafredda di Maratea, Italy, September 1991), ISSN 1018-4554.

Wyatt J. (1987) Improving the Usability of Knowledge-Based Medical Decision-Aids, paper represented at IKBS in Medicine, EEC, Brussels, November 1987.

An object oriented approach to distributed problem solving

A. Eliëns

Vrije Universiteit, Department of Mathematics and Computer Science

De Boelelaan 1081, 1081 HV Amsterdam The Netherlands

email: eliens@cs.vu.nl

Abstract

One of the principal difficulties in developing a distributed problem solver is how to distribute the reasoning task between the agents cooperating to find a solution.

We will propose the distributed logic programming language DLP as a vehicle for the design and implementation of distributed knowledge based systems. The language DLP combines logic programming with *active objects*.

We will show how object oriented modeling may be applied for the specification and implementation of a distributed diagnostic (medical) expert system. The example illustrates how the diagnostic process is distributed over the agents participating in the diagnosis according to the structure of the knowledge of that particular domain.

Keywords: *object oriented modeling, distributed problem-solving, knowledge-based systems, expert systems, distributed logic programming*

1   Introduction

Logic programming offers a declarative way to solve problems in Artificial Intelligence. However, when implementing large (possibly distributed) systems, traditional software engineering problems such as modularization and the distribution of data and control reoccur. Cf. [Subrahmanyam, 1985].

One of the principal difficulties in developing a distributed problem solver is how to distribute the reasoning task between the agents cooperating to find a solution.

Due to its declarative nature, logic programming has become popular for implementing knowledge-based systems. However, lacking adequate modularization facilities, logic programming languages such as Prolog fall short in providing the mechanisms necessary to specify the distribution of data and control.

Object oriented modeling   To tackle these problems, we suggest in this paper to embed the logic programming paradigm into an object oriented approach. Such an approach encourages to design a system — which consists of a collection of objects and relations between them — so that its structure corresponds with the natural structure of the problem domain. An object oriented decomposition of a system may thus reflect in a declarative way the structure of the reality it models. From this perspective, we may regard *object oriented modeling* as complementary to the declarative description provided in a logic program, since it directly expresses the structural characteristics of the problem domain. In our view, these structural characteristics may serve as a guideline in deciding how to control the activity of the agents taking part in the process of problem solving. Cf. [Booch, 1991].

DLP   As a vehicle for the design and implementation of distributed knowledge-based systems, we will propose the distributed logic programming language DLP [Eliëns, 1992]. The language DLP combines logic programming with object oriented features and parallelism.

To enable abstraction and encapsulation, DLP supports objects, which are basically named sets of clauses. Also, an inheritance mechanism is provided as to specify the relations between objects.

DLP supports *active* objects. Method calls for such objects result in a rendez-vous. In order to allow for search-based techniques, DLP supports (distributed) backtracking over the results of a method call by rendez-vous.

Related work   As related approaches in combining logic programming, object oriented programming and parallelism, I wish to mention first of all Delta Prolog that also supports distributed backtracking, but in the context of a less powerful communication mechanism. [Pereira et al, 1986]. Delta Prolog does however not provide any modularization construct.

Modularization in an object oriented style is offered by MultiLog, a multi-tasking object oriented Prolog developed to support prototyping embedded systems, that are (eventually) to be implemented in Ada. [Karam, 1988]. The distinguishing feature of DLP with respect to MultiLog however is that DLP supports backtracking over the answers of a method call by rendez-vous, whereas MultiLog proceeds from the assumption that such backtracking is not needed.

Other efforts at extending logic programming with object oriented features are reported in [Shapiro and Takeuchi, 1983], [Zaniolo, 1984], [Davison, 1989] and [Moss, 1990].

Also related is the work on distributing (medical) reasoning tasks reported in [Gomez and Chandrasekaran, 1981]. A logical basis to this approach has been provided in [Kowalczyk and Treur, 1990].

The DLP approach to the issue of defining generic reasoning tasks comes from a programming perspective. In this respect DLP may be compared to the proposal in

[Hynynen and Lassila, 1989], exploring the use of the object oriented programming paradigm in a distributed problem solver.

The structure of this paper is as follows. We will start by investigating the support that the object oriented paradigm offers to tackle the problems occurring in distributed problem solving. Next, we shall describe the distributed logic programming language DLP. Then we will describe the specification and implementation of a distributed medical expert system, illustrating our use of object oriented modeling techniques to arrive at a proper distribution of the diagnostic process. Finally, we will discuss the current status of our work and our plans for future research.

2   Distributed problem solving

From a software engineering perspective the issues that arise in developing a distributed knowledge based system are no different than in developing any distributed system: the distribution of *data* and *control*. Cf. [Smith and Davis, 1981]. The distribution of data involves decisions concerning shared resources and protocols that enable a safe use of these resources. To properly distribute control requires to partition the reasoning process into appropriate subtasks that may be distributed over the agents participating in this process.

Static knowledge   The actual distribution of static knowledge may be suggested by the way the knowledge is structured for domain experts. As an example, in the realm of medical diagnosis systems an early attempt at distributing knowledge can be found in [Gomez and Chandrasekaran, 1981]. They propose to structure the knowledge as a hierarchy of medical concepts. They moreover suggested to associate with each concept a process that is busy checking whether the observed symptoms justify the diagnosis of the disease represented by that concept. Another approach at distributing knowledge can be found in [Aikins, 1980], where a frame-like system supporting prototypes is used to model the diagnosis of lung diseases.

Specialists   In the medical expert system that will be described in section 4 we introduce *specialists* (in its literal meaning) to explore classes of diagnoses. In contrast with the approach described in [Gomez and Chandrasekaran, 1981], where each concept actively searches for symptoms fitting its diagnosis, our specialists are general purpose problem solvers capable of generating diagnoses within a particular medical area. An instance of a specialist, with knowledge of a specific field, is created in order to explore a subtree of the hierarchy embodying the static knowledge, the medical concepts applying to that particular field. Specialists are created only when during the diagnostic process the need arises to refine a given diagnosis. The specialists operate quasi-independently. They cooperate implicitly, however, by virtue of sharing the dynamic data storing the

observed symptoms and the derived intermediate diagnoses. An important feature
of our approach is that the creation and activity of the agents cooperating to find a
solution is governed by the structure of the static knowledge concerning that domain.
See [Fox, 1981] and [Davis, 1980] for alternative approaches.

3   The language DLP

The language DLP may be regarded as an extension of Prolog with *object declarations*
and *statements* for the dynamic creation of objects, communication between objects
and the assignment of values to non-logical instance variables of objects.

3.1   Object declarations

Object declarations in DLP have the form

object

> *object* name {
> *var* variables.
> clauses
> }

Both *object* and *var* are keywords. The variables declared by *var* are non-logical variables that may be assigned values by a special statement.

Objects act as prototypes in that new copies may be made by so-called *new* statements. Such copies are called *instances*. Each instance has its private copy of the
non-logical variables of the declared object. In other words, non-logical variables act
as instance variables.

3.2   Statements

DLP extends Prolog with a number of statements for dealing with non-logical variables,
the creation of objects and the communication between objects. These statements may
occur as atoms in a goal.

Non-logical variables   For assigning a term t to a non-logical variable x the statement

- $x := t$

is provided. Before the assignment takes place, the term t is simplified. The non-logical
variables occurring in t are replaced by their current values.

For accessing the value of a non-logical variable x of some object O a term of the form

$$O@x$$

is used. This term is simplified to the value of that non-logical variable when the atom in which it occurs is evaluated.

New expressions   For dynamically creating instances of objects the statement

- $O = new(c)$

is provided, where c is the name of a declared object. When evaluated as an atom, a reference to the newly created object will become bound to the logical variable O. For creating active objects the statement

- $O = new(c(t_1, ..., t_n))$

must be used. The activity of the newly created object consists of evaluating the *constructor* goal $c(t_1, ..., t_n)$, where c is the object name and $t_1, ..., t_n$ denote the actual parameters. The constructor goal will be evaluated by using *constructor clauses*, which are clauses defining a predicate with the same name as the object.

Method calls   A method call is the evaluation of a goal by an object. To call the method m of an object O with actual parameters $t_1, ..., t_n$ the statement

- $O!m(t_1, ..., t_n)$

must be used. It is assumed that O is a logical variable referring to the object to which the request is addressed. When such an atom is encountered, the object O is asked to evaluate the goal $m(t_1, ..., t_n)$. If the object to which the call is addressed is willing to accept the request then the result of evaluating $m(t_1, ..., t_n)$ will be sent back to the caller. After sending the first result, subsequent results will be delivered whenever the caller tries to backtrack over the method call. If no alternative solutions can be produced the call fails.

Active objects must explicitly interrupt their own activity and state their willingness to accept a method call by a statement of the form

- $accept(m_1, ..., m_n)$

which indicates that any request for one of the methods $m_1, ..., m_n$ will be accepted.

3.3   The computation model of DLP

The computation model of DLP combines the computation model underlying Prolog and the model underlying a parallel object oriented language. Parallel object oriented processing must support objects, processes and communication between objects.

Objects   contain non-logical data, persisting during the life time of the object, and clauses defining the functionality of the object.

Objects may be *active* or *passive*. The activity of an object is defined by *constructor clauses* that describe the own activity of an object. Apart from constructor clauses, active objects may also contain *method clauses* that are used when the object receives a method call. A *method call* is simply the request to evaluate a goal.

Processes   are created when creating a new active object and for the evaluation of a method call. The process executing the own activity of an active object is called the *constructor process*. For each method call a process is created to enable backtracking over the results of a method call.

Passive objects have no activity but answering to method calls. Active objects must explicitly interrupt their own activity to indicate the willingness to answer a method call. Because of this feature active objects provide strong encapsulation.

Communication   with another object takes place by engaging in a (synchronous) rendez-vous. In order to achieve compatibility with the ordinary Prolog goal evaluation, DLP supports global backtracking over the results of a rendez-vous. With respect to backtracking, it is transparent whether a goal is evaluated remotely, by another object or locally, provided the necessary clauses are defined. This transparency holds for both passive and active objects.

Below it is pictured what happens when a process issues a method call to an active object.[1]

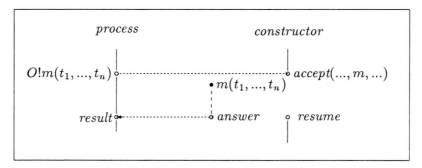

As soon as both the process calling the method and the constructor process of the object to which the call is addressed have synchronized, the activity of the constructor is interrupted and a process is created to evaluate the goal $m(t_1, ..., t_n)$. The constructor is interrupted for safety reasons, in order to guarantee that no other method call will be accepted.

---

[1]In the diagram, vertical lines represent computations. A node represents a particular state in a computation. A horizontal line between two nodes represents a communication taking place between the processes to which these nodes belong.

3.4   Inheritance

An essential feature of the object oriented approach is the use of inheritance to define relations between objects. C.f. [Wegner, 1987]. From the perspective of modeling, inheritance must be regarded primarily as a means to refine behavior. Cf. [Halbert and O'Brien, 1987]. From an implementation perspective, inheritance is a facility to share code.

The declaration for an object inheriting from an object *base* is

inheritance

```
object name : base {
var variables.
clauses

}
```

This declaration will result in adding the non-logical variables and clauses declared for the object *base* to those of the declared object.

4   The specification and implementation of a distributed medical expert system

In modeling medical diagnosis it seems appropriate to assume that a doctor comes to a conclusion concerning a certain disease by applying *knowledge* to *facts*. The assumptions with respect to how this takes place are embodied in the reasoning component that consists of the objects *infer* and *facts*. The *knowledge* that is needed to make inferences belong to the area of medical practice itself. The reasoning component, however, is dependent on the format of the knowledge.

In our medical (toy) expert system we employ a simple rule-based reasoning component. In addition we introduce a number of objects to model the (structure) of the knowledge involved and the behavior of the agents participating in the diagnostic process. The medical knowledge presented here is purely fictional.

4.1   The reasoning component

The reasoning component of our expert system consists of two parts: a store of *facts* that initially contains the observed symptoms and an *inference engine* that deduces new facts by using knowledge rules embodying the expertise.

Knowledge rules of the form

$$conditions \rightarrow conclusion$$

are used by the system to add new facts when the given facts satisfy the conditions of
the rule.

Facts   Facts are stored in the object declared below.

```
object facts {
var data=[].

facts(D) :−  data  :=   D, run.

run :−  accept(holds, add), run.

holds(X) :−  member(X,data).
add(X) :−
        append([X],data,R),
        data  :=   R.

}
```

The object *facts* has a non-logical variable *data* containing an initially empty list of
facts. When creating an active instance of *facts* the instance variable *data* is initialized
to the given facts. The object may then be asked whether a particular fact holds, or
it may be asked to add a new fact.

Inference engine   The inference engine operates on a collection of facts, by applying
knowledge contained in rules. A derivation is successful if the item that must be derived
either holds as a fact or is derivable by recursively applying a knowledge rule.

```
object infer {
var knowledge, facts.

derive(H) :−  facts!holds(H),!.
derive(H) :−
        knowledge!rule(P,H),
        test(P),
        facts!add(H).

test([]).
test([X|R]) :−
        derive(X),
        test(R).

}
```

The strategy by which new facts are derived may be characterized as *backward reasoning*. It proceeds by taking the conclusion of a rule, for example as a possible diagnosis, and checking the conditions of the rule. A condition is satisfied when it is either a fact, or it may be derived as a fact by applying some of the other rules.

The object *infer* as presented is of an abstract nature. It has non-logical variables to store knowledge and facts. However, these variables can only be given a value by an object inheriting the capabilities of *infer*.

4.2   Modeling medical practice

The agents that play a role in our conception of medical practice are *doctors*, having general knowledge of diseases, and *specialists*, having knowledge of special diseases. We will also introduce a *clinic* to assign doctors and specialists to patients for consultation.

An object oriented modeling technique has also been applied in the hierarchic representation of knowledge about diseases.

Doctor   A *doctor* inherits the reasoning capacity needed to derive a diagnosis from the object *infer*. In other words, a doctor is a straightforward modification of an inference engine. C.f. [Wegner and Zdonik, 1988]. A doctor possesses knowledge about diseases as represented by the object *disease* described below. This knowledge is also used to suggest the possible diagnoses the doctor will look for.

doctor

```
object doctor : infer {

doctor() :-
        knowledge  :=  disease,
        accept(diagnosis),
        doctor().

diagnosis(F,D) :-
        facts  :=  F,
        member(D,knowledge@diagnoses),
        derive(D).

}
```

Before being able to accept the request for a diagnosis, the non-logical variable *knowledge*, inherited from *infer*, must be initialized to *disease*. The non-logical variable *facts* is updated when starting to search for a diagnosis. All possible diagnoses a doctor knows of will be tried.

Disease   Knowledge concerning diseases is structured as an inheritance tree with at the top node the most general knowledge that is refined for specific diseases further down the tree. C.f. [Gomez and Chandrasekaran, 1981].

At the root of the tree we have the object *disease*, that represents the most general knowledge of diseases.

This knowledge is laid down in rules that enable to assess whether a patient has the symptoms of someone who is ill.

disease

```
object disease {
var diagnoses = [disease],
      causes = [liver,lungs].

rule([high_temperature],fever).
rule([fever],disease).
}
```

Apart from the rules that contain the knowledge needed to establish a diagnosis, the object contains also a list of possible *diagnoses*, which for the generic case simply states that a patient may have a disease. These diagnoses function as hypotheses when searching for the actual diagnosis. The rules inform us that a patient has a disease if he has fever, that is a high temperature.

Diagnosis   Before we proceed, let us see what a doctor can do.

```
?-
      F = new(facts([high_temperature,yellow_skin])),
      M = new(doctor()),
      M!diagnosis(F,D).
```

The diagnosis delivered will be *disease*, since the doctor is not assumed to know anything about other diseases. The patient needs a (in this case a *liver disease*) specialist for a more refined diagnosis.

In addition, the knowledge concerning a disease contains an indication of its possible *causes*. Such knowledge is included to allow specialists to give advice about the further examinations.

4.3   Refining knowledge

Other diseases are specializations of the generic object *disease*. The objects representing specific diseases share by inheritance the more general knowledge. This knowledge is, for each disease, augmented with a number of rules embodying the specific knowledge concerning that disease. Each specific disease contains also a list of possible diagnoses in order to direct the search for a diagnosis. This list overwrites the list of diagnoses pertaining to the more general case.

As an example of refining the generic object disease to a particular case consider the declaration for a liver disease.

```
object liver : disease {
var diagnoses = [liver_disease],
      causes = [intrahepatic, extrahepatic].
rule([disease,yellow_skin],liver_disease).
}
```

Notice that, in accordance with our discussion of inheritance, the values of the variables *diagnoses* and *causes* are determined by the object containing the knowledge of a liver disease.

We may now further enlarge our body of knowledge.

```
object lungs : disease {
var diagnoses = [tuberculosis, asthma],
      causes = [].
rule([coughing,bleeding],tuberculosis).
rule([coughing,red_eyes],asthma).
}
```

The knowledge added contains some fictional rules concerning lung diseases. Also we add some knowledge refining the knowledge about liver diseases.

```
object intrahepatic : liver {
var diagnoses = [intrahepatic],
      causes = [].
rule([liver_disease,sweating],intrahepatic).
}
```

Intrahepatic liver diseases represent one particular variant of liver diseases. Another variant is represented by *extrahepatic* liver diseases.

```
object extrahepatic : liver {
var diagnoses = [extrahepatic],
    causes = [].

rule([liver_disease,bleeding],extrahepatic).
}
```

Neither for lung diseases nor for the intrahepatic and extrahepatic variants of liver diseases are any causes known. As a remark, distributed backtracking may occur for instance when more than one of the possible diagnosis for a lung-disease applies.

Specialist   The hierarchical structure of medical knowledge suggests to distribute the search for possible diagnoses over a number of specialists.   A *specialist* is a doctor having specific knowledge of a certain class of diseases. Apart from giving a diagnosis, a specialist also gives advice for further examination. This definition of a specialist enables to search, for the most specific diagnosis, taking the most general disease as a starting point. In this search, the possible *causes* indicate how to traverse the hierarchy of diseases.

```
object specialist : doctor {

specialist(K)  :-
        knowledge  :=   K,
        accept(diagnosis),
        accept(advice).

advice(A)  :-   A = knowledge@causes.
}
```

The non-logical variable *knowledge*, inherited from *infer* (by being a *doctor*), is assigned the object representing a particular class of diseases. The constructor for a *specialist* further enforces that advice may be asked for only if a diagnosis has been given. Here we have an example how a protocol of interaction may be enforced by *active objects*.

4.4   The diagnostic process

The distributed nature of our diagnostic system comes to light in the definition of a *clinic*, that handles the distribution of tasks among the specialists.

Clinic   A clinic receives patients and assigns to each patient a doctor. This doctor is a specialist knowing all about diseases in general. When the specialist comes to the conclusion that the patient has a disease, he gives advice for further examinations.

clinic

```
object clinic {

case(C,D) :-
        F = new(facts(C)),
        examine(disease,F,D).

examine(K,F,[D|R]) :-
        M = new(specialist(K)),
        M!diagnosis(F,D),
        M!advice(A),
        explore(F,A,R).

examine(K,_,[]).

explore(F,[],[]).

explore(F,[K|T],[D|R]) :-
        examine(K,F,D) & explore(F,T,R).

}
```

The advice given by a specialist is used to consult other specialists, having more specific knowledge of the diseases listed in the advice. An examination results in listing all the diagnoses that apply to the case. The advice given by a specialist consists of a list of possible causes. For each possible cause a specialist is created to examine the patient. Exploring the possible causes may occur in parallel, as indicated by the use of the parallel &-operator.[2]   The result of exploring the possible causes is a (possibly empty) list of diagnoses.

Below I present the worst case that I can imagine.

?- clinic!case([high_temperature,yellow_skin,sweating,coughing,bleeding],D).

The reader is invited to compute the appropriate diagnoses by hand.

5   Conclusions

We have illustrated how object oriented modeling techniques may be used to represent knowledge and to direct the search for a solution. Our approach allows to control the

---

[2]The language DLP supports *and*-parallelism in a straightforward way. See [Eliëns, 1989]. Another feature supported by DLP is the allocation of processes to nodes in a network in order to arrive at a proper distribution of the reasoning process.

creation of the agents participating in a reasoning task and the distribution of sub-tasks over these agents by means of a suitable representation of the domain knowledge reflecting the structure of that knowledge in a natural way.

As a vehicle for the specification and implementation of distributed knowledge based systems we have proposed the distributed logic programming language DLP. Currently, there exists only a rather inefficient prototype implementation of DLP. See [Eliëns, 1992]. The prototype has been implemented in a variant of the language described in [America, 1987]. Recently, we developed Active C++, an extension of C++ with active classes and communication by rendez-vous [Eliëns and Visser, 1992]. We are now in the process of implementing a more efficient version of DLP in Active C++.

References

[Aikins, 1980] J.S. AIKINS, *Prototypes and Production Rules: A knowledge representation for consultations,* Report STAN-CS-80-814 (1980) Stanford

[America, 1987] P. AMERICA, *POOL-T: a parallel object oriented language,* in: [Yonezawa and Tokoro, 1987]

[Booch, 1991] G. BOOCH, *Object oriented design with applications,* Benjamin Cummings (1991)

[Davis, 1980] R. DAVIS, *The Contract Net Protocol: High Level Communication and Control in a Distributed Problem Solver,* IEEE Transactions on Computing C-29 (12) (1980) pp. 1104-1113

[Smith and Davis, 1981] R.G. SMITH AND R. DAVIS, *Frameworks for Cooperation in Distributed Problem Solving,* IEEE Transactions on Systems, Man, and Cybernetics 11 (1) (1981) pp. 61-69

[Davison, 1989] A. DAVISON, *Polka: A Parlog object oriented language,* Ph.D. thesis, Dept. of Computing, Imperial College, London (1989)

[Eliëns, 1989] A. ELIËNS, *Extending Prolog to a Parallel Object Oriented Language,* Proc. IFIP W.G. 10.3 Working Conference on Decentralized Systems (1989) Lyon

[Eliëns, 1991] A. ELIËNS, *Distributed Logic Programming for Artificial Intelligence,* AI Communications Vol. 4 No. 1, 1991, pp. 11-21

[Eliëns, 1992] A. ELIËNS, *DLP - A language for Distributed Logic Programming,* Wiley (1992)

[Eliëns and Visser, 1992] A. ELIËNS AND C. VISSER, *Active C++, active classes and communication by rendez-vous,* Technical Report Vrije Universiteit (to appear)

[Fox, 1981] M. FOX, *An organizational view of distributed systems,* IEEE Transactions on Systems, Man, and Cybernetics 11 (1) (1981) pp. 70-80

[Gomez and Chandrasekaran, 1981] F. GOMEZ AND B. CHANDRASEKARAN, *Knowledge Organization and Distribution for Medical Diagnosis,* IEEE Transactions on Systems, Man, and Cybernetics 11 (1) (1981) pp. 34-42

[Halbert and O'Brien, 1987] D. HALBERT AND P. O'BRIEN, *Using types and inheritance in object oriented programming,* IEEE Software 4 (5) (1987) pp. 71-79

[Hynynen and Lassila, 1989] J. HYNYNEN AND O. LASSILA, *On the use of object oriented paradigm in a distributed problem solver,* AI Communications, 2 (3/4) (1989) pp. 142-151

[Karam, 1988] G.M. KARAM, *Prototyping Concurrent systems with Multilog,* Technical Report Dept. of Systems and Computer Engineering Carleton University (1988)

[Kowalski, 1979] R. KOWALSKI, *Logic for problem solving,* North Holland (1979)

[Kowalczyk and Treur, 1990] W. KOWALCZYK AND J. TREUR, *On the use of a formalized generic task model in knowledge acquisition,* in: Proc. EKAW 90, IOS Press (1990) pp. 198-220

[Moss, 1990] C. MOSS, *An introduction to Prolog++,* Report Imperial College 90/10

[Pereira and Nasr, 1984] L.M. PEREIRA AND R. NASR, *Delta Prolog: A distributed logic programming language,* in: Proc. FGCS, ICOT (1984) pp. 283-231

[Shapiro and Takeuchi, 1983] E. SHAPIRO AND A. TAKEUCHI, *Object-oriented programming in Concurrent Prolog,* New Generation Computing, Vol. 1, No. 2 (1983) pp. 5-48

[Subrahmanyam, 1985] P.A. SUBRAHMANYAM, *The Software Engineering of Expert Systems: Is Prolog appropriate?,* IEEE Transactions on software engineering 11 (1985) pp. 1391-1400

[Zaniolo, 1984] C. ZANIOLO, *Object oriented programming in Prolog,* in: Proc. Int. Symp. on Logic Programming, Atlantic City, IEEE (1984) pp. 265-270

Intelligent User Interface
for Multiple Application Systems

X. ZHANG, J.L. NEALON, R. LINDSAY

Knowledge Engineering Research Group
School of Computing & Mathematical Sciences
Oxford Polytechnic

Abstract: Current intelligent user interfaces have two limitations: (i) They are domain specific and mainly built for existing database management systems. (ii) They are specific to the target systems for which they are constructed. However, user goals, which motivate interactions with a computer, are likely to be complicated and to require the use of multiple target systems in various domains. In this paper, we discuss the development of intelligent user interfaces which are not subject to the limitations identified. An architecture is proposed, the major function of which is the dynamic integration and intelligent use of multiple target systems relevant to a user's goals. Other important features of the proposed system include its theoretical orientation around relevance relationships, mental models and speech acts, and the introduction of "system experts" and "goal manager". A prototype Intelligent Multifunctional User Interface, (IMUI), is briefly described which indicates that the proposed architecture is viable, the methodology is promising, and the theoretical ideas introduced are worthy of further investigation.

1   INTRODUCTION

Computer-based systems are coming to play an ever more important part in our society, and as they do so, they become increasingly complicated and difficult to use effectively. As a consequence, the need to develop flexible and versatile intelligent interfaces has become more crucial than ever.

What would an ideal interface look like, and how can such a system be designed and implemented? Most investigators would agree that it should behave like an intelligent human assistant who has expert knowledge both of user characteristics and requirements, and of target system(s)[1]. The interface should thus be an "intelligent intermediary" between user and target system able to effectively integrate their capacities so as to achieve the user's goals. Recently, the design of intelligent interfaces has

---

[1]Target systems refer to the computer-based systems the interface is built for.

begun to attract increased attention from AI and cognitive scientists. For example, research has been reported on the development of natural language interfaces which can translate the user's natural language input into formal commands acceptable to the target system, and translate the target system's output into natural language sentences. [Wal84, DB88]; and there has been research on the development of on-line and off-line help systems [JV91, Chi91].

Generally speaking such systems continue to be monofunctional, i.e. they only provide single assistant functions for the use of single target systems. Like a good human assistant, an ideal intelligent user interface must provide a multiplicity of assistant functions for the use of multiple target systems. The intelligent user interface should be able to help us to communicate with the target systems, answer our questions, and provide appropriate advice or warnings; it should not be confined to helping us to use a single target system, but any and all target systems relevant to our current task. To increase naturalness and efficiency, the interface should also be able to *talk* with the user via a range of media, including written language, speech, graphics, gesture, and so on. In summary, an ideal user interface should be multifunctional across multiple dimensions. These requirements are illustrated in Figure. 1.

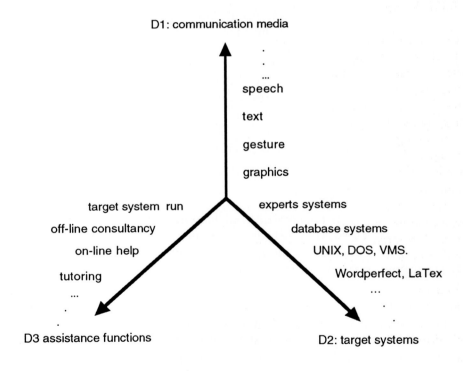

Figure 1: Multiple Dimentions of Multiple Functions

In the secions following, problems associated with the design and development of an Intelligent Multifunctional User Interface, (IMUI), will be discussed. An architecture and its operating principles are also proposed. This is followed by discussion of processing components required by the design, illustrated by a running example. The present paper concentrates on the second dimension of multifunctionality illustrated in Figure 1 (D2): the dynamic integration of multiple target systems. A more comprehensive discussion of multidimensional, multifunctional, intelligent interfaces is given in [Zha92].

2   SYSTEM DESIGN

Before getting involved with more technical issues, it is valuable to consider how a human expert can act as an effective interface between a user and a target computer system. First, the goals and intentions of the user must be established. This can only be done on the basis of such factors as the content of the user's discourse, knowledge about the user, current context and the interaction environment, commonsense and domain knowledge. Secondly, a relevant plan which is capable of achieving the goal must be formulated. Thirdly, it must be decided what functions, of which target systems are required. Finally, an efficient way to use the relevant target systems to help fulfil the user's goal must be established.

Figure 2 illustrates an architecture for a multifunctional intelligent user interface. It consists of a natural language parser, a pragmatic interpreter, a goal manager, knowledge bases, a response planner, a natural language generator and one or more "system experts", (depending on the number of target computer-based systems). Natural language commands or queries from the user are first passed to the natural language parser for syntactic and semantic interpretation; the result is a set of possible literal meanings represented in logical form [All87]. The pragmatic interpreter takes these logical forms as input and makes inferences based on general (commonsense) knowledge, the output is a candidate set of user goals and relevant plans. These goals and plans are then passed to the goal manager for further analysis and inference supported by domain knowledge. The output of this stage is a set of domain oriented metacommands (goals and plans), which are then sent to the appropriate system experts. A system expert is the local manager of an underlying target system and is capable of generating commands and queries acceptable to it. The system expert is also responsible for the generation of an appropriate reply for the goal manager, based on the response of the target system. When the goal manager receives a reply message from the relevant system experts, it makes inferences and analysis based upon this message and other relevant knowledge, such as the context model, user model, domain knowledge and general knowledge. The normal output of the goal manager is a set of strategic goals and associated plans which are appropriate for response generation. Based on these "meta-goals and plans", the response planner generates refined (tactical) plans and subgoals for the natural language response generator, which in turn, generates natural language utterances.

What is described above is a simplified single directional flow of information through the system. In practice things are much more complicated. We cannot expect the user to "talk" correctly all the time in respect of syntax, semantics, pragmatics and the technical features of the query domain. Even if the user's natural language input is correct, it might be full of ambiguity, which must be filtered out at different comprehension phases. And we should recognize that the capacity of the system is necessarily limited. Hence, feedback paths are provided for discovery and recovery of errors, as shown in Figure 2. Detailed discussion of these issues are outside the scope of this paper.

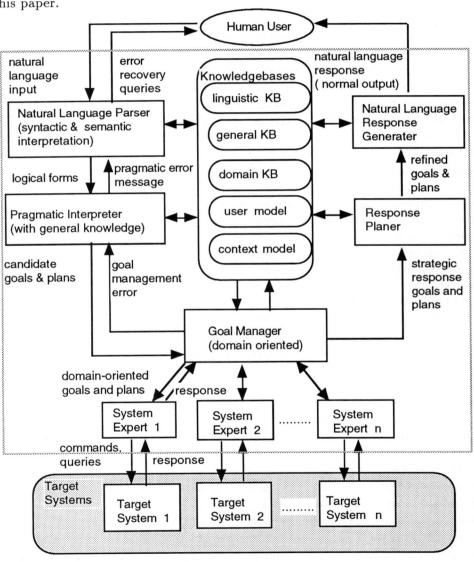

Figure 2: System Architecture

3   INDIVIDUAL COMPONENTS

The last section provided a general description of the architecture and operating principles of a multifunctional intelligent interface. In this section, we will discuss some of the more important components in greater detail.

3.1   Knowledgebases

The capabilities of the intelligent multifunctional user interface are determined by the knowledge which is available to it. Different kinds of knowledge are kept in distinct knowledgebases. They are used and updated by other system modules to help achieve user goals and determine the mental models of the world with which the system can operate.

The first category of knowledge in a system such as IMUI, is knowledge about language. The linguistic knowledgebase contains syntactic, semantic and lexical knowledge. This is mainly used by the natural language parser and natural language generator for the interpretation and production of natural language.

The "general" knowledgebase contains the commonsense knowledge required by the application. It seems beyond reasonable doubt that commonsense knowledge is essential for non-trivial problem solving and natural language understanding. [LG90, Hay90]. However, the quantity of commonsense knowledge available to humans is enormous, and its structure and the mechanisms by which it is manipulated are still not well understood. It is not practical to build a huge knowledgebase such as the *Cyc* system to support IMUI. Fortunately, any particular application of a computer system does not require the whole set of human commonsense knowlege, instead only a small fraction is needed. So it is reasonable to put only such relevant commonsense knowledge into the system as is convenient for the user and the system to maintain and update.

Another kind of knowledge is domain knowledge, i.e., knowledge about the application domain of an intelligent system. For example, an intelligent library inquiry system has its domain knowledge about general library information, and various target application systems.

If a computer system is to interact intelligently with a user, it must have some knowledge about its interlocutor. User models are used to represent the computer system's understanding of the user. Such models include the system's knowledge about the user's goals and plans, preferences, capacities, characteristics, knowledge about the domain, and knowledge about the computer system, etc.

The context model contains two kinds of knowledge: the discourse model and the environmental model. The former is the system's understanding of the user's discourse, which represents the historical, (vertical), context. It is a mental model represented as a network of the user's goals and plans integrated with the system's goals and plans which functions to assist the user in achieving goals. The environmental model reflects the horizontal dimension of context, i.e., the current state of world. For a robotic system in a workshop, this might include the current locations of machines it is to use, and of the objects upon which it is working, whether the robot's own hand is empty or not, etc.

3.2   Pragmatic Interpreter

The major function of this module is to further analyse the literal meanings provided by the syntactic-semantic parser in the light of general world knowledge, user models and the model of context. The theories of mental models [Joh83], speech acts [All87], goal dependent-expressions and relevance [GL89, SW86] are all utilised during this stage, and the next. (The latter concerns domain oriented goal management and is discussed in the next subsection). The output of the pragmatic interpreter is the candidate goals and plans implied by the user's utterance.

3.3   Goal Manager

The goal manager is the most important element of the system. Its first major function is to carry out speech action analysis based on relevant domain knowledge, user models and the contextual model; and to plan actions accordingly.

- If the analysis fails, then try to recover from failure locally.

- If the local error recovery fails, generate an error message which helps the pragmatic interpreter to recover from error.

- If the analysis is successful, that is to say, the user's real plans and goals are found, the goal manager will check if the user's intended goals and plans are legal.

    - If the goal is illegal or unattainable (such as trying to delete some body else's file without authorisation, or asking the computer to print a 1000-page file within 20 minutes), refuse to attempt the task and explain it to the user.

    - If the user's goal is legal but the plan is illegal or impractical, then try to help the user find a practical way to achieve the goal.

    - If the user's plan and goal are legal and implementable, set up corresponding system goals and plans to help achieve the goal, and assign subtasks among the relevant system experts. The goal manager is responsible for organising and scheduling the underlying target systems to help achieve the user's goal through different system experts.

The second major function of the goal manager is the maintenance of the user model, context model and domain knowledgebases. For example, the interpretation of the user's intended goals and plans, or responses from the system experts normally produce a change in the current state of the system's mental world, and so leads to the updating of appropriate knowledgebases or mental models.

The third major function of the goal manager is to provide strategic goals and plans to the response planner to guide the generation of acceptable natural language output. These are a kind of metainstruction, the detailed plans and goals for generating natural language output will be worked out by the response planner.

3.4   System Experts
These are domain-oriented expert systems with expertise about individual target systems. They sit between the goal manager and the target systems, as shown in Figure 2. There is one system expert for each target system. The introduction of system experts brings several advantages.

- By separating the target-system-oriented knowledge and functions from the goal manager, a more uniform and higher lever interface is formed between the target systems and the goal manager. That gives more flexibility and adaptability to the whole intelligent interface system. It also means that the goal manager is freed from the trivial tasks of direct communication with different target systems at lower levels, and can concentrate on strategic planing and reasoning.

- As a local expert with the expertise about its corresponding target system, (including the target system's knowledge, state, functions, and effective domain strategies,) a system expert is capable of working out more effective commands and queries for the target system.

- Finally, our system will not only help the user to use one target system more intelligently, but also make it possible to integrate a flexible number of independent application systems under the same goal manager, which can use them in a coordinated manner to achieve a wider range of goals, and to achieve particular goals more efficiently.

3.5   Response Planner
The response planner is responsible for producing detailed (tactical) goals and plans which are compatible with the metacommands (i.e., strategic response goals and plans) provided by the goal manager. The knowledge required includes general knowledge, domain knowledge, user models, and the context model. The output provides specific pragmatic information to the natural language generator about: what to say, how it should be said, what are the system's current goals, which goals are to be achieved by the utterance to be generated, etc. In a sense, the response planner carries out operations which are the inverse of those carried out by the pragmatic interpreter.

4   AN EXAMPLE

To help make these ideas clear, this section presents a simple example of how the intelligent interface works within the domain of library inquiry servicing[2]. The target systems for this application include, among others, the database management systems (DBMSs) for each subject section (such as computer science, psychology, linguistics, etc.) and a means-ends planner to plan a route between two given locations on a map of the library. They are all integrated via the intelligent interface, as shown in Figure 3.

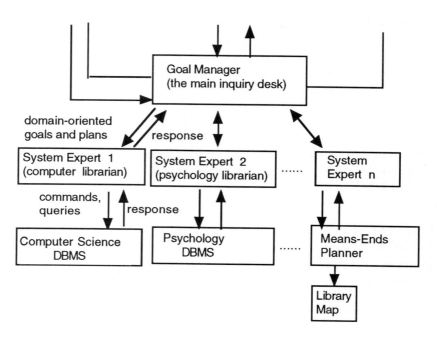

Figure 3: IMUI's Application in Library Inquiry

Suppose a user is interested in books on "expert systems". Without the intelligent interface, users must decide for themselves which database(s) to use. If they lack domain knowledge, they might have to try every one. Then retrieval must be carried out with the formal query language or menus provided by the database systems. Probably the best thing which can be done, is to use key words to retrieve those books whose titles include the noun phrase "expert system". Obviously, this will locate only a limited subset of the relevant books in the library's stock. The database fails to retrieve many of the relevant references because of its lack of any real knowledge about expert systems. The retrieval operations carried out used only blind pattern matching. After accessing appropriate reference information, the user will probably

---

[2]This example is based on the Headington Campus Library of Oxford Polytechnic

want to know how to get to the place where the books are physically located. This requires finding and using the route planner. If the user do not know of the existence of the planner, he/she cannot not benefit from it at all.

Within the present architecture, all the functions useful to the user are integrated behind a single intelligent interface. A user can talk to the interface by simply typing "I would like to read some books on expert systems.", just as if they were talking to a human assistant at the information desk of the library. The system will look after the rest. The utterance input by the user is first sent to the natural language parser for syntactic and semantic interpretation. The parsing procedure will generate the following logical form representing the literal meaning of the utterance:

```
(PRES w1 WANT
        (AGENT user22 PERSON)
        (OBJECT
              (INF r1 READ
                      (AGENT user22)
                      (OBJECT b1 BOOK
                              (FIELD es1 EXPERT-SYSTEMS)))))),
```

which can be paraphrased as

> There is a PRESent WANT event **w1**. The AGENT of **w1** is **user22** who is a PERSON. The OBJECT of **w1** is a READ event **r1** that **user22** reads BOOKs **b1** in the FIELD of EXPERT-SYSTEMS.

The logical form expression is then sent to the pragmatic interpreter for further interpretation in the light of more general knowledge. According to the commonsense rule:

$$\text{want}(\text{agent, event}) \& \text{practical}(\text{event}) \rightarrow \text{goal}(\text{agent, event}).$$

the pragmatic interpreter finds that the user's goal is the reading event which he/she wants to achieve, i.e.,

$$\text{read}(\text{user, books}) \& \text{in-field}(\text{books, expert-systems}).$$

This is regarded as the current goal of the user and added to the user model. Since the goal is legal, the system sets a new goal for itself: to help the user fulfil their current goal. The new system and user goals (as well as any relevant plans once they become available) are then integrated into the context model. Two general rules will be available from the "General" Knowledgebase, (See Fig. 2, above), which will help the user to achieve a particular goal, G:

Rule 1
> If the system can directly achieve G by itself through some implementable plan, P, then do it.

Rule 2

If the user is pursuing G through a plan P, and some, but not all of the elements in the plan are achievable by the system, then achieve these elements and cooperate with the user to achieve the rest.

In the present example, since the system cannot do the reading for the user, Rule 1 is not satisfied. The commonsense plan for the goal of reading books involves two steps:

Step 1 get the books, and

Step 2 read them.

This is the plan which the user must be supposed to be pursuing. The first step of the plan is where the system can help, while the second step falls entirely within the user's capabilities. Therefore Rule 2 is satisfied, and Step 1 of the plan becomes the system's current goal. Again, according to commonsense knowledge, there are several candidate plans for this subgoal, including:

1. get the books for the user.

2. tell the user the particular locations of the books and assist in getting there.

These candidate goals and associated plans are passed to the goal manager for further interpretation taking domain knowledge into account. In the light of its domain knowledge about library services, the goal manager regards the second candidate plan as preferable. Again, according to its domain knowledge, the goal manager knows that books on expert systems may be found in the computer section or the psychology section of the library. Therefore, domain-oriented goals and plans are generated and sent to the system experts in charge of the computer science DBMS and the psychology DBMS respectively, asking them to provide details of the locations of the books on expert systems under their local management.

Since the system experts are experts on the target systems with which they are associated, they are much more intelligent and powerful than simple DBMSs. In the present example, when the computer science system expert is given the task of providing the locations of books on expert systems, it will attempt to retrieve all those books which *actually* deal with the subject. Many such books might not contain the term "expert systems" in their titles at all. Instead, they might be on "knowledge-based systems", "knowledge engineering", or "rule-based systems". Since research on expert systems is an important part of artificial intelligence, the system expert will also consider general books on "artificial intelligence". It should be clever enough not to retrieve older books because books on expert systems did not appear until early 1970's. These intelligent actions are possible because the system expert has knowledge about computer science and the books under its management. This knowledge can be continually improved.

The system experts interact with the target database system through its specific query language. In the case of the prototype system IMUI described here, the target system is a typical relational database (called CS), with an SQL interface. The output of the system expert will be:

(select * from CS where subset([expert, system], TITLE))

(select * from CS where subset([knowledge-based, system], TITLE))

(select * from CS where subset([knowledge engineering], TITLE))

(select * from CS where subset([rule-based systems], TITLE))

(select * from CS where (subset([artificial, intelligence], TITLE) &(PUB-TIME > 1970)))

In exactly the same way, the system expert on the psychology DBMS will find the required books under the subsections of cognitive psychology and cognitive science. The goal manager is analogous to the library's main inquiry desk, and the two system experts have functions which are similar to the computer science and psychology subject librarians.

Once the appropriate information (including each relevant book's title, author, publication time, location, etc) has been retrieved from the database systems and sent back to the system experts, it is integrated with any necessary additional domain information, (such as the general locations of the AI books and the relation between expert systems, knowledge engineering, knowledge-based systems, AI, etc), before being passed back to the goal manager .

The goal manager next consults the user model to see whether there is any reason to believe that the user knows how to get to the place where the books are physically located. If no such reason exists, the goal manager will call the system expert in charge of the route planner to find an efficient route. Since the target system is a general means-ends planner, it lacks domain knowledge and its performance may be very poor if it is left to work alone. The first route found may be very inefficient. For example: it may move up and down between floors several times before reaching the destination. If the planner is required to generate the shortest route, it will seek to examine possibilities exhaustively, and as a consequence, will probably do a great deal of unnecessary computation. Supplementary domain knowledge can be provided for the system expert on route planning, which allows it to use the general planner in a more efficient way. For example, when calling the planner to find a route, the system expert will additionally supply useful hints (or constraints), such as " Don't go up one staircase and down another stairs.", "Use the nearest staircase available", etc. In general, system experts allow general purpose software to be used for specific purposes in an efficient way.

Once an efficient route is found and passed to the goal manager, it will work out a strategic goal and set of associated plans for generating a reply to the user. This goal

```
Expert systems  is a subfield  of artificial  intelligence
(AI), which is in turn a subfield of computer science. You
can find the following relevant books on the AI shelves in
the computer science section.
```

Author	Title	Pub_Time	State
Waterman, A.	A Guide to Expert Systems	1986	borrowed
Oshea,T.	Intelligent Knowledge-Based Systems	1987	3 available
So&so	Knowledge Engineering	1990	1 available
Rich, R.	Artificial Intelligence	1991	2 available
...	...	...	...

```
Research on  artificial intelligence and expert systems is
also  done  in  the  field  of  psychology,  especially on
cognitive  psyshology and cognitive science.  You can find
the following relevant books  on the AI  bookshelf  in the
psychology section of our library.
```

Author	Title	Pub_Time	State
Somebody	Psychology Background of Knowledge-Based Systems	1980	2 available
Scort, L.	Cognitive Science Projects in Prolog	1991	1 available
...	...	...	...

```
The  locations  of  both  the  computer  section  and  the
psychology section are shown in the following map. A route
to visit them from here is also suggested.
```

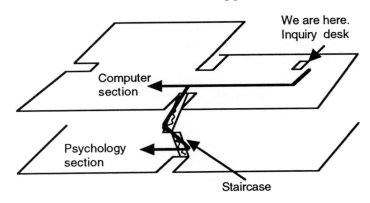

Figure 4: Final Output for the User

and plan complex will contain information such as: what to tell the user, how to tell the user, etc. These plans are constructed in the light of knowledge available in the user model, the context model and any other knowledgebases which are relevant.

If the user is a novice in the domain of expert systems, the goal manager is capable of adding extra information, such as text describing the relationships between computer science, artificial intelligence, expert systems, psychology, cognitive science, etc. In the current example, the strategic response messages generated by the goal manager for the response planner might be:

> **Goal:** Help the user find books on expert systems(higher level goal: to help the user know more about expert systems).
>
> **Plan:**
>
> 1. State the relationship between expert systems, artificial intelligence, and computer science.
>
> 2. Present the title, author, publication date and state of availability of each book about expert systems located in the computer science section.
>
> 3. State the relationship between expert systems, artificial intelligence, psychology and cognitive science.
>
> 4. Present the title, author, publication date and state of availability of each book about expert systems located at the psychology section.
>
> 5. Provide the user with an efficient route to the computer science section and the psychology section of the library.

The response planner is responsible for working out detailed (tactical) plans and goals. It may decide for example, that the route can best be explained with a brief map; that information about individual books can be presented in the form of a table; and that natural language will be used to convey other information.

All of these detailed goals, plans and other requirements are now fed into the natural language generator to generate the system's natural language response to the query. The natural language generator is responsible for making linguistic decisions which effectively carry out the input plans, based on the goals of the system, the user model, the context models, etc. These will include

1. syntactical decisions such as sentence voice (active or passive), tense (present tense), mood (declaration), word order in a sentence, etc.;

2. semantic decisions such as concept (or word sense) usage, the use of anaphoric expressions, ellipsis, etc.;

3. decisions concerning multimedia communication such as the format of tables containing book information, the layout of the map, etc.

The form of output resulting from these decisions is illustrated in Figure 4.

The example presented above illustrates only a simple, one-shot dialogue between a user and the intelligent interface. The interface system has the potential for involvement in much richer dialogue.

5   IMPLEMENTATION

A prototype of IMUI has been developed in Prolog within the application domain of library inquiry servicing. It consists of the three lower layers of the architecture proposed earlier. They are

- goal manager layer:

  a goal manager.

- system expert layer:

  3 target software system oriented expert systems:

  - the computer science subject librarian expert system,
  - the psychology subject librarian expert system
  - the expert system of a typical means-ends route planner.

- target system layer:

  target systems:

  - a relational database system for computer science AI books
  - a relational database system for psychology AI books
  - a means-ends route planner.

In its present form, the prototype demonstrates the principles and techniques described above. It accepts general goals and plans as input and generates useful output for the user.

6   DISCUSSION AND FURTHER RESEARCH

The example discussed above shows how an intelligent multifunctional system can provide better service to users by effectively organising and coordinating the functions provided by individual target systems. As pointed out at the beginning of the paper, this discussion only reflects one dimension of the concept *multifunctional*, namely, the integration of multiple target systems behind a uniform interface. The other two dimensions can also be realized within the system architecture proposed. To support multimedia communication with the user, the natural language parser and generator must be augmented to deal with information represented in other forms than written sentences, such as speech, graphics, gestures, etc. Different assistance modes are also possible: the intelligent interface can help the user achieve a goal by actually executing a relevant plan (or part of the plan) on the target systems. But the system is also capable of providing consultancy or giving advice, on for example: how to solve a problem or achieve a goal. IMUI can also provide advice at different levels with different granularity of details.

The development of a practical multifunctional intelligent system is by no means an easy task. Quite a few problems need a good deal of further research. Some of the more important ones are:

1. what is an optimal design for the goal manager;

2. how should the knowledgebases be developed and maintained, especially the user model and the context model;

3. how to provide the specific definition and formalism of the interface between the goal manager and the system experts;

4. how can the system experts communicate with the target systems more efficiently.

7   CONCLUSION

Current intelligent interfaces are mainly uni-functional: they are usually dedicated to a single application target system to provide a single type of assistance. This paper first argues for the importance and feasibility of implementing a multifunctional intelligent interface. The term *multifunction* has three underlying dimensions:

1. Support of multimedia communication.

2. Integration of multiple target application systems behind a uniform intelligent interface, which is competent to understand both the target systems and the user, and which can help users achieve a goal by coordinating the individual functions of target systems.

3. Provision of different types of help in interfacing with the application domain, such as acting as a consultant, a practical assistant, or an actual task executor.

Secondly, a methodology and architecture for the design of the proposed intelligent interface is described, and a simple example is presented and discussed. Some outstanding research problems associated with the proposed intelligent interface are itemised. The paper concentrates on the dynamic integration of multiple target systems and describes an already implemented proof-of-concept prototype as evidence that the approach is workable and promising.

References

[All87] Allen, J. *Natural Language Understanding*, Benjamin/Cummings, 1987.

[Chi91] Chin, D. N, Intelligent Interfaces as Agents, in Sullivan, J. W. and Tyler, S. W(edt.) *Intelligent User Interfaces*, ACM Press (frontier series), 1991.

[DB88] Debille, L. and Binot, J.-L, LOQUI: a natural language interface to databases, *Proceeding of the Sun User Group European Conference*, March 1988.

[GL89] Gorayska, B. and Lindsay, R, On Relevance: goal dependence expressions and the control of planning processes. Research Report 16, Dept. of Computing and Mathematical Sciences, Oxford Polytechnic, 1989.

[Hay90] Hayes, P. J. The Naive Physics Manifesto, in Boden, M. A,(ed.), *The Philosophy of Artificial Intelligence*, Oxford University Press, 1990.

[Joh83] Johnson-Laird, P. N, *Mental Models: Towards Cognitive Science of Language, Inference, and Consciousness*, Cambridge University Press, 1983.

[JV91] Jones, J., and Virvou, User Modelling and Advice Giving in Intelligent Help Systems for Unix, in *Information and Software Technology*, vol 33 no. 2 March 1991.

[LG90] Lenat, D. B and Guha, R. V, *Building Large Knowledge-Based Systems(Representation and Inference in the Cyc Project)*, Addison-Wesley Publishing Company, Inc., 1990.

[SW86] Sperber, D. and Wilson, D., *Relevance: Communication and Cognition*, Basil Blackwell, 1986.

[Wal84] Wallace, M, Communicating with Databases in Natural Language, Ellis Horwood Limited, 1984.

[Zha92] Zhang, X, Intelligent Multifunctional User Interface, Research Report (6), Knowledge Engineering Research Group, Oxford Polytechnic, 1992.

Combining Qualitative and Quantitative Information for Temporal Reasoning

H. A. Tolba, F. Charpillet and J.-P. Haton

CRIN-CNRS and INRIA-Lorraine
Campus Scientifique - B.P. 239
54506 Vandœuvre–lès–Nancy Cedex, FRANCE

1 Introduction

Time is an important aspect of any intelligent knowledge representation. This has led to a rising need for reasoning about time in various applications of artificial intelligence such as process control or decision making. Different schemes for temporal information representation have been proposed so far. A natural way to refer to a temporal event consists in making references to a clock providing a quantitative or numerical representation of time, as well as several concepts such as duration and calendar. However, a clock reference is not always available or relevant. In such cases, a qualitative (symbolic) representation of time can be used to describe the situations in question.

In spite of the different representations of temporal information proposed, most are not completely satisfactory. Looking at existing work, Allen's representation [Allen 83] is a very powerful representation in describing the relativity between intervals. Vilain and kautz proposed a subinterval algebra [Vilain & Kautz 86], Ghallab and Mounir [Ghallab & Mounir 89] based on the notion of subinterval algebara, have also proposed a model with symbolic relations but within the framework of subinterval algebra. However, these models don't address numerical aspect of time. On the other hand, the time map of Dean and McDermott [Dean & McDermott 87], Rit geometrical model [Rit 86] and the temporal constraint networks [Dechter, Meiri & Pearl 91] are designed for handling metric information and can't handle in a good way symbolic ones.

We propose in this paper a new temporal representation combining the notions of intervals, dates and durations. Our model [Tolba, Charpillet & Haton 91] is based on constraint representation. We highlight in this paper the integration in a single framework of both quantitative temporal information (tempoal windows and durations) and qualitative ones (Allen's 13 relations). A powerful language has been defined for representing both kinds of constraints: symbolic and numeric. The reasoning procedure is based on constraint-propagation algorithms. These algorithms are a generalization of AC4 an optimum algorithm for arc-consistency and can handle n-ary constraints. The manipulation of both symbolic and numerical temporal information is done via two temporal constraints propagation levels. This original method of propagating temporal constraints permits flexible control over both levels as well as the independence between those two levels.

There are relatively few related works in the literature. Meiri [Meiri 91] has proposed such a model, capable of handling both qualitative and quantitative temporal information. However contrary to our approach his model is based on a single network managing both constraints. It uses the usual arc-consistency algorithms converting AC-3 to a path consistency one. Thus, it suffers from the fact that it is local consistent and the solution is incomplete. However, new classes of tractable problems have been discovered, some of which can be solved in polynomial time using arc and path consistency. In such cases Meiri's algorithms are complete. A second approach very close to ours has been described in [Kautz & Ladkin 91]. The authors presented an idea separating the two types of constraints. However, in this work the information exchange is not complete. The only exchange done is the translation carried out from Allen's primitives to point algebra. It also, suffers from the incompleteness of conventional CSA. In [Dechter, Meiri & Pearl 91] the authors present the TSCP. This model is an equivalent approach to Dean's time map manager and based on propagation of constraints. This approach is based on representing temporal numerical constraints in form of inequalities. Thus, no symbolic constraints are available in this case.

2 Knowledge Representation

We propose a discrete model of time which relies on a partition of R, the set of real numbers. We define a temporal reference **Tr** (Cf. figure 1) as the maximal set of discrete and adjacent temporal units **uj** . Each unit represents the smallest discrete portion of time that can be obtained over the temporal reference. Using these units another temporal entity is defined : the interval. An interval **I** is represented by a couple of units (u_i, u_j), where u_i and u_j are the start and end times respectively. U_O represents a particular reference.

Each interval I is identified with a lower-bound and an upper-bound identified with relative offsets (est, lst) and (eet, let). The precision of the starting and ending points of an interval depend obviously on the size of the unit **uj.**

This model relies on the definition for each interval **I** of the Sets Of Possible Occurences (SOPOs) where it can take place. In our model a SOPO O is restricted to be a temporal window; i.e. a set of intervals with a constant duration. Our SOPOs are defined by couples of units (u_i, u_j), where u_i and u_j are the start and end time respectively of the specified window. An instance of an interval taking place in a SOPO is called an occurrence. Events represent intervals that take place during windows. Between any two events we can define any number of Allen's thirteen primitives. Every event is self constrained by its duration and the window in which it takes place. The propagation of constraints is used to deduce all the possible relations between any pair of events leading to a consistent labeling. The events which are numerically self constrained use the result of the propagation to eliminate the impossible numerical constraints represented in the windows in function of the existing symbolic constraints between events.

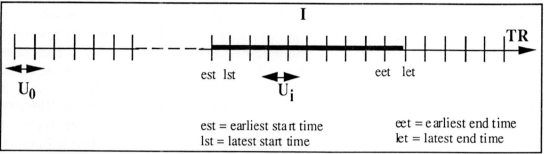

Figure 1. Time-line partition

More formally, on each couple $O_1 \times O_2$ of SOPOs (windows), a relation R is defined. This relation is composed of a disjunction of the 13 Allen primitives. A primitive is defined by:

`P  :  O₁xO₂` $\rightarrow$ `{F, T}`

`(O₁xO₂)` $\rightarrow$ `P(I₁,I₂)  and  I₁ in O₁ and I₂ in O₂`.

where O_1 and O_2 are SOPOs, I_1 and I_2 are intervals and P one of the 13 primitives of Allen. The primitive `P` expresses a constraint over the beginning and the end of the occurrences with respect their SOPOs. For example, let P be the `meet` or `after` Allen's primitive, `b(I)` the beginning of `I` and `e(I)` the end of `I` :

`meet(I₁,I₂)=T` $\Leftrightarrow$ `b(I₂)=e(I₁);`

`after(I₁,I₂)=T` $\Leftrightarrow$ `b(I₂)<e(I₁).`

The goal of the constraint propagator is then to delete from all SOPOs O_1, O_2, ..., O_n the occurrences which do not respect the constraints expressed by the edges of the temporal graph. The disjunctive relations are handled by considering the union of the SOPOs allowed by each relation of the disjunction.

3 Propagating Temporal Constraints

3.1 Introduction

Let N be a set of variables x_i, each defined on a discrete domain $\{a_{i1}, ..., a_{in}\}$ and R a set of constraining relations on a subset of theses variables. A constraint satisfaction problem (CSP) consists in finding all sets of values $\{a_1j_1, ..., a_nj_n\}$ for $\{x_1, ...,x_n\}$ satisfying all relations belonging to R. The network G=(N, R) characterizing the CSP is generally a hyper-graph in which the vertices represent variables and hyper-edges represent relations. Since the CSP is NP-complete, algorithms assuming only local consistency were invented. These algorithms aim at transforming the network G into an equivalent and simpler one G' by removing from the domain of each variables all values that cannot belong to any global solution. A k-consistency algorithm removes all inconsistencies involving all subset of k variables belonging to N. When k=2 and k=3 we say that the solution is respectively arc and path consistent. The k-consistency problem is in polynomial time $O(n^k)$ where n is the cardinal of N. Among the arc consistency algorithms found in the literature, Ac4 [Mohr & Henderson 86] developed in our laboratory has been proved optimum for discrete relaxation. This algorithm was extended in Gac4 [Mohr & Masini 88] to handle n-ary constraints. This algorithm is also optimum. We have extended in a first step [Tolba, Charpillet & Haton 91] a version of Gac4 for handling temporal constraints. However, GAC4 suffers from many short comings. Indeed, it's simple but it consumes a lot of memory space. Furthermore, Gac4 does not provide us with a good solution to address the world's evolution [Bessière 91]. For these two reasons, we chose to develop a new algorithm called ANGEL [Tolba, Charpillet & Haton 91]. This algorithm can be used for both symbolic and numeric constraint propagations.

3.2   A Two Level   Constraint Propagator

Our temporal propagator works in two steps. First it tries to complete and deduce all missing information between events. Then, deduced information is used to reduce the size of the temporal windows and the symbolic relations linking every pairs of events. The numerical and symbolic temporal constraints are handled by two separate communicating TMM.

The symbolic and numerical TMMs operate in an interactive manner. The symbolic relations which cannot be satisfied by the numerical level are deduced and fed back to the symbolic propagation level via a communication module. Inversely, the symbolic relations which are eliminated by the symbolic level are communicated to the numerical level. This feed-back operation provides a solution refinement and a flexible method to control the problem reduction. This procedure ends when there are no more results to be processed. Figure 2 illustrates this process.

3.2.1Ssymbolic propagation

Allen has proposed a path consistency algorithm with a complexity of $O(n^3)$. However, no proof of its optimality exists. Fortunately, it is possible to transfcrm Allen's algorithm into a CSP. This algorithm relies on a graph G where nodes represent intervals and arcs are labelled by a set of Allen's primitives. For each triplet of nodes (i,j,k) for which the admissible relations between (i,j) and (j,k) are known, the transitivity table allows the admissible relations between (i,k) to be computed. As we have to find the actual relations between events, the relations should be considered as the labels by the propagation algorithm. (G) is thus transformed into another graph A(G) in which a node noted (ij) represents the set of relations {Rij} constraining the intervals i and j. A node (ij) is linked with any node (ik) and (kj) by the hyper-edges (ijk) of A(G). An hyper-edge (ijk) specifies the following constraint : {Rij} o {Rjk} = {Rik}

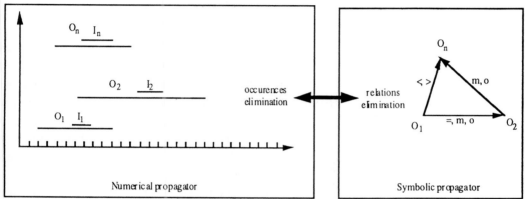

Figure 2. A Two Level Constraint Propagator.

3.2.2 Numerical propagation

The numerical level propagates the numerical constraints represented by windows to find out the precise date of events. The numerical propagation consists in finding for each event all occurrences satisfying locally the temporal constraints (3-consistency). The symbolic constraints and the occurrences which cannot be satisfied are eliminated. Traditionally the propagation algorithm relies on a graph where nodes are events (with a domain in the form of a window) and edge are symbolic constraints. In order to transform this representation into a CSP one, a similar transformation as the one used for Allen's algorithm is needed.

3.2.3 GAC4

GAC4 handles relations such $R\{i,j,... k\}$ specifying the admissible labels for the nodes i,j,...k. It is represented by an edge in a hyper-graph. $R\{i,j,... k\}$ can be defined as the enumeration of all the p-tuples of labels admissible for $\{i,j,...k\}$: $((i,a),(j,b),...(k,c))$. GAC4 works as a recursive label pruning. When a label a has to be removed from the set L_i of admissible labels for i, all the p-tuples including a have to be discarded. When a p-tuple is discarded from a relation R, it may happen that this p-tuple be the last of R which was supporting a particular label. This label has thus to disappear, and so on. An efficient implementation of the algorithm is described in [Mohr & Masini 88]. The algorithm, in fact, runs in two steps. The first step consists in building the data structure from the list of admissible labels for all the hyper-edges R. The second step prunes the labels which are not admissible.

The complexity of GAC4 is $O(n^3)$, where n is the number of nodes of (g). However, as Allen's relations are oriented, we have to deal with their symmetry, i.e. compute three labellings for each hyper-edge. Also, GAC4 gives us the possibility of choosing the consistency order in which the propagation is to be done.

3.2.4 ANGEL

We have designed the path consistency algorithm called ANGEL which is capable of propagating n-ary constraints. It runs on the graph which has been processed by the other special purpose of the algorithm or GAC4 in the previous tool version. The principles demonstrated for GAC4 are thus also true for it: the final result is a path-consistent graph. Contrary to most existing constraint propagation algorithms, ANGEL is dynamic, i.e. it dynamically builds the graph on which it works by progressively processing the constraints one by one. Whereas the input of GAC4 is the set of non-admissible relations delivered by the initialization step, it receives admissible set of relations under the form of a set of all the possible occurrences for a given event. The constraints received by the algorithm (propagator) are placed in a input-diary to be processed in the order of arrival. If the hyper-edge corresponding to the current constraint does not exist yet, it is created.

If the set of occurrences is modified for any of the edges of the current hyper-edge, all the hyper-edges having the edge in question in common are to be loaded into the input-diary in order to be examined later. When the input-diary becomes empty, the propagation stops, waiting for a new input. The symbolic relations which cannot be satisfied are deduced and fed back to the symbolic propagation level via a communication module. This feed-back operation presents a kind of solution refinement allowing this one pass procedure to be repeated till no more possible solutions or problem reduction can be obtained.

Algorithm:

```
while input-diary <> nil do
   hyper-edge = pop(input-diary)
   verify-constraints(hyper-edge)
if modified(hyper-edge) then
   push(input-diary, succ(hyper-edge)
```

where *verify-constraints* applies the constraints specified by an hyper-edge, *modified* checks if the nodes linked by an hyper-edge have been modified and *succ* returns all hyper-edges having a common arc with a given hyper-edge.

Evaluation for numerical propagation:
Since there is a finite number of labels and hyper-edges, ANGEL is guarantied to terminate. As for the complexity, the fact that it is a dynamic algorithm led us to consider it from the following point of view. We normally start with an empty input-diary and the algorithm stops working when this diary is empty or when there are no more hyper-edges to be processed. Thus the complexity problem is controlled by the number of hyper-edges formed from the triplet of nodes *(i,j,k)* defining an interval. The number of updates for an arc *(i,j)* is limited, due to the limited number of intervals found in the temporal graph. Therefore, the possibility for an hyper-edge to return in the agenda is limited. The complexity cost in this case is bounded by the number of hyper-edges and it will be in the order of $KO(n^3)$ where *n* is the number of the graph nodes.

4 TOOL DESCRIPTION

The **TemPro** tool is based on a dynamic arc-consistency algorithm characterized by its ability to manipulate n-ary constraints. A control procedure to build the time map and exchange information between the two propagators encloses both constraint propagators.

4.1 Communication Module

The communication module carries out important functions of the TemPro. It is responsible for passing the results from the output of each module to the input of another. During this operation, it matches the numerical and symbolic constraints resulting from both propagation modules. Thus, in case either of numerical or symbolic constraints are determined to be impossible by a verification module, the labels are eliminated. The verification module matches the symbolic constraints with numerical constraints for given events (nodes on the time map). This is done over the hyper-edges propagated. If the symbolic constraints cannot be satisfied via the numerical ones, the symbolic are removed from the event's labels. The communication module then stacks all the hyper-edges in common with the events being tested in the algorithm's queue to be examined later.

The input agenda (algorithm's queue) are the surveyed by this module. It acts as the door-keeper looking after the loading of agenda for both propagators. It detects if a stability point is reached and thus the TemPro becomes passive. This termination process is done when the agenda becomes empty.

The complexity of such an algorithm si equal to that of the propagators multiplied by a coefficient. The verification step complexity is dependent on the size of step granularity σ, number of intervals in a window for an event ν and the number of symbolic constraints ρ. Therefore constant coefficient K is $\sigma * \nu * \rho$. The complexity of this algorithm in general is: K O(complexity of the propagator). The termination of this algorithm is guaranteed since both propagators work on a finite number of nodes in a time map and consequently terminates when the communication module algorithm terminates.

4.2 Propagators

The propagator's role is to propagate temporal constraints, and to detect if any modification on the labels of a hyper-edge it processes. If a modification is detected it returns a list of the hyper-edges having an edge in common with the one it processes to the communication module.

3.2.1 Symbolic propagator

0) While Next (Com-Agenda) <> End Of List do
1)   W-hyper-wdge := Next (Com-Agenda);
2)   Composition (w-hyper-edge);
3)   If Modified (w-hyper-edge) Then
4)   Return Related-Edges(w-hyper-edge)
5)   end if;
6) end While.

The *Composition* function we define here has the ability of treating n-ary constraints. That means it is defined in the traditional sense as defined by [Allen 83] or it is able to achieve more than 3-consistency. This is done using the definition in [van Beek 89]. The difference is done over the length of a hyper-edge passed to the function to be propagated. *Modified* is a function where intersection is defined between the result of composition and old labels given for a hyper-edge. Related-Edges returns the list of hyper-edges to be examined in the following propagation cycle.

4.2.2 Numerical propagator

The numerical propagator is similar to that of symbolic propagator except for one modification. This modification takes place in the functional propagation step. Step 2 in the last propagator is changed with the following line: Apply-constraints (w-hyper-edge). The function *Apply-constraints* matches the symbolic and numerical constraitns for a hyper-edge processed.

4.2.3 Conclusion

We can conclude from the last sections the importance of the separation of both constraints types from each other. In fact, it is the key to our representation and TemPro. The idea of the two propagation levels allows us to perform a sort of progressive reasoning while propagating. Also, such reasoning can give us the possibility of refining the solution of the problem on which we are working. Another aspect is the fact of separating the complexity and the modular nature of the tool. The complexity of each module can be calculated separately which leads of an over all acceptable complexity. The most important issue, is that of the completeness. We know that the symbolic propagator is not complete. However, the numerical one is. This fact leads us to use the numerical propagation to complete the symbolic one via the communication module. This is due to the fact that each constraints type is separated and independent thus allowing the exchange of information between both of them in order to complete the propagation till stability.

4.3 Query Language

Modifying, updating and querying the time map are important aspects neglected by several temporal representation models. We propose an interface and a language built over our TemPro. This is missed in the similar representations discussed earlier. The syntax of this language is a *lisp-like*. This language is used to command the TemPro as well as its interrogation. It takes the form of functions call to modify an entry or update it. This language also can be used by an inference engine to pilot the tool. Several query types are supported by the tool. For example we can ask the tool to add a new node to the graph or to use only one propagator. We can ask it to check the possible relations or to give the different forms of a temporal window of an event: disjunctive or window form. Asking the tool to find a possible solution according to a given condition is also possible. This query is an important one especially in a planning type application. The tool can provide the user with a limited number or all the possible solutions of the problem in question. Thus allowing the user or the interrogating part to take more accurate decisions. This was implemented by a improving a forward checking like algorithm. An X-window graphical interface has been developed. Its goal is to illustrate the reasoning process and to allow the user to easily interact with the TemPro shell.

5 Tool Evaluation

Several tests to analyze the performance and the capacities of the tool were carried out with random data and according to the following procedure. The numerical and symbolic Time Maps are randomly initialized 100 times. As we want to consider only the consistent Time Maps, we have introduced the label *bef* in the randomly generated labels of an event over the time map. Thus, we guarantee at least an ordered possible solution and a coherent graph. This was for symbolic initialization. For the numerical one, we generate windows and durations for the ordered events found previously. Both windows and duration are randomly generated and the only fixed obligation is the size of a window: it is at least ten times that of an interval's duration. These tests must evaluate the dynamic, static features of the TemPro. Also, the execution time (CPU time) is calculated for them as well as both propagators. The TCP is subjected to different conditions : step changing increasing and decreasing its size. Also, the confidence interval is calculated for the important features. These results represent the average calculated time over 100 tests for every feature analyzed. The TemPro propagates a completely connected graph. It is written in Common Lisp and runs on a SUN Sparc2 workstation.

We will present limited number of tests, because of the space limits, in order to give the reader a sufficient idea of its capacities. Figure 3 shows curves for a symbolic time map; its maximum size is 200 nodes. Sample results varying from 5 to the 200 nodes are shown over the curves. For every sample chosen the number of labels over the nodes, representing events now, are varied from one label to the thirteen labels (labels are Allen's primitives). All curves provide us with a clear view of the execution time of the time map. This execution time is influenced by the number of labels existing over the events propagated. This is due to the time spent in the *composition* function. That is why every time the number of labels increases the execution time, directly proportional in this case, increases. So, the curve propagating 13 labels is the highest one although logically the composition function should spend its least effort to calculate the new labels. We can not due this result as a problem of interval algebra. However, an algorithm or a more intelligent function can give us better results in such a case.

The performance of the numerical part is shown in figure 4. Another important aspect shown here is that of the varying time step. The time step reduces the number of intervals in a window. This has a direct effect on the complexity coefficient factor and reduces the execution time considerably. As it is clear by the curves for nodes carrying 5 labels. Changing the step causes the execution time to decrease by a factor of 3 to 4 between curves. We must note that the interval's duration in this case, for every event is at least 10 times that of a window.

To give an idea of the performance of the tool in general, figure 5 shows the overall performance of the tool's three blocks: the two propagators and the communication module. The curves of figure 5 show the results of propagating events over a time map carrying 4, 7, and 11 labels through symbolic and numerical propagators and the verification step. As we mentioned that the propagation steps execution time can be compared with that of the communication exchange step. There, the TemPro passes a considerable part of its time. Also the numerical step time is much more important than that of symbolic. Although we could not determine, or estimate, the number of passes needed by the time map to reach stability, which may be considered as a disadvantage. However, compared with the results gained by information exchange and leading to solution refinement is more importante, the time spent in the last step is worth.

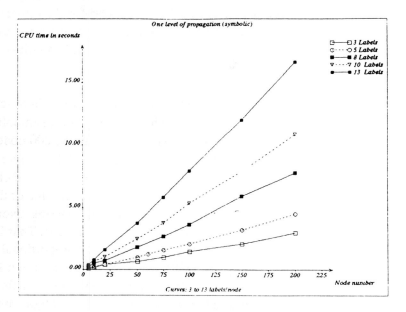

Figure 3. Symbolic propagator

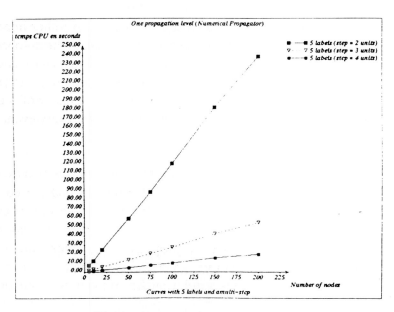

Figure 4. Numerical propagator

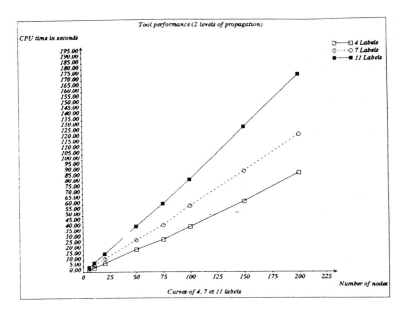

Figure 5. Tool performance curves

6. Conclusion and Future Work

In this paper we have proposed a new representation of time which combines both symbolic and numerical temporal information. We have also presented an original constraint propagation strategy based on two levels of propagation. The ANGEL algorithm presents the new feature of being dynamic, thus allowing to be used with an inference engine. A tool has ben presented. It provides any potential user with a useful interface language allowing interfacing the tool with other modules or exploiting the advantages of the temporal model. Such tool was missing in the previous representations.

Presently, we are working on improving and providing a more powerful interrogation language. The language extension is to support more complex queries. The improvement of the graphical interface is also previewed. The integration of this tool in a functioning expert system application is one of our near future goals.

References
[Allen 83] J. F. Allen, "Maintaining Knowledge about Temporal Intervals," *Communications of ACM*, 26(11):832--843, November 1983.

[Bessier 91] C. Bessiers, Arc Consistency in Dynamic Constraint Satisfaction Problems, In AAAI, pages 329-335, 1991.

[Dean & McDermott 87] T. L. Dean and D. V. McDermott, "Temporal Data Base

Management," *Artificial Intelligence*, 32:1--55, 1987.

[Dechter, Meiri, & Pearl 91] R. Dechter, I. Meiri and J. Pearl," Temporal Constraints Networks," *Artificial Intelligence*, 49:61--95, 1991.

[Ghallab & Mounir 89] M. Ghallab, A. Mounir-Alaoui, "Managing efficiently temporal relations through indexed spanning trees," In IJCAI89, pages 1297--1303, 1989.

[Kautz & Ladkin 91] H. A. Kautz and P. Ladkin, "Integrating Metric and Qualitative Temporal Reasoning," In AAAI, pages 241--246, 1991.

[Meiri 91] I. Meiri, "Combining Qualititaive and Quatitative Constraints in Temporal Reasoning," In AAAI, pages 260--267,1991.

[Mohr & Henderson 86] R. Mohr and T. C. Henderson, "Arc and Path Consistency Revisited," *Artificial Intelligence*, 28:228--233, 1986.

[Mohr & Masini 88] R .Mohr and G. Masini, "Good Old Discrete Relaxation," In 8th ECAI, pages 651--656, 1988.

[Rit 86] J.F. Rit, "Propagating temporal constraints for scheduling", in AAAI, pp. 383-388.

[Tolba, Charpillet & Haton 91] H. Tolba, F. Charpillet and J-P. Haton, "Representing and propagating Temporal Constraints," *AICOM*, vol 4, No. 4, pages 145--151, 1991.

[Vilain & Kautz 86] M. Vilain and H. Kautz, "Constraint Propagation Algorithms for Temporal Reasoning," In AAAI, pages 377--382, 1986.

[van Beek 89] P. van Beek, "Approximation Algorithms for Temporal Reasoning," In IJCAI, pages 1291--1296, 1989.

Documents as Expert Systems

BRIAN R GAINES & MILDRED L G SHAW

Knowledge Science Institute, University of Calgary
Calgary, Alberta, Canada T2N 1N4.
gaines@cpsc.ucalgary.ca & mildred@cpsc.ucalgary.ca

This paper is written in a document production tool that appears to a user as a word processor but also acts as an expert system shell with frame and rule representations supporting deductive inference. The electronic version of the document is active, providing typographic text and page layout facilities, versioning, hypermedia sound and movies, hypertext links, and knowledge structures represented in a visual language. It can be read as a hypermedia document and also interrogated as a knowledge-based system for problem-solving. The paper version of the document, which you are now reading, is produced by printing the electronic version. It loses its active functionality but continues to act as a record of the knowledge in the document. The overall technology has been developed as an alternative approach to the dissemination of knowledge bases. It also provides a different interface to knowledge-based systems that emulates document interfaces with which many users are already familiar.

1 INTRODUCTION

The knowledge document publication system emulates conventional word-processing packages as closely as possible to require the minimum of new skills in the user. It produces documents that are formatted and paginated for printing so that parallel publication of paper and electronic documents is available. It allows diagrams, pictures, video and sound to be integrated in documents, with their preparation and editing being based on existing packages so that again the user has the minimal learning requirements. For example, the

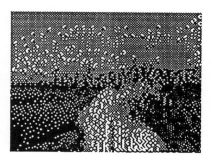

picture inset in this paragraph is a QuickTime video with moving picture and sound commentary that may be played by double clicking in the picture. The mechanism for linking to multi-media material is also used to provide simple and versatile hypertextual linking. Formal knowledge structures may also be embedded in documents, represented as semantic networks in a visual language easily understood by people. The same knowledge structures may also be accessed through computer programs to provide the decision support and problem solving capabilities of an expert system.

The knowledge document publication system is part of a research program on general 'knowledge support systems' integrating many information technologies to support knowledge processes in human society (Gaines, 1990). Since the intended users are not computer specialists, our objective has been to achieve all the functionality outlined above through an environment that appears simple and natural to the user. That is, the project is successful to the extent that the system appears like a conventional word processor rather than an over-engineered concatenation of multi-media and artificial intelligence functionality. This paper focuses on the expert system functionality of the system and illustrates this through some studies of organizational modeling and problem solving which were reported in greater detail in an (inactive) paper at the Conference on Organizational Computing Systems (Gaines, 1991d).

The problem considered is one of room allocation from an ESPRIT project (Voß, Karbach, Drouven, Lorek & Schuckey, 1990) that has recently been made part of Project Sisyphus. Sisyphus is a research program to encourage international collaboration in knowledge-based system development initiated by the European Knowledge Acquisition Workshop in 1989. A number of problem datasets have been made available through Sisyphus, and a major part of the EKAW'91 program was devoted to reports on the solution of these problems using different approaches and techniques (Linster, 1991).

What is remarkable about the document you are reading is that the paper version of it reports a solution to the problem, giving all the knowledge structures involved in visual form, and the electronic version of it *is* the solution. That is, if you opened this paper in the associated word processor you could interrogate it to solve room allocation problems. You could edit the visual knowledge structures within the document, for example by adding additional rules, and when you interrogated it again those rules would be in effect. Thus, the document itself provides an active, editable knowledge base and problem-solving inference engine.

The next section gives an overview of the architecture of the system, followed by the visual language for knowledge representation and the problem formulation and solution in this language.

2 KSSn ARCHITECTURE
KSSn (Knowledge Support System n) is the latest in a series of developments deriving from our initial implementation of KSS0 (Gaines, 1988a,b) and KSS1 (Shaw & Gaines, 1987). These early knowledge support systems focused on knowledge acquisition and conceptual modeling, and have been extended through heterogeneous integration to offer close integration with hypermedia and expert system shells (Gaines, Rappaport & Shaw, 1989; Gaines & Linster, 1990). KSSn is designed as a C++ class library implementing KRS (Gaines, 1991a), a KL-ONE-like (Brachman & Schmolze, 1985) knowledge representation server, and a set of associated functional modules for knowledge elicitation, text analysis, empirical induction, graphic knowledge base editing, and so on.

Figure 1 shows the architecture of KSSn as a family of modules attached to the knowledge representation server, KRS. The modules are (reading clockwise from the top left):

- Interface modules to other knowledge bases and servers, including databases.
- A hypermedia module allowing informal knowledge structures in text and images to be captured, accessed and linked. The linkage structure itself is held as a knowledge base.
- A text analysis module allowing documents to be analyzed in terms of word usage, and associations between significant words to be graphed—based on TEXAN in KSS0. This enables protocols and technical documents to be used to initiate knowledge acquisition.
- A repertory grid expertise transfer module allowing graphic definition of concepts and graphic creation and editing of individuals—based on the elicitation screens of KSS0.
- A conceptual clustering module allowing interactive definition of new concepts—based on the hierarchical and spatial clustering from KSS0.
- A knowledge editing module allowing the interactive development and editing of knowledge structures through a visual language.
- A conceptual induction module creating rules about specified subsets of individuals and transforming them to a minimal set of concepts and default rules—based on the Induct algorithm.
- A problem solving module supporting frame, rule and case-based inference from the knowledge structures.
- A grapher laying out specified parts of the concept subsumption graph, concept structures and individual structures—based on an incremental layout algorithm that can be used interactively to support the production of clear visual knowledge structures.
- A language interface accepting and generating definitions and assertions in formal knowledge representation languages, both textual and visual.

The knowledge representation services of KRS, the central server module, correspond to those of CLASSIC (Borgida, et al, 1989), augmented with inverse roles, data types for integers, reals, strings and dates, and with rule representation that allows one rule to be declared an exception to others. KWrite, the document production tool used to produce this paper, may be seen as providing a word processing user interface to the functionality shown in Figure 1.

3 KDRAW VISUAL LANGUAGE
An important component of KWrite and KSSn in the context of this paper is the graphic knowledge editor, KDraw, at the right of Figure 1. This is a drawing tool designed for ease of use that provides a visual structure editor for semantic networks representing classes, objects and rules in KRS. Nosek and Roth (1990) have demonstrated empirically that the visual presentation of knowledge structures as semantic nets leads to more effective human understanding than does textual presentation of the same structures. We have developed a formal visual language that corresponds exactly to the underlying algebraic semantics of KRS that has remarkably few visual primitives and is easily learnt and understood (Gaines & Shaw, 1990).

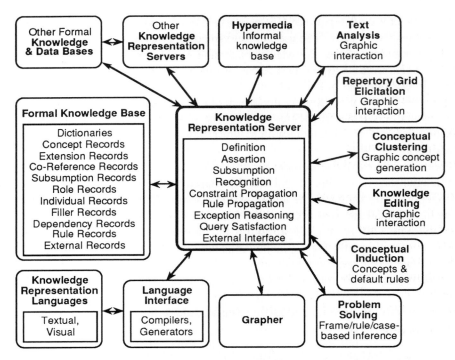

Figure 1 Architecture of the knowledge representation server

Visual representation of knowledge structures has been common since the early development of diagrams and taxonomies, and was associated with semantic networks in the early days of artificial intelligence (Quillian, 1968). The early development of such nets resulted in criticisms that the semantics of particular diagrams was not well-defined (Woods, 1975; Brachman, 1977). Nodes, arcs and their labels could be used very freely and ambiguously and diagrams were subject to differing interpretations. In the 1970s there were proposals for network formalisms with well-defined semantics (Cercone & Schubert, 1975; Fahlman, 1979; Brachman, 1979). However, these preceded two important developments in computing: first, the ubiquity of personal workstations with high resolution graphics supporting visual languages as operational editors (Glinert, 1990); second, the studies of complexity issues in knowledge representation, leading to the simplified and tractable semantics of CLASSIC (Borgida et al, 1989).

Computer production of visual forms of knowledge represented in a computer has been a topic of research since the early days of knowledge representation research (Schmolze, 1983) and a feature of many research systems (Kindermann & Quantz, 1989) and commercial products. Abrett and Burstein's (1988) KREME system graphically displays the computed subsumption relations between concepts so that those entering knowledge structures can see the consequences of definitions and detect errors due to incorrect or inadequate definitions.

The KDraw design (Gaines, 1991c) has drawn upon this previous research and experience to develop the visual syntax and underlying semantics of a visual language for term subsumption knowledge representation languages in the KL-ONE family. It focuses on the use of the language to enter and edit knowledge visually, and on its application in a highly interactive graphic structure editor. KDraw may be used just to support the entry of conceptual structures and facts in a knowledge base. However, it is capable of going beyond this and accepting problem solving knowledge structures in the form of concepts defining the premise and conclusion of rules. The rule structure provided in KDraw and KRS is itself powerful in both its representational and inference capabilities in supporting exceptions and defaults (Gaines, 1991b).

The structures below show the top level conceptual structures of an organizational domain. The visual language used in these diagrams is precisely defined. Concepts are ovals, primitive concepts are ovals with small horizontal lines inside each side, individuals are rectangles, roles are unboxed text, rules are rectangles with double lines at the sides, constraint expressions are rounded-corner boxes. Lines without arrows connecting primitive concepts denote that the concepts are disjoint, and those connecting roles denote that they are inverse. The interpretation of the arrows in the editor is overloaded but well-defined by the types of the objects at their head and tail, e.g.:

concept → concept	definitional subsumption
concept → role → concept	definitional role with conceptual constraint
concept → role → constraint	definitional role with extensional, cardinality or numeric constraint
constraint → individual	extensional constraint
individual → concept	asserted constraint on individual
individual → role → individual	asserted value of role for individual
concept → rule → concept	production rule
rule → rule	first rule exception to second

Thus knowledge structure 1 defines "animate" and "inanimate" to be disjoint primitive concepts of type "Individual"; "person" and "organization" to be disjoint concepts inheriting from "animate"; and "location" and "activity" to be disjoint concepts inheriting from "inanimate". Knowledge structure 3 further defines "general organization" as an "organization" (nodes may be freely duplicated for the sake of visual appearance) to have the role "head" filled by exactly one individual of type "head", to have the role "secretary" possibly filled by individuals of type "secretary", and to have the role "member" possibly filled by individuals of type "person". A project, since it is shown to inherit from "organization" also has these roles and constraints but is further constrained to have its "head" role filled by a "group head" and its "member" role filled by individuals of type "researcher".

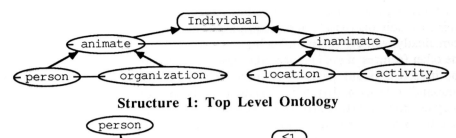

Structure 1: Top Level Ontology

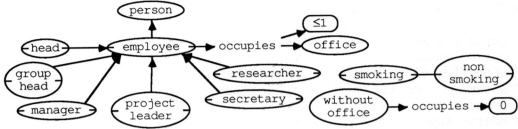

Structure 2: Employee Ontology

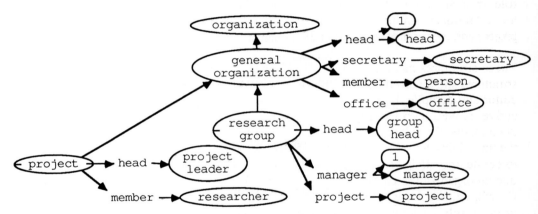

Structure 3: Organization Ontology

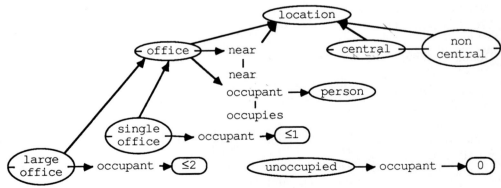

Structure 4: Office Ontology

The underlying knowledge representation inference engine propagates constraints so that defining an individual as a "project" and then filling its "member" role with "Marc M." will automatically lead to "Marc M." being inferred to be a "researcher". Structure 4 shows some other features of the language. For example "occupant" and "occupies" are defined to be inverses, as are "near" and "near". Hence, if "Marc M." is asserted to fill the "occupant" role of office "C5-120" then it will be inferred that "C5-120" fills the "occupies" role of "Marc M.", and if "C5-119" is asserted to fill the "near" role of office "C5-120" then it will be inferred that "C5-120" fills the "near" role of "C5-119."

Structures 5 and 6 show the way in which facts may be asserted about individuals in the visual language. For example, the "RESPECT Project" in structure 5 is shown to be one of the fillers of the "project" role of "YQT Research Center" which is defined to be an instance of a "research group" defined in structure 3. This concept instantiation has the consequence that the conceptual constraints defined in structures 1 through 3 will be inherited appropriately by individuals in structure 5. For example, from structure 3 it will be inferred that "Thomas D." is "group head", "head", and the only filler of the "head" role, from structure 2 that he is an "employee" and a "person", and from structure 1 that he is "animate" and of type "Individual". Structure 6 supplies further facts about the project and the rooms that will be needed in the problem-solving activity.

These structures have a number of significant features as semantic networks. First, the structures shown are fully operational. They were created in the KDraw graphic structure editor and compile directly into knowledge structures in KRS. In this document they are active as well as operational, and can be edited with immediate impact on inference. Second, the visual language used is completely formally defined and intertranslatable with the underlying KL-ONE knowledge structures. Third, the freedom in layout has been used to create knowledge structures that are natural to the people involved. Structure 5 looks like an organization chart. Structure 6 is based on the actual room layout in the building. Fourth, editing these structures changes the ontologies and facts, and hence any related problem solving activity. For example, at the top right of the room layout, room "C5-119" is the only room asserted to be "central". If this appears to be restrictive when the room allocation rules are run then it is easy for the user to add arrows from "C5-117" and "C5-120" to"central" and see what changes result in the room allocation behavior.

Double-clicking in the structures above brings up a floating dialog box allowing them to be edited as shown in Figure 2. Human-computer interaction in the editor is modeled on Apple's MacDraw with additional features appropriate to the language such as arcs remaining attached to nodes when they are dragged. A popup menu that appears when one mouses down on the right edge of a node allows connecting lines to be entered easily. The syntax of possible node interconnections and constraint expressions is enforced—it is not possible to enter a graph that is syntactically incorrect. Cut-and-paste of graphs and subgraphs is supported, and scroll and fit-to-size capabilities allow large structures with a thousand or more nodes to be edited in KDraw.

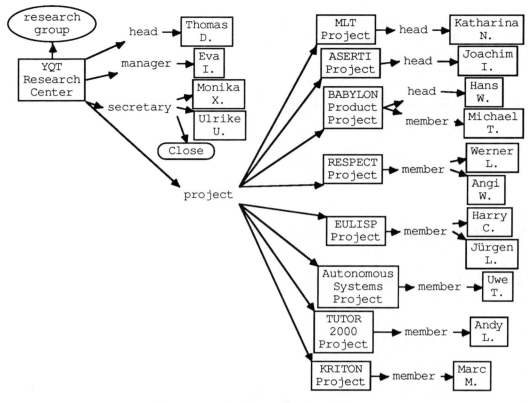

Structure 5: Organization Chart

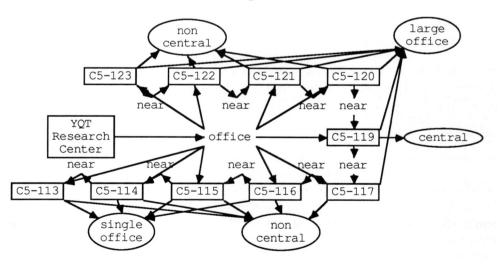

Structure 6: Room Layout

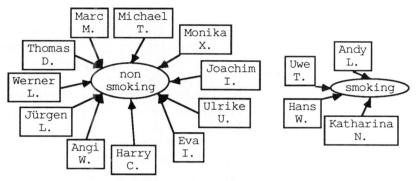

Structure 7: Smoking Employees

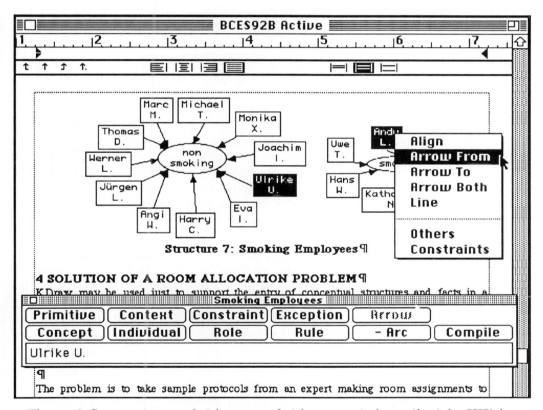

Figure 2 Screen dump of this page of this paper being edited in KWrite. Double clicking on knowledge structure 7 above has brought up a floating dialog box to edit it. A popup menu has been accessed at the right edge of a particular graphic item in order to enter a connecting arrow. Some of the word-processing features of KWrite are also apparent in this figure.

4 SOLUTION OF A ROOM ALLOCATION PROBLEM

The problem is to take sample protocols from an expert making room assignments to researchers occupying a new building. The rules derived from the expert protocols are, in order of declining priority:

A large, central office should be allocated to the Head of Group.

A large office already occupied by a secretary should be allocated to another secretary.

A large office near the Head of Group is suitable for the secretaries.

A single office near the Head of Group is suitable for the Manager.

A single office near the Head of Group is suitable for a Project Leader.

An office with one smoking researcher occupant should be allocated to another smoking researcher.

An office with a non-smoking researcher occupant should be allocated to another non-smoking researcher.

A large office should be allocated to researchers.

It is not sufficient just to implement these rules. Resource allocation problems tend to be either over-determined, and hence notionally insoluble, or under-determined, and hence subject to combinatorial explosion. People deal with this by problem reformulation, which is a strongly knowledge-based process, and this is expedited by systems that generate meaningful partial solutions that indicate the sources of obstacles to solution. What is required is a system that uses the rules to suggest allocations, allowing the user to make choices when the problem is under-determined, and to resolve conflicts when the problem is over-determined. The system should support retraction and backtracking if the user wishes to explore alternative solutions, perhaps involving considerations not expressed in the knowledge base. An agenda mechanism to support this approach is itself programmed as knowledge structure 8, with the concept of a prioritized task defined at the top and appropriate tasks and priorities defined at the bottom.

Structure 9 shows a rule used to determine if a room is "near" to that of the "group head". The upper left concept defines a "head office" as an "office" with at least one occupant and such that every occupant is a "group head". The rule "near head office" then asserts that an office "near" such an office is "near head office", that is the concept "near head office" will be asserted of it. The lower left concept defines an "occupied near head office" office as one which is "near head office" and has at least one occupant. Such an office again has its neighbors classified as "near head office". This captures the expert's reclassification of offices further away from head office as being "near" to it as intervening offices are filled.

Structures 10 and 11 show the representation of the rules above. For example, at the top of structure 10, if an individual is a "group head" and "without office" (both defined in structure 2) then that individual is classified as "group head without office" and the "group head request" rule fires placing "group head task" in the "person recommended" role of the individual. Hence, since this role is defined as self-inverse in structure 8, the individual is inferred to be in the "person recommended" role of "group head task".

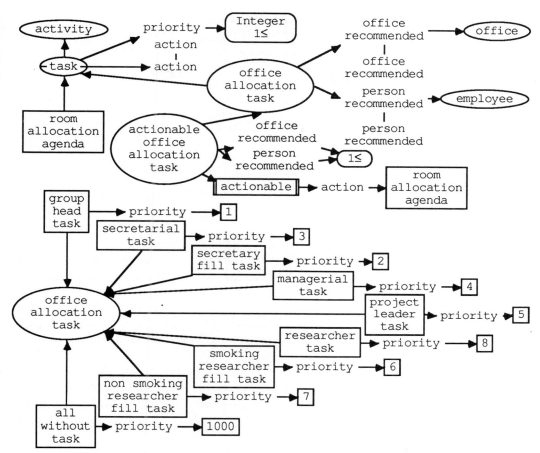

Structure 8: Agenda Mechanism for Room Allocation

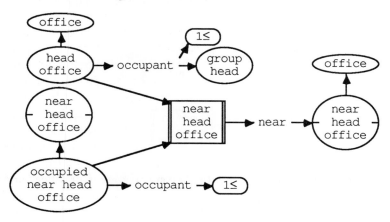

Structure 9: Rule for Room "Near Head Office"

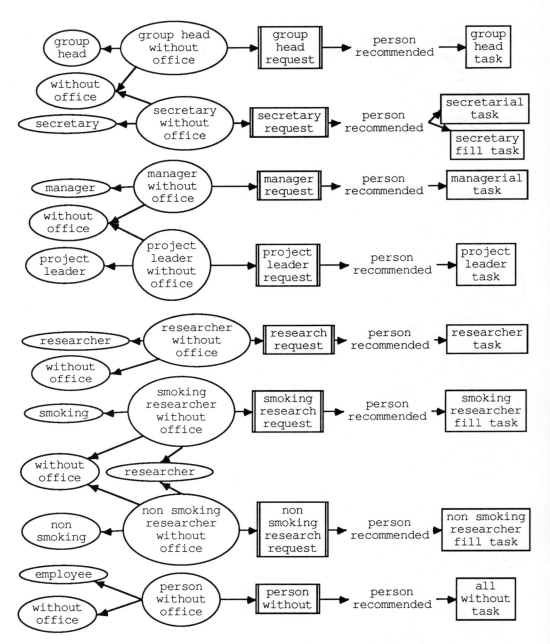

Structure 10: Rules for Employee's Office Requirements

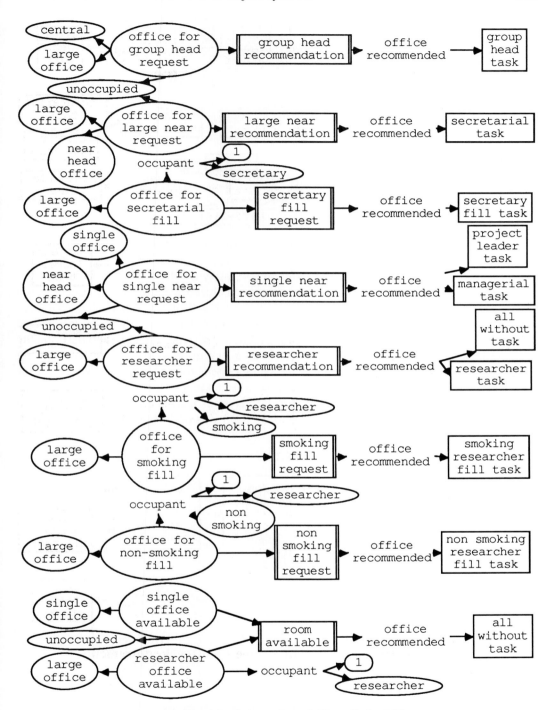

Structure 11: Rules for Office Suitability

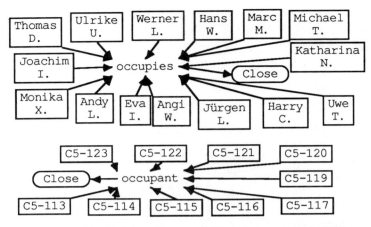

Structure 12: Initial State of Employees and Offices

Structure 12 shows an initial state for problem solving when no one has been allocated a room and no rooms are occupied (the roles have been closed with no fillers). Other initial states are possible corresponding to partial allocation. All of the knowledge structures required for the room allocation problem are in this paper. They provide the user interface for domain, problem-solving and particular problem description. It remains to describe the user interface for problem solving. KRS is a server providing problem-solving capabilities, and KWrite and KDraw provide knowledge entry and editing sub-systems for creating a knowledge base. It is possible to use either textual or graphic querying of KRS to solve a particular problem. However, for the Sisyphus example the use of HyperCard to provide an open architecture user interface to KRS was demonstrated. Figure 3 shows the overall architecture.

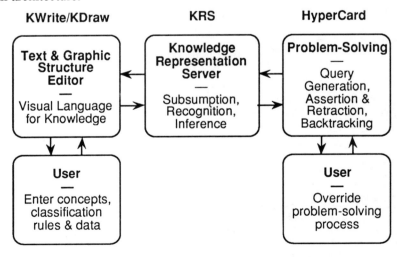

Figure 3 System architecture, functions and user interaction

HyperCard communicates with KRS, as do KDraw and KWrite, through Apple's System 7 inter-application communication protocol. This allows a server instantiation to exist anywhere on a network and be accessed locally or remotely. The electronic version of this document serves as the knowledge base for KRS, and the visual knowledge structures shown above are compiled directly into concepts, roles, individuals and rules in KRS.

Figure 4 shows the initial screen in HyperCard. The fields at the lower left list the knowledge bases embedded in this paper that will be used in problem solving. The user clicks on the "Solve" button to load these into a KRS server and commence inference. A sequence of recommended room allocations is then shown. If the problem is under-determined, this will involve some choice. Figure 5 shows the screen when the group head has been allocated and now the secretarial allocations are possible and top priority.

The person and room recommended for allocation are highlighted but users can over ride these by clicking on their own choices if they wish. Clicking on the "Allocate" button sends a message to KRS allocating the highlighted room to the highlighted person. The windows on the right in Figure 5 show all the employees without rooms and all the rooms available so that the user can override the recommendation process completely if desired. The user can also go to the screen shown in Figure 6 at any time, see the allocations already made, select any number of them and retract them if desired. The KRS truth maintenance system automatically undoes any conclusions based on retracted data.

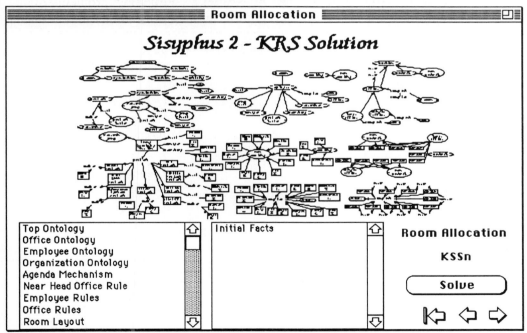

Figure 4 Initial HyperCard screen

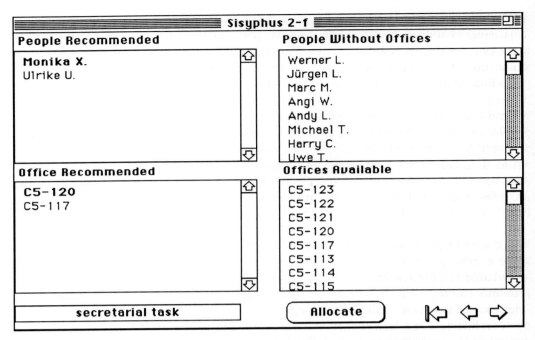

Figure 5 Secretarial room allocation recommendations

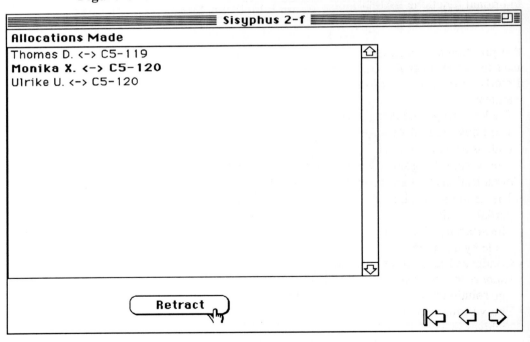

Figure 6 Allocations and retraction

4 CONCLUSIONS

This paper is written in a document production tool that appears to a user as a word processor but also acts as an expert system shell with frame and rule representations supporting deductive inference. The electronic version of the document is active, providing typographic text and page layout facilities, versioning, hypermedia sound and movies, hypertext links, and knowledge structures represented in a visual language. It can be read as a hypermedia document and also interrogated as a knowledge-based system for problem-solving. The paper version of the document, which you have just read, is produced by printing the electronic version. It loses its active functionality but continues to act as a record of the knowledge in the document. The overall technology has been developed as an alternative approach to the dissemination of knowledge bases. It also provides a different interface to knowledge-based systems that emulates document interfaces with which many users are already familiar.

In addition to demonstrating the knowledge document system, this paper has reported some experience in the design and implementation of a lightweight, object-oriented knowledge representation server, and its application to organizational modeling and problem solving. The primary user interface is through a formal visual language implemented simply and naturally as a drawing environment on graphic workstations. The open architecture implementation of the server allows it to be integrated with existing applications, such as corporate database and accounting systems, and also allows additional functionality to be added through self-contained modules requiring no changes in the kernel system.

The problem solving example given has shown how knowledge entered visually can be used to model organizational structures in a way that is simple and natural, and leads directly to operational problem solving. The process described here has the following features:
- The knowledge and data structures are totally overt and easily edited
- The knowledge document format allows a single instance of them to be disseminated both as an active knowledge base and as a passive paper report
- The visual language allows knowledge associated with structures such as the organization chart and room layout to be presented very naturally
- The problem solving strategy is incremental and can be applied to extend an existing partial solution
- The arbitrary choices that arise in undetermined problems can be made by the system or made by a person with, perhaps, additional considerations in mind
- Condensed and understandable information is available through the agenda items to support an attractive presentation of the problem solving process to the user
- The solution developed is a highly generic problem solving strategy
- The various components of the solution may be envisioned as coming from different archives in a corporate knowledge repository

ACKNOWLEDGEMENTS

Financial assistance for this work has been made available by the Natural Sciences and Engineering Research Council of Canada. We are grateful to many colleagues for discussions that have influenced the research described. We are particularly grateful to Marc Linster, the GMD and the Esprit Reflect Project for making the dataset available. The research reported here would not have been possible without access to the word processing and page makeup software developed by Gary Crandall of Datapak, and much of the significant document processing functionality is a direct consequence of his work.

REFERENCES

Abrett, G. & Burstein, M.H. (1988) The KREME knowledge editing environment. In Boose, J.H. & Gaines, B.R., Eds. Knowledge Acquisition Tools for Expert Systems. pp.1-24. London, Academic Press.

Borgida, A., Brachman, R.J., McGuiness, D.L. & Resnick, L.A. (1989). CLASSIC: a structural data model for objects. Clifford, J., Lindsay, B. & Maier, D., Eds. Proceedings of 1989 ACM SIGMOD International Conference on the Management of Data. pp.58-67. New York: ACM Press.

Brachman, R.J. (1977) What's in a concept: structural fondations for semantic nets. International Journal of Man-Machine Studies 9, 127-152.

Brachman, R.J. (1979). On the epistemological status of semantic nets. In Findler, N.V., Ed. Associative Networks: Representation and Use of Knowledge by Computers. pp.3-50. New York: Academic Press.

Brachman, R.J. & Schmolze, J. (1985). An overview of the KL-ONE knowledge representation system. Cognitive Science, 9(2) 171-216 (April-June).

Cercone, N. & Schubert, L. (1975). Towards a state-based conceptual representation. Proceedings of AAAI75. pp.83-90. Los Altos: Morgan Kaufmann.

Crandall, G. (1990). Word Solution Engine Programmer's Manual. Vancouver, Washington, DataPak.

Fahlman, S.E. (1979). NETL: A System for Representing and Using Real-World Knowledge. Cambridge, Massachusetts: MIT Press.

Gaines, B.R. (1988a). Structure, development and applications of expert systems in integrated manufacturing. Kusiak, A., Ed. Artificial Intelligence Implications for CIM. pp.117-161. Bedford, UK: IFS Conferences.

Gaines, B.R. (1988b). Knowledge acquisition systems for rapid prototyping of expert systems. INFOR, 26(4), 256-285 (November).

Gaines, B.R. (1990). Knowledge support systems. Knowledge-Based Systems 3(3) 192-203.

Gaines, B.R. (1991a) Empirical investigation of knowledge representation servers: design issues and applications experience with KRS. AAAI Spring Symposium: Implemented Knowledge Representation and Reasoning Systems. pp. 87-101. Stanford (March)—SIGART Bulletin 2(3), 45-56 (June).

Gaines, B.R. (1991b). Integrating rules in term subsumption knowledge representation servers. AAAI'91: Proceedings of the Ninth National Conference on Artificial

Intelligence. pp.458-463. Menlo Park, California: AAAI Press/MIT Press (July).

Gaines, B.R. (1991c). An interactive visual language for term subsumption visual languages. IJCAI'91: Proceedings of the Thirteenth International Joint Conference on Artificial Intelligence. San Mateo, California: Morgan Kaufmann.

Gaines, B.R. (1991). Organizational modeling and problem solving using an object-oriented knowledge representation server and visual language. COCS'91: Proceedings of Conference on Organizational Computing Systems. pp.80-94. ACM Press.

Gaines, B.R. & Linster, M. (1990). Integrating a knowledge acquisition tool, an expert system shell and a hypermedia system. International Journal of Expert Systems Research and Applications 3(2) 105-129.

Gaines, B.R., Rappaport, A. & Shaw, M.L.G. (1989). A heterogeneous knowledge support system. Boose, J.H. & Gaines, B.R., Eds. Proceedings of the Fourth AAAI Knowledge Acquisition for Knowledge-Based Systems Workshop. pp.13-1-13-20. Banff (October).

Gaines, B.R. & Shaw, M.L.G. (1990) Cognitive and logical foundations of knowledge acquisition. Boose, J.H. & Gaines, B.R. (Eds) Proceedings of the Fifth AAAI Knowledge Acquisition for Knowledge-Based Systems Workshop. pp. 9-1-9-25. Banff (November).

Glinert, I.P., Ed. (1990) Visual Programming Environments: Paradigms and Systems. Los Alamitos, California: IEEE Computer Society Press.

Kindermann, C. & Quantz, J. (1989) Graphics-oriented user interfaces for KL-ONE. KIT Internal Report 23. Technical University of Berlin.

Linster, M., Ed. (1991) Sisyphus Working Papers Part 2: Models of Problem Solving. EKAW91, Glasgow: University of Strathclyde.

Nosek, J.T. & Roth, I. (1990) A comparison of formal knowledge representations as communication tools: predicate logic vs semantic network. International Journal of Man-Machine Studies 33, 227-239, 1990.

Quillian, M.R. (1968). Semantic memory. Minsky, M, Ed. Semantic Information Processing. pp.216-270. Cambridge, Massachusetts: MIT Press.

Schmolze, J. (1983). KLONEDRAW—a facility for automatically drawing pictures of KL-ONE networks. Research in Knowledge Representation for Natural Language Understanding. pp.41-44. Report No.5421, Cambridge, Massachusetts: Bolt Beranek and Newman Inc.

Shaw, M.L.G. & Gaines, B.R. (1987). KITTEN: Knowledge Initiation & Transfer Tools for Experts & Novices. International Journal of Man-Machine Studies, 27, 251-280.

Voß, A., Karbach, W., Drouven, U., Lorek, D. & Schuckey, R. (1990) Operationalization of a synthetic problem. ESPRIT Basic Research Project P3178 REFLECT Task I.2.1 Report (July).

Watanabe, H. (1989). Heuristic graph displayer for G-BASE. International Journal of Man-Machine Studies, 30(3) 287-302 (March).

Woods, W.A. (1975) What's in a link: Foundations for semantic networks. Bobrow, D.G. & Collins, A.M. (Eds) Representation and Understanding: Studies in Cognitive Science. pp.35-82. New York: Academic Press.